About Island Press

Island Press is the only nonprofit organization in the United States whose principal purpose is the publication of books on environmental issues and natural resource management. We provide solutions-oriented information to professionals, public officials, business and community leaders, and concerned citizens who are shaping responses to environmental problems.

In 2005, Island Press celebrates its twenty-first anniversary as the leading provider of timely and practical books that take a multidisciplinary approach to critical environmental concerns. Our growing list of titles reflects our commitment to bringing the best of an expanding body of literature to the environmental community throughout North America and the world.

Support for Island Press is provided by the Agua Fund, The Geraldine R. Dodge Foundation, Doris Duke Charitable Foundation, Ford Foundation, The George Gund Foundation, The William and Flora Hewlett Foundation, Kendeda Sustainability Fund of the Tides Foundation, The Henry Luce Foundation, The John D. and Catherine T. MacArthur Foundation, The Andrew W. Mellon Foundation, The Curtis and Edith Munson Foundation, The New-Land Foundation, The New York Community Trust, Oak Foundation, The Overbrook Foundation, The David and Lucile Packard Foundation, The Winslow Foundation, and other generous donors.

The opinions expressed in this book are those of the author(s) and do not necessarily reflect the views of these foundations.

NATURE-FRIENDLY COMMUNITIES

NATURE-FRIENDLY COMMUNITIES

Habitat Protection and Land Use

CHRISTOPHER DUERKSEN

and

CARA SNYDER

ISLAND PRESS
Washington • Covelo • London

Library of Congress Cataloging-in-Publication data.

Duerksen, Christopher J., 1948-
Nature-friendly communities : habitat protection and land use / Christopher Duerksen and Cara Snyder.
    p. cm.
Includes bibliographical references and index.
    ISBN 1-55963-593-2 (hardback : alk. paper) — ISBN 1-55963-865-6 (pbk. : alk. paper)
1. Habitat conservation—Economic aspects—United States. 2. Habitat conservation—United States—Case studies. 3. Land use—United States—Planning—Case studies.
I. Snyder, Cara. II. Title.
    QH76.D84 2005
    333.95'16—dc22

2005003191

British Cataloguing-in-Publication data available.

Printed on recycled, acid-free paper ♲

Design by Schawk, Inc.; Publishing Solutions for Retail, Book, and Catalog

Manufactured in the United States of America
10 9 8 7 6 5 4 3 2 1

CONTENTS

ACKNOWLEDGMENTS

It has been a privilege and pleasure to work with a distinguished consortium of conservation organizations to produce this book on nature-friendly communities. We count the members of the project management team—Laura Watchman of Defenders of Wildlife, Jim McElfish of the Environmental Law Institute, Bruce Stein of NatureServe, and Kristy Manning of Island Press—as good friends and teachers. Kristy Manning deserves special mention and thanks for her thoughtful orchestration of this effort. It gives us great comfort to know that these bright and dedicated people are working tirelessly to protect the wild things, and that institutions like the Doris Duke Charitable Foundation are making this and other efforts possible with generous financial support.

A number of leading lights in the fields of planning, law, and wildlife biology offered invaluable counsel in helping us identify and select the case study communities. Paul Farmer and Bill Klein of the American Planning Association, Edward McMahon, late of the Conservation Fund and now with the Urban Land Institute, and Peter Howell, formerly of the Doris Duke Charitable Foundation and now at the Open Space Institute, were particularly helpful. Kudos are also in order for the editorial staff at Island Press, especially Jessica Poppe, Jeff Hardwick, and Mary Anne Stewart for their heroic efforts to make us sound more cogent and erudite, and James Nuzum, for his invaluable help with graphics.

And in each case-study community, we received generous assistance from key individuals, without whose help this book simply would have not been possible. We particularly appreciate the way they freely and honestly allowed us to have an insider's look at how things really worked in their jurisdictions. They are acknowledged in the notes to the case studies.

Several of our colleagues at Clarion contributed to the research and writing of the case studies and helped keep the project on schedule. We are deeply in debt to Ben Herman (Placer County), Matt Goebel (Austin), Craig Richardson and Chad Meadows (Charlotte Harbor), and Marlise Fratinardo (Teton County and Powell County) for their work and insights. Darcie White, Lesli Ellis, Elizabeth Boyd, Molly Mowery, Renae Pick, Gretchen Wrede, and Jill Nobles also helped with graphics, illustrations, and other important odds and ends.

Indeed, we would like to dedicate this book to all the partners and associates at Clarion for supporting this effort and allowing us to slip away and write and think while they kept up the billable hours! They are a rare and inspiring bunch, and work hard to make the world a little bit better place every day.

Christopher Duerksen and Cara Snyder

INTRODUCTION

Surely the rest of life matters . . .

—EDWARD O. WILSON, *Harvard biologist*

The United States has a remarkable array of wildlife and wild places, equal to those of any nation in the world. This astounding variety goes beyond those unique and remote places like Alaska and Hawaii. From the coastal forests of the West to the desert ecosystems of the Southwest to the rich marshes of Florida and all those wetlands, prairies, and woodlands in between—we are blessed by nature's bounty.[1] The more than 200,000 species of plant and animals in the United States make up over 10 percent of species worldwide. America is the hotspot for many species, especially aquatic species like freshwater turtles.

This largesse adds much to our quality of life. Survey after survey in cities as well as rural areas confirms that wildlife occupy a special place in the hearts of Americans of every age group, every income level, and every region of the country. Americans want wildlife protected and are willing to pay for it. And increasingly there is hard evidence that living in harmony with nature and protecting habitat make good sense in dollars and cents. As documented later in this book, protecting our natural habitat helps generate tourist dollars, can in fact save local governments money in terms of the cost of providing services and infrastructure, and actually increases private property values in many instances.

However, the signs are mounting that the country is truly at a crossroads when it comes to preservation of this largesse. Unlike the last century, when overfishing and overhunting and the large-scale exploitation of timber and minerals were the culprits in the demise of many species, today the main threat is well documented: the destruction and degradation of habitat, often associated with conversion of vast stretches of land to housing and commercial development and transportation projects. Scientists tell us that about one-third of the best-known groups of plants and animals are at risk and that more than 200 species of U.S. flora and fauna are already extinct. More worrisome is the fact that, according to a 1995 report issued by the National Biological Service, 27 ecosystems have declined by 98 percent or more since the European settlement of this country. Prairies, sagebrush steppe, and oak savannas are just a few of the ecosystems that have been almost completely wiped out, along with the wildlife that called them home. No part of the nation has been immune.

In addition, the first "State of the Birds USA" report, released by the National Audubon Society in 2004, documents significant declines for almost 30 percent of North American bird species. These declines are abnormal, are not part of any natural population cycle, and are due to outside factors such as loss of wetlands, loss of native grasslands, and poor land use decisions.

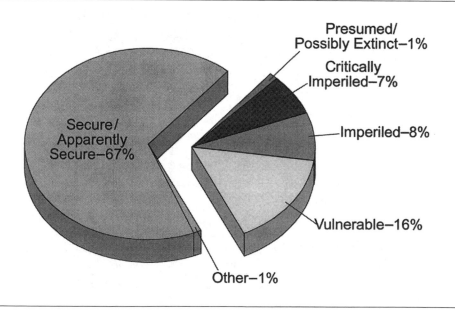

U.S. NATIVE SPECIES AT RISK
According to an assessment by natural heritage programs and The Nature Conservancy, a surprisingly high one-third of the native species of U.S. flora and fauna are at risk. Chart courtesy of Precious Heritage, ©2000 The Nature Conservancy and NatureServe.

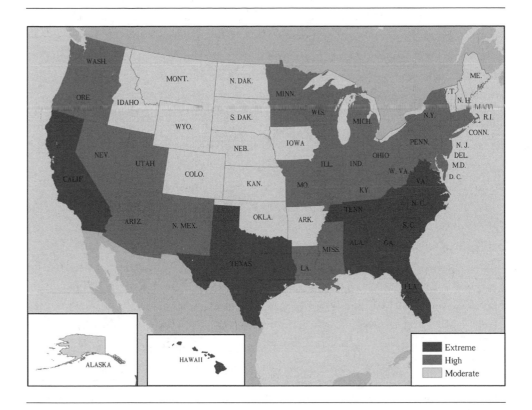

OVERALL RISK TO U.S. ECOSYSTEMS

Although the loss of native ecosystems has been most severe in the Northeast, South, Midwest, and California, no state has escaped damage. The overall risk to each state's ecosystems was determined by Defenders of Wildlife in 1995 by combining three factors: the number of most-endangered ecosystems, the percentage of species that are imperiled, and the overall development risk. This national study determined that there are 21 most-endangered ecosystems in the United States (e.g., tallgrass prairie; large streams and rivers as well as coastal communities in the lower 48 states and Hawaii; ancient eastern deciduous forest); how many of these 21 most-endangered ecosystems exist in each state was the first factor considered. Extensive data for plants, vertebrates, and aquatic invertebrates were used to determine the second factor: the percentage of species that are imperiled in each state. Finally, development risk was determined by considering both the development status in each state in the early 1990s (population density, percentage of state developed, percentage of state in farms, and rural road density in miles per acre) as well as the development trend in each state during 1982–1992 (absolute number of people added per square mile, percent change in population density, percent of state developed, and percent increase in the total amount of developed land). NatureServe is preparing a more current, comprehensive ecosystem evaluation, but data were not yet available when this book went to press. Map by Darcie White, based on data from *Endangered Ecosystems,* ©Defenders of Wildlife, 1995.

Invasion of nonnative species is another major and growing threat across the United States. Everyone is familiar with how English sparrows and starlings have crowded out native birds, but the problem is far more serious—especially with plants. Nonnative species now make up about 5 percent of the total U.S. continental biota, and in some states almost 50 percent of the flora.

The good news is that local governments—cities, towns, and counties—and regional agencies throughout the United States are stepping forward to meet the challenge as never before. Some are doing it because wildlife is a key feature in the local economy. In 2001, 82 million U.S. residents fished, hunted, and watched wildlife, spending over $108 billion on equipment and trips associated with those activities. Of that total, $40 billion was linked to wildlife watching alone. But just as many local governments have adopted nature-friendly policies because their citizens place a very high value on wildlife from a quality-of-life perspective. While it may be hard for economists or appraisers to put a price on seeing a fox on a stroll through a local nature preserve or catching a trout or bass in an urban lake, most citizens know the value intuitively. The innovation and ingenuity that local governments are bringing to this task are truly inspiring, a story told in the pages of this book.

The increased role of local governments in habitat protection is fortunate, because it appears that state and federal governments are pulling back from the task of wildlife habitat preservation, weakening protective regulations and cutting back on funding sources. At the federal level, funds to survey threatened and endangered species have fallen far short of demand over the past decade, and programs to add land to national wildlife refuges and national parks have been on low-dollar diets. Under the radar screen, administrative changes are being pushed through to wedge exemptions into roadless forest protection and to suspend some environmental laws to permit logging in the name of wildfire prevention. A 2001 U.S. Supreme Court decision held by the narrowest of margins that "isolated" waters and wetlands are not subject to federal protections, putting 30 to 60 million acres of wetlands at risk. At best, it might be argued that things are at a standstill, with assaults on protective programs like the Endangered Species Act being blunted for the most part over the past 20 years despite repeated attempts by opponents and so-called property rights advocates.

But there is no denying that, at the state level, gains of the 1970s and 1980s are being eroded. As the case studies amply illustrate, states like Wisconsin have cut back on funding for habitat acquisition programs, and others, like Colorado, have weakened state protective standards or hog-tied local governments and made their ability to enact protective regulations and funding programs ever more difficult. This is a

The Bush administration pushed through exemptions to roadless area rules and has made numerous other changes in federal regulations that weakened habitat protection. Courtesy of: Jack Ohman, ©2004, Tribune Media Services. Reprinted with permission.

dramatic reversal from the state of affairs in the early 1970s, when, as documented in books like *The Quiet Revolution in State Land Use Controls,* many state governments, such as Wisconsin, Maryland, and Washington, actually took the lead in wildlife habitat protection and in urging local governments to act. They provided regulatory authority and funding for a host of innovative programs. Some, like Florida, took a direct role in protecting critical natural areas.

The same story has played out with most regional governmental efforts. Taking a regional approach to nature protection is absolutely essential until wildlife learn to read maps and can tell where one jurisdiction starts and another stops. But just as state government initiatives in wildlife habitat protection peaked in the 1970s, so did efforts to promote regional land use planning. Indeed, in many ways, regional governance is probably at its weakest point in this country in the last 40 years. In some of the case study communities, regional land use planning agencies have been abolished. In others, they have been neutered or silenced when it comes to effective regional land use planning and growth management. The absence of effective regional land use planning agencies often leaves local governments to their own devices when it comes to coordinating habitat protection programs with their neighbors.

The pressures on wildlife and habitat are not likely to abate. Alone among Western industrialized nations, the population of the United States will continue to mushroom, growing from around 280 million people today to almost 400 million by 2050—an increase of over 40 percent. In many places, the easy development sites are gone, and now projects are being proposed along streams, on steep slopes, and in other spots whose remoteness and inaccessibility provided protection for flora and fauna. Places

U.S. Total Population Projections

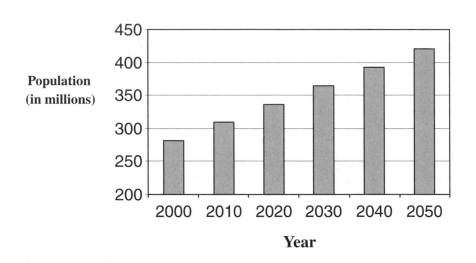

The population of the United States is expected to reach approximately 420 million by 2050. Graph based on data from *United States Census 2000*.

like Arizona, Texas, and California, with some of the most sensitive environments and declining species, will face the most pressure as their populations continue to expand.

So . . . there is no arguing that the task is daunting, but the communities featured in this book should give us all great hope. Overcoming obstacles, forging alliances, exhibiting innovative approaches—they represent the best in the country when it comes to nature protection and can serve as models.[2] Our search for the best was not an easy one, but we found some gems, and they are being joined daily by other communities that are getting on the nature protection bandwagon. Perhaps most encouraging are the thousands and thousands of citizens who are volunteering their time and working with local governments to manage nature preserves, fight invasive species, and serve as protective watchdogs. Their accomplishments are chronicled here.

Following this introduction and overview, Chapter 1 documents the economic and other benefits of nature protection. These benefits can be direct in terms of spending—for example, by tourists or visitors participating in outdoor recreation involving wildlife. Tips are offered to local officials who want to conduct their own local economic benefits assessment. But the chapter goes beyond this to explore the substantial cost savings for local governments in protecting what is coming to be known as "green infrastructure." Mounting evidence reveals that in many instances it is more cost-effective for local governments to protect than to exploit. Finally, Chapter 1 provides some useful references to sources that substantiate the public's willingness to pay for natural resource protection programs.

Chapter 2 distills lessons from the case studies about what makes for a good local nature protection program—the best practices and best tools that will protect wildlife and advance biodiversity, including innovative approaches to regional cooperation. The chapter is organized around what we call the key elements of a successful local program, including fundamentals like regulations, acquisition, and education. We address the basics of each element and discuss effective implementation tools in detail, with references to the case studies that follow in the remainder of the book. In many ways, Chapter 2 is the heart of the book and provides the reader with a summary of what it takes for a local government to put together an effective nature protection program. The chapter concludes with discussion of how to design an overall wildlife preservation strategy at the local level that is tailored to local realities. We offer practical benchmarks for evaluating local programs in each of the key element areas and underscore a major message of this book—that there is no such thing as a one-size-fits-all nature protection program. Jurisdictions can and should, of course, engage in the time-honored practice of borrowing or copying what has worked for their neighbors. But experience shows that these programs must be customized so that they are a good fit financially, legally, socially, and politically.

The rest of the book offers an insider's look at some of the best local and regional nature protection programs in the nation. The Major Case Studies section (Chapters 3–11) explores nine communities that were chosen after a lengthy investigation into which local governments had the best, most comprehensive nature protection efforts in the United States. A concerted effort was made to select communities that represent a range of governmental types and sizes (township, city, county, etc.); geographic locations; environments (mountains, coastal, etc.); and economies (university towns, blue-collar cities, etc.). Each chapter provides a quick overview of one community and its nature protection efforts, followed by a detailed discussion of how the particular local government addresses the key elements of a successful program. While some stellar examples— such as Boulder County, Colorado, and Portland, Oregon, were omitted from the list because of time and resource limitations or because they have been amply reviewed in other publications, in truth the number of exemplary communities across the country is relatively small, and for that reason all the more worthy of attention and study.

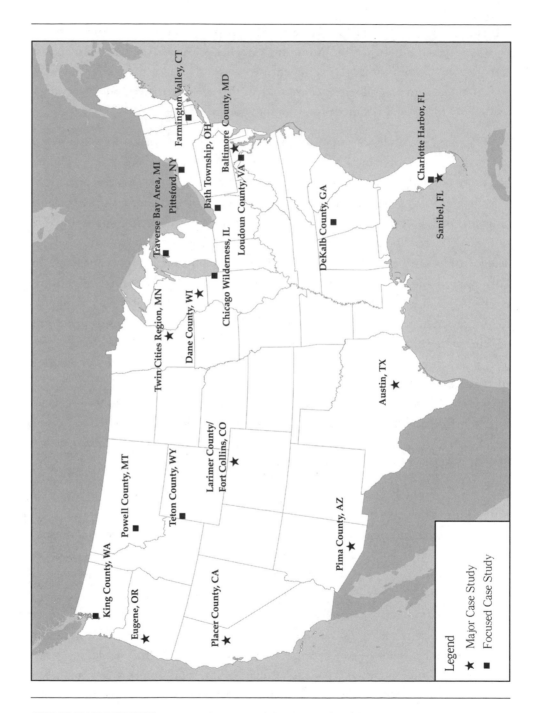

CASE STUDY COMMUNITIES
Major case studies are presented in Chapters 3–11, focused case studies in Chapters 12–22. Map
courtesy of Clarion Associates.

Former Denver mayor Federico Pena (holding eagle) was committed to wildlife habitat protection in the area around Denver's new airport. Photograph by Chris Duerksen.

The Focused Case Studies section (Chapters 12–22) concentrates on one or more particularly successful or noteworthy elements of 11 local or regional programs, even though the community might not yet have a comprehensive nature protection program. These include innovative mapping efforts, creative regulatory programs, and effective regional wildlife habitat planning efforts. As with the major case studies, we made a concerted effort to select a representative group of communities from across the spectrum.

The Conclusion offers some overall observations drawn from the case studies. We attempt to identify what we believe are some of the most critical challenges that must be dealt with if nature protection is to succeed at a local and regional level.

Notes

[1]In 2000, NatureServe and The Nature Conservancy published an excellent comprehensive assessment of the extent and condition of America's biological riches, *Precious Heritage: The Status of Biodiversity in the United States,* which documents the full breadth and complexity of wildlife resources in America.

[2]Throughout this book, the phrase "nature protection program" is used interchangeably with "nature-friendly" and "natural resource and biodiversity protection program."

CHAPTER 1

The Benefits of Nature Protection

Why would a community, especially elected officials, want to protect nature and natural resources? In these economic times, local governments find it difficult to make ends meet and to avoid budget overruns, much less provide more of what might be seen as a luxury to some people. However, along with the myriad intrinsic values people often place on nature, there are a host of economically important reasons for protecting natural resources and biodiversity. This chapter focuses on these benefits. Some are readily measured and well established, while the merits of others are just beginning to be recognized. Altogether, evidence continues to mount that protecting nature and promoting biodiversity make not just good sense but good dollars and cents.

For local or regional governments to seriously consider protecting nature, the bottom line must be considered. Will the costs outweigh the benefits? Can the community afford the investment? The short answer is that each community has a different set of circumstances, and ideally each community would evaluate its own overall goals, its economic realities, and its valuable characteristics. Some specific tools are available to evaluate a community's economic situation and to gauge the benefits of nature protection programs to the community.

Often, protecting nature is an obvious good investment. Resort communities have known this for a long time. If you protect nature, more tourists will want to visit, stay longer, and spend more. Although many resort areas draw on public land outside their community's boundaries, it can make financial sense to protect critical areas on private lands and ensure that visitors have a positive experience with nature within the local government boundaries as well. Of course, wildlife don't read maps—they wander in and out of public lands. But what about the majority of communities around the nation that are nonresort communities? Even then, there are many economically compelling reasons for protecting nature.

Some examples of protecting nature as a good investment—to be discussed in more detail in this chapter—include lower infrastructure service costs, benefits of green infrastructure,[1] and increased property values. Studies of costs of facilities and infrastructure such as roads, schools, water/sewer, and emergency services have repeatedly shown that preserving open space can be more cost-effective than building a residential development on the same property. Recent experience has shown that the value of services provided by green infrastructure, such as stormwater filtration, may far outweigh the value of developing the land. Just as important, there is increasing proof that protecting natural resources is a vital factor in attracting and retaining businesses and jobs.

Americans have demonstrated that they endorse and will pay for protecting natural resources. There has been strong support for preservation of open space and habitat from voters nationwide as well as in surveys of the general public. We will delve into these topics more closely in the following pages, to remind communities why protecting nature is good for business and local economies and to give local officials the ammunition they need to make the case in persuading their colleagues and citizens to adopt effective protection strategies.

An initial decision and action to protect habitat may need to be followed by planning for future pressures on the protected area. When communities successfully preserve natural areas, that very success can increase the use of those areas, and degradation may become a pressing issue. Having mechanisms in place to prevent killing the golden goose can be just as vital as protecting the resource in the first place.

A final note: Although we focus here on the aspects of protecting nature that are most suited to quantification, as Pittsburgh mayor Tom Murphy observed at the 1999 symposium of the City Parks Forum,[2] "Parks and many cultural events should not be forced into this kind of economic analysis mold but should have value for their own purpose."[3] Natural areas have many undefinable benefits, and so protection efforts may lose out to more quantifiable services like highways and schools, but that does not mean communities should not value and protect natural areas.

Positive Economic Benefits

Growing evidence illustrates that nature-friendly communities can realize substantial economic benefits. From attracting and retaining employers and employees to bringing in potentially millions of tourist dollars, an investment in nature can provide measurable payoffs in the short and long term. The beauty of investing in biodiversity protection is that it provides long-lasting benefits and returns—it is not just a one-shot deal.

Attracting Businesses/Capital Investment

Study after study documents that preservation of natural resources and provision of open space are important factors in helping a region to retain existing jobs and businesses and to attract new ones. Quality-of-life matters and natural amenities are high on the list of quality-of-life ingredients. For example, the Center for the Continuing Study of the California Economy found that conservation of open space was critical for ensuring a higher quality of life, which the center documents as one of the most important components for attracting employers and employees to California communities.[4]

Although quality of life is valuable in both rural and urban areas, the type of employers and their priorities may be slightly different in each area. Urban areas tend to draw more of the larger or high-tech companies, while rural areas tend to see more growth in small businesses.

Urban Areas

Today, there are more fast-growing entrepreneurial companies, more telecommuters, and less economic stability than in previous eras.[5] The marketplace is global, and technology is key. Despite the failure of many dot-com start-up companies in 2000–2002, information technology is here to stay. This is the "new economy," and there are implications for communities wishing to attract employers and employees alike, especially when it comes to quality of life.

High-technology companies treasure natural amenities and in national and local surveys have rated environmental quality ahead of housing costs, cost of living, commuting patterns, schools, climate, government services, and public safety in making location decisions.[6] As Bill Calder, a spokesperson for computer chip manufacturer Intel, told the *New York Times* in the late 1990s, "Companies that can locate anywhere will go where they can attract good people in good places."[7] Many of the "good people" are creative, educated high-technology workers. And, increasingly, the "good places" are those that value and protect natural resources and open space, because those are the places where high-technology workers want to live.

A survey of more than 1,200 young high-technology workers found that "community quality of life" was the second most important factor in evaluating jobs after salary considerations, and more important than benefits, stock options, or company stability. Focus groups further revealed that young high-technology workers wanted easy access to a wide range of outdoor activities and a clean, healthy environment with a commitment to preserving natural resources for enjoyment and recreation. A vibrant music and performance scene with a wide range of live music opportunities and a wide range of nightlife experiences were also part of the perceived quality of life.[8]

Rural Areas

In rural America the situation is slightly different. Small businesses are even more crucial to rural economies. A 2003 study in the Greater Yellowstone region showed much higher growth rates in small businesses than in any other group—there were 2,781 new firms with fewer than five employees in the previous ten years.[9] Nationally, small businesses create more jobs than large businesses.[10] The types of small businesses vary from the low-wage service and trade sectors to high-end service providers in real estate and finance.[11] Preferences of small companies and their employees are thus a critical economic fact of life, and they place a high value on open space.

In one study, companies with fewer than 8 employees rated "quality of life" as their number one concern, while companies with more than 88 employees chose operating costs.[12] "Recreation/parks/open space" was the top quality-of-life element preferred by the small companies, with cost of living/housing a close second.[13] Similarly, the results of a survey of 500 businesses in the Greater Yellowstone area—largely rural—showed that amenities like parks, trails, and rivers were relatively more important than traditional profit-maximizing reasons, both as a draw for new businesses that relocated to the area and as a magnet for retaining existing businesses. Yet another study asked participants to rate the relative importance of 15 business location variables; the results showed the highest-ranking variable to be "scenic beauty," followed by "quality environment."[14]

Oakhurst is a small California tourist town near Yosemite National Park that began attracting small high-tech companies in the 1990s. Mike Jones, a Seattle native who moved to Oakhurst to work for a computer game company, pointed out in 1998: "I've had offers to go elsewhere and work for a lot more money, but I'd rather be in Oakhurst. The property values are good, people are nice, and *this* [rolling Sierra Nevada foothills] is what you see from the window!"[15] Proximity to natural areas can play a critical role in attracting and keeping employees and contributes to a new theory of economic development that considers "migration first, then jobs" as a basis, instead of the previous "jobs first, then migration."[16]

Of course, rural communities should recognize that while natural amenities are a key ingredient, they will not guarantee economic growth by themselves. Although economic growth has been linked positively to the amount of protected land in an area, other factors are also critical in attracting and keeping businesses. Having a nearby airport, an educated workforce, and a local college or university were the top three other factors found by the Sonoran Institute in their studies.[17]

Still, as discussed previously, there is no denying the growing link between economic development and natural area protection in rural America.

Direct Economic Activity

From the most remote rural towns to the most dense urban areas, nature attracts visitors. Humans cannot resist being in and near nature, delighting in it. And when Americans visit, they spend money. The burgeoning economic impacts of tourism and outdoor recreation (such as mountain biking, skiing, hiking, fishing, or bird-watching) are impressive.

Tourism Dollars Nationwide

Tourism is the largest sector of the nation's economy. The U.S. travel industry received more than $545 billion in 2002 from domestic and international travelers, which generated about 7 million jobs.[18] Evidence shows that nature and open space are a key to those big numbers: A 1998 survey revealed that an impressive 48 percent of mainland U.S. residents participated in nature-based activities on their last vacation.[19]

Visitors to natural areas can be locals taking a day trip to a nearby park or tourists flying in from far away to enjoy a week's vacation; they both bring much-needed dollars into the local economy. People living adjacent to a natural area may not even have to leave their homes to enjoy nature but may still purchase outdoor equipment such as binoculars or walking shoes. No matter what type of activity, money spent on recreation associated with wildlife and nature can have a tremendous impact. According to a U.S. Fish and Wildlife Service survey, nationwide, more than 82 million U.S. residents fished, hunted, and watched wildlife in 2001, spending over $108 billion on equipment and trips associated with those activities.[20] The same study documented annual national expenditures amounting to $40 billion associated with wildlife watching alone.[21] Interestingly, the study used a very strict definition of wildlife watching: participants must either take a "special interest" in wildlife around their homes or take a trip for the "primary purpose" of wildlife watching. In another arena, about 147 million people in 2002 participated in outdoor recreation such as hiking and bicycling.[22] That number represents about 67 percent of the nation's population! Corresponding sales for the outdoor recreation industry (specifically, human-powered recreation) were about $18 billion in 2001.[23]

Local Examples

Looking beyond the big national numbers is instructive. Local economies can benefit in several ways from tourism and outdoor recreation associated with natural areas, open space, and wildlife. Direct expenditures can include durable goods such as outdoor equipment, as well as nondurable goods like food, beverages, and gas for the car. Indirect impacts may include the creation of jobs in nearby businesses owing to increased visitor activity and other trickle-down effects of having more money in the economy, and can be calculated and quantified using economic multipliers. (Multipliers are tools commonly accepted and widely used by economists to estimate how much indirect economic activity is generated by the original expenditure. For example, a tourist may purchase a sandwich—a direct impact—but the purchases made by the restaurant to locally produce the sandwich are indirect impacts.) The economic benefits of protected natural areas can seem too numerous to count.

However, these benefits can be counted, and many studies document the local impact of nature-based tourism. For example, the cumulative total economic impact of birding along the Platte River in Nebraska in 1998 ranged between $21.8 and $48.5 million, with the average visitor contributing from $1,276 to $1,814 per year to the Nebraska economy.[24] The East Bay Regional Park District, which operates over 91,000 acres of park lands near San Francisco, undertook an economic evaluation in 2000. The study showed that total expenditures on all goods in the East Bay were $74 million higher per year because of the presence of these lands; when multiplier effects were taken into account, the total economic impact was $148 million per year.[25] Another study revealed that the economic impact of wildlife-related recreation on a four-county region in northeastern Florida (Clay, Duval, St. Johns, and Putnam

Watching wildlife, such as these pronghorn in Wyoming, generated more than $40 billion nationally in 2001. Photograph by Lokey Lytjen.

counties) was close to 10,000 jobs and over $500 million dollars in 2000.[26] Near Dayton, Ohio, an estimated 150,000 people per year visit the Little Miami Scenic Trail and spend an average of $13.54 each per visit just on food, beverages, and transportation to the trail. They also spend about $277 per person per year on clothing, equipment, and accessories related to trail use.[27] Nature-based tourism in the Sierra Vista, Arizona, area (southeast of Tucson), especially visitors to Ramsey Canyon, in one year generated $1 million in value-added activity.[28]

Having such local data can help sell a nature protection program, and an expanding number of local governments and nonprofit organizations are undertaking targeted studies. Box 1.1 briefly summarizes the steps locals can take to carry out their own economic benefits assessment.

Cost Savings for Governments

Protection of natural areas can provide big cost savings for communities, on both a local and a regional basis. Avoiding the costs of unchecked sprawl is one way a community can use open space and natural areas to save taxpayers' money. Additionally,

BOX 1.1

DOING YOUR OWN LOCAL ECONOMIC BENEFITS ASSESSMENT

Evaluating the economic impacts of a new natural area on your local economy can be as simple as making some educated guesses about how many tourists might visit the new park area and what they might spend during their visit. Or it can be quite a bit more complex and can involve visitor surveys and the determination of indirect impacts on the economy using complicated economic modeling software. Impacts other than tourist dollars can also be evaluated, such as expenditures by local residents; revenues of commercial businesses that might benefit by having the natural area nearby (e.g., recreational equipment rentals and sales, food services, lodging); or expenditures by the agencies that manage the property (e.g., the local park district provides jobs and purchases supplies locally).

The most common type of economic impact assessment is determining what out-of-town visitors (tourists) spend because of a visit to a natural area or park. This is typically estimated by some variation of the following simple equation:

**Economic impact of tourist spending = number of tourists ×
average spending per visitor × multiplier***

These three key inputs are listed in their order of importance:

1. Number and types of visitors
2. Average spending per visitor
3. Multipliers

A reasonable estimate of the number and types of tourists is essential, with an estimate of average levels of spending following close behind in importance. Multipliers are the least important and are only needed if secondary effects are desired (how the tourism dollars "ripple" through the local economy). However, experts recommend using a measure of the impact in terms of "income" to the community, also known as "value added" to the community, which will require the use of multipliers. The "income" measure of economic impact shows the effect of an extra unit of tourist spending on the level of personal income in the visited community. It enables local government officials to relate the economic benefits received by residents to the money (e.g., taxes) they invested initially. Sales data that show the economic activity resulting from tourist visits (just multiplying the number of visitors by the average spending per visitor) can be helpful if a more simple approach is desired but have limited use in determining the true effects of tourism on the local economy.

*A multiplier is a number that estimates the ripple effect in the economy.

—continued—

Box 1.1 *(continued)*

Tourism economic impact assessment can vary in complexity from using educated guesses for all three variables to using scientific surveys and models for all three variables. The bulletin *Approaches to Estimating the Economic Impacts of Tourism,* available from the Michigan State University website noted under "Resources," contains a table illustrating the range of options.

Resources

Crompton, John. *Measuring the Economic Impact of Visitors to Sports Tournaments and Special Events.* Ashburn, Va.: National Recreation and Park Association, 1999. Available from the National Recreation and Park Association: 703-858-0794; www.nrpa.org.

Topics include repositioning park and recreation departments as contributors to economic development, understanding economic impact studies, and data collection and procedures. The focus is on sporting events and special events, but most of the methods are also relevant for non-event-related evaluation.

Crompton, John. *Parks and Economic Development.* PAS Report No. 502. Chicago: American Planning Association Planning Advisory Service, 2001. Available from the American Planning Association: 312-786-6344; www.planning.org/bookservice.

Main sections deal with real estate values/property taxes, attracting tourists (with valuable information on how to conduct your own survey of the economic impact of special events), attracting businesses, and attracting/retaining retirees. Traditional parks are not always distinguished from natural open space.

Leones, Julie, and Douglas Dunn. "Strategies for Monitoring Tourism in Your Community's Economy." Tucson: University of Arizona, Arizona Cooperative Extension, March 1999. Available on the web at http://ag.arizona.edu/pubs/marketing/az1113.

An excellent summary of ways to measure levels of tourism activity in a community.

Michigan State University, Department of Community, Agriculture, Recreation and Resource Studies (formerly Department of Parks, Recreation, and Tourism Resources); www.carrs.msu.edu.

The department provides several useful guides regarding the economic impacts of recreation and tourism. The department's website contains an introduction to economic impact concepts and methods for noneconomists, a summary of basic methods, and the following bulletins in PDF file format:

1. *Economic Impacts of Tourism.* This bulletin is aimed at tourism industry managers and analysts. Economic impact concepts and methods are introduced, along with the key issues that arise in assessing the economic impacts of tourism. The bulletin covers typical costs and the preliminary design decisions without getting into technical details of models and methods.

2. *Approaches to Estimating the Economic Impacts of Tourism: Some Examples.* This bulletin goes into greater detail on specific methods for estimating economic impacts of tourism. Three examples are presented to cover a range of approaches.

—continued—

Box 1.1 *(continued)*

---

3. *Guidelines for Measuring Visitor Spending.* This bulletin provides guidelines for conducting visitor spending surveys. It focuses especially on the key requirements for spending surveys gathering data to be used in an economic impact assessment. Segmentation strategies are recommended. Suggested survey designs, sampling procedures, and a survey instrument are included.

Murray, Ray, et al. *Economic Impacts of Protecting Rivers, Trails, and Greenways Corridors.* 4th ed. Washington, D.C.: National Park Service, Rivers and Trails Conservation Assistance Program, 1995; www.nps.gov/pwro/rtca/econ_index.htm. Available in hardcopy (free) from Rivers and Trails and Conservation Assistance, National Park Service: (510) 817-1446.

Sourcebook developed by the Western Region of the National Park Service. The information is easily accessible to the average citizen, and though some data are older, they are comprehensive. The study concentrates on linear recreational green spaces. However, it also provides substantial guidance in finding sources of information on economic studies focused on traditional parks and similar spaces. Particularly relevant are the sections about expenditures by residents, commercial uses, agency expenditures, tourism, and estimating the effects of spending.

---

natural areas provide a green infrastructure—services that are vital to a healthy, functioning community, such as water filtration and stormwater management. These tasks have been taken for granted and seem invisible. Only recently has the value of these green services been studied and quantified. Another area of potential enormous savings is avoiding damage due to natural disasters such as flooding and wildfires, which have cost local economies billions of dollars in the past few years. These cost savings provide another incentive for protecting natural lands.

Curbing the Costs of Sprawl

Numerous studies have been undertaken to examine the fiscal and other impacts of sprawl on local governments.[29] How do local benefits from development such as an increased tax base compare to costs such as building new roads or schools? There continues to be considerable debate over the benefits and consequences of controlling sprawl and fostering "Smart Growth," but the weight of evidence and opinion is that Smart Growth offers some modest, but nevertheless substantial, potential benefits to communities in terms of reduced dependence on automobiles, reduced infrastructure costs, and protection of open space.[30]

Community Infrastructure Services

Many studies show that it may actually be more cost-effective for communities, especially those on urban fringes and rural areas, to preserve or buy open space rather than permit it to be developed. Several types of fiscal impact analysis are available to help communities make decisions about costs and benefits of growth—either on a case-by-case basis, or by projections for the entire jurisdiction (see Box 1.2).

BOX 1.2

FISCAL IMPACT ANALYSIS

Fiscal impact analysis—also referred to as *cost-revenue analysis* or *cost of community services analysis*—has been in use since the 1930s. Direct current public costs and revenues associated with residential or nonresidential growth are projected to determine the net fiscal impact of development in the local jurisdiction(s) in which the growth is taking place. More and more local governments are either undertaking or hiring consultants to perform such studies for a particular development all the way up to assessments of the fiscal impact of long-range comprehensive plans. Such studies can be extremely valuable tools in effective growth management and economic development strategies.

There are two general types of fiscal impact analysis: (1) jurisdiction-wide and (2) new-development-specific. In both types there are four basic steps:*

1. Estimate the population generated by growth or by a particular development (i.e., number of new residents, school-age children, employees).
2. Translate this population into consequent local public service costs (e.g., roads, schools, emergency services).
3. Project the tax and other local revenues generated by growth.
4. Compare development-induced costs to revenues and, if a gap exists, determine how to address the shortfall.

*Charles J. Fausold and Robert J. Lilieholm, "The Economic Value of Open Space: A Review and Synthesis," Lincoln Institute of Land Policy research paper published in *Environmental Management* 23, no. 3 (Spring 1999): 307–320.

—*continued*—

Box 1.2 *(continued)*

Resources

Many books and other sources explain how to conduct fiscal impact studies, such as several coauthored or edited by Robert Burchell: *The Fiscal Impact Handbook: Estimating Local Costs and Revenues of Land Development* (New Brunswick, N.J.: Rutgers University Center for Urban Policy Research, 1978, 480 pp.); *The New Practitioner's Guide to Fiscal Impact Analysis* (New Brunswick, N.J.: Rutgers University Center for Urban Policy Research, 1985, 73 pp.); and *Development Impact Assessment Handbook* (Washington, D.C.: Urban Land Institute, 1994, 326 pp.).

Paul Tischler provides an overview in "Analyzing the Fiscal Impact of Development," *Management Information Service Report* **20, no. 7 (July 1988).**

Another source is "Assessing the Impacts of Development Choices" by Linda Hollis, Douglas Porter, and Holly Stallworth, April 1997, available at the Growth Management Institute's website; www.gmionline.org.

Julia Freedgood discusses the American Farmland Trust approach in *Cost of Community Service Studies: Making the Case for Conservation* **(Washington, D.C.: American Farmland Trust, 2002).**

In 2002 the State of Florida commissioned the development of a fiscal impact analysis model with the goal of making fiscal impact analysis a routine part of land use planning in the state. This innovative program should provide further insight into the practice of fiscal impact analysis. For progress on this model, see www.fishkind.com/dep/home.html.

At the national level, a 2002 report by a highly respected organization demonstrated that a controlled-growth scenario through 2025 could save the United States as a whole $110 billion total for road infrastructure, $12.6 billion total for water/sewer infrastructure, and $4.2 billion annually in other public service costs (schools, police, fire, etc).[31] Another study determined that the State of South Carolina would save $2.7 billion in capital infrastructure over 20 years by encouraging higher-density development at a moderate level.[32] Eighty-three cost-of-community-services studies conducted in 19 states at a county or municipality level show that farms and open lands have a positive fiscal impact and more than pay for the public services they receive, while residential developments have higher service costs, causing a net drawdown on local budgets.[33] One study in DuPage County, Illinois, outside of Chicago, found that even nonresidential development did not necessarily pay for itself, often resulting in a need for increased taxes.[34] Finally, in Lancaster County, Pennsylvania, the fiscal impacts of providing township services under three different residential scenarios were assessed. The annual deficit per household for each scenario was $40 for urban infill; $147 for the sprawling subdivision option (scattered subdivisions of 1 acre average); and $1,133 for sporadic development (random development pattern with lots from 1/4 to 20 acres).[35]

In the short run, development may increase the local tax base, whereas protected land does not, except for its effect of increasing the property value of nearby lands. However, development—particularly residential—often demands expensive improvements in local infrastructure and services that frequently exceed net tax revenues. In the early 1990s, the City of Huntsville, Alabama, purchased a 547-acre tract on Mount Sano for $3.3 million. The annual maintenance costs for the land were about $75 an acre. Residential development would have cost about $5 million for roads, sewers, and other infrastructure—or about $2,500 per acre per year.[36]

Moreover, in the long run, open land requires a much lower level of public services, which limits cost increases for the local government. In contrast, residential developments require services, often increasing from year to year, necessitating increased taxes or public borrowing. A 1999 study from Massachusetts makes this connection clear. It found that towns with the most open space per capita have the lowest tax bills; towns where open lands are a higher proportion of the tax base have lower tax rates than more developed towns; and towns with the most permanently protected land have lower tax rates.[37] This is not to say that cities and counties should not grow—only that they should realistically assess the costs of growth and how to pay for it, as well as consider options such as preservation.

Other Costs of Sprawl

By pursuing more compact development and preserving more open space, communities could avoid or mitigate other costs of sprawl, such as traffic problems, air pollution, water issues, and species loss.

A comprehensive research study published in 2002 shows that the most sprawling cities in the United States have 13 more traffic fatalities per 100,000 people, 41 parts per billion more ozone, and the same level of traffic congestion (not less, as is usually assumed) as the least sprawling cities.[38]

Drought around the nation in 2001–2003 brought water supply worries to the forefront. Sprawl often makes the water supply situation worse, because it increases impervious land cover, thus forcing valuable water to flow out of the region rather than allowing it to percolate down through the soil to recharge groundwater resources. In 1982–1997 in Atlanta, the potential amount of water not infiltrated because of increased imperviousness ranged from 56.9 billion to 132.8 billion gallons annually. Atlanta's losses of water not infiltrated in 1997 amounted to enough water to supply the average daily household needs of 1.5 million to 3.6 million people per year. Dallas was at the lower range of the 20 cities studied, with infiltration losses estimated to be from 6.2 billion to 14.4 billion gallons.[39] Often the only alternatives are to build expensive dams and to increase local water rates.

The same impervious land cover associated with sprawl also threatens water quality. The Denver Regional Council of Governments estimates that sprawling development could affect water quality in 60 subwatersheds in the region—about 25 percent of which could be protected through more compact forms of development.[40] Water rates in the Denver area skyrocketed in 2000–2004, and the state is considering spending billions of dollars to find new water sources and build new dams.

In addition, and certainly pertinent for a nature-friendly community to consider, sprawl is the leading cause of species imperilment in California, affecting 188 of the state's 286 threatened or endangered species.[41] A 1997 Environmental Defense Fund study found that over 85 percent of endangered species in the United States are threatened by habitat degradation and loss, much of which is a result of urbanization.[42]

Green Infrastructure Value

Natural ecosystems can provide building blocks for successful communities just as much as traditional infrastructure such as roads, bridges, and wastewater treatment plants. This natural green infrastructure, consisting of functioning ecosystems, provides many services that we have taken for granted in the past but are now beginning to acknowledge. Some community-scale examples of these services are groundwater recharge and floodwater management (discussed in other sections of this chapter); filtration of pollutants from the soil, water, and air; pollination of food crops and other plants; and soil and water conservation.[43]

Green infrastructure acts as "an interconnected network of green space that conserves natural ecosystem values and functions and provides associated benefits to human populations."[44] This definition encompasses the ecosystem services element mentioned previously and a corresponding economics element (money saved by utilizing nature's help with various services), as well as an important design element—planning how to intentionally incorporate nature with the built environment. Loudoun County, Virginia, has embraced green infrastructure as a basic building block in its Revised Comprehensive Plan. The county broadly defines green infrastructure as follows: "A predominantly natural system of environmental, natural and heritage resources, open space assets and complementary elements that serves as the underlying structure for general land use, planning, and development in the county." Ideally, these should provide the context in which the built environment relates to the natural environment and should guide where and how development and redevelopment are to occur.

Other places recognize the monetary value of open space as well. For instance, a 1992 study calculated that wetlands in California provided up to $22.9 billion in value annually to the state (not including the indefinable value of biodiversity), including water supply, water quality, recreation, and fishing-related jobs.[45]

Although economists may debate about how to place an exact value on nature and the services it provides, the bottom line is hard to ignore.

About two-thirds of U.S. residents rely on surface water for drinking water. Although many cities already have filtration plants, they often need to be expanded to

Loudoun County, Virginia, containing both bucolic rural areas and bustling suburbia, has embraced green infrastructure as a basic building block in its Revised Comprehensive Plan. Photograph by Craig Richardson.

serve new development. Instead of costly new construction, over 140 cities have considered the option that New York City has been pursuing since the early 1990s: protecting drinking water by preserving the watershed. New York City is spending $1.5 billion to protect land upriver instead of building a new water filtration system for $6 to $8 billion. The largest portion of this budget, $260 million, is dedicated to buying land to provide undeveloped buffers around reservoirs. Other significant dollar amounts are earmarked to help farmers reduce pollution, build new storm sewers and septic systems, and update existing sewage plants.[46] Between 1997 and 2004, the city secured over 59,000 acres in land purchases and conservation easements throughout the watershed and will continue to work with willing sellers and to identify strategic properties through 2006.[47]

In another instance, concern about the water supply also led to land conservation. After development was proposed for the Sterling Forest (about 17,000 acres) on the New York–New Jersey border, the two states worked together with private support to purchase the watershed. The results were protection of the water supply for one quarter of New Jersey's residents, recreational open space for both states (the Appalachian Trail crosses the forest), and preservation of the last remaining intact forest in the region. Learning from past experiences, New Jersey developed a new water management master plan in 1996 that, instead of calling for increased capacity (which would have required costly new reservoirs and treatment facilities), contains provisions for resource protection, management, and conservation. The protection element proposes funding watershed acquisition to protect both surface water and groundwater.[48]

After a hard-fought political campaign, voters in Austin, Texas, approved a $13.4 million bond in November 2000 to preserve land in the Barton Springs watershed in order to protect the city's water source. Other bonds were approved in the 1990s for similar purposes, including $23 million in 1992 and $65 million in 1998. Surface water and the underlying Edwards Aquifer are the only sources of drinking water for the arid region, making protection of watershed and recharge areas a high priority.[49]

Trees are another aspect of green infrastructure and help conserve energy by providing shade, absorbing pollutants, stabilizing soil, offering wind protection, reducing noise, and providing habitat for wildlife. For example, the estimated value of 500,000 mature mesquite trees in Tucson is $90,000 per year for runoff control and $1.5 million per year for particulate matter removal.[50] Benefits may be more local and personal— yet very important to the average citizen. To illustrate, some studies suggest that belts of trees 100 feet wide and 45 feet high can cut highway noise in half. A coniferous hedge can reduce the noise of a garbage truck at 90 feet by up to 50 percent.[51] Noise consistently ranks as the number one irritant for urbanites.

American Forests, the nation's oldest nonprofit citizens' conservation organization and a pioneer in the science and practice of urban forestry, has developed the Urban Ecosystem Analysis process to study the quantifiable green infrastructure benefits of forest canopy. The benefits relate primarily to residential summer energy impacts, air pollution removal, and stormwater management. For example, residents of Atlanta save $2.8 million annually on their energy bills owing to shade from Atlanta's current tree canopy.[52] Similarly, the Denver metro area's current tree cover is about 6 percent and provides $2.6 million of air pollution removal benefits annually. If this tree cover were increased to 25 percent, the benefit would be worth $4.4 million annually, removing 1.8 million pounds of pollutants from the atmosphere.[53] And finally, stormwater flow in the Puget Sound metro area (Seattle and other cities surrounding the sound) during a heavy rain has increased about 29 percent since 1972, during which time heavily vegetated areas have decreased 37 percent. To replace the lost stormwater retention capacity with reservoirs and other engineered systems will cost the local communities $2.4 billion.[54]

Avoiding Natural Disasters

The rash of floods and wildfires throughout the country in 2000–2003 has heightened awareness of the cost to governments of such catastrophes. Nature-based alternatives to traditional approaches (such as building more levees or spending more on fire suppression) are becoming more attractive. For example, it may be cheaper to buy floodplain or fire-prone open space and natural areas and leave them undeveloped than to build and pay the consequences.

Floodplain Management

The Great Midwest Flood of 1993 was a turning point for flood control in the United States. The preferred methods of the U.S. Army Corps of Engineers were to construct tall levees and to undertake deep dredging. These clearly did not meet flood prevention goals along the Mississippi River. The Corps had taken some steps before then to use nature for floodplain management—for example, restoring wetlands along the Charles River in the Boston area at a tenth of the cost of a proposed dam.[55] Since the 1993 flood, the federal government has focused more on utilizing nature and has pursued voluntary property buyouts in flood-prone areas. Since then the government has acquired easements on approximately 400,000 acres of flood-prone farmland in 14 states. An additional 200,000 acres of high-risk farmland are being considered in Minnesota and Illinois.[56]

Napa County, California, is one of the first communities in the nation to initiate a "living river" approach for flood control. The county voted in 1998 to raise taxes to pay to take out its flood control system and let the river run free. The Napa Valley had endured 27 floods in less than 150 years. With traditional flood controls in place since the 1960s, resulting property damage costs were more than $500 million in that same time frame.[57] The living river project will cost about $255 million total. The federal government is funding half of this amount, leaving about $127.5 million to come from county and state sources. The project is estimated to result in an annual savings of $26 million in flood damage costs, with a total savings of $1 billion not paid out in insurance claims. New local investment along the river has been stimulated, with $196 million invested since 1999 in the downtown area.[58]

Pima County, Arizona, has a Floodprone Land Acquisition Program that is increasingly used to preserve natural floodplain characteristics in upstream areas. Photograph courtesy of the Pima County Flood Control District.

Fire Management

Suppressing wildfires is expensive. Federal agencies spent $1.4 billion in 2000, $918 million in 2001, and an estimated $1.6 billion for 2002 on suppression efforts.[59] This does not include state and local costs. Even more is being spent on other wildland fire programs. Annual National Fire Plan appropriations now surpass $2 billion on a regular basis.[60] For example, over $50 million was given to state and federal agencies in Colorado alone in 2000 and 2001 as part of the National Fire Plan.[61] The costs are not all financial: in 2002, at least 21 firefighters lost their lives, thousands of people evacuated their homes, hundreds of structures were destroyed, and 6,400,000 acres burned.[62]

The wildland-urban interface, where human development mixes with forests and grasslands, is of most concern to all wildfire suppression agencies, and increasingly for local governments. The 1996 Federal Fire Policy transferred the majority of interface fire protection responsibility to local fire control organizations. While state crews are generally ready for this responsibility, many of the nation's 26,000 rural volunteer fire departments are not as well equipped or as well trained.[63]

Complicating the issue further is that more and more people are moving into the wildland-urban interface. According to 2000 census figures, the number of people living in Colorado's red zones (the areas at risk for catastrophic wildfires) increased by one-third between 1990 and 2000, to 1 million residents.[64]

One potential option for addressing this issue is similar to the strategy for floodplains: plan land use to avoid the problem—designate fire-prone areas as open space or very low-density development (1 unit per 40 acres or more). Congress requested a report in 2002 to explore options for cost containment. A panel of the National Academy of Public Administration concluded that the only way to significantly reduce fire suppression costs is to deal with the root causes. One of these is the increasing community development occurring in and near wildlands. The panel recommends "strategies to avoid development that is hard to protect in fire prone areas."[65] A novel thought!

Increased Property Values

One of the clear benefits of open space and natural resource protection is the positive effect on nearby properties. Residential lots near open space, parks, and woodlands are worth substantially more than those only a short distance away. Residential property values increased by $1,915 per acre for every acre closer to the greenbelt in Boulder,

Colorado, all other factors being equal.[66] In Portland, Oregon, a public park of any kind (including those with recreational facilities) within 1,500 feet of a home served to increase a home's sale price by about $2,200.[67] Further analysis showed more specifically that homes within 1,500 feet of a natural area park (where more than 50 percent of the park is preserved in native and/or natural vegetation) had the largest increase in sale price compared with urban parks (where more than 50 percent is landscaped and developed for recreation—e.g., ball fields) and specialty parks/facilities (i.e., areas having primarily one use—e.g., boat ramp facilities).[68]

Similarly, lots with mature vegetation in a new subdivision command a premium over those that have been denuded and replanted with smaller trees and bushes. Perhaps most compelling are the testimonials from developers who grab a market advantage by building environmentally sensitive developments. And, of course, increased property values generally mean increased tax revenues for local governments, offsetting somewhat the costs of protection.

A study in Indianapolis, Indiana, showed that conservation corridors (greenways that do not provide public access) had a greater effect on housing prices than greenways with multiuse recreational trails. The average premium paid for a home within one-half mile of a greenway trail was $4,384, while homes within one-half mile of conservation corridors garnered a premium of $5,317. Overall, greenways, with or without trails, increased property values by nearly $285 million.[69]

Finally, a study of 4,800 parcels surrounding an 8,300-acre nature reserve in the rapidly urbanizing oak woodlands in Riverside County, California, determined that property closer to the reserve is more valuable. Specifically, a decrease of 10 percent in the distance to the nearest oak stands and to the edge of the permanent open space land resulted in an increase of $4 million in total home values and an increase of $16 million in total land value in the community.[70]

Not only homeowners and municipalities benefit economically from the protection of open space. In Apex, North Carolina, a developer marked up the price of 40 homes in the Shepherd's Vineyard housing development by $5,000 because they bordered a regional greenway, and still those homes were the first to sell.[71] A survey of home buyers cosponsored by the National Association of Home Builders and the National Association of Realtors confirmed that home buyers want to be close to trails: jogging and bicycle trails ranked second in importance behind highway access out of 18 community amenities in the survey.[72] Another study, in Tucson, Arizona, found that homes located within one-half mile of riparian areas proposed for protection commanded a 3 to 6 percent higher sales price than comparable homes that were

Greenways, such as the Monon Trail, shown here, increased property values in Indianapolis by nearly $285 million. Photograph courtesy of Indy Greenways.

not located near riparian areas.[73] Additionally, in a study of the town of Greece, a suburb of Rochester, New York, treed lots sold for an average of $9,500 more than untreed lots.[74]

Nearly 70 percent of developers from around the country said in a 2001 survey that the supply of alternative developments—for example, communities with conserved open space, higher-density developments, and pedestrian- and transit-oriented developments—is inadequate. These developers thought that between 10 and 25 percent of households in their own market areas would be interested in alternative development forms.[75]

Indirect Benefits

In addition to the direct economic benefits of open space and resource protection, a number of reports document a host of other indirect benefits that are harder to quantify but that are nevertheless real and important. These include improved public health, enhanced community character, and benefits for urban residents. For example, there are more indications that compact development patterns may not only save open space and wildlife habitat but also improve the health of residents by encouraging walking or other physical activity. There is also evidence that compact development can actually lower the cost of housing in some instances—just the opposite of what some development advocates assert. Additionally, nature protection provides recreational opportunities for urban residents, such as public parks and low-cost outdoor activities.

Public Health

Land use patterns can also contribute to how much people exercise. American obesity has become headline news, and the leading cause is lowered activity levels. Environmental health experts at the Centers for Disease Control and Prevention published a report that asserts suburbs are designed in such an auto-oriented fashion that residents don't regularly bike or walk.[76] People living in the most sprawling areas of the United States are likely to weigh six pounds more than people living in the most compact county (Manhattan—also known as New York County). Similarly, the odds that a county resident will be obese increases 10 percent with every 50-point rise in the degree of sprawl on the county sprawl index.[77]

One solution is to provide active recreational opportunities close to home, work, and school. Studies have documented that trails near one's home will lead to increased exercise. For example, in studying seven trails in Indiana, researchers found that 74 percent of users of the Monon Trail lived within four miles of the trail, and that for all seven trails, at least 70 percent of users indicated that their participation in some form of physical activity was increased owing to the trail.[78] Other researchers surveyed adults in six North Carolina counties to measure the association between environmental factors and leisure time physical activity. The results indicated that people with access to trails and places to exercise were more likely to engage in recommended levels of physical activity.[79]

Protection of natural resources also contributes to human well-being in that various species of plants and animals serve to protect human health. Sometimes the health benefits are indirect—for example, a rich diversity of animal species existing in a Lyme disease area lessens the risk of humans contracting Lyme disease. In contrast, in a disturbed ecosystem, infectious diseases are able to travel more quickly to human hosts.[80] At other times the health benefits of nature have a very direct connection to humans, as when chemical components from animals or plants are used in medicine. For example, the drug paclitaxel (Taxol), now widely used in cancer therapy, was isolated from the bark of the Pacific yew tree in 1969 as part of a random plant screening process. Because the number and distribution of the Pacific yew was unknown, the National Cancer Institute developed a semisynthetic version of the drug, using yew needles as a base. This chemical compound is very complex, making it unlikely to have been created without the original plant template and highlighting the importance of preserving biodiversity for precisely this reason—access to unusual chemicals that could benefit humankind. [81]

Enhanced Community Character

Thoughtfully preserving natural areas and focusing instead on more compact development patterns can contribute to community character. Critics of low-density, dispersed development decry its ugliness. Visual preference surveys that have been used to gauge the reaction to sprawl typically show that a majority of citizens favor traditional communities over sprawl developments.[82]

Studies have also shown that low-density developments weaken a sense of community or make community building more difficult. One study showed that residents in low-density areas rely more on their cars for shopping and recreation trips and thus are less likely to develop contacts and friendships with neighbors.[83] Another study assessed the psychological sense of community across different neighborhoods and housing conditions in Columbus, Ohio, and found that residents of mixed-use areas had significantly more sense of community than residents of single-family neighborhoods.[84]

The presence of trees and grass in a neighborhood may also contribute to a sense of community and increase the vitality of a neighborhood by increasing the number of social interactions. People are attracted to greenspace and then tend to interact more when they are in the greenspace. Researchers found that the residents of buildings with surrounding greenspace (instead of barren land) in public housing in Chicago had a stronger sense of community and better relationships with their neighbors and reported using less violent ways of dealing with domestic conflicts.[85]

Benefits for Lower-Income Citizens

Being a nature-friendly community does not mean being unfriendly to humans. There are advantages of protecting natural areas for all residents, but especially for lower-income residents, and especially in urban areas. These can include more affordable housing options (if Smart Growth tools are used) and readily accessible and inexpensive recreational opportunities.

Housing Options

No single type of housing can serve the varied needs of the diverse households of the twenty-first century. However, communities that utilize Smart Growth tools as part of a nature protection strategy may be able to address this situation in several ways. First, mixed-use developments can be designed to provide a range of housing types—single family, townhomes, and multifamily developments on a variety of lot sizes. Second, because Smart Growth developments tend to be denser, housing within them will typically be more affordable. All of this is counter to the arguments of some pro-development forces who claim that growth management drives up housing costs.

The assertion that growth management can actually reduce housing costs is supported by major studies by Robert Burchell of Rutgers University.[86] Burchell looked at overall housing costs in a larger area governed by managed growth (at the state or regional level), where development would be restricted in certain locations (e.g., environmentally sensitive lands) and encouraged in others (areas with existing or excess infrastructure capacity). These large-scale studies developed housing cost models to estimate the likely housing price increases in the more restricted outlying areas and the likely housing price decreases in targeted-growth areas (owing to their inherent higher densities and the proposed housing type mix—e.g., more attached housing). Under the planned-development scenarios in Burchell's studies, more housing would be built in core areas than in more rural outlying areas. The studies concluded that overall private housing costs under the planned-growth scenarios would be between 2 percent and 8 percent lower than under the sprawl development scenarios. Thus communities concerned with the affordability of their housing stock could realize savings through the use of less land per home.

Recreational Opportunities for Low-Income Citizens

A visit to urban parks and rivers reveals an undeniable fact—lower-income citizens and their children are heavy users of these "free" recreational opportunities and open space. The positive impacts include the health and social effects mentioned previously, as well as purely recreational benefits.

About four out of five North Americans use their local government recreation and park systems, a relatively high percentage of use compared with other local government services. This percentage includes lower-income residents: 69 percent of

U.S. citizens with household incomes of less than $20,000 used local parks. Nine out of ten persons report significant benefits to themselves, their household, and their community from use of local government recreation and park services, primarily health benefits in the form of physical exercise and stress reduction.[87]

Many states sponsor urban fishing programs to achieve goals such as youth mentoring, environmental education, and water quality protection. Although the results of these efforts are difficult to quantify, participation is increasing. For example, over 40,000 urban anglers in 11 cities participated in Arizona Game and Fish Urban Fishing programs in 2003, including fishing clinics for all ages and capabilities.[88]

Although it is easy to assume that it is good for kids to be active in nature, a research project started in 2003 in the Pacific Northwest to attempt to quantify more clearly the social benefits of youths working in nature programs such as trail building, tree planting, ecosystem restoration, habitat creation, and parks maintenance.[89]

Youth fishing in Kill Van Kull, which separates the City of Bayonne, New Jersey, from Staten Island. The city is one of several partners with the New Jersey Department of Environmental Protection in an urban fishing program. Photograph by Lynette Lurig, courtesy of the New Jersey Department of Environmental Protection.

Paying the Piper: Is the Public Willing?

While many local officials might agree that protecting open space and natural resource areas is good policy, an oft-heard remark is, "We can't afford it. We need new development to pay the bills and to create jobs." And while fiscal impact analysis can help make the case that new development will not necessarily pay its way, in some instances protection and preservation will involve public acquisition of land—which can cost substantial sums. Local elected officials in many jurisdictions quake at the thought of raising taxes or spending more public dollars for open space. However, increasingly, citizens are willing to step up to the plate and tax themselves to preserve open space and natural resource lands. According to a national bipartisan poll conducted in early 2004, 65 percent of American voters would be willing to support modest increases in taxes to pay for programs to protect water quality, wildlife habitat, and neighborhood parks. There was particularly strong support for conservation funding measures from Latino voters—77 percent.[90] An earlier survey by the National Association of Realtors found that more than 80 percent of voters support preserving farmland, natural areas, stream corridors, true wilderness areas, and historic sites in areas under pressure from development, although support decreased among lower-income residents when property tax increases were added in other survey questions.[91]

Many other surveys illustrate that Americans are willing to pay to protect nature. Residents of three counties near Chicago (Kane, McHenry, and DeKalb) were willing to pay $484 per year for five years to permanently protect about 20,000 acres of farmland in their county from development. Concern was so great that protecting farmland and open space was ranked up with reducing crime and improving schools, issues that have historically been most important in the area.[92] Another study found that U.S. households were willing to pay $50 to $330 per year to protect habitat critical to the survival of at-risk fish in the Southwest.[93] California residents indicated they were willing to spend $177 million to $448 million per year to support legislation to protect 6.9 million acres of the state's desert lands.[94] Also, the annual net willingness of Florida residents to pay for the restoration of the Florida Everglades was $70 per household for wildlife species attributes and $59 per household for hydrologic attributes for 10 years (about $7.5 billion total including both items over 10 years). The most highly rated option for both items was the complete restoration alternative.[95]

Although it may be easy to support nature protection in hypothetical situations such as a poll or a "willingness to pay" survey, many Americans are backing up their opinions by actually casting their votes for spending money on nature protection.

"American voters are remarkably consistent in approving three out of every four fund-ing measures for land conservation, both before 9/11 and after, whether in recession or recovery," according to Will Rogers, president of The Trust for Public Land, which tracks ballot measures through its LandVote program.[96]

Many communities over the past decade have passed tax and bond issues to fund open space acquisition—a key element of successful nature protection programs. In fall 2004, voters in 121 communities in 24 states voted to create $3.25 billion in new public funding to protect land as parks and open space. [97] Despite a weak economy in 2003, U.S. voters showed overwhelming support for conservation. One hundred measures in 23 states were approved by voters, with about $1 billion specifically ded-icated for purchase of land for parks, open space, and farmland.[98] Data for 2002 show that three-fourths of all local and state conservation-related ballot measures passed (141 of 189), generating approximately $5.7 billion specifically for land acquisition and restoration. In 2001, over 70 percent of open space financing measures won at the polls, worth an estimated $1.7 billion.[99] Voters have been considering not only nature protection specifically, but also growth issues in general. For example, on November 7, 2000, there were 553 state and local ballot measures (in 38 states and hundreds of communities) dealing with how and where communities grow.[100]

More tourism dollars, enriched quality of life, enhanced property values, more recreational opportunities for local residents, improved flood control, reduced capital infrastructure costs: What community would not want any one of these things? Nature protection can provide all of these benefits and more. From direct economic impacts to less quantifiable social effects, protecting the habitat that a community already has can provide real benefits. How can local jurisdictions incorporate nature protection into their efforts? The next chapter shows how.

BOX 1.3

Resources

General References

Crompton, John. Parks and Economic Development. PAS Report No. 502. Chicago: American Planning Association Planning Advisory Service, 2001.

Main sections deal with real estate values/property taxes, attracting tourists (with valuable information on how to conduct a survey of the economic impact of special events), attracting businesses, and attracting/retaining retirees. Traditional parks are not always distinguished from natural open space.

Lerner, Steve, and William Poole. *The Economic Benefits of Parks and Open Space.* San Francisco: Trust for Public Land, 1999.

Very good overall summary of why it makes sense for local governments to protect open space, with extensive examples of communities.

National Park Service. *Economic Impacts of Protecting Rivers, Trails, and Greenway Corridors.* 4th ed. National Park Service, Rivers, Trails and Conservation Assistance, 1995.

Extensive list of ways to look at economic impacts geared toward concerned citizens, with helpful sections on how to actually use the tools in local communities.

Rasker, Ray, et al. *Prosperity in the 21st Century West: The Role of Protected Public Lands.* Tucson: Sonoran Institute, July 2004.

This report verifies a clear connection between the prosperity of western communities and the vast, publicly owned open spaces that surround them. Filled with important facts on today's economy, with case studies of communities and individuals in business, this study offers recommendations for rural westerners who want to protect their environment and grow their economy at the same time.

Tibbetts, John. "Open Space Conservation: Investing in Your Community's Economic Health." Cambridge, Mass.: Lincoln Institute of Land Policy, 1998.

Good overview of methods for measuring the economic value of open space and alternatives for open space financing.

—continued—

Box 1.3 *(continued)*

Examples of Local Efforts

Economic & Planning Systems. "Quantifying Our Quality of Life: An Economic Analysis of the East Bay's Unique Environment." Oakland, Calif.: East Bay Regional Park District, November 2000.

ECONorthwest. "Economic Benefits of Protecting Natural Resources in the Sonoran Desert." Report prepared for the Coalition for Sonoran Desert Protection, Tucson, Arizona, 2002.

Kiker, Clyde, and Alan Hodges. "Economic Benefits of Natural Land Conservation: Case Study of Northeast Florida." Gainesville: University of Florida, Food and Resource Economics Department, December 2002.

Green Infrastructure

Benedict, Mark A., and Edward T. McMahon (The Conservation Fund). *Green Infrastructure: Smart Conservation for the 21st Century.* Sprawl Watch Clearinghouse Monograph Series. Washington, D.C.: Sprawl Watch Clearinghouse, May 2002.

Daily, Gretchen, and Katherine Ellison. *The New Economy of Nature.* Island Press, 2002.

Ernst, Caryn. *Protecting the Source: Land Conservation and the Future of America's Drinking Water.* 2nd ed. San Francisco: Trust for Public Land and American Waterworks Assoc., 2004.

Heal, Geoffrey. *Nature and the Marketplace: Capturing the Value of Ecosystem Services.* Washington, D.C.: Island Press, 2000.

Notes

[1] We will use the phrase "green infrastructure" in this chapter to mean "an interconnected network of green space that conserves natural ecosystem values and functions and provides associated benefits to human populations," as defined in Mark A. Benedict and Edward T. McMahon (of The Conservation Fund), *Green Infrastructure: Smart Conservation for the 21st Century,* Sprawl Watch Clearinghouse Monograph Series (Washington, D.C.: Sprawl Watch Clearinghouse, May 2002).

[2] The City Parks Forum is a fellowship of mayors, park advisers, and community leaders administered by the American Planning Association.

[3] John Crompton, *Parks and Economic Development,* Planning Advisory Service Report No. 502 (Chicago: American Planning Association, 2001), p. 69.

[4] Steve Lerner and William Poole, *The Economic Benefits of Parks and Open Space* (San Francisco: Trust for Public Land, 1999).

[5] Doug Henton and Kim Walesh, *Linking the New Economy to Livable Community* (San Francisco: James Irvine Foundation, 1998).

[6] Richard Florida, *Competing in the Age of Talent: Quality of Place and the New Economy* (Pittsburgh: R. K. Mellon Foundation, 2000); Paul D. Gottlieb, "Amenities as an Economic Development Tool: Is There Enough Evidence?" *Economic Development Quarterly* 8, no. 3 (August 1994): 270–285.

[7] Timothy Egan, "Drawing a Hard Line Against Urban Sprawl," *New York Times,* December 30, 1996, p. A1.

[8] Florida, *Competing in the Age of Talent.* (See n. 6.)

[9] Ray Rasker and Ben Alexander, *Getting Ahead in Greater Yellowstone: Making the Most of Our Competitive Advantage* (Tucson: Sonoran Institute and Yellowstone Business Partnership, 2003).

[10] Crompton, *Parks and Economic Development,* PAS Report No. 55. (See n. 3.)

[11] Alexander Vias, "Jobs Follow People in the Rural Rocky Mountain West," *Rural Development Perspectives* 14, no. 2 (September 1999); Ray Rasker et al., *Prosperity in the 21st Century West: The Role of Protected Public Lands* (Tucson: Sonoran Institute, 2004).

[12] Crompton, *Parks and Economic Development,* p. 55 (See n. 3.); John L. Crompton, Lisa L. Love, and Thomas A. More, "An Empirical Study of the Role of Recreation, Parks, and Open Space in Companies (Re) Location Decisions," *Journal of Park and Recreation Administration* 15, no. 1 (1997): 37–58.

[13] Crompton, *Parks and Economic Development,* p. 55 (See n. 3.); Crompton, Love, and More, "Empirical Study." (See n. 12.)

[14] Ray Rasker and Andrew Hansen, "Natural Amenities and Population Growth in the Greater Yellowstone Region," *Human Ecology Review* 7, no. 2 (2000): 30–40.

[15] Henton and Walesh. *Linking the New Economy to Livable Community* (see n. 5).

[16] Rasker et al., *Prosperity in the 21st Century West.* (See n. 11.)

[17] Ray Rasker and Ben Alexander, *Working Around the White Clouds: County and Community Profiles Surrounding Idaho's Boulder, White Cloud, and Pioneer Mountains* (Tucson: Sonoran Institute, 2003).

[18]Travel Industry Association of America, "Economic Research: Economic Impact of Travel and Tourism"; www.tia.org.

[19]Bruskin Goldring Research of Edison, New Jersey, "Nature-Based Activities and the Florida Tourist" (Visit Florida Research Office, 1999), as quoted in Ecotourism Society, "USA Ecotourism Statistical Factsheet," 1999; www.ecotourism.org.

[20]U.S. Fish and Wildlife Service, *2001 National Survey on Fishing, Hunting, and Wildlife-Associated Recreation* (Washington, D.C.: U.S. Fish and Wildlife Service, 2002).

[21]Ibid.

[22]Outdoor Industry Association, "Planning for 2004? Stay Informed and Get Ahead of the Trends with the Fifth Edition of the Participation Study," press release, September 17, 2003; www.outdoorindustry.org.

[23]Ibid., "Outdoor Industry Association (OIA) Releases 2002 State of the Industry Report," press release, February 12, 2003; www.outdoorindustry.org.

[24]Fermata, Inc., *The Economic Impact of Wildlife Watching on the Platte River in Nebraska,* report prepared for U.S. EPA Region VII, 1998.

[25]Economic & Planning Systems, "Quantifying Our Quality of Life: An Economic Analysis of the East Bay's Unique Environment" (Oakland, Calif: East Bay Regional Park District, November 2000).

[26]Clyde Kiker and Alan Hodges, *Economic Benefits of Natural Land Conservation: Case Study of Northeast Florida* (Gainesville: University of Florida, 2002).

[27]Trails and Greenways Clearinghouse, "Economic Benefits of Trails and Greenways," fact sheet (n.d.); www.trailsandgreenways.org.

[28]Julie Leones, Bonnie Colby, and Kristine Crandall, "Tracking Expenditures of the Elusive Nature Tourists of Southeastern Arizona," *Journal of Travel Research* 36, no. 3 (1988): 56–64, as quoted in ECONorthwest, *Economic Benefits of Protecting Natural Resources in the Sonoran Desert,* report prepared for the Coalition for Sonoran Desert Protection (Tucson: Coalition for Sonoran Desert Protection, 2002).

[29]The reader should be aware that critics of Smart Growth maintain that in some cases Smart Growth has increased traffic congestion, raised housing and land costs, and created unmarketable housing products and commercial spaces.

[30]Smart Growth principles include compact growth and preservation of open space/environmental resources; mix of uses; cost-efficient provision of public services and infrastructure; quality design, community character, and sense of place; transportation options; housing choice; and efficient, predictable development processes. These principles have been culled from several sources, including the Maryland Department of Planning, "What Is Smart Growth?" (2002); American Planning Association, *The Principles of Smart Development,* PAS Report No. 479 (1998); and Florida Center for Community Design and Research at the University of South Florida, "Guides for Sustainable Community Development" (2002), www.fccdr.usf.edu.

[31]Robert Burchell et al., *Costs of Sprawl—2000,* TCRP Report 74 (Washington, D.C.: National Academy Press, 2002), p. 281.

[32]Amanda Sauer, "The Value of Conservation Easements: The Importance of Protecting Nature and Open Space," World Resources Institute discussion paper, April 9, 2002.

[33]Julia Freedgood, "Cost of Community Service Studies: Making the Case for Conservation" (Washington, D.C.: American Farmland Trust, 2002), p. 8.

[34]Elizabeth Brabec, *On the Value of Open Spaces,* Technical Information Series (Washington, D.C.: Scenic America, 1992).

[35]Paul Tischler, "Fiscal Impact Analysis of Residential Development Alternatives, Lancaster County, PA" (Bethesda, Md.: Tischler & Associates, 1998).

[36]Benedict and McMahon, *Green Infrastructure: Smart Conservation for the 21st Century.* (See n. 1.)

[37]Deb Brighton, "Community Choices: Thinking Through Land Conservation, Development, and Property Taxes in Massachusetts" (Boston: Trust for Public Land, 1999).

[38]Reid Ewing, Rolf Pendall, and Don Chen, *Measuring Sprawl and Its Impact* (Washington, D.C.: Smart Growth America, 2002).

[39]Betty Otto et al., *Paving Our Way to Water Shortages: How Sprawl Aggravates the Effects of Drought* (Washington, D.C.: American Rivers, Natural Resources Defense Council, and Smart Growth America, 2002).

[40]Ann Livingston, Elizabeth Ridlington, and Matt Baker, *The Costs of Sprawl: Fiscal, Environmental, and Quality of Life Impacts of Low-Density Development in the Denver Region* (Denver: Environment Colorado, 2003).

[41]National Wildlife Federation, *Paving Paradise: Sprawl's Impact on Wildlife and Wild Places in California* (Washington, D.C.: National Wildlife Federation, 2001).

[42]David S. Wilcove et al., *Rebuilding the Ark: Toward a More Effective Endangered Species Act for Private Land* (New York: Environmental Defense Fund, 1997).

[43]Gretchen C. Daily et al., "Ecosystem Services: Benefits Supplied to Human Societies by Natural Ecosystems," *Issues in Ecology,* no. 2 (Spring 1997).

[44]Benedict and McMahon, *Green Infrastructure: Smart Conservation for the 21st Century.* (See n. 1.)

[45]Jeff Allen et al., *The Value of California Wetlands: An Analysis of Their Economic Benefits* (Oakland, Calif.: Campaign to Save California Wetlands, 1992), quoted in Save the Bay, *Protecting Local Wetlands: A Toolbox for Your Community* (Oakland, Calif.: Save the Bay, 2000), p. 4.

[46]Gretchen Daily and Katherine Ellison, *The New Economy of Nature* (Washington, D.C.: Island Press, 2002).

[47]City of New York, Department of Environmental Protection, "New York City Acquires 187 Acres in East Fishkill," press release, July 13, 2004.

[48]Richard M. Stapleton, *Protecting the Source: Land Conservation and the Future of America's Drinking Water* (San Francisco: Trust for Public Land, 1998).

[49]Trust for Public Land, *Local Greenprinting for Growth,* vol. 1 (San Francisco: Trust for Public Land, 2002).

[50]Douglas Krieger, *Economic Value of Forest Ecosystem Services: A Review* (Washington, D.C.: Wilderness Society, 2001).

[51]Christopher J. Duerksen with Suzanne Richman, *Tree Conservation Ordinances,* Planning Advisory Service Report No. 446 (Chicago: American Planning Association, 1993), p. 12.

[52]American Forests, *Urban Ecosystem Analysis: Atlanta Metro Area* (Washington, D.C.: American Forests, 2001).

[53]Ibid., *Regional Ecosystem Analysis for Metropolitan Denver and Cities of the Northern Front Range, Colorado* (Washington, D.C.: American Forests, 2001).

[54]Ibid., *Regional Ecosystem Analysis for Puget Sound Metropolitan Area* (Washington, D.C.: American Forests, 1998).

[55]Daily and Ellison, *New Economy of Nature.* (See n. 46.)

[56]National Wildlife Federation, *Higher Ground: A Report on Voluntary Property Buyouts in the Nation's Floodplains: A Common Ground Solution Serving People at Risk, Taxpayers and the Environment* (Reston, Va.: National Wildlife Federation, 1998).

[57]Timothy Egan, "For a Flood-Weary Napa Valley, A Vote to Let the River Run Wild," *New York Times,* April 25, 1998.

[58]Napa County Flood Control and Water Conservation District, "Napa River Flood Protection Project: Progress and Plan Summary 2004"; www.napaflooddistrict.org.

[59]Wildland Fire Statistics, National Interagency Fire Center website; www.nifc.gov.

[60]National Academy of Public Administration, *Wildfire Suppression: Strategies for Containing Costs* (Washington, D.C.: National Academy of Public Administration, 2002), Foreword.

[61]Theo Stein and Jim Hughes, "'Red Zone' Is Burning Problem," *Denver Post,* April 28, 2002.

[62]National Academy of Public Administration, *Wildfire Suppression,* Foreword. (See n. 60.)

[63]National Association of State Foresters website; www.stateforesters.org.

[64]Stein and Hughes, "'Red Zone' Is Burning Problem." (See n. 61.)

[65]National Academy of Public Administration, *Wildfire Suppression,* p. 40. (See n. 60.)

[66]Amanda Sauer in "The Value of Conservation Easements: The Importance of Protecting Nature and Open Space" (World Resources Institute discussion paper, April 9, 2002) references the following source and notes that the data have been converted to 1996 dollars per acre: Mark Correll, Jane Lillydahl, and Larry Singell, "The Effects of Greenbelts on Residential Property Values: Some Findings on the Political Economy of Open Space," *Land Economics* 54, no. 2 (1978): 207–217.

[67]Ben Bolitzer and Noelwah R. Netusil, "The Impact of Open Spaces on Property Values in Portland, Oregon," *Journal of Environmental Management* 59, no. 3 (2000): 185–193.

[68]Margot Lutzenhiser and Noelwah R. Netusil, "The Effect of Open Spaces on a Home's Sale Price [in Portland, OR]," *Contemporary Economic Policy* 19, no. 3 (July 2001): 291–298.

[69]Greg Lindsey et al., *Public Choices and Property Values: Evidence from Greenways in Indianapolis* (Indianapolis: Center for Urban Policy and the Environment, Indiana University—Purdue University Indianapolis, 2003).

[70]Richard B. Standiford and Thomas Scott, "Value of Oak Woodlands and Open Space on Private Property Values in Southern California," USDA Forest Service Gen. Tech. Rep. PSW-GTR-184 (2002).

[71]Don Hopey, "Prime Location on the Trail," *Rails-to-Trails* [quarterly magazine of the Rails-to-Trails Conservancy] (Fall/Winter 1999): 18.

[72]Consumer survey conducted by the National Association of Home Builders and the National Association of Realtors, April 22, 2002; www.americantrails.org/resources/benefits/homebuyers02.html.

[73]Bonnie Colby and Steven Wishart, *Riparian Areas Generate Property Value Premium for Landowners* (Tucson: University of Arizona, College of Agriculture and Life Sciences, 2002).

[74]Brabec, *On the Value of Open Spaces* (See n. 34.); ibid., *Trees Make Sense,* Technical Information Series (Washington, D.C.: Scenic America, 1992).

[75]Jonathan Levine and Aseem Inam, "Developer-Planner Interaction in Accessible Land Use Development," paper presented at the Conference of the Association of Collegiate Schools of Planning, November 2001, Cleveland, Ohio, as quoted in David O'Neill and Victoria Wilbur, *Environment and Development: Myth and Fact* (Washington, D.C.: Urban Land Institute, 2002).

[76]Richard J. Jackson and Chris Kochtitzky, *Creating a Healthy Environment: The Impact of the Built Environment on Public Health,* Sprawl Watch Clearinghouse Monograph Series (Washington, D.C.: Sprawl Watch Clearinghouse, 2001).

[77]Barbara A. McCann and Reid Ewing, "Measuring the Health Effects of Sprawl: A National Analysis of Physical Activity, Obesity, and Chronic Disease" (Washington, D.C.: Smart Growth America and the Surface Transportation Policy Project, September 2003).

[78]Hugh Morris, *Trails and Greenways: Advancing the Smart Growth Agenda* (Washington, D.C.: Rails-to-Trails Conservancy, September 2002), p. 18.

[79]Sara L. Huston et al., "Neighborhood Environment, Access to Places for Activity, and Leisure-Time Physical Activity in a Diverse North Carolina Population," *American Journal of Health Promotion* 18, no. 1 (September–October 2003): 58–69.

[80]Eric Chivian, ed. "Biodiversity—Its Importance to Human Health: Interim Executive Summary," a project of the Center for Health and the Global Environment, Harvard Medical School, 2003, p. 35. The final report will be published as a book (working title, *Sustaining Life: How Human Health Depends on Biodiversity*) by Oxford University Press in 2005.

[81]Ibid., pp. 20–21.

[82]On the other hand, the literature fails to indicate any significant causal relationship between sprawl and aesthetically less pleasing low-density development. Indeed, in one survey in the early 1990s, Americans favored homogeneous neighborhoods over mixed ones by a margin of two to one, according to Lloyd Bookout, "Neotraditional Town Planning: The Test of the Marketplace," *Urban Land* 51, no. 6 (1992): 12–17.

[83]Jack L. Nasar and David A. Julian, "The Psychological Sense of Community in the Neighborhood," *Journal of the American Planning Association* 61, no. 2 (1995): 178–184.

[84]Thomas Glynn, "Psychological Sense of Community: Measurement and Application," *Human Relations* 34, no. 7 (1981): 789–818.

[85]The following sources were consulted: USDA Forest Service bulletin dated January 1996, "Do Trees Strengthen Urban Communities, Reduce Domestic Violence?" as quoted in Jackson and Kochtitzky, p. 14 (See n. 760.); William C. Sullivan, Frances E. Kuo, and Stephen F. DePooter, "The Fruit of Urban Nature: Vital Neighborhood Spaces," *Environment and Behavior* 36, no. 5 (September 2004): 678–700; Frances E. Kuo and William C. Sullivan. "Environment and Crime in the Inner City: Does Vegetation Reduce Crime?" *Environment and Behavior* 33, no. 3 (May 2001): 343.

[86]Robert W. Burchell, *Impact Assessment of the New Jersey Interim State Development and Redevelopment Plan, Report III: Supplemental AIPLAN Assessment* (Trenton: New Jersey Office of State Planning, 1992); ibid., *Fiscal Impacts of Alternative Land Development Patterns in Michigan: The Costs of Current Development Versus Compact Growth* (Detroit: Southeast Michigan Regional Council of Governments, 1997).

[87]Jack Harper, Geoffrey Godbey, and Stephen Foreman, "Just the Facts: Answering the Critics of Local Government Park and Recreation Services," *Parks and Recreation* 33, no. 8 (August 1998): 78–81.

[88]Urban Fishing Fact Sheet, Arizona Game and Fish website; www.azgfd.com.

[89]Kathleen L. Wolf, "Youth and Mental Health: Work Projects in Urban Green Space" in C. Kollin, ed., *Engineering Green: Proceedings of the 11th National Urban Forest Conference* (Washington D.C.: American Forests, 2003).

[90]Trust for Public Land, "Poll Shows Bipartisan Support for Conservation," press release, April 19, 2004; www.tpl.org.

[91]National Association of Realtors, "NAR Survey Shows Public Support for Open Space Depends on Use and Cost." press release, April 25, 2001; www.realtors.org.

[92]Douglas J. Krieger, "Saving Open Spaces: Public Support for Farmland Protection" (Center for Agriculture in the Environment, April 1999); American Farmland Trust, www.farmland.org; accessed November 2002.

[93]Earl R. Ekstrand and John Loomis, "Incorporating Respondent Uncertainty When Estimating Willingness to Pay for Protecting Critical Habitat for Threatened and Endangered Fish," *Water Resources Research* 34, no. 11 (1998): 3149–3155.

[94]Jerrell Richer, "Willingness to Pay for Desert Protection," *Contemporary Economic Policy* 13, no. 4 (October 1995): 93–104.

[95]J. Walter Milon et al., *Public Preferences and Economic Values for Restoration of the Everglades/South Florida Ecosystem,* Economic Report 99-1 (Gainesville: University of Florida, Food and Resource Economics Department, 1999).

[96]Trust for Public Land, "A Clear Victory for Land Conservation: Americans Approve $2.4 Billion in New Open Space Funding," press release, November 4, 2004; http://sev.prnewswire.com/environmental-services/20041104.

[97]See Trust for Public Land under LandVote; www.tpl.org.

[98]Land Trust Alliance and Trust for Public Land, *LandVote 2003: Americans Invest in Parks and Open Space* (San Francisco: Land Trust Alliance and Trust for Public Land, 2004).

[99]Ibid., *LandVote 2002: Americans Invest in Parks and Open Space* (San Francisco: Land Trust Alliance and Trust for Public Land, 2003).

[100]Phyllis Myers and Robert Puentes, *Growth at the Ballot Box: Electing the Shape of Communities in November 2000* (Washington, D.C.: Brookings Institution Center on Urban and Metropolitan Policy, 2001).

CHAPTER 2

Key Program Elements and Best Tools

What is the hallmark of successful nature protection programs? The case studies show that it is savvy, energetic people—politicians and citizens alike—who know how to pick and choose among a menu of tools and tailor them to the local political, social, and environmental conditions. They recognize that one-shot approaches will usually fall short, and instead opt to weave together a number of key elements and tools.

Regulations in the form of zoning controls and other land use standards are often the foundation of these programs, but the track record shows they probably will not succeed alone because of legal constraints like the "takings" issue and political boundaries. And even regulatory hawks have come to realize that strong protective regulations can be loosened quickly if the local political winds change.

Acquisition of sensitive wildlife habitats is another important tool and an effective supplement to regulations. But again, there are serious limits to this tool—raising the money for acquisition and ensuring a steady stream of funding over time is a challenging task, as anyone who has asked voters to pony up at tax time can attest.

However, the truly effective, balanced programs, such as those exemplified by the case study communities, make clear that while these two traditional tools are often indispensable, more well-rounded programs have a better chance of success. Drawing on the know-how from numerous local government nature protection programs over the past years, we have found that a number of additional key elements are inevitably part of the strongest biodiversity protection initiatives.

Program Structure and Administration

How is the local program structured? What resources in terms of staff and budgets are available? Who are the key players, and what about relationships with other organizations and institutions? These indicators relate to how the local program is structured, staffed, and administered. For example, a very good indicator of local interest and efforts in the land use planning sphere is the number of qualified professionals on staff and whether any have natural resource training. Beyond that, have staff in other departments been educated and imbued with a sense of ecological responsibility?

On the institutional side, are there organizations or other agencies in existence that work with the local government toward protection of natural resources? Does the local government lend support to such organizations as land trusts? And do the protection programs go beyond the purely local through regional governmental or intergovernmental agreements? The most effective programs are those that build partnerships and take a regional focus.

Planning

Effective regulatory and acquisition strategies need to be based on careful planning and background work. Has the local government inventoried and mapped natural resource areas before it regulates or acquires land? On the basis of these inventories/ mapping, has the local government adopted a resource protection element in its comprehensive and open space plans that is based on sound ecological principles (e.g., preserving critical lands in blocks versus fragmentation)? Are the plans used as a template for acquisitions? How do the plans tie into regional habitat protection plans?

Acquisition/Funding

Successful programs inevitably have a strong acquisition element to purchase critical habitat, backed by permanent funding sources (e.g., dedicated sales taxes). Land dedication/impact fee programs that require new development to mitigate impacts by setting aside open space or providing funds for that purpose are also becoming increasingly important facets of acquisition strategies.

Regulations

Zoning and land development regulations are typically the backbone of local government resource and wildlife habitat protection programs. They can take many forms, ranging from riparian setbacks to conservation subdivision options to resource conservation overlay districts. Additionally, fiscal impact assessment tools that gauge the true cost of development can be a valuable element. Such tools often work to discourage unwise development or lay the groundwork for mitigation requirements. Typically, the existence of a number of such regulatory regimes is a good indicator that the local government is serious about habitat protection, especially if implementation is strong and effective.

Restoration

Particularly in older urban and suburban jurisdictions, a good deal of habitat has been degraded. A good indicator for these communities is attempts to restore damaged habitats (e.g., eroded stream banks along urban drainages). An increasing number of greenfield communities require restoration of habitat and vegetation damaged or destroyed during the development process.

Leading by Example

A probative test of local resolve is often whether local governments follow their own rules (e.g., zoning regulations) and take good care of the lands under their jurisdiction (e.g., parks). This section emphasizes the importance of "walking the talk."

Social Indicators

Some critics claim that biodiversity and nature protection are only for the well-to-do. Smart communities embrace programs that attempt to ensure that everyone benefits from habitat protection and that such programs don't have adverse impacts on working-class families. Some of these efforts encourage infill development and urban revitalization that can help limit sprawl and preserve open space. Others enact inclusionary housing programs that require new developments to include a fair share of affordable housing. A growing number of cities and urban counties have initiated park and recreation programs that support fishing and similar activities that are easily accessible to lower-income city dwellers.

Education

Education programs for local government employees and citizens can be essential to laying a strong foundation of respect for local habitat protection regulations. Programs in local schools can help create an educated citizenry. Ambitious education and involvement programs can provide political support and invaluable volunteer time to resource protection efforts.

Results

In the final analysis, results speak loudly of a community's commitment to resource protection. How much land is actually being protected? What is the condition of local environmental resources like water? Is the area losing species or are they holding their own? Communities are beginning to use more than just anecdotal information to gauge progress in their nature protection programs.

Innovative Approaches

In addition to the more traditional indicators discussed previously, local governments around the country have demonstrated a great deal of creativity in implementing a variety of other programs, policies, and laws that support resource protection. Some have effective landowner outreach programs. Others have native plant nurseries that support local vegetation protection and mitigation requirements. Other jurisdictions have funded estate planning for ranchers to help them craft plans to protect open space. Existence of such efforts is a good indicator of local government commitment in this arena.

These key elements, discussed in greater depth below, make up a successful nature protection program. Implementing these tools can help spell success. However, each tool can also pose challenges from a variety of perspectives—legal, political, and financial.

Tables 2.1 and 2.2 (see end of the chapter) summarize how the each of the individual communities in the case studies approaches the use of these key program elements and best tools.

Program Structure and Administration

Local elected officials are usually can-do people who are impatient to get things done—and rightly so. If a tract of prime wildlife habitat is being threatened with development, they will often spring into action to purchase it or enact protective regulations. However, in the long run, a solid nature protection program structure that is staffed by knowledgeable professionals will trump one that is reactive and piecemeal; the case studies amply demonstrate this. If the protection efforts are scattered among several agencies with weak coordination or key departments are starved for help, then almost inevitably programs will suffer and fail to reach their full potential. By the same token, a well-oiled local protection machine that does not mesh gears with regional preservation initiatives will fall short.

Local governments need to pay attention to three basics of program administration and structure: staffing, internal program organization, and partnerships and regional alliances.

Staffing

There are two things to look for when it comes to staffing of nature protection programs. First, does the local government take the issue seriously enough to hire adequate staff? Baltimore County, Maryland, is a perfect example of a community that backs its initiatives with a sufficient number of staff in key departments. The consolidated agency that oversees resource protection has over 100 trained staff, with another 50 in the land use planning department. Not surprisingly, the county has one of the most effective biodiversity protection programs in the nation, with well-rounded regulatory, acquisition, and restoration elements. But what of those smaller jurisdictions that can barely afford one planner, let alone 100? Sanibel, Florida, shows that it can be done with a few good men and women. This city of just over 6,000 people makes do with a staff of only five planners and a couple of natural resource specialists to handle one of the country's most ambitious resource protection agendas. How? Hard work by staff—*and* with the helping hands of hundreds of volunteers courtesy of nonprofit organizations like the Sanibel-Captiva Conservation Foundation.[1] Sanibel has even delegated some important monitoring and enforcement programs to volunteers.

Where money is tight—most everywhere—smart jurisdictions are looking to tap steady funding streams that are resource related. One prime candidate in many places is water and utility funds and fees that pay for water plants, wastewater treatment, and similar facilities. In Austin, Texas, for example, the major nature preserve is managed by the Austin Water Utility instead of the Parks and Wildlife Department because the utility has a steady independent stream of funding through water tap fees. The essential linkage is that protection of the natural area helps to protect the city's water sources.

Internal Structure/Organizational Framework

Because resource protection is a relative newcomer in terms of local government organization and responsibility, responsibility for it has often been fragmented among several agencies. Planning, parks and recreation, and public works/utilities are often all involved. While the case studies suggest there is no "right" way to marshal a successful biodiversity protection effort, they do provide some important do's and don'ts. Fort Collins, Colorado, with its streamlined Department of Community Planning and Environmental Services, has successfully combined development review and long-range planning—two critical pieces that are sometimes divorced in other jurisdictions. Similarly, in Baltimore County, development review finds a home in the same consolidated agency as does watershed management and land preservation. And in Dane County, Wisconsin, there has been a high degree of coordinated land use planning and development review between the Planning and Development Department and Parks (which oversees land acquisition and open space management).

These more efficient structures compare favorably to the multiplicity of agencies involved in resource protection in places like Austin, where the very fragmented structure of the program is a drag on an otherwise impressive effort. In other places, lack of

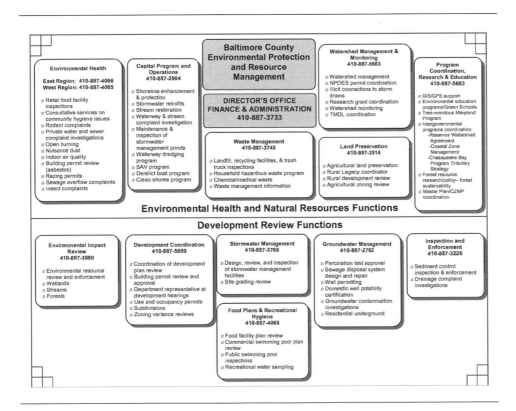

Organizational chart for the Department of Environmental Protection and Resource Management in Baltimore County, Maryland. Chart courtesy of Baltimore County, Maryland.

coordination and even interdepartmental warfare between planning and public works or utility departments responsible for building roads and water facilities can sometimes encourage growth, even in places with high natural values. Eugene, Oregon, has had more success in this arena than most, albeit somewhat serendipitously. Wetlands protection and parks staff are housed in the public works department, in part because when the wetlands program was set up in the 1990s, stormwater fees, administered by public works, offered a reliable funding source for the new initiative. The presence of these resource-oriented programs and personnel in public works has made for easier coordination with the planning department on nature protection endeavors. Additionally, city staff have taken the initiative to form several interdepartmental teams to coordinate environmental activities both internally and externally.

One particularly important linkage that is emerging in several jurisdictions, such as Loudoun County, Virginia, is a good working relationship between planners and economic development specialists. Loudoun County has several economic development staffers dedicated exclusively to working with rural landowners to promote rural economy uses (e.g., vineyards, Christmas tree farms, rural conference centers) as alternatives to residential subdivisions—a key facet of the county's comprehensive plan and development regulations.

Partnerships/Intergovernmental Cooperation

No city or county is an island—either geographically or politically—when it comes to resource protection. Critters just do not seem to be able to read maps to see where one local government's jurisdiction ends and another's starts. Unfortunately, as the case studies so vividly attest, cooperation on regional resource protection is probably at its lowest ebb since the 1970s in this country. Regional government powers and planning are on the wane, and many state programs for local resource protection are slowly being starved by shortsighted state legislatures.

A good example of the challenges facing even the strongest regional planning and governance bodies can be seen in the Minneapolis/Saint Paul case study. The Metropolitan Council has long been the shining light of regional planning advocates. Its regional plan, to which local governments must conform their plans and regulations, has a newly formed resource protection goal. The council also has a say in extension of water and sewer services that can spur growth in the wrong places if not scrutinized. While the council has carried out a successful regional parks initiative since the 1970s, local governments are increasingly ignoring the council's plans, and a more conservative governor and his appointees sporadically place less emphasis on land use planning and natural resource protection. The council is hardly alone in facing political animosity toward regional planning.

So, just as scientists are telling us that nature protection strategies must take a bigger-picture regional view (what they call a landscape level), local governments are being increasingly left to their own devices to forge the regional links essential to successful biodiversity strategies. Indeed, many, like the township officials in Dane County, Wisconsin, actively oppose any type of regional initiatives, viewing them as unholy assaults on local autonomy.

As the case studies illustrate, however, there are several notable exceptions. One is the habitat conservation plans being implemented in several of the case study communities. These plans, driven by the need to comply with the federal Endangered Species Act, often take a truly regional perspective, focusing on where the habitats and wild things are rather than artificial government boundaries.

Another bright spot is in places like Florida, where state critical area legislation gives local governments the choice of cooperating to protect resources or facing state intervention—which to most local officials is like waving a red flag in front of a bull. The Charlotte Harbor is an exemplary multijurisdiction habitat resource planning and management effort involving three counties.

But these are not the rule, and resource advocates might be wise to take a close look at several voluntary cooperative efforts at regional resource protection. Dane County, Wisconsin, offers a good lesson on how one local government can, with a small investment, coax other local governments into a productive regional planning partnership. In Dane County, a smart county executive has initiated several modestly funded programs to assist its constituent towns and townships in their land use plans, with encouraging results. For example, the county helps fund local programs aimed at revitalizing small-town downtowns, thereby helping to reduce sprawl and resource damage outside their borders. An increasing number of counties nationwide are realizing that it is more cost-effective to help fund such planning efforts and infrastructure capacity building in towns rather than to allow large-lot development to sprawl throughout rural areas—which are expensive to serve and often have adverse impacts on sensitive natural areas.

The Northeastern Illinois Planning Commission and the Chicago Wilderness Coalition (with its 170+ public and private organization members) have produced a biodiversity atlas and adopted a regional biodiversity plan, all on a voluntary basis. Similarly, Placer County, California, and Grand Traverse Bay, Michigan, provide exemplary public-private programs that look beyond the boundaries of one jurisdiction.

Planning

While it sounds obvious, sound planning is an absolutely essential foundation of any successful implementation strategy, particularly those involving growth management regulations and acquisition programs. In some places, the ruling credo seems to be ready, shoot, aim—new regulations are imposed or land is purchased hastily with only minimal forethought. As a result, the essential foundation for regulations and acquisition programs is weak, often leading to legal troubles later on or erosion of political support.

Planning as used here means a variety of things. Mapping and an understanding of the location and extent of critical resources are the bedrock of most successful nature protection programs. Planning also means building on that essential information and identifying important demographic and economic trends to craft comprehensive protection strategies.

Good planning also means linking land use planning with capital facilities planning, so when lands are identified as worthy of protection from a natural resource perspective, sewer lines and roads are not extended willy-nilly into the area, thereby making preservation dicey at best.

Mapping and background environmental studies, comprehensive land use and habitat protection plans, and acquisition planning are the essential ingredients of good planning.

Mapping and Environmental Studies

One of the most important developments over the last 20 years of natural resource protection efforts has been the ever-increasing amount of basic background information available to local governments in their habitat protection planning programs. Prior to the landmark 1970s Sanibel Plan—the nation's first comprehensive land use plan, based on identification of six ecological zones—most local nature protection programs were based on a brew of anecdotal observations of wildlife patterns and hopeful guesses. Since then, many state governments through their natural resource departments have produced increasingly sophisticated maps and backup information on the location and extent of critical wildlife habitats. Many local governments have built on this information and have gone several steps further, solidifying the foundation of their protection plans—on both the regulatory and the acquisition fronts. These efforts have been buttressed by the increasing availability of accurate habitat information produced by satellite imagery and aerial photos.

Pittsford, New York, is a prime example of a relatively small jurisdiction spending the time and money to produce a solid footing for the use of regulatory and acquisition tools. As part of its Greenprint Program, Pittsford citizens identified key parcels throughout its jurisdiction—about 2,000 acres—that appeared to be worthy of protection. All of these undeveloped pieces of land were evaluated and ranked by a consulting biologist on the basis of available background information and a site visit. The highest-value sites were included in the Greenprint Program, which combined development rights purchase and land use regulation to protect them. Sites that were not considered to be of high value were designated for development.

Farmington Valley, Connecticut, communities have undertaken a similar resource identification project that augmented simple mapping with field visits and ranking of sites. The resulting profiles helped communities in identifying sites to protect as well as tracts that were more appropriate for development.

Several other case study communities such as Eugene, Oregon; Fort Collins, Colorado; and Baltimore County, Maryland, are also good examples of local governments that have based their habitat protection regulatory agendas on detailed mapping and background studies.

Comprehensive Plans/Habitat Conservation Plans

Thirty years ago, ecologically based planning was in its infancy. Then came the Sanibel Plan, which was grounded in an analysis of habitat and ecological zones. The plan was implemented directly by a set of zoning regulations that restricted uses and densities on the basis of the area's environmental sensitivity. That plan continues to guide growth on Sanibel Island today and has served as the template for many other habitat protection efforts across the United States. It is still the shining example of how a local government and its citizens can translate habitat mapping and environmental background studies into a clear vision for a community. With its specific goals and objectives, the plan has been implemented through regulations, acquisition, and other tools.

Many states now *require* local governments to include a natural resources element in their local comprehensive plans. Many communities do so without state prompting. It is the important middle step in the mapping/study-to-implementation continuum. In addition to setting the stage for specific implementation tools, a strong natural resources element also helps to reconcile competing community objectives, such as affordable housing, economic development, and recreation. Potential conflicts can be identified before a controversial development is proposed in the wrong place. Indeed,

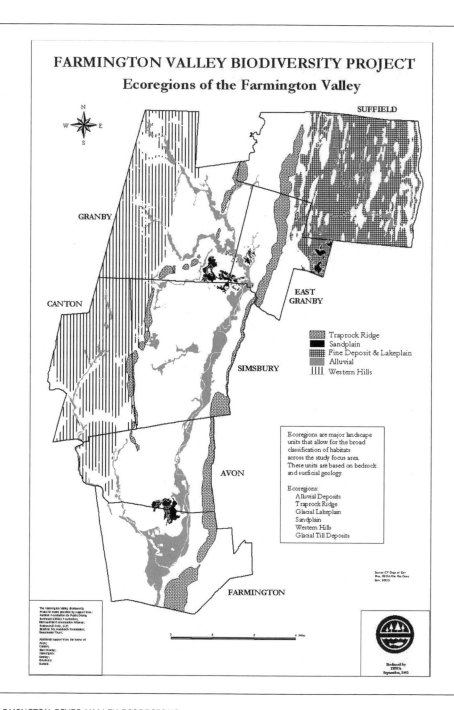

FARMINGTON RIVER VALLEY ECOREGIONS
This map of ecoregions in the Farmington River valley in Connecticut shows citizens why one town has different habitats and species than another nearby town. Map courtesy of Alex Persons, Farmington River Watershed Association.

as the Farmington Valley case study demonstrates, a plan can be valuable not only because it identifies important habitats that should be preserved but also because it targets those areas that are appropriate for development. The comprehensive planning process also throws light on the importance of linking disparate elements of a community's growth. For example, Baltimore County, Maryland, successfully melded rural protection strategies and urban infill.

An increasing number of communities are taking their resource protection plans to the next level by crafting specific area plans for high-value habitat that focus on protection of a specific resource (such as rivers or wetlands) throughout a jurisdiction. Eugene, Oregon, and Austin, Texas, are two excellent examples of cities that have focused on a particular resource as a springboard to more protection. The primary advantage of this targeted approach is that it is often easier to rally citizens around protection of a specific resource than to create a more broad-based coalition. Thus, in Eugene, wetlands have been used as an effective rallying cry, while both Austin and the Chesapeake Bay in Baltimore County have rallied behind protecting sensitive aquifer recharge areas. Indeed, the case studies teach an important lesson in this regard. While generating citizen support for generic plans and implementation strategies can be challenging, those programs that have an iconic resource—a big animal like an elk or a major river or body of water—have a much greater chance of lasting success.

In some communities, the targeted planning approach has been carried much further, thanks to the dictates of the federal Endangered Species Act. As witnessed by the Placer County, California, and Austin, Texas, case studies, communities have a tremendous incentive to develop detailed habitat conservation plans that preserve large, connected swathes of critical habitat for threatened and endangered species. The alternative is to have the federal government exercise direct land use permitting authority through the U.S. Fish and Wildlife Service. While these habitat conservation plans can be time consuming and expensive to prepare, they represent some of the most sophisticated land use planning for natural resource protection now being undertaken in this country. They often cut across multiple jurisdictional boundaries and involve all three levels of government. Their resource focus is often on multiple species and multiple habitat types. The clear benefit of this cooperative approach is that local governments share the burden of implementation and that planning and protection are not artificially constrained to one jurisdiction.

The Sonoran Desert Conservation Plan adopted by Pima County, Arizona, is an interesting example of a local government that has gone beyond the dictates of the federal Endangered Species Act. That plan has won regional, national, and international awards for its scope. The most impressive aspect of this plan is that it considers biodiversity protection at an ecosystem level, rather than simply at a species level. Although the plan was developed because of federal endangered species pressures, the county chose to adopt a stronger conservation plan than might otherwise have been required by the federal government. The plan and its data are now being used as the basis for the federally required multispecies conservation plan that will be adopted separately in the future.

Acquisition and Planning

Sound mapping and identification of key resources have also been an essential building block of some of the best local government habitat acquisition programs. In Fort Collins, Colorado, the city's extensive mapping efforts have not only been used in the regulatory review process but have played a key role in setting priorities for the community's extraordinary open space acquisition program. Similarly, in Dane County, Wisconsin, mapping has helped redirect the county parks program more toward preservation and protection and away from "boat launches and picnic tables."

DeKalb County, Georgia's, programs demonstrate the value of involving citizens in the process of identifying lands to be preserved through acquisition. In 2000, after the State of Georgia set aside $30 million for open space acquisition, DeKalb County adopted a comprehensive parks and open space strategic plan. A key feature of the plan was a citizen survey that identified priorities for facilities and protection. Walking and biking trails as well as nature preserves ranked high in the survey, setting the stage for a $125 million bond referendum to fund the county's greenspace program. The referendum passed, and citizens then nominated sites for inclusion in the system. Two criteria for selection were directly relevant to biodiversity protection—improving water quality and protection of scenic and natural features such as wildlife habitat, wetlands, and stream buffers.

Acquisition/Funding

Experience demonstrates that a variety of tools is necessary for the "compleat" resource protection program. Regulations are often essential, but successful programs inevitably have a strong acquisition element backed by reliable, long-term funding sources (e.g., dedicated sales taxes) or land dedication/impact fee programs that require new development to mitigate impacts by setting aside open space or providing funds for that purpose. Why cannot regulations alone do the job? First, it may be necessary for a jurisdiction to forbid any development whatsoever in a particularly critical area—a breeding or nesting area, for example. Such restrictions might raise difficult constitutional "takings" issues involving the right to make a reasonable economic use of a property. Second, there may be instances in which the lands being acquired should be opened to the public or need to be subject to intense management and oversight. In such cases, regulations would fall short because it is difficult to require access without compensation. Finally, in some instances, tough regulations to protect critical habitats might pass legal muster but generate intense political opposition. In such instances, the local government's best option may be to purchase development rights or the entire parcel to defuse any controversy.

Some of the more innovative local and regional strategies to provide adequate funding for land acquisition and other resource protection programs concentrate on long-term funding sources that have worked around the country, open space dedication and impact fee requirements, transferable development rights programs, and funding and incentives for infill development.

Long-Term, Reliable Funding

Just as sensitive-area acquisition programs are essential complements to regulatory programs, so too are reliable funding sources an indispensable facet of successful acquisition efforts. Jurisdictions that get caught up in a reactive, crisis mode of purchasing sensitive natural areas when threatened by development find that they may pay extortionate prices for last-second purchases and that these types of piecemeal acquisitions make it difficult to assemble an ecologically functioning system of open space reserves. Local jurisdictions have grappled with this challenge in myriad ways.

Not to be overlooked is the importance of state and federal assistance for open space and critical habitat acquisition. Many of the most successful case study community acquisition programs—Baltimore County, Maryland; DeKalb County, Georgia; and Dane County, Wisconsin—quickly point to the strong financial incentives created by their state governments. Maryland's Rural Legacy and GreenPrint programs provide substantial matching funding to local governments to save unprotected natural lands and link them together through a system of corridors. The State of Wisconsin earmarked $10 million annually for 10 years for open space acquisition from a voter-approved state stewardship fund—money that Dane County leverages as part of its ambitious land protection strategy. A number of states also tap into state lottery funds for open space acquisitions. The State of Colorado is the most impressive in this regard:

Its lottery will generate over $100 million for open space preservation over the next decade. And as Eugene, Oregon, demonstrates, there are significant pots of money within the federal government available to local governments with grantsmanship savvy.

The best local programs build on outside funding sources. Some, like Baltimore County's, have established a sterling track record of annual appropriations from general revenues for land acquisition. In this case, the county uses its cut of the state real estate transfer tax. Dane County has ponied up $1 million annually since 1990 from its general funds. But that is the exception rather than the rule. Acquisition programs left to the vagaries of annual funding quite frequently tend to be put on a starvation diet. Moreover, as Loudoun County, Virginia, illustrates, annual appropriations can be slashed by a new, less sympathetic governing body.

An alternative approach that has been successful is the passage of major bond referendums for long-term open space purchase programs in places like Dane County, Wisconsin, and DeKalb County, Georgia. In April 1999, Dane County citizens approved a $30 million bond issue that has significantly ramped up the county's ability to acquire critical pieces of habitat and open space that are under development pressure. A small property tax increase will retire the bonds. Similarly, in March 2001, DeKalb County citizens overwhelmingly approved a $125 million bond issue that has already enabled the county to acquire thousands of acres of open space, including several sensitive habitats. Key to the success of both of these programs were plans and studies that helped to assure citizens that funds would be spent carefully and thoughtfully for land acquisition—they were not writing a blank check for a local spending spree. The same is true for Pima County, Arizona, where years of study for the Sonoran Desert Conservation Plan (SDCP) had identified priority habitat that the county should acquire to meet the goals of both the SDCP and the county's federally required multispecies conservation plan. When Pima County voters went to the polls in May 2004, 65.7 percent of them agreed to spend $112 million for these high-priority habitat lands, with the potential to acquire up to 600,000 acres.

Still, these bond-funded programs can have their ups and downs. Eugene, Oregon, is a prime example of the vagaries of using occasional bond referenda to fund open space purchases. The city has a history of periodic bond-funded open space acquisition initiatives dating back to the 1940s. Several bond issues in the 1970s helped protect ridgelines and riparian habitat along the Willamette River. But a sluggish economy in the 1980s and 1990s hampered passage of any bond issues for open space for a long period. Only in 1998 did the city get back on track with another bond issue that focused primarily on recreational needs.

The City of Fort Collins, Colorado, started its acquisition program by purchasing riparian areas along the Poudre River, which runs through town. Photograph by Lesli Ellis.

Jurisdictions like Larimer County and Fort Collins, Colorado, have taken advantage of state enabling legislation to earmark part of their local sales tax for land acquisition and habitat protection purposes. Because they are based on taxation of retail sales rather than real property, these taxes seem easier for voters to digest. Moreover, while they are typically adopted by a local referendum, they tend to provide funds for a longer period than bond referendums—usually from 5 to 10 years. And perhaps most importantly, a small-percent sales tax levy will usually generate hefty sums of money. In Fort Collins, a regional market center, the city projects that a voter-approved ¼-cent sales tax levy through 2030 will generate by 2013 $55 million dollars for natural areas, trails, and parks. A similar levy in Larimer County produced $50 million in only 6 years between 1996 and 2002.

One important point local governments with aggressive acquisition programs and dedicated funding sources need to keep in mind—those lands being acquired will need to be managed. Some will need to be restored. Others will require limiting and managing public access. All of these can be expensive propositions. Jurisdictions like Fort Collins that have a decade of experience in this arena are beginning to set aside a significant slice of this acquisition funding for long-term care and management. In Larimer County, about 15–30 percent of the funds are set aside each year for staff and management. The ability to allocate funds to these purposes should be made clear in any enabling referenda language.

Another promising long-term, reliable source of open space acquisition and management funds that local governments are tapping into is local utility revenues. Local utility funds are huge cash generators, as people pay their water/sewer bills monthly. While water and sewer tap and use fees by law usually must be spent for improvements and programs related to the provision of these services, cities like Austin, Texas, have established the necessary legal and policy links between utilities and open space preservation. In this instance, water tap fees are used to manage lands to protect aquifer recharge areas—Austin pumps much of its water from wells. It just so happens that these recharge areas are prime wildlife habitat, so the purchases serve double duty. Similarly, an increasing number of communities are using stormwater utility funds to restore damaged drainage ways to their natural conditions—which dramatically improves both riparian and aquatic habitats.

A final important aspect of local funding for acquisition programs relates to assistance for local nonprofit land preservation organizations. Both Dane and Baltimore counties have provided annual funding for such groups. Baltimore County, for example, has provided county funds for conservation easement purchases made by local land trusts as part of the state's Rural Legacy Program. Dane County has allocated about 20 percent of its new pot of acquisition money (about $600,000 annually) to local nonprofit land conservation groups and local governments that are attempting to acquire and protect resource lands identified in the county open space plan. Recipients must match the county dollars, among other grant criteria. All parties agree that this kind of seed money can produce huge benefits and a good deal of leverage.

Land Dedication, Mitigation, and Impact Fees

Often different protection tools can be designed to interact and support one another. Such is the case with land acquisition and land use regulations. In many jurisdictions, hard-cash acquisition programs are supplemented by land use regulations that require developers to dedicate land or pay impact fees to address demands for open space and recreational lands necessitated by their projects. Such programs are subject to legislative and judicially imposed limits that allow local governments to exact only an amount of land/fees that is reasonably related to the demand created by a particular development. Also, an increasing number of communities require developers to mitigate the impacts of their developments on wetlands, vegetation, and other sensitive habitats by replacing them on- or off-site. While the experience in the case study communities shows that these tools will rarely be the backbone of a strong acquisition program, they can be useful supplements to purchase programs.

Most of the case study jurisdictions require residential subdivisions to dedicate a specified amount of land for open space and recreation. Reference is often made to national standards that call for up to 10 acres of parkland to be set aside for every 1,000 project residents (a good example of this is Placer County, California). Typically, fees may be paid in lieu of land dedication. One of the real problems with many of these dedication requirements is that they give the developer a free hand in choosing what lands to set aside or whether simply to pay the in lieu fee. Sometimes this works well, because the developer wants to dedicate lands that are unbuildable, which are often those most sensitive from an environmental perspective. But in some instances, the developer chooses to carve into the best habitats because they are attractive parcels (e.g., treed lots, next to a stream) and to dedicate the leavings to the locality. Jurisdictions like Fort Collins have altered this equation by giving the city the authority to select the property to be dedicated, based on a priority list that ranks natural habitats and other sensitive parcels identified in city open space plans at the top.

Increasingly, communities are requiring residential developers not only to dedicate to the public a small percentage of land for open space, but also to set aside additional acreage for *private* open space to which the public does not have access. These set-aside requirements typically run from 10 to 40 percent of the site, depending on location—with larger set-asides being required in rural areas. Priority is usually given to protection of sensitive natural areas in selecting land for the set-aside. These private land set-aside regulations can be extremely effective in protecting large tracts of open

Placer County, California, acquired the Towle property next to Tahoe National Forest as part of its Placer Legacy Open Space Conservation Program. Photograph by Loren Clark.

space important as wildlife habitat. They can generate opposition from the development community because such standards, in effect, reduce allowable density on a property unless the developer is allowed to shift such density to smaller lots on the remainder of the parcel. Additionally, care must be taken to ensure that there is some entity responsible for managing the resulting open space and ensuring that it is not used for non-open-space purposes.

A number of the case study jurisdictions also have imposed mitigation requirements on developers to offset the adverse environmental impacts of their developments. In Placer County, California, for example, the county already requires replacement of trees removed from a site and is proposing to tighten those standards and add a strong open space conversion fee to offset impacts to open space that cannot be mitigated on-site. Other local governments, like Dane County, Wisconsin, are following the lead of the federal government by pushing for "no net loss" of important habitat—wetlands, for example. In Dane County, one enterprising developer has established a wetland mitigation bank by creating wetlands and then selling pieces of it to other developers to help them meet their regulatory mitigation requirements. Eugene, Oregon, has gone even further by establishing a municipal wetlands mitigation bank. The bank provides mitigation credits to developers who under local and federal regulations need the credits to offset impacts to wetlands on their building sites. Costs are about $50,000 per credit to reflect the expense associated with development, design, planning, and construction of the wetlands as well as monitoring. About $2 million in credits have been sold over the past 10 years.

Land dedication and mitigation requirements are often supplemented or superseded by park and open space impact fees in many jurisdictions. In Larimer County, Colorado, for example, every residential developer must pay an impact fee of up to $700 per unit toward regional park expansion. The county shares a portion of this fee with Fort Collins in recognition that the city's parks and open space programs serve county residents. Legally in most states, open space impact fees can usually be used only for acquisition, not for park maintenance or management. While impact fees can generate modest sums of money for land acquisition and can be useful in a land acquisition program, they are one-shot affairs and do not provide a reliable, stable funding source. Moreover, developers and residents of new subdivisions not unexpectedly put pressure on local officials to spend those fees close to home in a way that clearly benefits the new developments. While not a legal requirement, that pressure can make it difficult to rely primarily on impact fees for a comprehensive open space and habitat protection program. The other limitation on open space and park impact fees is that, despite background studies justifying substantial fees, because of political considerations they are rarely set high enough to truly offset development impacts.

Purchase of Development Rights: Stretching the Acquisition Dollar

A growing number of jurisdictions, like Baltimore County, Maryland, are using a technique to stretch their land acquisition dollars—purchasing development rights on key parcels rather than buying the entire fee. Experience shows that communities can save anywhere from 25 to 50 percent over fee purchase, depending on development demand. King County, Washington, has been one of the national leaders in using purchase of development rights (PDR) as a land protection tool. This is a technique that works when a local government wants to protect open space but keep land in agriculture or other active use. Loudoun County, Virginia, initiated a promising purchase of development rights program that was helping to augment its strong protective regulations, taking the sting out while providing options for willing sellers. Unfortunately, that program has been targeted for elimination by a new pro-growth board of supervisors who see it as a program to subsidize wealthy landowners.

Here is how purchase of development rights can work. In return for an agreement not to develop houses or commercial uses, a farmer gets cash based on an appraisal of the value of the land without restrictions and with development rights stripped away. Thus the tool puts money in the farmer's pocket, retains the land on the tax roles, and keeps the family on the land to manage it, which saves the government even more money. Pittsford, New York, is using a PDR program funded by a $9.9 million bond issue to preserve 1,000 acres of land on seven farms. If the development restrictions can also address preservation of key habitats (e.g., wetlands, stream buffers), then everyone wins. However, the tool is more limited where the goal is to preserve large tracts of wildlife habitat untouched or to provide public access. Then full-fee purchase will probably make more sense. PDR will also be less likely to be attractive in situations in which the development value of a property is low because it is already subject to significant zoning restrictions (like large minimum lot sizes and environmental standards).

Purchase of development rights can also be an important supplement to regulations in situations in which some development on a property may be appropriate, but at lower densities than allowed under the existing zoning. A farmer might agree, for example, to reduce the allowable number of homes that can be built on his property substantially, but still retain the right to build at very low densities in selected locations that avoid adverse impacts on key natural resource areas. In return, the development rights on the critical areas are purchased by the locality. Thus the sweetener of development rights purchase may be the key ingredient that makes a conservation-oriented planned development agreement work.

Public-Private Funding Partnerships

All of the most successful land acquisition programs featured in the case studies share the common feature of substantial private contributions—either in terms of land or money. Sanibel's impressive land acquisition efforts in Florida were jump-started by over $1 million in private contributions. Staff in Dane County, Wisconsin, point to the generous contributions by private parties of land to create or expand several major county parks and nature reserves. Baltimore County's partnerships with local land trusts in Maryland has resulted in the donation of over 12,000 acres protected by conservation easements—allowing the landowners to take advantage of an array of federal and state tax credits. In Placer County, California, a unique partnership with the business community produced upwards of $2 million for land acquisition. Each one of these programs came about under different circumstances, so there is no standard template for involving private donors and the private sector. The right approach will vary from place to place. Nevertheless, the potential to tap into the deep reservoir of good will toward wildlife and nature in most communities should not be underestimated or ignored.

Regulations

The case study communities make clear that protective land use regulations are an essential element of local government nature protection programs, establishing a minimum code of conduct for protecting these resources while setting the stage to make other tools more effective. Experience shows that not only are effective regulatory systems important in their own right in protecting sensitive natural resources; they also set the stage for effective use of other tools, such as transferable development rights and acquisition programs.

Land use regulations in the form of zoning have been around close to a century. The first comprehensive zoning laws were implemented by New York City in 1916. Zoning was then approved by the United States Supreme Court in the 1920s in the landmark case of *Village of Euclid v. Ambler Realty.* Since then, the vast majority of cities, towns, and counties have adopted basic zoning regulations to control the location of development as well as permissible densities. But as the most successful communities demonstrate, modern land use regulations are much more sophisticated, focusing not only on the basic attributes of development and growth, but also on development quality, impacts, and costs. In addition to being broad based, they are built on a solid foundation of comprehensive land use plans, ecological studies, or sound fiscal impact analysis.

Land use regulations can be broken down into three basic categories, with numerous tools available under each: zoning and subdivision controls, development standards, and fiscal impact assessment.

Zoning and Subdivision Controls

Zoning and subdivision controls are the workhorse of most land use regulatory systems. Almost all jurisdictions in the United States have zoning or something akin to it. As noted previously, zoning typically focuses on allowable uses and densities in various locations of a jurisdiction. Subdivision regulations address the process of dividing a parcel into salable lots. Traditional subdivision regulations address such issues as minimum lot frontages, road location and dimensions, and similar physical features of a development. While some communities have become enamored with land use regulations that might be termed cutting edge and that have more sizzle to them, case study communities like Baltimore and Dane counties make abundantly clear that basic zoning regulations have an important role to play in nature protection strategies.

Large-Lot and Conservation District Zoning

Early zoning ordinances in suburban and rural jurisdictions often addressed the issue of development density by setting a minimum lot size of 1 acre or less and leaving it at that. But as Baltimore County discovered, what on the surface would appear to be a rather large lot size in actuality is a recipe for sprawl and loss of wildlife habitat. In reaction to its farms and the countryside being carved up into suburban cookie-cutter subdivisions, Baltimore County revamped its zoning several times in the 1970s and 1980s, eventually ramping the minimum lot size up to 50 acres in rural and resource conservation areas. Similarly, Loudoun County, Virginia, learned the hard way that 3-acre minimum lot zoning was not up to the task of protecting rural resources in the county's western reaches. In a bold, controversial move, the county board in 2002 increased the minimum lot size to 1 unit per 20 acres in rural areas and 1 unit per 50 acres in resource conservation zone districts.

The experience in Baltimore County and other jurisdictions has been revealing, demonstrating that the simple act of dramatically reducing allowable densities is probably the most effective tool to preserve agricultural lands and sensitive natural areas in the zoning toolbox. Some counties, intent on preserving their farming base in the face of suburban growth, have gone even further, setting minimum lot sizes of

160 acres and forbidding any type of uses or housing not directly related to agriculture. Dane County is an example of that approach, but with an important twist.

In the early 1970s, spurred on by a Wisconsin state law that created income tax incentives for farmers who put their land in exclusive agricultural districts, Dane County and many of its constituent townships created zone districts that restrict most nonagricultural uses and set a minimum lot size for houses at 35 to 75 acres. As a result, there has been very little intrusive development in most of the rural reaches of Dane County, which retains a strong agricultural economy despite booming growth around Madison. A spin-off benefit has been the protection of sensitive natural areas because development intensities are very light. Many observers doubt whether the agricultural zoning would have been politically feasible without the state income tax credits.

While it is a proven, effective tool, large-lot zoning can create intense controversy. When a community is first considering zoning or reducing densities from, say, 1 unit per 10 acres to 1 unit per 50 acres, the political opposition may be manageable. But if

In Dane County, Wisconsin, agricultural zone districts restrict most nonagricultural uses and set a minimum lot size of from 35 to 75 acres. Photograph courtesy of Dane County.

rural landowners have been handed 1 unit/acre zoning and have come to rely on it like money in the bank, and the locality proposes a major downzoning and potential reduction in value, as did Loudoun County, it can expect heavy political weather. For example, in Hall County, Georgia, a fast-growing jurisdiction in Atlanta's orbit, a proposed reduction of densities in rural areas from 1 unit/acre to 1 unit/10 acres resulted in cries of foul. In the end, the county barely was able to muster political support for a reduction to 1 unit/3 acres—what Loudoun County found to be a sprawl-inducing density.

In those instances, the Dane County experience suggests a potential alternative— use of local tax credits or perhaps coupling the downzoning with the purchase of development rights program to take the sting out. Loudoun County took a somewhat different but equally effective tack. The county allowed landowners to recoup some of the lost density by agreeing to cluster development on a smaller portion of the tract with smaller lots while preserving a significant portion of the property in open space.

While large-lot and conservation district zoning can be very effective, it is not a panacea. It typically does not address the location of a house or structures on a lot or restrict disturbance of sensitive natural areas such as wetlands. Other tools are needed to deal with these aspects of developments, as discussed below.

Conservation Overlay Zoning

Zoning ordinances typically establish what are called base zoning districts across a community—residential, commercial, and industrial are the three most common types of base districts. Another form of zone district is the overlay district, which typically focuses on a particular resource or feature that stretches across several base districts. Floodplain overlay districts that impose additional protective regulations on lands in a floodplain, no matter what base district they lie within, are a common example. Historic preservation districts are another. Overlay districts have become popular tools for protecting sensitive natural areas, because they can be put in place without a controversial downzoning to lower densities, a war cry to many landowners.

One good example of an effective overlay approach to protect natural resource areas is the environmental corridors overlay designated by Dane County. Dane County has mapped sensitive environmental resources such as lakes, wetlands, floodplains, steep slopes, woodlands, and unique vegetation. The corridors are then used by the county in development reviews—most are off-limits to development even though development might be allowed in the underlying zone district. Similarly, the City of Austin created drinking water/aquifer recharge protection zones that significantly limit the amount of impervious cover within the overlay. Because less land may be disturbed or paved over in the development process, wildlife benefit directly because more habitat is protected.

Smaller communities have also used the overlay district approach successfully, as witnessed by the Riparian Overlay District enacted by Bath Township in Ohio. Based on thorough environmental background studies, Bath Township put the new district in place in 2000. The overlay, which applies to major watersheds within the community, prohibits certain land uses allowed in the underlying base district that might have adverse impacts on the waterways and imposes a streambank buffer within which development or disturbance is prohibited.

Teton County, Wyoming, has over 10 years of experience with its detailed Natural Resource Overlay (NRO) District, which has served as a model for other communities in the West interested in protecting wildlife. The overlay district protects wildlife habitat throughout the county for several major species such as elk, moose, trumpeter swans, and cutthroat trout. All developments within the overlay district must carry out an environmental analysis, including a habitat inventory and a development impact assessment. Development is prohibited in certain areas (e.g., within 150 feet of cutthroat spawning areas and elk migration corridors) in most instances, and other requirements address issues such as fencing. The NRO District has proven to be a powerful and highly effective tool in protecting critical wildlife habitat.

Overall, overlay districts have proven to be very effective on the ground and politically palatable because they are targeted at protecting specific resources in a specific area—an approach that the citizens and landowners alike can understand. One of the few pitfalls associated with overlay districts is a situation in which property is subject to multiple overlays. Those situations can become an administrative headache for both staff and applicant alike.

Conservation/Cluster Subdivisions

Cluster development (also called conservation subdivisions) is a trend that is widely becoming accepted practice in many American communities. The concept is simple—housing sites are clustered closer together on smaller lots than might otherwise be allowed in a zone district; the remaining portion of the land not taken up in building lots is protected from future development by easements designed to preserve it as open space. Although some communities design clustering so that the overall density of the development parcel remains the same, other communities provide a bonus by allowing a few more lots to be created if they are clustered. The issue in many communities is not whether to cluster, but how to cluster. There are vast differences

Moose habitat is protected by Teton County's Natural Resource Overlay District. Photograph by Lokey Lytjen.

between suburban residential clustering designed to allow for future urbanization, and rural clustering designed to maintain open character and wildlife habitat values. For example, rural clustering often places an upper limit on the number of homes that can be clustered in order to protect rural character. Similarly, there are significant differences between programs that require clustering, and those that provide incentives for clustering or simply allow it as a landowner option.

Baltimore County has used the conservation subdivision option successfully to protect over 2,000 acres of open space. Interestingly, however, county staff do not favor using this technique for protection of active farms because introduction of houses into agricultural areas has resulted in conflicts with existing farming operations. The county staff feel that this approach works better to create transition areas between suburban and rural areas and to promote the connection of environmental corridors.

Similarly, Loudoun County has made clustering a very attractive option in the western portion of the county, making it the only way landowners can "recoup" density lost. However, it has discovered what many other communities are learning about cluster subdivisions—the tool has generated some heated opposition in more suburban areas in which existing landowners have built on larger tracts and object to

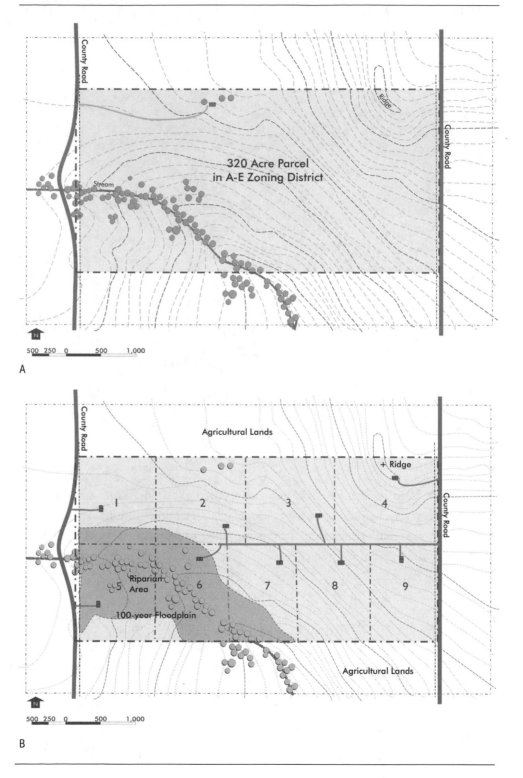

RURAL CLUSTERING
A, Hypothetical 320-acre parcel in a rural zone district with a stream and ridgeline. B, Without a cluster option, the applicant would be eligible for nine 35-acre parcels on the 320-acre parcel.

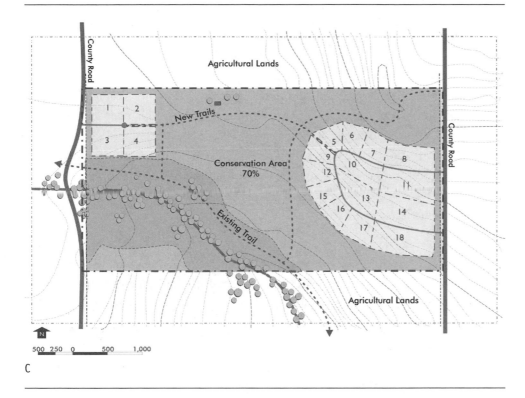

Labels within the map:
County Road
Agricultural Lands
New Trails
Conservation Area 70%
Existing Trail
Agricultural Lands
County Road

Map scale: 500 250 0 500 1,000

C

RURAL CLUSTERING
C, A cluster option allows the applicant to locate 18 lots on the site and to conserve 70 percent of the parcel as open lands. Natural features such as the stream corridor and ridgeline are undisturbed. Maps courtesy of Clarion Associates.

conservation subdivisions that allow development on lots smaller than theirs. These landowners view the smaller lots as an erosion of their semirural lifestyle despite the large tracts of open space that must be preserved.

The Rural Land Use Process established by Larimer County, Colorado, is an interesting and innovative variation on the conservation subdivision theme. Voluntary in nature, the process invites the landowner to submit to county review of large-lot (35-acre) subdivisions that are normally partially exempt from land use regulation under state law. Landowners who agree to set aside blocks of open space and to protect natural resources are eligible for density bonuses. The bonuses plus free site planning assistance from staff dedicated to the task by county officials have helped preserve several thousand acres since the program was begun in the late 1990s.

There is little debate that conservation subdivisions can be an important tool in habitat protection efforts, providing for the preservation of large contiguous blocks of open space while still allowing a significant economic return on a property. But the tool should be approached with caution. First, no one should be surprised if existing property owners view having a cluster near them with a jaundiced eye. Second, and even more important, effective conservation subdivision ordinances can be fairly complicated if they adequately address key issues such as location and configuration of the actual development, location and configuration of the resulting open space, and long-term use and management of preserved lands.

Transferable Development Rights (TDRs)

TDRs are a preservation tool that has received significant attention over the last decade and are the subject of several detailed and excellent books. (See Box 2.2, "Resources," at the end of the chapter.) In concept, they are simple. Landowner A's property, on which are located high-value natural resource areas, is subject to significant development restrictions, such as large-lot requirements or stringent development standards, putting much of the site off-limits to development (the sending area). To take the sting out of these regulations, Landowner A is allowed to sell his previously existing development rights to Landowner B or a developer who desires to build at a higher density than allowed under the current zoning in an area designated for development (the receiving area). Landowner B pays A and builds his project—and everyone goes home happy. In practice, a growing number of jurisdictions are successfully utilizing TDR programs, but the number is still relatively small.

The granddaddies of TDR programs are New Jersey's Pinelands and Montgomery County, Maryland. (Neither are case study communities, but both are subjects of numerous excellent publications.) In the Pinelands, rural lands were downzoned from

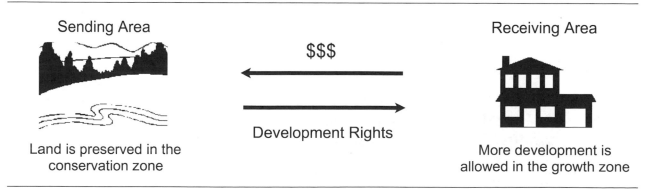

Sending Area   Receiving Area

$$$

←——————————————

——————————————→

Development Rights

Land is preserved in the   More development is
conservation zone   allowed in the growth zone

TRANSFERABLE DEVELOPMENT RIGHTS
In a transferable development rights (TDR) program, a landowner in a sending area is allowed to sell development rights to a landowner in a receiving area. Illustration by Chris Sturm, courtesy of New Jersey Future.

1–5 units/acre to 1 unit/25 acres to protect the region's drinking water supply and natural areas. To take the edge off the regulations, rural landowners can sell the development rights that were stripped away by the downzoning to developers who want to build higher-density residential projects in towns and villages targeted for growth. The program has helped protect over 10,000 acres of land with little controversy.

Larimer County, Colorado, has adopted a similar program in its Fossil Creek area, albeit on a much reduced scale. The sending area is a community separator between the cities of Fort Collins and Loveland where existing county zoning (1 unit/2 acres) allows development at densities that does not conform to the applicable comprehensive plan. The area includes some sensitive bald eagle habitat around a reservoir. The receiving zone is a newly annexed area in Fort Collins called Fossil Creek, where the city desires higher densities than allowed under the previously applicable county zoning. Because of conservative politics, the county did not want to downzone the property within the community separator. Instead, it collaborated with the city to establish a TDR program. The result has been the protection of several hundred acres, including the eagle habitat.

An increasing number of communities are adopting TDR programs, but only a few are producing tangible results. Unfortunately, the programs are often designed hastily without a clear understanding of how large sending and receiving areas should relate to one another to create a viable market for the development rights. Additionally, not enough attention is paid to the mechanics of the process—that is, how to determine how many development rights are assigned to a particular parcel. Still, when approached methodically, TDR programs can be an effective melding of regulations and incentives that may be more palatable than regulatory and acquisition programs in conservative jurisdictions with strong property rights leanings.

Development Standards

Early zoning ordinances contained only minimal development standards, which addressed features like the height and setback of buildings. Modern development codes have evolved far beyond these humble beginnings to include standards addressing a wide variety of development impacts ranging from lighting to building appearance to environmental impacts. These standards may apply across the board to all projects or may be targeted at commercial or residential developments only. They are typically applied in the normal course of development review. Before an applicant can get approval to proceed with construction, a site plan must be submitted for review to determine if the proposal meets applicable standards.

When it comes to natural resource protection and development standards, communities have taken three basic approaches. The first—and most common—is to enact a variety of standards to address specific types of natural features of a development. For example, many local governments have added tree protection regulations, floodplain standards, and wetlands buffers to their zoning ordinances. Other regulations may focus on features of a project, such as fencing and lighting, that can have significant impacts on wildlife. The second approach looks more directly at the issue of protecting wildlife habitat as a single element rather than at its constituent pieces. While far less common, this approach is gaining an increasing number of adherents. Finally, an increasing number of communities have developed infill incentives and standards to foster development in preferred locations.

Targeted Protection Standards

Most of the case study communities have enacted a wide variety of development standards that protect different types of wildlife habitat or attempt to mitigate potential adverse impacts from some feature of a development. The advantage of this approach is that it is relatively easy to administer if the standards are written clearly and quantifiably. For example, the simple act of requiring all development to be at least 100 feet from streams and wetlands can have enormous beneficial results in protecting wildlife habitat while being quite easy to administer. Listed below are some of the most effective development standards from a perspective of nature protection. It is important to realize, however, that the list is only a starting point and could be much longer. (Box 2.2, "Resources," lists many good sources that discuss and assess the experience of local governments in this arena.)

- *Stream, wetland, and lake buffers.* One of the most common and effective nature protection tools, these buffer regulations came on the scene in the 1970s. The shoreline protection regulations that are part of Dane County's highly effective regulatory triumvirate are a prime example, enacted in response to State of Wisconsin legislative requirements. As in Dane County, this type of regulation typically requires a linear setback from various water bodies accompanied by a ban on vegetation removal or land disturbance within the buffer. Loudoun County, Virginia, adopted some of the most extensive and detailed river and stream corridor protection standards in 2003, only to have them struck down on a legal technicality relating to notice. Those proposed standards are still worthy of study by other communities that are committed to protecting riparian habitats and water quality.

Riparian setbacks are required in Bath Township, Ohio. Photograph courtesy of Bath Township.

- *Tree and vegetation protection.* According to the National Association of Home-builders, tree preservation was one of the hottest environmental issues facing its members in the 1990s. Literally hundreds of local governments adopted tree and vegetation protection regulations during that period, and the march continues today. These ordinances run the gamut from older ones that protect individual large trees from cutting to more modern approaches that require a specified percentage of existing vegetation on a site to be preserved or do not allow any disturbance outside carefully established building envelopes on a site. Three of the case study communities—Baltimore County, Maryland; Austin, Texas; and Sanibel, Florida—have what are widely recognized to be the most ambitious and effective vegetation protection standards in the nation. All link their vegetation protection requirements to protection of the most valuable wildlife habitat or sensitive natural areas on a site. Baltimore County's regulations even allow it to require revegetation of sites that have been denuded.

- *Hazard-area protection.* Numerous communities have adopted standards to protect against development in so-called hazard areas—steep slopes, hillsides, floodplains, and the like. Very often these areas have high wildlife habitat values. The protections can range from simple to stringent. Many communities, for example, prohibit or severely restrict most development on slopes in excess of 30 percent, thereby protecting what is often important wildlife habitat from disturbance. Dane County's environmental corridor regulations focus on keeping development off of steep slopes and out of other potentially hazardous areas. Similarly, floodplains are almost universally regulated by local governments because of federal insurance requirements. Some of these ordinances allow development in floodplains, but an increasing number place severe limitations on density and site disturbance in floodplain areas, all of which help to protect what is often critical wildlife habitat.

- *Site features.* When development is allowed within or near important wildlife habitats, careful site planning and control of site features like fencing and lighting can be critical. A growing number of jurisdictions, particularly in the West, are regulating fencing that can injure wildlife and fragment important habitat areas. Teton County, Wyoming, for example, strongly discourages fencing near such areas and has established standards to control residential fencing in the Natural Resource Overlay District.

  Based on growing evidence of potential adverse impacts on wildlife, night lighting limitations are finding their way into local development codes. While most communities have very vague lighting controls in their codes—for example, prohibiting "glare" on adjacent properties—many are beginning to realize the serious limitations of this first-generation approach. More and more are adopting standards that specify the use of special fixtures that limit light trespass, control the height of lighting poles, and regulate the hours during which lighting can be turned on. Initially, this new generation of lighting standards was designed primarily to reduce nuisance impacts on residential properties and (especially in the West) to preserve the dark night sky. However, communities concerned with protecting wildlife now recognize that glaring night lighting can have serious adverse impacts on wildlife behavior and are responding accordingly by applying these standards not only to protect neighborhoods but to protect habitat as well.

The use of development standards that directly protect wildlife and their habitats is growing markedly as communities place more value on biodiversity protection. But one important lesson from the case study communities is that wildlife protection advocates should not be shy about piggybacking their protection efforts on regulations designed to address other issues. Austin is a prime example of this point. There some of the most important habitat protection measures (a bond issue to fund land acquisition and aquifer protection regulations) won support because they were linked to protection of the city's drinking water supply. As one observer noted, "In Texas it is not hard to explain the need to have good water. But birds and bugs are harder."

Dane County offers another good lesson in that regard. The county was able to pass a very strong and progressive stormwater management ordinance because of concerns over water quality in lakes and streams, much beloved by citizens. The new ordinance adopts regulations aimed at preventing soil erosion and runoff of chemicals. The additional benefits to wildlife and aquatic species promise to be enormous. Limitations on land disturbance to reduce soil erosion will reduce habitat disturbance, and aquatic habitats should get healthier as runoff of chemicals is reduced. Baltimore County's experience with similar controls to protect the Chesapeake Bay is very similar.

Wildlife-Specific Regulatory Systems

A number of local governments have gone beyond targeted development standards to develop more sophisticated regulatory systems that look more broadly at wildlife protection during the development review process. While the numbers are relatively small, they point the way to a new generation of wildlife-friendly local regulatory systems that are proving to be more effective in protecting natural habitats because they are based on sound biological principles. (See Box 2.1.) Two of the case study communities—Fort Collins and Teton County—are excellent examples of future directions in habitat protection strategies.

Teton County's approach provides a bridge between second-generation strategies involving overlay districts and targeted development standards, and more comprehensive approaches that focus on maintaining intact ecosystems. As discussed previously, Teton County has enacted a Natural Resources Overlay District that includes strong standards protecting critical habitat areas through development setback requirements. Other regulations address site features like fences. But Teton County has taken a further step that allows decision makers to get a broader view of development impacts: All proposed projects in the overlay district must carry out an environmental analysis, including a habitat inventory and a development impact assessment. This assessment helps the county tailor mitigation measures in addition to the setback and site planning standards.

Fort Collins has also augmented its standards-based approach with additional authority that grants city staff the power to require an ecological character study providing more detailed information on the extent and quality of habitat on the site. A broad development standard has also been adopted that allows review staff to look

BOX 2.1

FIVE BIOLOGICAL PRINCIPLES FOR WILDLIFE CONSERVATION

Principle 1. Maintain buffers between areas dominated by human activities and core areas of wildlife habitat.

Principle 2. Facilitate wildlife movement across areas dominated by human activities.

Principle 3. Minimize human contact with large native predators.

Principle 4. Control numbers of midsize predators, such as some pets and other species associated with human-dominated areas.

Principle 5. Mimic features of the natural local landscape in developed areas.

Source: *Habitat Protection Planning: Where the Wild Things Are,* APA PAS Report 470/471 (Chicago: American Planning Association, Planners Press, 1997), p. 17.

---

beyond the boundaries of the development site and consider protection of habitats in the vicinity of the proposed site as well. This general standard also permits decision-making bodies to require enhancing existing conditions on a site for wildlife and restoring or replacing lost resource values as a condition of approval.

Infill Development Incentives and Standards

Smart jurisdictions like Dane and Baltimore counties recognize that protecting important resource areas and wildlife habitat is only half the battle. Local governments must play an "inside" game that focus on fostering and encouraging development in the *right* place, where it will have few adverse impacts. Often this means encouraging development on infill sites within already developed areas, where impacts on wildlife will be minimal. In addition to designating growth areas where development is encouraged, thereby taking the pressure off for sprawling development in rural areas, these communities have revamped their development codes to remove impediments to infill. Some of the usual suspects found in most local codes include the following:

- Parking standards designed for greenfield locations that are excessive for constrained infill sites served by mass transit and pedestrian links. Finding land and building parking beyond what is necessary is an expensive proposition and is one of the real roadblocks to infill in many areas.

- Landscaping and buffering standards better designed for suburban campus-style office parks are often applied to infill areas, which not only drive up the cost of development but thwart the compact development pattern desired in most infill situations.

- Commercial and residential building design standards that are much tougher on infill and mixed-use developments than on the run-of-the-mill strip development on the urban edge. Such standards often drive developers to the easier, cheaper alternative—which likely will have more significant impacts on wildlife habitat.

To the extent that local governments can designate appropriate growth areas and then remove unnecessary hurdles to development in the right place, there will likely be less pressure to develop in sensitive natural areas. Many communities are, for example, tailoring parking and landscaping standards to better accommodate infill development while still ensuring that new development is compatible.

Example of development in one of Baltimore County's targeted growth areas. Photograph by Chris Duerksen.

Fiscal Impact Assessment

Due to increasing financial constraints, frequently associated with statewide tax limitation measures, local governments are more sensitive than ever to the costs associated with development and who pays those costs. As a result, many local governments routinely require a fiscal impact assessment of larger developments to get a better sense of the ramifications of a new project on the community's financial health. These impact assessments often show that new developments will not pay their own way in terms of tax and other revenues and thus lead to permit denials or requirements for compensating amenities or financial contributions from the applicant. These fiscal impact assessments often support habitat protection measures.

The use of fiscal impact analysis by Pittsford, New York, is particularly instructive. Faced with residential development on thousands of acres of sensitive wildlife habitat and scenic lands, the town undertook a fiscal analysis that showed it would cost an average of $250 in taxes annually for all town homeowners if new houses were built on those parcels. In contrast, the same study showed that it would only cost an average of $50 annually per homeowner to fund a purchase of development rights program that would prevent most development and preserve the wildlife habitat. This information was very persuasive in helping garner a successful vote for a bond referendum to fund the purchase of a development rights program.

Fiscal impact analysis can also be used on a site-by-site basis so that the local government can see the actual financial benefits of a major development in terms of local revenues and the fiscal burden in terms of costs of services that will be demanded by new residents and businesses (e.g., roads, schools, community facilities). Often the developer will pay for the cost of this analysis, which should be performed by consultants reporting to the local government to ensure an impartial study. With these numbers in hand, the local government is in a much better position to negotiate compensating revenues or community amenities, which in many instances take the form of additional open space.

Restoration

An often-overlooked feature of an effective nature protection strategy is restoration of damaged habitats. Restoration programs can take a number of forms. In older urban and suburban areas, a good deal of natural habitat has often been degraded, particularly along streams and rivers that have been turned into convenient stormwater ditches and convenient trash and rubble dumps. Development may have also allowed the invasive species to get a foothold through land disturbance or landscaping. More and more local governments are responding by establishing successful programs to clean up and restore urban watersheds. Others have adopted aggressive strategies to root out invasive plant species and replace them with native vegetation that better supports native wildlife.

In suburban and rural areas, new development sites are often the focus in order to ensure that adverse impacts are mitigated. For example, requiring disturbed wetlands to be replaced on at least a one-for-one basis elsewhere in the jurisdiction will ensure that critical wetland habitat is not lost. A few local governments also have enacted regulations requiring new development sites that have been denuded of vegetation to plant new trees to stop soil erosion and create habitat for wildlife.

Habitat Restoration

A growing number of local governments are beginning to recognize that even if they have effective regulatory and land acquisition programs, they must still deal with the "sins of the past" if they are to have really successful nature protection programs. Several of the case study communities have exemplary habitat restoration programs that can serve as models for other local governments.

Baltimore County has one of the most sophisticated, well-funded stream and shoreline restoration programs in the nation. It has resulted in the restoration of miles of urban/suburban streams damaged by prior development and accelerated runoff. In 2003, the waterway improvement program had a staff of six people and a budget of almost $8 million. Some of these fees are paid by developers in lieu of on-site stormwater management. Most of the actual restoration projects are undertaken by contractors under supervision by county staff. The county has assessed 700 miles of streams, and 26 restoration projects have been completed with almost 10 miles of streams rehabilitated, at a cost of $12.4 million.

Additionally, the county has an ambitious forest and tree restoration program that is paid for in significant part by mitigation fees from developers who remove trees when constructing a project, and by state funds. Baltimore County also coordinates delivery of trees to citizens and community groups participating in the State of Maryland's Tree-Mendous Program. This state program was designed as an inexpensive way to enable citizen groups to obtain trees and shrubs for planting on public land and within community open spaces. Baltimore County is unique in that it is one of the few jurisdictions in the country to maintain its own native tree nursery, which helps accelerate reforestation. Also, the county has a full array of heavy equipment to assist in planting.

Dane County has been a leader in water-oriented restoration efforts since the 1970s, when it won national attention for its trout stream rehabilitation efforts. Initially, these efforts focused on fencing streams to protect them from damage by cattle. Today, Dane County has gone much further with projects that involve removal of streamside trees—which, surprisingly, actually do more harm than good. The county is now spending about $250,000 annually to rehabilitate streams and completed work on 12 miles of stream restoration between 1999 and 2004.

The result, when combined with stormwater management controls on developments, has been steadily improving water quality in streams like the West Branch of Sugar Creek, a trout stream south of Madison. The stream has been removed from the state impaired list, where it had been relegated owing to sedimentation and bank erosion.

Regional restoration efforts in Minneapolis/Saint Paul have also been encouraging and notable for their use of volunteers. A shining example here is a nonprofit citizen group, Great River Greening. This organization came together in the 1990s, when a vision for Saint Paul's downtown waterfront led to massive native plant restoration locally and now throughout the region. Great River Greening restores valuable and endangered natural areas and open spaces in the greater Twin Cities by engaging individuals and communities in stewardship of the Mississippi, Minnesota, and Saint Croix river valleys and their watersheds. Since 1995, the nonprofit has engaged more than 12,000 volunteers and planted more than 37,000 native trees and shrubs. A key component of its volunteer work groups is education. Workshops are provided for supervisors and other volunteers on native ecology as well as restoration techniques.

Exotic Species Eradication

Sanibel, Florida, has complemented its pioneering ecological planning and protection programs with a very ambitious habitat restoration program that involves a major exotic species eradication aspect. Surprisingly, one of the biggest threats to the island's ecosystems has been exotic vegetation. The warm, inviting climate is at the southernmost range of many temperate plant species and the northernmost for subtropical ones. The result is what a city brochure on exotics terms the "alien invasion." Literally hundreds of introduced species—some benign, like bananas and citrus, and others, like the Brazilian pepper—are terribly destructive. The invasive exotics pose a real threat to the island's ecosystems and wildlife as they crowd out native vegetation on which native wildlife depend.

In response, the city has adopted some of the strictest laws regulating eight invasive pest species. These eight species (Brazilian pepper, air potato, earleaf acacia, exotic inkberry, melaleuca, Java plum, lead tree, and mother-in-law's tongue) are not permitted to be grown, propagated, or sold on Sanibel and must be removed from a property

Volunteers (coordinated by Great River Greening) replant prairie plants at Harriet Island Regional Park on the Mississippi River across from downtown Saint Paul. Photograph courtesy of Great River Greening, Saint Paul, Minnesota.

that is given a development permit. Furthermore, homeowners on existing lots must remove all Brazilian pepper and melaleuca even if they do not apply for some sort of development permit. The city has a financial assistance program for those in the latter category, because removal of Brazilian pepper can be very difficult and expensive.

To assist in revegetation, the city has a vegetation committee staffed by volunteers who give advice on proper plants for native landscaping, and the Sanibel-Captiva Conservation Foundation maintains a native plant nursery that provides a ready source of native vegetation for residents and also larger restoration efforts.

Mitigation Programs

Many communities, including case study jurisdictions like Placer County, California, and Eugene, Oregon, use regulatory standards to require mitigation of adverse impacts of development on habitats such as wetlands. This approach was discussed in detail in the regulatory element section above. Two other case study mitigation programs are worth highlighting. One focuses its attention on a particular resource, and the other involves a novel reforestation requirement.

The cooperative effort by the City of Sanibel and the Sanibel-Captiva Conservation Foundation to restore the flows of the Sanibel River is particularly noteworthy. A slow-moving stream that would hardly qualify as a river in most places, nevertheless, the Sanibel River is a critical piece of the ecological puzzle on Sanibel. It has been routinely diked, ditched, and diverted over the last century, thereby disrupting Sanibel's interwoven hydrologic system. Today, both organizations are undertaking river restoration on property they own, such as Sanibel Gardens. Additionally, the city is insisting on restoration when it receives a private development application for land through which the river meanders.

The revegetation mitigation program in Baltimore County is part of that jurisdiction's efforts to comply with state law that focuses on protection of the water quality in the Chesapeake Bay. Under county regulations, a specified percentage of existing tree cover on a site must be retained to reduce runoff and encourage infiltration to help maintain water quality. If no trees exist on a site, the applicant may be required to revegetate either on- or off-site. Other jurisdictions around the country have taken a similar approach by specifying a minimum vegetation "stocking" requirement on any site. If an existing site does not meet these minimum standards, the applicant must plant additional trees and shrubs to satisfy the regulatory floor.

Leading by Example

A good litmus test of how serious and dedicated a local government is to habitat protection is the energy it devotes to managing its own lands and programs in an environmentally sensitive manner. While some jurisdictions seem to follow a "do as I say, not as I do" philosophy in this regard, a number of the case study communities have noteworthy programs that are good models.

Most of the case study communities—but not all—require that major city projects go through the normal course of development review. This is an important first step in leading by example. Others have taken additional steps.

Eugene, Oregon, leads by example in several different ways. In 1999, when the chinook salmon was listed as an endangered species, the city first looked at its own practices. The city paid for independent studies of both its *regulations* and its city *activities* to see what affect they had on the environment. This self-examination was one result of an in-house environmental policy team. The team has pushed for the city to (1) create a body to coordinate environmental activities—externally and internally; (2) adopt an environmental policy; and (3) show the public that it is complying with the same rules as the public. As a result of this team's initiatives, the city now has a formal environmental policy, an Endangered Species Act team, an environmental review team, and a green buildings team.

Eugene also put in place an integrated pest management program that is one of the oldest in the nation, with over 20 years in practice. Although pesticides are still used, they are used only sparingly, and less hazardous compounds are chosen. Crews have had to spot-spray for weeds only once on three playfields out of Eugene's 25 fields in the last 16 years. Given that most of the threatened and endangered species in the Eugene area are water related (wetlands plants/animals and salmon), the city is a role model for the region in reducing one aspect of threats.

One glaring shortcoming of many local nature protection programs is the lack of coordination between preservation efforts (regulations and acquisition) and capital improvement projects like roads, water, and sewer. Too often preservation programs are undermined when a local government builds a new road or extends a sewer line into a sensitive area, thereby dramatically increasing growth pressure.

The City of Eugene paid for independent studies of both its regulations and its city activities to see what effect both are having on the environment. Photograph courtesy of the City of Eugene Wetlands Program.

The City of Austin has a good approach to this problem—requiring formal assessments of the environmental impacts of capital improvement projects. Austin's Capital Improvement Plan outlines the scheduling, coordinating, and funding of the construction of public facilities, ranging from bridge and road construction to installation of playground equipment in public parks. As part of the development of public facilities, the Watershed Protection and Development Review Department (WPDR) reviews all proposed projects and determines whether an environmental assessment is required during the project's planning phase.

Under the Land Development Code, environmental assessments are required for projects in sensitive areas. The goal of the environmental assessment is to avoid losses of significant natural resources or degradation of water quality that might result from a public project. The assessment also recommends alternatives if negative impacts cannot be avoided. The city attempts to incorporate review of all projects by WPDR as early as possible to ensure that projects are constructed in the most environmentally sensitive manner.

The variety of approaches that local governments are taking to lead by example is encouraging. An increasing number of communities are realizing that these initiatives help provide a sense of balance and equity to strong development regulatory programs that often are aimed at the private sector.

Social Indicators

The rap against some local wildlife and nature protection efforts is that they are only for the rich and hurt the average working family by driving up the cost of housing or raising taxes. The experience and practice of many of the case study communities, plus scores of others around the United States, refute this assertion. Several have aggressive infill development and urban revitalization programs to encourage growth in existing neighborhoods while discouraging sprawling subdivisions in rural areas. Others have targeted open space acquisition programs to inner-city neighborhoods. Some have adopted inclusionary housing regulations that require developers to build a minimum percentage of affordable units. All of these facets help to counter the misperception that wildlife protection is an elitist sport.

Perhaps most innovative of all the aspects of Dane County's multifaceted approach to land protection is what might be called its "inside" game. Led by a savvy county executive who is a former environmental attorney with a strong track record in social justice issues, the county has aggressively worked to encourage redevelopment and growth within the borders of its constituent cities and towns. By creating incentives for infill and removing unnecessary roadblocks to redevelopment, the county helps take pressure off for sprawling, greenfield development in rural areas. The county executive also wants less well-off inner-city neighborhoods to benefit from growth and government investment in infrastructure. To this end, the county has a successful grants program to encourage planning and redevelopment within its municipalities. The county also supported Madison's controversial affordable housing linkage regulations, which require developers to provide a percentage of affordable units in every project.

Baltimore County tells another interesting story. One of the most striking aspects of the county is that this is not a wealthy community or a jurisdiction with a college or a tourism-based economy. To the contrary—while the county does have its horse country with large estates, the average family income is only about $65,000, second lowest of the six jurisdictions in its region, reflecting the many working- and middle-class families and the large minority population. Its land preservation strategy has had two fundamental themes—protect land in rural areas and encourage development in existing neighborhoods and areas with infrastructure readily available. To this end, the county designated growth areas into which it has poured millions of dollars of infrastructure investment to support higher-density development. The objective has been to direct development to areas that can be served in a cost-effective manner and to avoid inefficient development in more rural areas. These growth areas have relatively high densities, a good mix of housing types, and a diverse group of residents, all with access to ample parks and recreational facilities. Going a step further, the county executive proposed a "renaissance" strategy to further jump-start development on vacant infill and redevelopment parcels within urban services area. A renaissance development would receive speedy county approval for building in targeted areas.

In Minneapolis/Saint Paul, the Metropolitan Council Livable Communities Program is using incentives (not regulations) to encourage brownfield redevelopment, affordable housing, and infill. This voluntary program has disbursed funds from its three grant accounts to approximately 106 communities in the region so far. To be eligible for any of these grants, a community must work with the council to set affordable housing goals. About $5 million in grants is available every year to communities to help clean up polluted land. Another $1.5 million is awarded for development or preservation of affordable housing, and $42 million has been provided to encourage efficient land development patterns and reinvestment initiatives.

The Livable Communities Program received a U.S. Environmental Protection Agency Smart Growth Achievement Award in 2003. Some critics say that this award was given more because there are so few places attempting this kind of program than because the program itself was exemplary. The primary drawbacks are that the state legislation that created this program does not require any quantitative goals, and there is no measuring to see if affordable housing needs are actually being met.

The City of Austin adopted an award-winning S.M.A.R.T. Housing Policy in April 2000 to provide new housing that is safe, mixed-income, accessible, reasonably priced, and transit oriented. The program was expected to have 600 new housing units in the development review process in its first year (2001) but instead had more than 6,000 single-family or multifamily housing units. The program also provides fee waivers for developments where at least 40 percent of the units meet the "reasonably priced" standard, meaning that the development serves families at or below 80 percent of the Austin area median family income. Other incentives include faster plan reviews and advocacy throughout the development process. In its first three years of existence, the incentive-based S.M.A.R.T. Housing Policy in Austin appears to be assisting in the construction of more reasonably priced new single-family and multi-family housing units on an annual basis than any other housing program in the country that attempts to achieve the same goals through mandatory zoning strategies.

Placer County, California, has implemented a number of programs to encourage redevelopment and the building of affordable housing. The county considers these measures to be part of a total package that along with preservation of open space will limit sprawl. These programs include an aggressive set of policies designed to increase the supply of affordable housing. For example, redevelopment projects designed to stimulate economic growth are connected to the construction of low- and moderate-income housing (California redevelopment law mandates that 20 percent of tax increment funds generated by redevelopment be set aside for affordable housing). The county has adopted a housing ordinance that requires 15 percent of housing units in all market-rate developments to be affordable.

Many cities have attempted to make outdoor activities more accessible for their residents. In 1998, Austin voters approved a $40 million bond issue to acquire greenways and parks. To address social equity concerns, the city directed that most purchases occur in the lower-income Latino eastern part of the city to balance out the large sums that were being spent for habitat protection in the more affluent western part. Acquisition efforts are focusing on land along major creeks and linear greenbelts to connect major parks.

Rosemont at Oak Valley is a unique blend of 120 apartments and 160 duplex units in Austin, Texas, reserved for families earning at, or below, 60 percent of the median family income, or about $42,650 for a family of four. Photograph courtesy of the City of Austin, Neighborhood Housing and Community Development—Public Affairs and Marketing Division.

Similarly, the Minnesota State Department of Natural Resources (DNR) provides programs that reach out to urban groups that might not otherwise get a chance to enjoy nature. Fishing in the Neighborhood (FiN) is a relatively new DNR program with admirable goals of increasing fishing opportunities, public awareness, and environmental stewardship within the seven-county metro region. DNR Fisheries staff have had an active urban fisheries program for many years. However, as the state's population has become increasingly urbanized, the need for angling options close to where people live became obvious. The 2000 Minnesota legislature provided funding for an expanded urban fishing program, which has evolved into FiN. FiN works with local partners to create safe family settings in residential areas where people can enjoy a day in the park and good fishing. Along with these local partners, FiN stocks fish, installs fishing piers and platforms, restores shoreline habitat, and sponsors aquatic education to create quality fishing opportunities.

Education

The most successful nature protection efforts stress the need for educational programs carried out by local governments, often in partnership with nonprofit organizations. Equally impressive is the effective use of legions of volunteers to accomplish habitat protection goals. These educational and volunteer programs have become essential elements in the success of nature protection efforts.

The Sanibel-Captiva Conservation Foundation (SCCF) successfully combines education with its conservation efforts. The foundation maintains an environmental education fund that reaches as many as 50,000 people annually. Programs include lectures, workshops, new-resident orientations, guided tours of SCCF properties, nature cruises, and beach walks. Participants include school kids, businesspeople, local realtors, church members, and civic groups, among others. The foundation's army of volunteers racked up over 20,000 hours of time in 2003, engaged in duties ranging from fund-raising to guiding nature walks to answering the phone.

The Traverse Bay area of Michigan has created several innovative educational programs since the mid-1990s as part of the New Designs for Growth Program. After investigating why a development guidebook for the region was not used by local jurisdictions, New Designs sponsored community workshops to train local stakeholders how to use the guidebook. Additionally, the Citizen Planner Program was begun with the help of the Michigan State University Extension and has since become a statewide land use training and certificate program for volunteer land use decision makers.

The Fort Collins Natural Areas Program has an educational arm: One of the management goals for natural areas is to provide citizens with educational and interpretive opportunities. Two educators are on staff and they operate a Master Naturalist Program, consisting of about 100 volunteers who speak to local groups and take people on guided tours of the natural areas. These volunteers are trained and certified in ecology, including the plants and animals found in the natural areas. They also provide many programs and educational materials that fit into local school curriculums and standards.

Results

In the final analysis, results speak loudly in any evaluation of a community's resource protection efforts. How much land is actually being protected, and how much is being lost to development every year? How good is water quality in streams and lakes? Are any species threatened or endangered?

A Citizen Planner program was started in the Traverse Bay region of Michigan to help preserve the region's natural resources and high quality of life, which are attracting a multitude of new residents. Photograph by John Robert Williams.

A weak point in land use planning and growth management efforts over the years has been lack of attention to measurable results. All of that is changing as elected officials and citizens ask for more than just anecdotal signs of progress.

This section focuses on measures that communities are using to gauge progress in their nature protection programs. It highlights a formal indicator project from the Seattle region that provides a good checklist of potential measures that other communities might use.

Land Protection

Some of the best gauges of progress relate to land protection—and they are relatively easy to measure. Baltimore County has done a good job of tracking progress in large part by keeping simple statistics that related to the key elements of a nature protection strategy:

- *Administration.* The county has information at its fingertips regarding the number of employees in the relevant departments and their training. It also keeps count of the number of volunteers and hours spent on nature protection tasks.

- *Planning.* The county has set goals and tracked progress in completing watershed management plans for its 14 major watersheds (10 have been completed). It also measures the total percentage of population living within the areas designated for urban growth versus the percentage living in rural conservation zones.

- *Acquisition.* Accurate count is kept of the number of acres of open space, agricultural lands, and sensitive areas protected through acquisition or easement, both by the county and by its cooperating nonprofit partners.

- *Regulations.* The county assesses the effectiveness of its regulations in several ways. Some measures look at the coverage of regulations—for example, strict resource conservation zoning covers more than 92 percent of the three drinking water reservoir watersheds—about one-half of the county's land area. On the results side, the county tracks how large a percentage of forests has been protected on development sites by the Forest Conservation Act—an impressive 65 percent. Similarly, the county keeps an eye on the health and extent of submerged aquatic vegetation in reaches of the Chesapeake Bay within its jurisdiction, as well as miles of trout streams—a clean water indicator that relates back to controls on vegetation clearing and land disturbance.

- *Restoration.* Restoration efforts are measured in several ways: miles of streams restored and number of trees planted/acres reforested.

There are many other ways that jurisdictions are using to measure progress. A good guiding principle is to select a benchmark that is (1) relatively simple to measure using readily available data; (2) understandable to the average elected official or citizen; and (3) trackable over time through data or statistics that are easily obtained or reproducible. Some communities have begun benchmark/measurement programs with great expectations and significant resources, but the programs have faltered as tracking costs mounted and staff resources were diverted to more immediate tasks such as development review. Keeping benchmark/measurement programs simple and easy to administer can help to assure their survival over the long term—which, of course, is essential if they are to have any real value. These other measures (with reference to communities in which they are being used) include:[2]

- *Acres of land converted from forests/agriculture to urban development compared with population growth* (Atlanta region): a good measure of sprawl versus compact development that protects rural high-value habitats.

- *Total number of acres in forests* (Seattle): a general indicator of preservation of an important habitat type.

- *Quality of sensitive habitat* (Eugene, Seattle): goes beyond simple acreage measure to track the health of specific sites/habitats, such as wetlands.

- *Density of development* (Las Vegas/Southern Nevada Region): comparison with other jurisdictions to assess whether land development is sprawling or more compact. Overall densities of less than 4 units per acre are low and will likely result in sprawl.

- *Presence/absence of desired species* (Seattle, Kenai): bird, fish, and animal counts can help to measure the health of local habitats (although other variables obviously may affect habitat health and need to be considered) and can indirectly measure the effectiveness of local protection efforts.

Environmental Quality

Data on water quality, air pollution, and habitat health can serve as useful surrogates to measure the effectiveness of nature protection programs. If water quality in streams and lakes is deteriorating, there is a good chance that aquatic habitats are being degraded. If wetlands show evidence of degradation, land use regulations may be too weak.

- *National water pollution statistics* available from the U.S. Environmental Protection Agency (EPA) and state departments of natural resources can provide a snapshot of how effectively controls on land disturbance and vegetation protection are working (Dane County).

- Several of the case study communities track the *health of particular types of habitats* and use them as indicators for the effectiveness of regulatory/restoration programs. Baltimore County keeps an eye on the health and extent of submerged aquatic vegetation in reaches of the Chesapeake Bay within its jurisdiction, as well as the miles of trout streams—a clean water indicator that relates back to controls on vegetation clearing and land disturbance. As noted previously, Eugene evaluates the quality and success of wetlands mitigation sites according to preestablished criteria.

- Many jurisdictions collect information regarding *total impervious area,* which indicates how much urbanization has occurred—how much of the land surface is covered by such features as roads, parking lots, and rooftops. A higher percentage of impervious area affects both water quality and groundwater recharge.

- An increasing number of local governments are documenting *species lost or endangered,* and whether the *full spectrum of species* is present and protected. This information can assist jurisdictions in protecting biodiversity as well as important economic resources. For example, the amounts of commercial fish and shellfish taken from waters nationwide and their populations are watched closely. Some noncommercial species are also tracked nationally by the EPA, such as the worms, clams, and other small animals that live at the bottom of estuaries, which can indicate habitat health as well as species diversity. In addition, NatureServe and its natural heritage member programs evaluate the status of about 22,000 at-risk native species throughout the United States.

King County, Washington, has one of the most ambitious and successful planning benchmark programs in the United States. Described in greater detail in the King County case study, this program is organized into 45 indicators for five general topic areas, including environmental issues and land use policy.

Many of these indicators have relevance for biodiversity in that they track growth, and several address species and habitat issues directly, such as under "environmental issues": land cover changes in urban and rural areas over time, surface water and groundwater quality, change in wetland acreage and functions, continuity of terrestrial and aquatic habitat networks, and change in number of salmon; and under "land use policy," the number of acres in forest land.

Originally a single annual publication (in 2003), the format of the Benchmark Report was changed to five bimonthly reports, one on each of the five topics. For each indicator, the reports also describe the data sources and the policy rationale. To illustrate: the salmon data sources are listed as the Washington Department of Fisheries, the Washington Department of Wildlife, and the Western Washington Treaty Indian Tribes. The policy rationale refers to sections of the Countywide Planning Policies and gives a summary of the importance of salmon to the citizens of King County for "recreational, economic, cultural and environmental values," as well as indicating the overall health of the waterways.

The King County Benchmark Program can be considered to be past infancy, but not yet mature. Staff offer the following words of wisdom: Any jurisdiction starting a benchmark program must understand it is a long-term commitment, and must be funded for at least 5 to 10 years to get good data and see trends. Ownership is critical to provide clear lines of reporting and to provide a possibility of the data actually being used to affect policy.

As with any indicator project, there are pluses and minuses. Choosing appropriate indicators and ensuring adequate data is one issue. Another concern is that the data may not be used to affect policy after all. However, the snapshots of various trends that can be seen in each of King County's Benchmark Reports are commendable and are an important start in monitoring the impact the county's policies may or may not be having on preserving the area's quality of life for all species.

Austin also has a noteworthy benchmarking program. Its State of the Environment (SOE) report is an annual undertaking to consolidate and publish information about the city's efforts to protect the natural environment. Various agencies contribute to the report, which is coordinated and published by staff from the Watershed

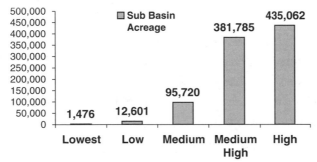

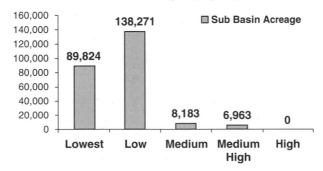

QUALITY OF HABITAT IN RURAL AND URBAN KING COUNTY, WASHINGTON
King County, Washington, has a benchmark program that evaluated habitat quality countywide in 2004. Graphs by Rose Curran, courtesy of the King County Benchmark Program.

Protection and Development Review Department (WPDR). A key goal behind the report is public education, and the report is intended to be publicly accessible. It is the city's main tool for pulling together all the various efforts underway to protect natural resources in the Austin area.

The original purpose of the SOE report was to provide a tool by which to measure progress in improving the quality of Austin's creeks and watersheds. Specifically, the WPDR staff developed an Environmental Integrity Index about eight years ago to help get a handle on the health of local creeks and to determine where funds should be spent. The index looks at five areas (e.g., sediment, aquatic life, recreational opportunities). The index is periodically tweaked and fine-tuned. Each watershed is examined once every three years, and so the SOE report discusses different results every year. Using a scoring system for all watersheds, the SOE report originally was intended as a motivating tool to increase scores in each overall watershed on an annual basis. In retrospect, staff today note that their original goals were too ambitious because of lack of resources to make significant changes; today, they have revised their goals to be more realistic and to focus on incremental progress in smaller geographic areas (e.g., moving scores for subareas from "poor" to "marginal").

Each year the report focuses on a new set of issues in depth. It is sometimes lengthy and sometimes brief, depending on the level of research and reporting available for the topics covered that year. Very little new research or reporting is created solely for the SOE report; instead, most elements of the report are created for other purposes and then reprinted in the SOE report.

Fort Collins is another jurisdiction that has adopted a monitoring effort to gauge progress on growth management issues. It started the City Plan Monitoring Project in 2001. The first report contained indicators for population growth, land use (e.g., housing density, infill development), housing (including affordability), transportation, employment, and environment. The two environment indicators were air quality and open lands management. The latter tracks how much natural habitat or rural/open lands have been protected. As of 2001, the city had protected about 55 percent of the areas identified as natural habitat or features on the city's Natural Habitats and Features Inventory map (which is also used to identify items that require buffer zones). The 2001 report also indicated that about 46 percent of the areas designated as rural/open lands on the city's Structure Plan had been publicly protected from development.

Case study communities like Baltimore County teach another important lesson—setting concrete goals at the *outset* of nature protection efforts can be a guiding light and inspiring objective that can sustain a program over time. In the 1990s, Baltimore County established a grand goal of protecting 80,000 acres (one-fifth of the county's total land area) through acquisition. Today, the county is over halfway there through a combination of land purchases and easement acquisitions. Much like United Way fund-raising campaigns, the land protection campaign rallies citizens by acreage "thermometers" that show progress toward meeting the goal. The 80,000-acre figure is the kind of simple, clear measure that citizens can identify with.

Landowner Outreach Programs

One of the most interesting and novel features of several case study community programs is an innovative landowner outreach program. These programs offer a variety of special services or benefits to farmers and other large landowners that help supplement—and to a certain extent take the sting out of—regulatory and land acquisition strategies. At the core of some programs has been the notion that unless landowners have viable alternative economic uses of their land other than residential or commercial development, protective growth management regulations would likely be little more than a short-term, stopgap answer. Other programs embrace the idea that large landowners need some special incentives to undertake land protection and restoration.

The PlacerGROWN initiative in Placer County, California, successfully addresses the issue of ensuring that farming and other uses that help maintain open space and wildlife habitat are economically viable. PlacerGROWN is a nonprofit organization formed to assist Placer County farmers and ranches with marketing of their produce and farm products. The idea behind the program is that Placer County's prized agricultural landscapes, which also provide a good environment for many species of wildlife, will survive only "as long as farms are financially viable."

The program has its roots in 1989, when the county board of supervisors initiated a farmers' market that grew to eight locations and 10,000 customers a week by 1994. PlacerGROWN now encompasses a dizzying array of programs and activities, including a Mountain Mandarin Festival that attracts 30,000 visitors over a two-day period each fall; a Placer Farm and Barn Festival, an educational and informational event that features Placer County agriculture and artists, including AGROart, a nationally known competition featuring sculptures created from locally grown and seasonal fruits and vegetables, farm tours, barn photo contest, art show, farmers' market and workshops; and a marketing program that produces an annual County Farm Trail Guide, directing consumers to local produce and agricultural markets and outlets. The program is beginning to show some benefits to farmers as well. When the program first began, there were 8 active mandarin orange producers in the county; today, they number more than 50. As a result of the PlacerGROWN County Farm Trail Guide and other marketing efforts, customer traffic for one iris grower in the county increased by 100 percent in the first year of involvement in the program; the second year, this grower's traffic increased another 50 percent.

Loudoun County, Virginia, has undertaken a program with similar roots. The county's economic development department has four employees who work with rural landowners to promote rural economic uses. As an alternative to a farm sprouting townhomes, the program works with farmers and other larger landowners on an array of alternative money-producing crops and activities—Christmas tree farming, wine growing, and rural conference and wedding venues are but a few of the many options that the county staff have studied and encouraged.

Dane County's Land and Water Conservation Department represents another cooperative approach with landowners that is paying dividends. One of the key environmental and habitat issues in the county is water quality. Much of Dane County's rich farmland is laced with high-quality trout streams that were threatened by soil erosion and chemical runoff from cropland. Under the tutelage of a director who has roots in the local agricultural community, the department has provided an array of soil conservation planning grants to farmers as well as assistance with stream protection fencing projects and stream restoration projects. Not only have these projects helped to protect and restore miles of aquatic habitat, they have helped to keep land in productive agricultural use, thereby protecting large tracts of open space throughout the county.

Putting It All Together: Tailoring the Right Nature Protection Program for Your Community

The case study local governments illustrate the rich diversity of programs and strategies being used around the country to protect natural resources and promote biodiversity. Indeed, the variety of options available to communities may be somewhat bewildering, particularly for smaller jurisdictions with limited resources or those just getting started with nature protection programs. For that reason, we do not recommend here a "model" program, a one-size-fits-all approach. What may work exceedingly well in one community with ample financial and staff resources as well as strong political support may be ill fitting in a smaller jurisdiction that is taking its first steps to promote biodiversity and protect natural resources.

Instead, we suggest here a hierarchy of best practices geared to the size, resources, and political support for nature protection in a community. We hope the following checklists will be useful for local officials and planners in tailoring a program for their jurisdiction and a valuable measure for gauging the effectiveness of their efforts. For ease of reference, we have categorized the checklists into an ascending hierarchy of bronze, silver, and gold programs, depending on the tools selected to address each key element.

- *Bronze standard.* This standard is designed primarily for local governments with limited resources or staff or those that are just getting their feet wet when it comes to nature protection. The bronze standard is marked by simple, straightforward—yet effective—protective standards supplemented by other programs such as modest land acquisition initiatives.

- *Silver standard.* Communities aspiring to the silver standard would typically be those that are upgrading their first-generation habitat protection regulations or bulking up modest land acquisition programs. They characteristically would have more resources and solid political support for comprehensive natural resource protection programs but might not be addressing some key elements such as restoration or education.

- *Gold standard.* The gold standard is for jurisdictions that have devoted ample resources and staff to administer state-of-the art regulatory and acquisition programs. Additionally, they have complete programs that involve nonprofit organizations and the private sector and address other key elements such as regional habitat planning, education, and landowner outreach.

Under each category we discuss the key program elements and suggest approaches that are most appropriate given the financial and political context. For example, for a novice jurisdiction, we recommend that the local government enact very simple, quantifiable development setback regulations to provide breathing room for wildlife habitats; for larger jurisdictions with more experience and resources, we suggest a more detailed site-by-site environmental analysis and application of more complex habitat protection principles. The three-tiered approach is not to suggest there are clear delineations between effective habitat and open space protection programs. In practice, some bronze programs may include a more sophisticated or ambitious element that would typically be found in a silver- or gold-level effort. Similarly, an effective gold standard regulatory program might make good use of simple regulatory standards that are easy to administer. In other words, mixing and matching will and should be the order of the day to craft a program that fits locally.

Bronze Standard

Communities that aspire to the bronze standard are those that are just getting started seriously in the business of habitat and natural resource protection. These would typically include rural counties and small towns/cities that have small planning departments, if any. The county or town manager may do double duty as the jurisdiction's land use planner. Annual budgets are typically small, with limited resources for land acquisition. While there may be political support for land protection regulations, just as often the tilt is toward nonregulatory techniques, or at least a light touch when it comes to land use controls. But even under these conditions, many smaller, less affluent jurisdictions have proven that they can put together an effective nature protection program. The following steps or initiatives under each key element define a bronze standard nature protection program:

Administration

- Seek assistance from state resources agencies in development reviews and assessment of habitat impacts.

- On larger projects, require the developer to provide funding that will allow the local government to retain a consulting planner or resource biologist.

- Charge adequate application fees to reflect the true cost of development reviews and to pay for staff time.

Planning

- Utilize available state resource maps and aerial photography to delineate critical habitats.

- Include natural resource element in comprehensive land use plan.

- In comprehensive plan, target growth to incorporated municipalities and designated development nodes.

- Limit county services (e.g., road plowing, fire protection) in remote areas with high habitat value.

Acquisition/Funding

- Enact land dedication and open space set-aside requirements for rural subdivisions.

- Provide seed financial assistance to local land trusts to help secure conservation easements.

- Use limited funding to acquire priority high-value habitats. Work with special water/sewer districts to use tap and other fees for targeted acquisitions. Solicit donations for targeted habitat acquisition.

Regulations

- Enact simple, quantitative development standards to protect critical habitats:
  - Require 100-foot stream/wetland development setbacks.
  - Establish percent vegetation retention requirements (e.g., retain at least 30 percent of native vegetation on a residential site).
  - Require full cutoffs on all outdoor lighting.
  - Prohibit development on very steep slopes (greater than 30 percent incline) or reduce allowable densities on slopes as steepness increases.
- Create and map large-lot zone districts in areas with high habitat value (e.g., 1 unit/60 acres)
- Restrict commercial/industrial uses in rural zone districts unless they require rural location (e.g., guest ranch).

Restoration

- Require restoration of damaged sites as part of development approval criteria for larger sites.
- Organize volunteer restoration projects with nonprofit organizations. Focus on high-value resource areas like streams.

Leading by Example

- Require county/town projects (especially public works and roads) to follow county land use and environmental regulations.
- Coordinate infrastructure provision policies with incorporated towns and special utility districts.

Social Indicators

- Target growth to incorporated towns.
- Provide financial assistance to towns to provide water/sewer services within urban growth boundaries.

Education

- Work with local nonprofits on habitat cleanup (e.g., river cleanup efforts) and restoration projects.

- Provide seed funding for local land trusts.

Results

- Target specific high-value, high-visibility resource areas for protection/acquisition. Publicize progress over time.

- Adopt simple success measures such as the number of acres converted from agricultural to nonagricultural uses or number of acres acquired for open space.

Silver Standard

Once a local government has experience with these basic, but effective nature protection program building blocks, it will typically begin to see ways to make further improvements. A rural county may find opportunities for more sophisticated land acquisition programs involving purchase of development rights. A growing suburban community may see the need to tune up its land development regulations to better protect critical habitat, perhaps by adopting mitigation requirements and special resource protection overlay districts. A big city may see the need for enhanced regional protection efforts. The case study communities offer many important lessons for local governments desiring to elevate their programs to the next level. The following steps or initiatives under each key element define a silver standard nature protection program. They are in addition to the steps necessary to attain the bronze ranking.

Administration

- Build a strong planning staff to undertake comprehensive and long-range planning in addition to day-to-day project reviews.

- Add natural resource planners to the staff to make review expertise available in-house for planning, public works, and parks departments.

- Organize interdepartmental review teams for larger projects to avoid conflicts and overlaps in project reviews.

Planning

- Augment state resource mapping with local vegetative cover and habitat surveys. Link maps to development review.

- Identify high-priority resource protection areas and undertake specific area plans to focus on key resources and necessary protection tools.

- Undertake comprehensive parks and open space planning. Identify key habitats to acquire. Involve citizens in priority-setting efforts.

- Require capital improvement plans to be coordinated with and respect land use plans that identify sensitive resource areas.

- Adopt infill development plans and enact incentives for redevelopment. Scrutinize land use regulations and building codes to identify unnecessary impediments to infill.

- Pursue identification of urban growth areas and urban growth boundaries with surrounding jurisdictions.

Acquisition/Funding

- Explore parks and open space impact fees.

- Secure stable, long-term funding sources (e.g., sales tax set-asides, bond issues). Base acquisition priorities on comprehensive parks and open space plan and comprehensive land use plan natural resource element.

- Seek major state grants and foundation assistance for acquisition programs. Engage local business community in fund-raising.

- Provide grants to local nonprofit land conservation organizations for land acquisition.

- Experiment with a purchase of development rights program to stretch the acquisition dollar.

- Counties: provide funding for municipalities to improve utility services that encourage compact development within urban growth boundaries.

Regulations

- Enact conservation/cluster subdivision regulations for development on the urban edge. Give priority to sensitive resource areas in delineating open space.

- Add mitigation requirements to the development code (e.g., replace any wetlands damaged or vegetation removed during development process).

- Adopt resource protection overlay zones based on mapping and special area plans.

- Adopt wildlife-specific regulatory review standards (e.g., setbacks from migration corridors or nesting areas).

- Undertake fiscal impact analysis for major projects. Deny projects with adverse fiscal impacts or require compensating amenities (such as open space).
- Forbid urban-intensity growth outside designated urban growth areas.

Restoration

- Create stream and other habitat restoration programs with local government funding.
- Provide funding for local nonprofit volunteer restoration programs.

Leading by Example

- Ensure that local government building projects are exemplary from a habitat protection and "green building" perspective.
- Provide for environmental review of all local government projects and capital investments by resource specialists.

Social Indicators

- Create formal urban growth boundaries in cooperation with surrounding jurisdictions. Target urban-intensity growth within these boundaries.
- Adopt a program of grants and incentives for infill development. Remove unnecessary regulatory barriers.
- Fund a program to acquire sites for affordable housing. Write-down land costs to spur affordable housing projects.

Education

- Work with school districts to address resource conservation issues in the curriculum. Use student volunteers for restoration projects.
- Organize volunteer corps to work with parks department to manage habitat and open space.
- Initiate a landowner outreach/involvement program. Provide information on estate planning, resource management, and alternative economic uses.

Results

- Adopt a more sophisticated benchmarking program. Include more specific measures tailored to wildlife habitat conditions within the jurisdiction.
- Create an awards program for exemplary habitat protection efforts by private sector and nonprofit organizations.

Gold Standard

Communities that successfully pursue the silver standard program elements discussed previously will build exemplary nature protection programs that will rank them among the best in the nation. But even the best of the case study communities recognize there are holes and gaps in their efforts that need to be addressed. In Dane County, Wisconsin, for example, a stronger regional protection initiative is sorely needed. Sanibel, Florida, must tackle its affordable housing problem and make sure that existing community-serving commercial businesses are not forced out by high-end retail businesses or risk gutting itself socially. Austin, Texas, has accomplished much but is hamstrung by a jerry-built planning and land protection organizational structure.

No community in the United States has yet attained the gold standard for nature protection programs set forth below. But many are close and, when they meet the standard, will serve as shining models for other local governments across the country.

Administration
- Integrate land use and resource planning/protection into a unified agency.
- Add resource professionals in public works and other agencies that engage in development/construction projects.
- Provide reliable funding for parks/open space resource management agencies.

Planning
- Undertake formal regional resource planning with neighboring jurisdictions.
- Identify preferred growth areas as well as resource protection areas. Steer growth to targeted areas through infrastructure investment, regulations, and other tools.

Acquisition/Funding
- Create transferable development rights to protect large tracts of open space and critical habitat.
- Seek broader enabling legislation at the state level to fund habitat acquisition (real estate transfer taxes, state bond issues, etc.).
- Provide a stable funding source for resource land management, not just for acquisition.

Regulations

- Adopt wildlife-focused regulatory systems based on key principles of habitat preservation, such as maintaining intact ecosystems and avoiding habitat fragmentation.

- Create ecologically based zoning districts that gear density and other elements to preserving ecological systems.

- Enact other regulations (e.g., stormwater management) to protect critical habitats (e.g., thermal controls on stormwater runoff to protect trout streams).

Restoration

- Adopt ambitious habitat restoration programs with a steady funding source and specific goals (e.g., restore *x* miles of streams within *y* years).

- Initiate habitat restoration research in cooperation with universities and other educational institutions.

- Undertake regional habitat restoration projects with other local governments and nonprofit organizations.

Social Indicators

- Adopt affordable housing linkage programs to help ensure adequate supply of reasonably priced housing in community.

- Pursue programs to involve lower-income residents in outdoor activities and nature protection.

Education

- Create an educational unit within planning or parks/open space departments.

- Work closely with schools, nonprofits, and other institutions on specific resource protection and habitat restoration projects.

Results

- Publish an annual local state-of-the-environment report focusing on variety of environmental and nature protection measures.

- Give local government departments and personnel awards for achieving specific habitat protection goals.

BOX 2.2

RESOURCES

Arendt, Randall. *Growing Greener: Putting Conservation into Local Plans and Ordinances.* Washington, D.C.: Island Press, 1999.

As described by the publisher: "*Growing Greener* is an illustrated workbook that presents a new look at designing subdivisions while creating open space networks. Randall Arendt explains how to design residential developments that maximize land conservation without reducing overall building density, thus avoiding the political and legal problems often associated with 'down-zoning.' He offers a strategy for shaping growth around a community's special natural and cultural features by incorporating a strong conservation focus into the municipal comprehensive plan and zoning and subdivision ordinances. . . . *Growing Greener* includes case studies of actual conservation developments, and exercises suitable for group participation."

Duerksen, Christopher J., et al. *Habitat Protection Planning: Where the Wild Things Are.* PAS Report 470/471. Chicago: Planners Press, American Planning Association, 1997.

As described by the publisher: "The report explains why it's crucial to protect habitat and establishes a practical framework for making local habitat protection decisions. It covers various legal issues, links specific problems with appropriate tools, and shows how to implement an effective protection program. It highlights such protection strategies as various forms of land acquisition and overlay zones, buffer zones, and limiting the number of domesticated animals in suburban/semi-wild areas. Arranged in a logical style, this report is an excellent primer for anyone concerned about how humans impact the natural environment in their quest to be closer to it. Great for both planner and concerned citizen."

Environmental Law Institute. *Conservation Thresholds for Land-Use Planners.* Washington D.C.: Environmental Law Institute, 2003.

Provides a review and synthesis of information from the most up-to-date scientific literature to provide basic thresholds to land use planners to rely on when making decisions affecting biodiversity.

Freilich, Robert H., and Michael M. Schultz. *Model Subdivision Regulations: Planning and Law.* Chicago: Planners Press, American Planning Association, 1995.

Leading legal publication on drafting defensible progressive subdivision regulations.

Kelly, Eric Damian. *Managing Community Growth: Policies, Techniques, and Impacts.* Westport, Conn.: Praeger, 1993.

This was the first broad evaluation of the implications and impacts of community efforts to manage or limit rapid growth. It describes the major types of growth management programs and includes evaluation of such related techniques as targeted capital investments, annexation policy, and public land acquisition. Also examined are the various costs and benefits— some obvious and some not—of growth management programs: development requirements, rate-of-growth controls, urban boundaries, mixed housing requirements, and regional planning.

—continued—

Box 2.2 *(continued)*

Mantell, Michael A., Stephen F. Harper, and Luther Propst (Conservation Foundation). *Creating Successful Communities: A Guidebook to Growth Management Strategies.* Washington, D.C.: Island Press, 1990.

Case studies of innovative growth management strategies.

Meck, Stuart, ed. *Growing Smart Legislative Guidebook: Model Statutes for Planning and the Management of Change.* Chicago: Planners Press, American Planning Association, 2002.

A compilation of recommended state and local land use regulatory provisions from APA's Smart Growth Project.

National Association of Counties. *Local Tools for Smart Growth: Practical Strategies and Techniques to Improve our Communities.* Washington, D.C.: National Association of Counties, 2001.

Stories, tools, and lessons learned from communities throughout the nation on how to employ planning and development policy to improve quality of life and achieve Smart Growth goals.

Nolon, John R. *Open Ground: Effective Local Strategies for Protecting Natural Resources.* Washington D.C.: Environmental Law Institute, 2004.

Comprehensive source of information about how strategies, including properly drafted land ordinances, land acquisition programs, and Smart Growth strategies, can protect critical landscapes and valued natural resources. The book discusses how these initiatives can counter the negative effects of polluted runoff, erosion and sedimentation, habitat removal, wetland disappearance, and more.

O'Neill, David. *Smart Growth Tool Kit: Community Profiles and Case Studies to Advance Smart Growth Practices.* Washington, D.C.: Urban Land Institute, 2000.

According to Amazon.com: "The Tool Kit provides step-by-step instructions to . . . get started and explains the strategies that have worked in other cities. Case studies help . . . make the case for Smart Growth by providing concrete examples of successful projects involving infill redevelopment, brownfields, conservation design, master-planned and New Urbanist communities, town centers, and transit neighborhoods. The final section includes a resource guide, program agendas, and a Smart Growth presentation."

Porter, Douglas R. *Making Smart Growth Work.* Washington, D.C.: Urban Land Institute, 2002.

This book provides an in-depth look at the underlying principles of Smart Growth, explains how developers and planners have applied them, and how the public and private sectors can collaborate to make Smart Growth effective. Topics include economically viable compact mixed-use development, conserving open space, expanding mobility options, creating livable communities, Smart Growth in suburban greenfields and infill areas, and the role of the players involved in putting Smart Growth to work

—continued—

Box 2.2 *(continued)*

Stark, Carole, and Barb Cestero. *Landscapes, Wildlife, and People: A Community Workbook for Habitat Conservation.* Tucson: Sonoran Institute, 2001.

Landscapes, Wildlife, and People outlines the steps for conducting an inventory of a community's ecological conditions. The community workshop approach and related activities presented in the workbook can help a community create an information base for use in local decision making, land use planning, and community building.

Trust for Public Land. *Local Greenprinting for Growth, vols. 1–4.* San Francisco: Trust for Public Land, 2002–2003.

Four-volume series that serves as a guide for communities seeking to create a greenprint conservation program. Greenprinting is The Trust for Public Land's term for a Smart Growth strategy that ensures quality of life, clean air and water, recreation, and economic health.

TABLE 2.1 MAJOR CASE STUDIES: Summary of Key Elements

Community/Type	Program Structure and Administration	Planning	Acquisition/Funding	Regulations
Austin, Texas Large Urban (Chapter 3)	• Uncoordinated efforts among many agencies • City planning responsibilities split—development review vs. planning • One environmental review officer	• Weak staffing • Poor resource planning • Embryonic regional effort	• Long history • Much driven by Endangered Species Act • Funding source for managing lands through tap fees	• Water quality protection, tree and natural area, & endangered species regulations • Much negotiation—PUD and development agreements • Smart Growth map is notable
Baltimore County, Maryland Urban/Rural County (Chapter 4)	• Significant staff • Unified conservation agency • Lack of coordination with planning • Hearing officer system	• Extensive mapping • Infill plans	• Several tools are used • Linked to down-zoning • Dedicated funding • State role critical • Local land trusts important—get state funds	• Very large lot zoning & regulations • Clusters good for transit • Resource protection standards, with wildlife added later
Dane County, Wisconsin Urban/Rural County (Chapter 5)	• Fragmented government structure • 3 key departments—planning, land conservation, parks	• Infill & sprawl control plans • Regional planning turmoil • State has good maps • Regional planning is weak	• Modest general revenue funding source • Recent bond issue • Grants to non-profits and municipalities are important • State stewardship fund	• Ag zoning has been key—very large lot; tax incentive helped • State shoreland law • Environmental corridors—regulations with maps • Stormwater management ordinance
Eugene, Oregon Medium Urban (Chapter 6)	• Significant staff • Reliable funding is key • Partnerships are important—exemplary wetlands collaboration	• Wetlands plan is role model • Regional open space vision plan	• Joint federal lobby for funding • Focus on wetlands is modest; otherwise no major source	• Strong wetlands regulations • Other regulations are weaker but will be addressed • Good tie to mitigation bank

TABLE 2.1 MAJOR CASE STUDIES: Summary of Key Elements *(continued)*

Restoration	Leading by Example	Social Indicators	Education	Results	Other
• Vegetation management is incorporated into land management plans for acquired lands	• Public projects must follow the same environmental protection standards as private projects • Good capital improvement coordinating effort	• Land acquisition in poorer neighborhoods • Focus on infill development	• Extensive watershed awareness programs • Native plant landscaping education program	• Produces State of Environment report	• Water quality as impetus
• Stream and shoreline restoration • Well funded; have funding source • Forest restoration efforts	• County projects must follow regulations • Review process is slightly different	• Infill efforts	• High participation in state Green Schools Program • Modest in-house environmental education effort	• Extensive annual data gathering for watersheds, land preservation, regulatory, and restoration programs	• State funding critical • Water quality as impetus • Chesapeake Bay is rallying point
• Major stream restoration	• County projects must follow regulations • No-phosphorus policy in parks	• Support infill as well as sprawl control • Incentives for infill	• Large volunteer program for parks • Nonprofit education efforts	• Uses state and federal water quality data to evaluate regulations	• Agricultural extension agent is important
• Strong wetlands restoration program • In-house ability to do large-scale wetlands restoration	• Integrated pest management • Regulatory self-examination • Natural resource protection applies to city lands	• Impressive affordable housing program • Land bank and incentives • Modest infill efforts	• City sponsors stewardship education program • Large wetlands educational facility underway • Many volunteers help with restoration	• Impressive wetlands monitoring system	

TABLE 2.1 MAJOR CASE STUDIES: Summary of Key Elements *(continued)*

Community/Type	Program Structure and Administration	Planning	Acquisition/Funding	Regulations
Fort Collins/Larimer County, Colorado Medium Urban and Urban/Rural County (Chapter 7)	• Significant staff for both city and county • City has natural resource staff member; county does not • Sales tax funds both city and county natural lands staff	• Extensive mapping in both used for regulations and acquisitions • Extensive comprehensive planning • Weak regional planning efforts	• Both have dedicated funding • City is doing regional scale acquisitions • Minor acquisitions from dedications and TDRs • Management costs need to be factored in • Much partnering for acquisitions	• County has conservation development and the Rural Land Use Process • Both have wildlife habitat regulations • Much staff administration
Pima County, Arizona Urban/Rural County (Chapter 8)	• 3 key departments are housed in Public Works • County administrator champions protection efforts	• Innovative Sonoran Desert Conservation Plan goes beyond federal requirements • Extensive mapping	• Modest general funding for acquisitions • Major bond issue recently approved ($112 million) • Flood control district and parks department are major players	• Riparian area protection regulations • Hillside, native plant, and natural area buffer regulations • Conservation Lands System being implemented
Placer County, California Urban/Rural County (Chapter 9)	• Unique public/private effort at outset • Not much regional cooperation yet	• Mix of local efforts & state/federal habitat planning requirements	• Modest funding from general fund revenue and private sources • County voted down sales tax • Land trust partners	• State/federal habitat mitigation compliance is critical tool • County also has own mitigation and other regulations • Traditional zoning also important

TABLE 2.1 S Summary of Key Elements *(continued)*

Restoration	Leading by Example	Social Indicators	Education	Results	Other
• City has restoration staff and funding • City has mitigation standards	• Both city and county follow their own environmental regulations for public projects	• City has infill & compact development regulations & incentives • City has good affordable housing program	• Both have active educational programs	• Both have modest monitoring programs	
• Small-scale riparian efforts in parks • Larger-scale riparian efforts planned with Corps of Engineers	• County transportation projects and river trails require native vegetation • Other modest efforts	• Tucson has infill program • County affordable housing situation is not promising	• Environmental education efforts are taking off • New environmental education center being built	• Monitoring programs are not in place yet • Federal habitat plan will include monitoring • County plans to produce state of the environment report	• Political will, ESA, and state plan requirements were impetus
• Watershed restoration planning • Implementation still to come	• County projects follow environmental regulations (as required by state law)	• Aggressive policies to increase affordable housing • State law requires link between redevelopment and housing • Mandatory inclusionary housing ordinance	• Both Placer Legacy and PlacerGROWN have public outreach programs	• No formal monitoring program yet • State/federal habitat plans may eventually require monitoring	• PlacerGROWN contributes to farmland preservation

TABLE 2.1 MAJOR CASE STUDIES: Summary of Key Elements *(continued)*

Community/Type	Program Structure and Administration	Planning	Acquisition/Funding	Regulations
Sanibel, Florida Small Resort (Chapter 10)	• Small but professional staff • Two full-time biologists on staff • Volunteer role key	• Ecological planning revolutionized the field • Maps are inadequate	• Much partnering for acquisitions • 2/3 of the island is permanent open space	• Regulations tied directly to plan • Use, density, & development standards
Twin Cities Region, Minnesota Urban/Rural Region (Chapter 11)	• Regional planning agency & state DNR are key and have extensive staff	• Mapping is strong & serves as basis for acquisitions • Good formal regional planning process • Regional property tax sharing	• Long history of acquisition • Capital funding for open space • Good state participation with expanding partnerships	• Indirect regulations through regional plan conformance

TABLE 2.1 MAJOR CASE STUDIES: Summary of Key Elements *(continued)*

Restoration	Leading by Example	Social Indicators	Education	Results	Other
• Very ambitious invasive species & habitat restoration program • Restoring Sanibel River flow	• City public projects are exempt from the land use code	• Very little affordable housing • Little city funding or regulatory incentives • Concern over loss of retail	• Impressive educational efforts for residents and tourists	• No formal monitoring program, but invasive species are tracked closely	
• Good regional examples of nonprofit restoration efforts	• Modest efforts	• Good infill and brownfield programs through council • Urban fishing program	• Innovative nonprofit outreach effort to involve citizens in land use decisions	• No formal monitoring program • Council may pursue benchmark program	

TABLE 2.2 FOCUSED CASE STUDIES: Key Elements Illustrated

Location	Key Program	Key Elements Illustrated	Discussion
Bath Township, Ohio (Chapter 12)	Riparian Overlay District	Regulations • Based on extensive ecological studies	• Strong zoning overlay and development standards in a Midwest setting
Charlotte Harbor, Florida (Chapter 13)	Ambitious Critical Area Protection Program • Area of Critical State Concern (ACSC)—Florida state program • Regional planning effort—3 counties	Planning • Planning with state involvement • ACSC has high level of development review and regulations—if locals don't adopt Resource Planning and Management Plan • Implementation items were identified	• State role is catalyst for forcing local action • Regional effort • Alternative to state intervention
Chicago Region, Illinois (Chapter 14)	Biodiversity Recovery Plan	Regional planning	• Good example of regional effort regarding biodiversity • Voluntary approach
DeKalb County, Georgia (Chapter 15)	Greenspace Program • Land acquisition program • Large acreage	Land acquisition • Plan first • Regional element • $125 million in bond funding	• Citizens can nominate land for acquisition
Farmington Valley, Connecticut (Chapter 16)	Farmington Valley Biodiversity Project • Mapping to guide growth	Planning/mapping • Mapping to guide growth Education	• Note that for implementation, the cookbook method was not chosen—tailoring was chosen instead
King County, Washington (Chapter 17)	Benchmark Program	Results/monitoring	• Excellent example of documenting results and tying to plan policies
Pittsford, New York (Chapter 18)	Greenprint • Ecological evaluation	Planning • Resource identification and ranking Regulations • Implementation tools • Tailored TDRs, clustering, large lot zoning	• Fiscal analysis shows cheaper to buy development rights

TABLE 2.2 FOCUSED CASE STUDIES: Key Elements Illustrated (continued)

Location	Key Program	Key Elements Illustrated	Discussion
Powell County, Montana (Chapter 19)	Rural County Wildlife	Regulations • Large lot zoning, easements	• Small jurisdiction has simple approach
Teton County, Wyoming (Chapter 20)	Natural Resource Overlay District	Regulations • Setbacks • Fencing • Open space requirement • Clustering	• Sophisticated approach • Significant staff resources
Traverse Bay Region, Michigan (Chapter 21)	New Designs for Growth	Program structure and administration • Public-private partnership Education • Technical assistance	• Good education example
Loudoun County, Virginia (Chapter 22)	No program is highlighted; instead the focus is the impact of political changes		• Land use plans and implementing regulations can be amended and repealed much more quickly than the time it usually takes to put them in place

Notes

[1]Sanibel and Captiva are sister islands, the latter under the authority of Lee County. The Sanibel-Captiva Conservation Foundation is dedicated to the preservation of natural resources and wildlife habitat on and around these two barrier islands.

[2]Please note that several of the communities cited, such as Las Vegas and Seattle, are not case study communities. Information on these programs can be obtained by contacting the planning departments in these jurisdictions.

MAJOR CASE STUDIES

These in-depth case studies showcase the comprehensive nature protection programs of several communities across the nation. Ranging from a seven-county regional planning agency in Minnesota to tiny Sanibel Island in Florida, and from a medium-sized college town in Oregon (Eugene) to a more blue-collar area in Maryland (Baltimore County), each of these communities has developed innovative strategies appropriate to its setting. Some have responded to federal listings of species within their boundaries; others have pursued habitat protection as a means to provide open space for residents or safeguard water quality. And others have carried out nature protection programs because of a deep feeling for nature or because it was the right thing to do, without any outside forcing. State support, local political will, development pressures, and available funding mechanisms vary. Although each story is unique, these efforts offer lessons and ideas for other communities wishing to move forward with nature protection.

CHAPTER 3

Austin, Texas: Two for the Price of One—Protecting Water Quality and Habitat Through Land Acquisition

ustin is a model nature-friendly community because of an impressive, multifaceted set of governmental and nongovernmental programs designed to protect natural resources, open space, and wildlife habitat. The city has overseen one of the most ambitious and successful land acquisition programs in the country, driven by the Endangered Species Act and water quality issues. The Balcones Canyonlands Preserve and other large-scale land acquisitions insulate sensitive lands from intense development pressures. Annual progress reports document the ongoing stabilization of endangered species populations in west Austin. The city's work has paid off in tens of thousands of acres being protected from future development, in development being limited on many more acres through environmental standards, and in increasing public awareness of the ecological importance of being a nature-friendly community. Further, the city's programs are supported by a wide-ranging network of nonprofit groups focused on environmental issues. The city has many key elements of a successful program—especially acquisition, regulations, and mapping—along with some noteworthy endeavors such as the Smart Growth map and the State of the Environment report. But coordination is loose and sporadic, with responsibility spread among many agencies with relatively weak regulatory tools. Surprisingly little attention is being given to the creation of overall environmental protection goals and policies. Yet this lack of coordination and long-term comprehensive planning should not minimize the many noteworthy programs underway, both inside and outside the city government that can serve as models for other communities.

While Austin is widely known as the Texas state capital and the home of the 50,000-student University of Texas flagship campus, the city has also for many years enjoyed a reputation as one of the most liberal cities in Texas and one of the most progressive communities nationwide in terms of land use planning and environmental protection.[1]

In the early to mid-1990s, Austin experienced a tremendous surge in growth and development thanks to a high-tech economic boom led by locally based Dell Computer, major local facilities for IBM and Motorola, and over 800 high-tech companies that moved to the region. High-paying jobs attracted new residents to Austin from all across the country, drawn to the area's natural beauty, extensive park system, laid-back lifestyle, and well-educated citizenry. Between 1990 and 2000, Austin's population grew from 465,000 to over 650,000. Much of the new growth and development spread out into environmentally sensitive west Austin and Travis County, home of several endangered species and recharge areas for major aquifers.

In the late 1990s, the city's growth rate slowed dramatically as a result of the nationwide bust in the high-tech industry, and the city's economy has yet to fully recover. A multistory metal frame skeleton stands silently downtown, on the site where Intel abandoned a major new office tower midway through construction, symbolizing how abruptly fortunes declined in the city. Austin today is faced with the consequences of its 1990s boom, including deteriorating air quality, increased traffic, and sprawling suburban development—all of which threaten the high quality of life that attracted so many new residents in the first place.

The city's population as of April 2003 was just over 687,700. Austin has a land area of about 275 square miles, and is located in the center of the state where several major ecosystem types converge, from the plains of north Texas and the forests of east Texas, to the wetter grasslands of southeast Texas leading to the Gulf of Mexico, to the more arid lands of west Texas. As a result, Austin features an intriguing and diverse mix of elements of all these landscapes.

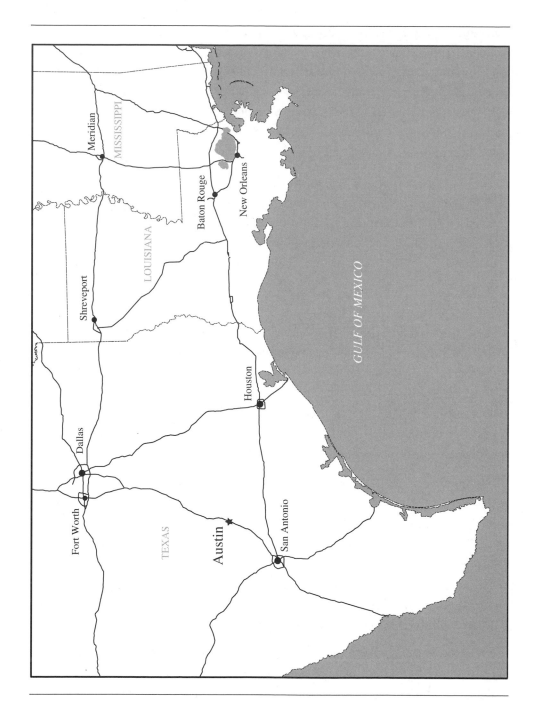

AUSTIN, TEXAS
Map courtesy of Clarion Associates.

The city is oriented north-south, bisected by Interstate 35. Areas to the east of the interstate are more flat, and traditionally the eastern part of the city has been home to a larger percentage of the city's minority population and less development pressure. The western half of the city spreads into the central Texas hill country, featuring rolling hills, impressive karst features, and the better-known Colorado River. Much of the western part of the city lies over a sensitive recharge zone for the Edwards Aquifer, which discharges water into the Colorado River and is a source of drinking water for many communities. The western areas are some of the wealthiest in the city, featuring new trophy homes and minimansions that have sprung up to take advantage of impressive hill country views and close access to the river and nearby lakes. Development pressures in the western part of the city accelerated in the 1990s, with new suburban neighborhoods stretching from Austin itself into adjacent western communities such as Bee Cave and Lakeway, and also into unincorporated Travis County.

Despite the fact that the growth pressures confronting Austin extend into Travis County and the entire central Texas region, there traditionally have been few examples of regional dialogue on growth issues or intergovernmental coordination. A new, nonprofit regional group called Envision Central Texas hopes to change that, however, and completed a regionwide survey in 2003 to help formulate a "shared vision" for all communities to accommodate anticipated future growth in central Texas (an expected 1.25 million people and 800,000 jobs over the next 20 to 40 years).

There is a high degree of public awareness about biodiversity and environmental issues in Austin, and land use debates have long dominated Austin politics. The city's mainstream and alternative newspapers cover such issues on a daily basis, more so than in many other communities nationwide and to a much greater extent than in other Texas cities. Despite Austin's national reputation as a green city, citizens by no means speak with one voice on environmental issues and sometimes do not support traditionally green programs. For example, in 2000 the citizens voted down a proposal to establish an ambitious new light rail system, putting the city behind the relatively more conservative cities of Dallas and Houston on that issue (though Austin voters did approve a slimmed-down light rail proposal in 2004).

Some observers note that environmentalism in Austin sometimes seems more rooted in politics than in ecology. Austin politics for years have been dominated by a contentious and somewhat simplistic split between "environmentalists" and "developers." Throughout the 1990s, many fiery debates ensued on growth and development policy as new residents flooded into the city and placed pressure on sensitive resources. Much of the focus has been on water quality issues. For example, increasingly frequent

The Edwards Aquifer is a source of drinking water for many communities in the area. Photograph by Matt Goebel.

closures of Barton Springs—a popular, spring-fed swimming pool at the heart of a major city park—because of high bacteria levels awakened many citizens to the consequences of sprawling subdivisions in sensitive watersheds. The Barton Springs closures led to volumes of news coverage and intense pressure by community activists to limit development over aquifer recharge zones, as well as the establishment of several powerful nonprofit groups focused solely on these issues.

In response to continuing growth pressures, Austin has developed an impressive, multifaceted series of nature-friendly programs. Numerous city agencies are using various tools to protect natural resources, such as zoning and subdivision regulations, development incentives, and public education campaigns. City programs are supported by a wide-ranging network of nonprofit groups devoted to environmental causes. Perhaps most importantly, the community has been working steadily for decades to purchase tens of thousands of acres to protect sensitive aquifer recharge areas and to set aside habitat for federally listed endangered species. Austin citizens have repeatedly supported attempts to protect natural resources through substantial land acquisitions. In one year alone, 1998, at the height of Austin's high-tech boom, citizens authorized over $113 million for open space acquisition.

If there is a criticism of Austin's various nature-friendly programs, it is that the activities discussed in this case study are loosely coordinated, and each is being undertaken in relative isolation. It appears that little attention is being paid to the development of overall goals and policies for protecting Austin's sensitive natural resources. This is symbolized by the city's highly decentralized planning structure and the decision not to revise the outdated comprehensive plan. Yet this lack of coordination should not minimize the many noteworthy programs underway, both inside and outside the city government, that can serve as models for other communities. This case study concentrates on the more significant of these programs.

Key Program Elements

Program Structure and Administration

While a variety of interesting and effective nature-friendly programs are in place in Austin, no one agency or group coordinates all the various activities. Instead, the work is carried out by a number of city agencies, as well as a wide range of quasi-public and nonprofit groups. Sometimes these agencies and groups work cooperatively, but more often each works independently on its own initiatives.

Within the city, responsibility for natural areas and natural resource protection is split among five main agencies. Two of these agencies have primary responsibility for land acquisition and management—the Parks and Recreation Department and the Austin Water Utility. On the land planning and development regulations side, responsibilities are scattered, and development review responsibilities are separated from planning.

There currently is no centralized land use planning agency in Austin, which is unusual for a city of its size and its progressive planning reputation. Instead, four planning-related departments make up Development, Environment and Transportation Services; all these departments report not to a central planning director, but rather to an assistant city manager. Two of these departments have specific responsibilities related to biodiversity protection: the Watershed Protection and Development Review Department and the Transportation, Planning and Sustainability Department.

Watershed Protection and Development Review Department

As its name implies, the Watershed Protection and Development Review Department (WPDR) has a dual focus: it monitors and protects local watersheds and also provides comprehensive development review and inspection services. (The department was created when the former water quality protection and environmental protection departments merged, since those issues were becoming dominant parts of the development review process.)

The watershed protection side, in particular the Environmental Resources Management Division, oversees issues such as flood control and safety, water quality protection, erosion control, and development of the Watershed Protection Master Plan. Biodiversity is not a central focus of the division, yet many of its watershed protection activities help protect habitat and undisturbed natural areas. The Development Review Division ensures that proposed development in Austin complies with the zoning and subdivision standards contained in the Land Development Code. A designated environmental officer oversees compliance with all environmental requirements, most of which are set forth in a detailed *Environmental Criteria Manual,* discussed later.

Transportation, Planning, and Sustainability Department

The Transportation, Planning, and Sustainability Department (TPSD) is an unusually multifaceted department with responsibility for a wide spectrum of activities, ranging from bicycle planning to urban design to Smart Growth programs. Reflecting the three areas of emphasis in the department's title, there are three divisions, two of which oversee biodiversity-related programs.

The Planning Division has responsibility for Austin's Smart Growth initiative, which resulted in the development of the Smart Growth map. This map identifies sensitive areas for protection and desired development zones. The Sustainability Division is headed by a sustainability officer, who in theory is responsible for overseeing the coordination of Austin's many diverse environmental and quality-of-life efforts, across multiple departments and agencies. In reality, however, the division had just one staff member as of late 2003, who was spending the bulk of his time on air quality issues.

Neighborhood Planning and Zoning Department

A third agency, the Neighborhood Planning and Zoning Department, has responsibility for long-range planning in Austin. This department currently is focused on preparing new plans for many Austin neighborhoods, all of which eventually are intended to be patched together, like a quilt, into a new citywide comprehensive plan.

Parks and Recreation Department

Within the Parks and Recreation Department, three divisions each have some responsibility for various biodiversity-related programs: the Austin Nature Preserves System; the Forestry Division; and the Design, Planning, and Construction Division.

The Austin Nature Preserves System manages and maintains fourteen natural areas in the city designated as nature preserves and wildlife sanctuaries. These relatively small preserves are typically open to recreational users and are located primarily in the central and eastern parts of the city. Activities inside the preserves include native plant rescues, biodiversity research, and wildlife monitoring.

The Forestry Division maintains trees in city parks and street rights-of-way, overseeing a citywide tree planting program, and also managing other tree-related projects (e.g., the city's Oak Wilt Program).

The Design, Planning, and Construction Division assists in the selection of new parklands, in consultation with the city's real estate officer, and designs facilities for active parks (e.g., ballfields, tennis courts).

Austin Water Utility

The Austin Water Utility also plays a significant role in biodiversity issues in the community as the manager of two large landholdings: the Balcones Canyonlands Preserve (BCP) and the Water Quality Protection Lands (discussed in more detail under "Acquisition"), close to 45,000 acres. Although other responsibilities may be scattered among various city departments, Austin Water Utility is the primary land manager, a wise choice due to its revenue-generating ability.

Public Works Department

Additionally, Austin maintains a full-time staff of real estate agents in the Public Works Department who have been instrumental in negotiating land acquisitions for conservation programs.

Nonprofit Groups

Complementing the work of city agencies, several nonprofit groups are engaged in biodiversity-related activities.

Austin is well known for its environmentally active citizenry. Dozens of nonprofit groups, such as the SOS Alliance, have played key roles in biodiversity-related environmental resource debates. In the mid-1990s, the Alliance was responsible for a successful citizen-led initiative to apply stricter limits on impervious surface cover in environmentally sensitive west Austin. Another example is the Hill Country Conservancy, a newly formed group billed as a collaboration between environmentalists and the local business community to form a consensus-based approach to environmental issues in the Austin region.

The Austin Water Utility's Center for Environmental Research is a collaborative program by the City of Austin, the University of Texas at Austin, and Texas A&M University. The center is located at Hornsby Bend, a 1,200-acre site in east Austin extending along 3.5 miles of the Colorado River. Although primarily used for sewage sludge recycling, Hornsby Bend is also a research site for urban ecology, biosolids, and ecological restoration. Understanding biodiversity in soil ecosystems is a principal research focus at the facility.

The Austin Biodiversity Project is a newly formed, cooperative undertaking organized by staff of the Center for Environmental Research and the Austin Nature Preserve System, as well as members of several local environmental organizations. Its organizers see the project as a tool for leveraging both public and private resources to protect biodiversity. One project is an ambitious biodiversity atlas that will catalog all elements of the natural environment in the Austin area. Another is the Austin to Bastrop River Corridor Project, established to restore habitat downriver from Austin.

Interagency Cooperation

While all communities periodically reorganize their administrative structure, Austin's organizational flowchart seems to have changed quite frequently over the past two decades. Perhaps as a result, there is surprisingly little coordination among agencies on natural resource and biodiversity issues. We heard many examples of poor coordination, such as the major open space land acquisitions that were made with apparently little planning department input. Almost all the city staffers we spoke with noted that interagency cooperation and coordination is one area where Austin could do better.

Nevertheless, this lack of coordination should not detract from the good work being done by individual agencies throughout the city. Plus, there are some examples of effective agency cooperation, such as the Green Garden initiative, which is a collaboration of six Austin agencies: Grow Green (from WPDR), Water Conservation (from TPSD), Green Building (from Austin Energy), Dillo Dirt (from the Center for Environmental Research), Composting (from Solid Waste Services), and Parks and Recreation. Watershed Protection staff also report that they coordinate regularly with Neighborhood Planning staff on environmental issues related to neighborhood planning (e.g., wildflower planting in street medians). Also, the various divisions within WPDR appear to do a good job with information sharing for development review purposes.

Some individual agencies appear to be doing well at coordinating their efforts with other local governments and nonprofit groups. The head of the Austin Nature Preserves System, for example, notes that he has extensive contact with surrounding jurisdictions (e.g., with Travis County and Rollingwood regarding security in parks). Similarly, the Center for Environmental Research has formed partnerships with dozens of local organizations for various activities (discussed below).

Planning

Austin's current comprehensive plan dates to the 1970s, and many sections are considered out of date by current officials, staff, and the public. The city has not undertaken a complete revision of the plan because of budget limitations and also because of hesitation about embarking on such a major new endeavor given the city's tough politics. Instead, the Neighborhood Planning and Zoning Department is preparing neighborhood plans for various geographic areas within the city, hoping that all the neighborhood plans ultimately can be pieced together like a quilt to form a new comprehensive plan. (This effort is criticized by many of those with whom we spoke, who note that the emphasis on specific neighborhoods allows each neighborhood to avoid tough decisions, such as placement of major communitywide infrastructure and utilities). Also, the Transportation, Planning, and Sustainability Department hopes to address some larger land use planning issues through development of a new comprehensive transportation plan.

Most current planning programs that focus on natural resource and habitat issues—on a citywide basis as opposed to the neighborhood scale—are being undertaken independently by the various agencies and groups discussed throughout this case study. For example, the Austin Water Utility conducts its own planning, focusing on habitat management and restoration for the BCP lands and the Water Quality Protection Lands, and also to identify additional parcels for future acquisition.

Because watershed management is such a key component of Austin's overall environmental focus, some of the most comprehensive planning for natural resources is being done by the Watershed Protection and Development Review Department, primarily through the Watershed Protection Master Plan. That plan inventories existing watershed problems and gauges the impact of future urbanization in 17 watersheds, including all the urban watersheds and 5 of the surrounding nonurban watersheds. The plan pulls together the various missions of the divisions within WPDR, including watershed protection and flood control. Habitat protection is discussed, though it has become a secondary focus now that the Austin Water Utility has assumed responsibility for the BCP, the city's primary species protection mechanism. The master plan is a continuing process that is reported on annually in the State of the Environment report (discussed below).

The findings of the plan provide sobering news. In the watersheds studied, as a result of urbanization, "flood, erosion, and water quality problems are pervasive and are expected to worsen if correction action is not taken." Over $800 million is required in capital funds over the next 40 years to address concerns raised in the plan (for example, to build new detention ponds); the amount is approximately twice the historical capital spending rate in Austin. The plan lays out a host of necessary code and criteria changes and suggested incentives to minimize additional watershed problems in the future, beyond those already identified.

Most of the planning done by WPDR and other city agencies focuses exclusively on land within Austin, and little to no cooperative planning is done with surrounding jurisdictions (beyond the county's cooperation in the BCP). Historically, there are few successful examples of regional planning and intergovernmental cooperation in Texas, though that is slowly starting to change. Envision Central Texas (ECT), formed in 2002, is a nonprofit entity established to prepare a new vision plan for the entire central Texas region, including the counties of Bastrop, Caldwell, Hays, Travis, and Williamson counties (the city of Austin lies at the heart of this region). Led by a diverse board of directors representing multiple perspectives (including the business community, environmentalists, social equity organizations, neighborhoods, and policymakers), the organization's goal is to "work in cooperative partnership with all entities and individuals to help guide the region toward a common vision." The group itself has no regulatory authority; its recommendations would have to be implemented by each of the participating local governments.

In December 2003, ECT published the results of a regionwide survey aimed at determining citizens' general preferences for future growth patterns. The main environmental focus was on how much development should be allowed over aquifers and in other sensitive areas. Over 12,000 people responded, with almost three-fourths of respondents preferring a scenario that would substantially increase density in Austin's core neighborhoods while concentrating suburban growth around existing roads or towns and away from environmentally sensitive areas. Already, the battle lines are being drawn over the survey's results, with some saying the survey is not a truly representative sample, and others saying the results provide a firm foundation for stronger environmental controls, and still others saying Austin's neighborhoods will never approve the densities contemplated in the survey.

ECT developed a "shared vision" for presentation and discussion by citizens in the region in May 2004. The main features of the central Texas vision include "an environment that is beloved and protected forever; an effective transportation system that is 'ahead of the curve'; an economy that is dynamic and diverse, with job opportunities across the region; a variety of housing choices affordable for everyone in the region; actions that demonstrate an understanding that social equity and racial harmony are important values that strengthen the region; the protection and enhancement of our neighborhoods, towns, rural areas, historic sites, and special sense of place; and regional understanding and the spirit that citizens fortunes are tied together."

Ultimately, many city staff members and officials hope that Envision Central Texas provides momentum and enthusiasm to undertake a new Austin comprehensive plan.

Acquisition/Funding

An aggressive land acquisition program, parts of which date back to the 1930s, is at the heart of Austin's efforts to protect natural resources, open space, and wildlife habitat. Early attempts to acquire sensitive lands relied on general revenue funds. In the 1990s, however, almost all of Austin's major public land acquisitions were the result of a series of successful bond issues, each of which has passed with high voter support (55 to 65 percent approval ratings). The more significant acquisitions and programs are described below.

Austin Nature Preserves

Austin began acquiring land to protect natural resources as early as 1934, when 80 acres adjacent to historic Zilker Park near downtown was acquired using New Deal funds and declared a nature preserve and bird sanctuary (today this is the home of the Austin Nature and Science Center). The next four decades saw periodic attempts to identify and set aside additional natural areas, though funds were limited.

By the early 1980s, as growth and development spread into the hills west of Austin, support grew both in the city administration and in the community to boost fundraising for land acquisition. In 1981, a neighborhood association proposed a successful citywide bond referendum to purchase about 40 acres of undeveloped land near their homes and set it aside as the Blunn Creek Nature Preserve, demonstrating the commitment of Austin neighborhoods to natural area protection. That same year, the city proposed a new capital improvements program to purchase and preserve the best examples of Austin's threatened natural areas throughout the city. Working in cooperation with local environmental groups, the city secured public approval of $5.7 million in bond money for the acquisition of nature preserves. An interdepartmental committee was established to recommend areas for acquisition. The group focused on acquiring lands of different ecological types (e.g., riparian areas, prairies). Though staff today note that the quality of some of the preserves acquired in the 1980s was mixed, the far-sighted program nevertheless formed the foundation of today's highly regarded Austin Nature Preserves System.

Today, the system's stated goal is to "acquire and manage the best examples of Austin natural resources and to increase the public knowledge and appreciation of Austin's natural's heritage." Properties have been acquired using bond money (and some general revenue funds), through redesignation of park lands as preserves, and through donations. The system's 14 areas (as of 2004) designated as nature preserves and wildlife sanctuaries cover 1,070 acres. According to the city, the preserves are "sanctuaries for native plants, native animals, and unique natural features. They provide educational and scientific opportunities for the people of Austin." Some form of public access is allowed on all of the preserves, ranging from guided tours to hiking to canoeing and kayaking. In addition to recreation, the preserves are managed for habitat protection and restoration, public access, recreation, and education. A management plan for each preserve was prepared in 1984; these currently are being updated to reflect current issues and new development pressures.

Remarkably, the system was staffed by just one person in late 2003, reflecting current city budget limitations and the fact that lands for endangered species (discussed below) are a higher priority in the budgeting process. The sole staffer is responsible for all activities and maintenance of the preserves. He seeks support from nonprofit and community groups to provide additional maintenance. For example, a neighborhood association and the Boy Scouts regularly volunteer to assist with cleanup in the Blunn Creek Nature Preserve.

Balcones Canyonlands Preserve

In addition to the Austin Nature Preserves, the city has a much larger set of landholdings, known as the Balcones Canyonlands Preserve (BCP), which were acquired primarily for habitat protection purposes. They form the heart of the city's biodiversity protection program. Comprising over 26,000 acres of land that cover much of western Travis County, the BCP was established in response to the listing of eight species as endangered under the federal Endangered Species Act (ESA) (two migratory songbirds and six karst invertebrates), plus an additional 27 plant and invertebrate "species of concern."

Under the ESA, no person may "take" a member of an endangered or threatened species. "Taking" is broadly defined (e.g., hunt, shoot, collect), and modifying or destroying habitat is considered a "take." Thus, any development that might damage potential habitat of the listed bird or invertebrate species in the west Austin hill country requires federal approval before proceeding.

The ESA does allow an individual, group, or community to prepare a plan that authorizes the taking of a listed species incidental to an otherwise lawful activity, provided the applicant obtains an Incidental Take Permit (also known as a "10(a) permit" after the ESA section under which it is authorized). The permit must be accompanied by a Habitat Conservation Plan (HCP) that outlines how species and habitat protection will occur, despite the proposed limited taking of the species. For a permit to be issued and an HCP to be approved, the proposed taking must be incidental to an otherwise lawful activity, the applicant must minimize and mitigate the impact of the taking, adequate funding for the plan must exist, and the taking must not reduce the likelihood of the survival and recovery of the species in the wild.

The City of Austin and Travis County applied for and obtained a 30-year 10(a) permit from the U.S. Fish and Wildlife Service in 1996, after several years of planning and negotiation. The accompanying Habitat Conservation Plan is known as the Balcones Canyonlands Conservation Plan (BCCP), and it identifies the species to be protected within the BCP and describes how the preserve is to be managed.

Under the terms of the permit, the city and the county agreed to set aside and manage 30,428 acres of habitat for two bird species, to manage populations of two rare plants, and to protect a total of 62 karst features known to contain populations of unique invertebrates. By the summer of 2002, about 26,000 acres of habitat had been set aside (grouped primarily into four separate "macro-sites"), the plant species were being managed, and 42 of the 62 karst features had received some level of protection.

Of the 26,000 acres under protection, 13,035 acres are held by the City of Austin and about 2,300 acres are held by Travis County. The city's land was purchased at a cost of about $28.5 million, assembled through a $22 million bond plus grants and other small sources. The bond measure passed despite some public skepticism about the value of the species being protected. (As one observer noted, "In Texas, it's not hard to explain the need to have good water. But birds and bugs are harder.") Tracts to be purchased were identified by a biological advisory committee, based on value as habitat.

The balance of the 26,000 acres is held by other participating organizations, including The Nature Conservancy of Texas, the Lower Colorado River Authority, and the Travis Audubon Society, which own and manage preserves dedicated to the BCP. No single parcel in the BCP is large enough on its own for complete ecosystem management, but the four major clusters of parcels are each managed based on their unique ecological characteristics.

The primary purpose of the BCP is species protection, which is accomplished through management, enhancement, monitoring, and protection of preserve habitats.

Management includes coordination among the various BCP land managers and with neighboring landowners. Enhancement activities focus on revegetation with native plant species and other improvement of habitat. Monitoring of the listed species is done through ongoing scientific data collection and publication in an annual report. Protection includes limiting recreational access, patrolling preserve lands to prevent inappropriate activities, and identifying boundaries and constructing fences.

While species protection is the primary purpose of the BCP, some public access and recreation are allowed on about 25 percent of the preserve system (primarily those areas that were public parks before becoming part of the BCP system). For example, hiking, mountain biking, swimming, tubing, canoeing, and dog walking are allowed in the popular Barton Creek Greenbelt, which runs through south Austin. Properties purchased with bond funds control or limit public access. The public process regarding public access to BCP lands was contentious and is still debated today. Staff members are researching the impacts of current recreational uses on habitat, and in the future the public access issue undoubtedly will be revisited.

Balcones Canyonlands Preserve lands, such as Reicher Ranch, shown here, are managed by the Austin Water Utility. Photograph by Carlos Abbruzzese, courtesy of the City of Austin, Balcones Canyonlands Preserve.

One of the few multispecies and multijurisdictional habitat planning projects in the country, the BCP is a collaborative effort between the city and the county (the two voting members), plus the other organizations previously noted. There appears to be a good working relationship among all the participating entities. However, most acquisition to date has been done by the city, and the city anticipates that future acquisition to obtain the total acreage called for in the BCCP will be primarily undertaken by the county. The county received $10 million in federal grant money in 2002 to support land acquisition within the preserve.

The BCP is managed by the Austin Water Utility, as opposed to the Parks and Recreation Department, which manages the Austin Nature Preserves System. This arrangement was selected apparently because the utility has a steady, independent revenue stream (from water tap fees), while Parks and Recreation is dependent on the city's annual budgeting process.

While some outside observers have criticized the BCP program (e.g., for failing to clearly coordinate conservation actions for species with different habitat requirements), staff managers feel that the BCP has been very successful in protecting habitat. Populations of the endangered species have stabilized and increased, as documented in the annual reports. Some habitat restoration is being done (e.g., by trying to increase woody canopy), though there is continuing debate about which restoration measures are most appropriate for the endangered species. In the future, staff members are anticipating increased community debate about the impacts of additional residential development near the BCP lands (e.g., how to deal with domestic pets).

Water Quality Protection Lands

In 1998, voters approved a $65 million bond offering to acquire land in the Barton Creek Watershed to protect land in the Drinking Water Protection Zone (mentioned as part of the Smart Growth map). This hourglass-shaped acquisition is known today as the "Prop 2 lands" after the proposition that authorized its purchase. Lands were identified for acquisition based on a combination of "art and science," according to city staff. In addition to practical factors such as tract availability, the city's Watershed Protection and Development Review Department developed a ranking score of 28 scientific indices to help select tracts for purchase. About 15,000 acres ultimately were acquired—a large area, though the size of a relative "postage stamp" in the massive watershed, notes one staffer.

Unlike the BCP lands, the Prop 2 lands are managed primarily to protect water quality, and habitat protection is a secondary consideration. Still, activities on the Prop 2 lands do have to comply with the ESA, and so the Austin Water Utility conducts informal consultations with federal officials regarding species and habitat protection issues. Some of the Prop 2 lands may ultimately be sold with conservation easements and development limits, in order to raise funds for additional acquisitions.

The issue of public access was not nearly as contentious with the Prop 2 lands as it was (and still is) with the BCP. Early on after acquisition of the site, it became clear that public access would be hotly debated. Water utility staff developed a more inclusive facilitation process than that used for the BCP, and the result is a public access program with more community acceptance and less controversy. The public process was honored with an award from a local mediation group.

Other Acquisition Programs

The Austin Nature Preserves, the BCP, and the Water Quality Protection Lands programs are the city's most significant examples of land acquisition. Yet there have been other notable acquisitions. One major example was the $20 million approved in 1992 for the Barton Creek Wilderness Park. Also, in November 1998, voters authorized $40 million in bonds to acquire land for greenways and destination parks for primarily the east side of the city, as discussed under "Social Indicators."

The city also acquires some land through dedications as part of the subdivision approval process (though most subdivisions pay a fee in lieu of dedication), the capital improvements plan budget, and individual donations. As of December 2002, staff note that just over 9,600 acres had been acquired through these various mechanisms.

The Mechanics of Major Land Acquisitions

Austin maintains a full-time staff of real estate agents in the Public Works Department who have been instrumental in negotiating the transactions for the BCP, the Prop 2 lands, and other acquisitions. The agents work for the city and bill their time to "clients" that include various city departments, such as the Austin Water Utility and Parks and Recreation.

In the case of the BCP, real estate agents selected possible sites based on species habitat criteria that were developed by a Biological Advisory Committee. In the case of the Prop 2 lands, an agent selected possible sites based on a threat matrix developed by the Watershed Protection and Development Review Department, which focused on areas of major biological interest or significance.

In all cases, the agents work as quickly and as stealthily as possible to identify sites that meet the applicable criteria. When a new funding source becomes available, such as through a major bond initiative, the money is spent as soon as it is available. City officials emphasized the secrecy of the site selection process as a key factor behind the overall success of the acquisition program. The real estate agents' goal is simply to get the best land available while spending the least money possible. When possible, the agents seek approval from the city manager's office for preliminary funding to put certain key parcels under option. Bond money is used for acquisition only. Other sources, including general revenue or special fees (e.g., water tap fees) cover ongoing costs like maintenance, restoration, and habitat enhancement. Condemnation is not used for any land acquisition. All transactions are done at arm's length.

There appears to have been little to no coordination between the real estate agents and Austin's planning agencies, though there has been extensive coordination between the agents and a handful of key officials from the agencies directly involved in the acquisitions, such as the water utility.

In retrospect, Austin's real estate agents and key agency officials believe that the BCP and Prop 2 land acquisition processes went about as well as possible, given the tight Austin real estate market at the time. City officials feel fortunate that the BCP and Prop 2 lands were acquired before land values in west Austin dramatically increased. One key success factor has been the active support of the city manager, who has always had an open-door policy and been very supportive of acquisition. The city council members also have always been supportive of acquisition, even in tough economic times. The council makes the final approval of any land purchase, on the advice of staff (particularly the real estate agent).

In an attempt to ensure better interdepartmental coordination of future acquisitions, key staff members report that they currently are assembling a strategic planning team (including representatives from the Austin Water Utility, WPDR, Development Review, and the city attorney's office) to decide how to set some general long-term goals to guide future acquisitions.

Regulations

In addition to its ambitious and wide-ranging land acquisition program, Austin protects open space and natural resources through a range of requirements embedded in its development review process.

The current land use code dates largely to the late 1980s; since then, periodic updates have occurred, but there has not been a comprehensive revision (which politically would be very challenging in Austin, staff believe). The city's environmental regulations include water quality, tree and natural area protection, and endangered species protection. A separate *Environmental Criteria Manual* contains extensive, detailed standards that implement the environmental regulations.

The water quality regulations apply in both the city and its extraterritorial jurisdiction area, and regulate the amount of impervious cover allowed with new development, setbacks from critical areas, and water quality. The regulations distinguish between the "desired development zone" (i.e., less sensitive areas where infrastructure and development should be concentrated) and the "drinking water protection zone" (see discussion of the Smart Growth initiative, below). The current regulations incorporate the Save Our Springs ordinance, developed by a coalition of environmental groups in response to the deteriorating water quality of Barton Springs and Barton Creek, and passed resoundingly by citizens in 1992. These regulations are the latest in a string of increasingly stronger ordinances drafted since the late 1970s to protect Barton Creek and the city's watersheds.

Barton Springs Pool is a beloved Austin landmark and the home of the endangered Barton Springs salamander. Photograph by Matt Goebel.

The tree and natural area protection regulations apply in the city only. They require site plan applications to include grading and tree protection plans that meet specified requirements and demonstrate how proposed development will preserve the existing natural character of the landscape. Existing trees eight inches or larger in diameter must be retained. The endangered species protection requirements require habitat surveys for species listed as endangered under the Endangered Species Act. Most enforcement of the environmental regulations occurs through the subdivision and site plan review processes. Both types of applications are required to identify critical environmental features and submit a tree survey and endangered species survey.

Though there are some alternative compliance provisions in the water quality and landscaping regulations, the environmental standards by and large are relatively basic and prescriptive—they do not allow for much administrative flexibility (e.g., tailoring to specific site attributes). This inflexibility is cited by both staff and developers as the reason why variances from the regulations are frequently sought, causing delays in the development approval process. Indeed, overall implementation of the environmental regulations reportedly is frustrated by the number of variances that are granted, as well as by a large number of developments that are building out under prior approvals granted under older, less rigid regulations.

The subdivision regulations contain parkland dedication requirements to help ensure that new development provides adequate parks for use by the residents that will live in the development. Five acres are required for every 1,000 residents. The parks department reports that they accept about a half-dozen parcels per year under this requirement, and accept fees in lieu of dedication for other projects (typically small projects that would yield substandard parcels).

Staff note that, for many years, the optional Planned Unit Development (PUD) process was used more frequently than the standard subdivision process for large developments. The flexibility of the PUD tool made it attractive to developers wanting to be creative in site design and also to staff looking to impose stronger open space and natural resource protection standards than were otherwise available in the code. In the early 2000s, however, thanks to several highly controversial PUD developments, the PUD tool has become less utilized, and developers report that they are returning to the standard subdivision process. Development agreements also are used frequently, though they are not fully described in the code. Developers note that they often will meet early in the site development process with staff managers to talk about environmental issues, and then the city attorney works with the developer to assemble a development agreement controlling the site and addressing pertinent environmental protection issues.

The Austin code authorizes cluster developments, in which a subdivision may be designed with smaller lot sizes than typically required, in exchange for setting aside 40 percent open space for use of the residents of the subdivision. However, staff and developers note that very little clustering is done, since the process laid out in the code is confusing and the standards for cluster development are not well defined.

The city has a designated environmental officer based in the Watershed Protection and Development Review Department. In place since the early 1990s, the position is intended to assign one official with responsibility for ensuring compliance with all the city's environmental regulations.

Beyond the environmental regulatory tools discussed previously, Austin also has tried to develop other mechanisms to protect sensitive natural resources through the development review process. In particular, the city experimented with a noteworthy Smart Growth initiative that attempted to direct growth away from environmentally sensitive areas and toward the urban core.

The Smart Growth initiative was established in the mid-1990s in response to the region's booming population growth and accelerating sprawl in environmentally sensitive west Austin. One key element got most of the attention: the Smart Growth Incentives. Underlying the incentives was a Smart Growth Map identifying the Desired Development Zone (DDZ) and the Drinking Water Protection Zone (DWPZ). The DDZ includes most of the urban core and already-developed areas and is where new development was to be targeted, while the DWPZ contains sensitive areas (primarily aquifer recharge areas, including wildlife habitat) to be protected. Within these areas, several types of incentives were created to encourage and direct development toward desired locations. An elaborate Smart Growth Matrix was developed to assist the city council in analyzing development proposals within the DDZ. It attempted to measure how well a project met the city's Smart Growth goals, such as proximity to mass transit and pedestrian-friendly urban design characteristics. The program offered financial incentives (fee waivers) to projects that scored high according to the Smart Growth criteria.

The Smart Growth initiative became quite controversial, as some observers accused the system of being overly complex and discouraging growth. The Smart Growth experience still frustrates many Austinites, especially city staff who worked on the program. Disappointed by what they say was widespread misunderstanding about how the program worked, staff members believe that the term "smart growth" was grossly misunderstood in Austin, and that as a result the term now is irreparably tainted. Nevertheless, there are valuable lessons in the Smart Growth experience. In particular, that the Smart Growth Map still is in place and has become an established

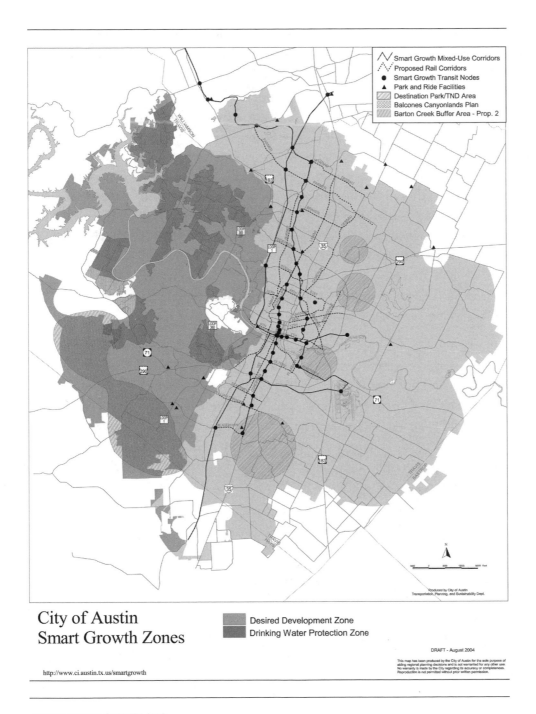

City of Austin
Smart Growth Zones

Desired Development Zone
Drinking Water Protection Zone

http://www.ci.austin.tx.us/smartgrowth

DRAFT - August 2004

AUSTIN SMART GROWTH MAP
Austin's Smart Growth Map has been used to direct development away from wildlife habitat and sensitive natural areas. Map courtesy of the City of Austin, Texas

part of the dialogue about future growth in Austin, and it still is a tool that can be used to direct development away from wildlife habitat and sensitive natural areas.

Restoration

The Austin Water Utility focuses on habitat management and restoration for the BCP lands and the Water Quality Protection Lands. Restoration and management activities for both programs are directed by land management plans. For BCP lands, restoration centers around vegetation management. This includes activities to plant or reestablish hardwood tree species to enhance habitat for golden-cheeked warblers. Another program strives to reduce overbrowsing by white-tailed deer, which can affect those same hardwood species. BCP land management plans also address plant communities that are favored by black-capped vireos. Restoration activities for BCP lands also involve removal of exotic invasive species, which compete effectively with native species that are important habitat components for protected species. Problem animal species such as feral hogs, brown-headed cowbirds, and imported fire ants are controlled to protect habitat preferred by protected species.

Restoration programs on Water Quality Protection Lands also include vegetation management. Efforts focus on reducing the tree canopy on upland sites to ensure that adequate recharge to the groundwater table occurs from the watershed. In the riparian areas, healthy plant communities are restored or protected, which helps the land area manage floodwaters (reducing sediment and pollutants) and enhances infiltration of water into the soil, which maintains stream flow. Selective methods of brush management, seeding, and protection from undesired disturbances are some of the techniques used.

Other restoration programs are being directed by the Center for Environmental Research, the most notable being the Austin Biodiversity Project (discussed under "Education"). The center also is involved in the Austin to Bastrop River Corridor Project, a partnership with federal, state, and local agencies and environmental groups to restore habitat along the 60-mile Colorado River corridor from Austin to Bastrop downstream. One result of this project is that the city of Austin began considering revisions to the waterway setbacks in fall 2004. Riparian buffers of 400 feet were proposed and could be implemented during 2005.

Leading by Example

The City of Austin requires that public projects be held to the same environmental protection standards as private projects and mandates formal assessments of the environmental impacts of capital improvement projects.

Austin's Capital Improvement Plan (CIP) outlines the scheduling, coordinating, and funding of the construction of public facilities, ranging from bridge and road construction to installation of playground equipment in public parks. As part of the development of public facilities called for in the CIP, the WPDR reviews all proposed projects and determines whether an environmental assessment is required during the planning phase of the project.

Under the Land Development Code, environmental assessments are required for projects in sensitive areas, including those projects over or draining to a karst aquifer; those in a floodplain, critical water quality zone, or water quality transition zone; and those projects on a tract with a gradient of more than 15 percent (steep slopes).

The goal of the environmental assessment is to avoid losses of significant natural resources or degradation of water quality that might result from a public project, and to identify alternatives if negative impacts cannot be avoided. The city attempts to incorporate review of all projects by WPDR as early as possible, to ensure that projects are constructed in the most environmentally sensitive manner.

Some agencies and departments have failed to get project information to WPDR early enough to budget for an environmental assessment and mitigation (if required). In response, the city currently is working on improving internal coordination to get forms to WPDR early enough for consideration in project budgets. One tool that has been recommended is an annual workshop for all departments' CIP project managers that would cover details of the environmental assessment permitting requirements and illustrate examples of sensitive environmental resources.

Social Indicators

In addition to improving overall coordination on natural resource protection issues, there are other steps that the city could take to improve the effectiveness of its nature-friendly programs. In particular, public education programs should target a wider range of city residents. The environmental community traditionally has drawn support from the university areas and the wealthier and whiter areas in the western part of the city, as opposed to the eastern side, which has a higher percentage of the minority population. Several observers noted that the community needs to do a better job in raising the environmental consciousness in the eastern side of the city. Some new efforts, such as the bond offering for new parks and preserves on the east side, hopefully should help to address this concern. In November 1998, voters authorized $40 million in bonds to acquire 4,000 acres for greenways and destination parks to implement a parks and greenways master plan prepared in the mid-1990s. The acreage acquired to date is 1,875; about $25 million has been spent so far. To address social equity concerns, the city directed that most purchases occur in the lower-income eastern part of the city to help balance out the large sums being spent on acquisition in the west. Acquisition efforts are focusing on land around major creeks and linear greenbelts to connect major parks.

The City of Austin also has an award-winning S.M.A.R.T. Housing Policy that was adopted in April 2000. The goal is to stimulate production of new housing that is *s*afe, *m*ixed-income, *a*ccessible, *r*easonably priced, and *t*ransit oriented. Housing also must meet Green Building standards. The program was expected to have 600 new housing units (that met the program's criteria) in the development review process in its first year (2001) and instead had more than 6,000 single-family or multifamily housing units, exceeding its goal by 1,000 percent. The program provides full-fee waivers for developments in which at least 40 percent of the units meet the "reasonably priced" standard, meaning that it serves families at or below 80 percent of the Austin area median family income. Other incentives include faster plan reviews, and advocacy through the development process. In 2003, the city's Neighborhood Housing and Community Development Department, which administers the S.M.A.R.T. Housing Policy, provided services to over 25,000 families, about 75 percent of whom were at or below 50 percent of the Austin-area median family income. These services included down-payment assistance, tenant-based rental assistance, and others.

In its first three years of existence, the incentive-based S.M.A.R.T. Housing Policy in Austin appears to be assisting in the construction of more new single-family and multifamily housing units on an annual basis than any other housing program in the country that attempts to achieve the same goals through mandatory inclusionary zoning strategies. Austin requires S.M.A.R.T. Housing™ development to meet higher environmental, energy efficiency, transit-oriented development, and accessibility standards than market housing is required to meet. S.M.A.R.T Housing Policy in Austin has demonstrated that environmental protection and housing affordability can be achieved through an incentives-based approach based on consistency and advocacy. S.M.A.R.T. Housing expects that more than 1,600 new units will be completed in 2004, with more than 70 percent of these being "reasonably priced" (ranging from $88,000 to $140,000).

Education

Environmental Education Programs

All the programs and entities discussed in this case study devote at least some resources to public education on environmental and natural resource issues. For example, both the BCP and the Austin Nature Preserves System provide kiosks at their accessible parks and open spaces to educate visitors about native species, habitat, watershed protection, and similar issues.

Perhaps the most comprehensive and impressive education program is overseen by the Watershed Protection and Development Review Department (WPDR), which focuses primarily on educating the public about the characteristics and health of local watersheds. They sponsor a variety of programs on pollution prevention designed to encourage environmentally responsible behavior. The department maintains an extensive website describing all its activities and public education programs, and handouts describing its activities are available throughout Austin (e.g., at the Barton Springs Pool).

Promoting the use of native landscaping is a major WPDR focus. Through its "earth-wise gardening" initiative, the department devotes significant resources (including the *Grow Green* handbook) toward educating the general public about the benefits of landscaping with native plant species, which require less care and water, versus imported species that require more care and water and that can introduce problematic nutrients into sensitive Austin watersheds. This initiative is seen as especially important given the high number of people moving to Austin from other parts of the country in the 1990s.

The "Splash! Into the Edwards Aquifer" exhibit offers a fun and exciting learning experience deep inside a simulated limestone cave. Photograph by Matt Goebel.

Other WPDR public education activities focus on children and youth. Earth Camp, for example, teams up WPDR staff scientists with local elementary schools, especially in poor and minority areas, for activities and education about local environmental issues. The program works with 500 students per year on programs such as setting up an organic garden. Other similar programs are geared to older age groups. Hydrofiles, for instance, works with high school students every year on more advanced, hands-on investigations of Austin watersheds. Students evaluate and analyze water quality trends and analyze historical case studies, and learn about possible careers in aquatic science.

Center for Environmental Research / Austin Biodiversity Project

The Center for Environmental Research focuses on scientific research into urban ecology and sustainability issues in the Austin area. The center is a joint effort of the Austin Water Utility, the University of Texas at Austin, and Texas A&M University. It represents an unusual example of direct cooperation among these groups, which have been competitive in the past.

Originally established in the 1980s for engineering research, the center today has evolved into more of an environmental research and educational facility. It emphasizes public education on biodiversity issues. For example, the center offers a regular series of lunchtime seminars and other programs to engage and educate the public. In April 2003 it held its first "BioBlitz," a 24-hour inventory of all species found at Hornsby Bend, the center's 1,200-acre headquarters site in east Austin along the Colorado River. The BioBlitz was sponsored by the center in partnership with city and state agencies, schools, museums, and nonprofit and environmental groups.

One of the major undertakings at the center is the Austin Biodiversity Project, which is a collaborative effort between the center, the Austin Nature Preserves System, and other nonprofit groups to, in their words, "leverage City of Austin and nonprofit resources to promote biodiversity in the Austin area through restoring and enhancing urban habitats." The project developed out of efforts by staff of the center and staff of the Austin Nature Preserves System working together to grow native plants for city projects, such as the nature preserves. Over time, the collaboration grew as the two staffs worked together and brought in new partners for activities such as developing educational materials about biodiversity issues and developing a core group of volunteers to assist with plant rescues and native plant restoration projects.

One of the key goals of the Austin Biodiversity Project is the development of an Austin Biodiversity Atlas, which is envisioned as a 100-year project cataloging all elements of the natural environment in the Austin area. Some elements already are in place (e.g., a bird atlas) that will be used as building blocks of the larger atlas. The Texas Memorial Museum is a major partner in the project, and its participation is seen as a key stabilizing force, helping to insulate the project from local politics. The project is intended to be citizen based as much as possible, both to lower costs and to help raise community awareness of biodiversity issues. A website ultimately will be developed to put the database online. The goal of the website will be to allow anyone to log in with their Austin address and find out what information has been found so far for their neighborhood. Eventually, interactive features will allow website users to report sightings of new species, and so forth. Certified users might even be able to use the website to add data to the environmental atlas.

Despite having formed partnerships with many local organizations, the center is not well integrated with the city's planning activities and with other city programs for protecting open spaces and natural resources. Center staff members recognize this and hope that the biodiversity atlas can, over time, serve as a foundation for integrating the center's work more with the city's. In fact, center staffers say that they are trying to develop projects that can leverage the resources from different city departments and agencies. They hope that, at some point in the future, city leaders will look up and realize that the center has quietly and effectively turned into a successful example of interdepartmental coordination.

Results

The State of the Environment (SOE) Report is an annual undertaking to consolidate and publish information about the city's efforts to protect the natural environment. Various agencies contribute to the report, which is coordinated and published by staff from the Watershed Protection and Development Review Department. It is the city's main tool for pulling together all the various programs underway to protect natural resources in the Austin area. A key goal behind the report is public education.

The original purpose of the SOE report was to provide a tool by which to measure progress in improving the quality of Austin's creeks and watersheds. Specifically, the WPDR staff developed an Environmental Integrity Index about eight years ago to help get a handle on the health of local creeks, and to determine where funds should be spent. The index looks at various indicators (e.g., sediment, aquatic life, recreational opportunities) and is periodically tweaked and fine-tuned. Each watershed is examined once every three years, and so the SOE report discusses different results every year.

Using a scoring system for all watersheds, the SOE report originally was intended as a motivating tool to increase scores in each overall watershed on an annual basis. In retrospect, staff today note that their original goals were too ambitious because of lack of resources to make significant changes; today, they have revised their goals to be more realistic and to focus on incremental progress in smaller geographic areas (e.g., moving scores for subareas from "poor" to "marginal").

Now the report focuses on a new set of issues in depth each year. It is sometimes lengthy and sometimes brief, depending on the level of research and reporting available for the topics covered that year. Very little new research or reporting is created solely for the SOE report; instead, most elements of the report are created for other purposes and then reprinted in the SOE report.

While the SOE report does appear to have evolved into an excellent tool for coordinating information about Austin-area environmental issues, it nevertheless still does not capture all the various local efforts underway to protect biodiversity and natural resources. Of the various agencies that we examined for this case study, some are usually covered in the SOE report and some are not. For example, the report usually covers the year's programs and activities conducted at Hornsby Bend by the Center for Environmental Research. The sustainability officer also regularly drafts a section on air quality issues. But the staff of the Austin Nature Preserves System, however, had not heard of the SOE report; they thought it would be a good place to publicize information about the current status of the city's nature preserves system.

Egrets are one of the many migrating waterfowl that can be seen at Hornsby Bend. Photograph by Kevin M. Anderson.

Note

[1]Primary sources for this case study include Austan Librach, Director, City of Austin Transportation, Planning and Sustainability Department; numerous other staff members at the City of Austin; the Austin City Code; and the city's website, www.ci.austin.tx.us.

CHAPTER 4

Baltimore County, Maryland: Using the Entire Toolkit for Habitat Protection

B altimore County, Maryland, has one of the most ambitious and successful land management and environmental protection programs in the country. An impressive combination of tools and strategies—land use regulations, land acquisition, an urban growth boundary, education, partnerships with private land trusts, and infill development initiatives—has been employed to preserve thousands of acres throughout the county and protect critical wildlife habitat. Agricultural land preservation and protection and restoration of the Chesapeake Bay have been two rallying points for continuing citizen support of these resource protection strategies. While changes in state government programs and politics since 2002 may make future progress more challenging, Baltimore County is in many ways a model for local governments everywhere when it comes to protecting nature and biodiversity.

Baltimore County, Maryland's third largest in land area and population, is a middle-class urban county located just north of Baltimore City, an independent jurisdiction.[1] With over 770,000 people, it has a substantial blue-collar population and maintains a significant manufacturing base. The county covers 607 square miles, running north of Baltimore to the Pennsylvania border. Despite its large size, the county

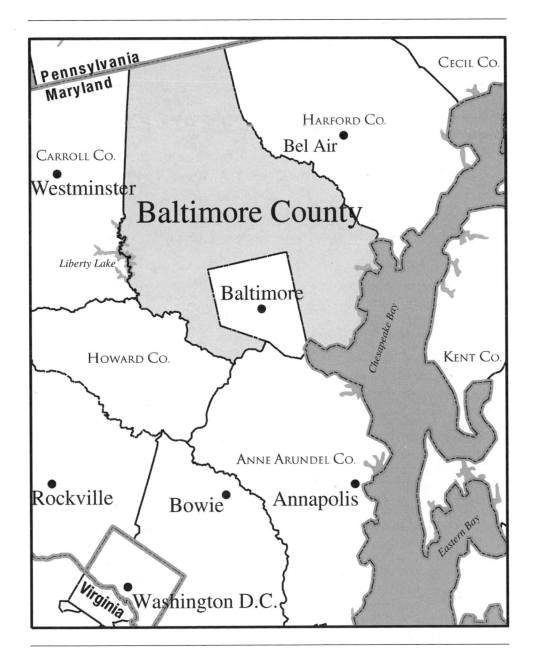

BALTIMORE COUNTY, MARYLAND
Map courtesy of Clarion Associates.

contains no incorporated municipalities or special utility districts, a fact that has made implementation of its growth policies and environmental programs much easier than in many places with fragmented government structures. It is governed by an elected county executive and seven county council district representatives.

Land cover in the county is evenly split among urban, agriculture, and forest. It has 2,100+ miles of streams and rivers and over 220 miles of shoreline on the Chesapeake Bay. About 80 percent of the county is within the Piedmont Plateau, with gently rolling hills; the remaining 20 percent is in the Coastal Plain region, with flat, sandy soils. The area adjacent to Baltimore City is highly developed at suburban densities, except for development nodes in places like Towson and Owings Mills. The rural hinterlands are a mosaic of fragmented forests and farms on limestone valleys and schist ridges.

The agricultural economy is diverse—the county is home to over 800 farms, and it is first in the state for equine production and fourth in vegetable acres harvested. Dairy products are the top farm commodity by value.

Common wildlife species are white-tailed deer and species that thrive in forest edges and fragmented forests. The larger, publicly owned forest blocks support populations of neotropical migrant birds. Black bear are even returning to the county. The county lies on the Atlantic Flyway for migratory songbirds and is ranked in the top 10 in number of trout streams in the eastern United States. Threatened and declining species include the cerulean warbler and bog turtle.

The county's growth rate has been a steady 1 percent over the past three decades. Its growth spurt came between 1950 and 1970 with white flight from Baltimore. Now, however, the white population continues to decline slowly, while the African American and Asian populations are on the increase. Blacks make up about 20 percent of the county. Seniors are the fastest-growing segment demographically.

The growth boom in the 1950s led to a concerted private attempt to protect the beautiful rolling valleys north of the I-695 Beltway, which opened during that decade and acted as a growth generator. Local residents retained planning icon Ian McHarg, who produced a Plan for the Valleys in 1963 that became a rallying cry for preserving the county's rural areas. Soon thereafter, in 1967, the county created an urban growth boundary (called the Urban-Rural Demarcation Line—URDL). Growth and public infrastructure investment were targeted inside the line. Areas outside the line were rezoned in 1975 to lower densities, and over time the county has purchased easements and development rights. Today, 85 percent of the county's population lives within the URDL on only 30 percent of the county's land.

This area in Worthington Valley is protected from intensive development by zoning and conservation easements. Photograph courtesy of Baltimore County, Maryland.

Since the mid-1980s, the county has adopted stiff environmental protection regulations (forest conservation, stream buffers, etc.) and further downzoned the rural areas, in part to protect the county's watersheds, water supply reservoirs, and the Chesapeake Bay. The URDL has stood the test of time and has even been strengthened in many ways since its creation. Currently, the county is considering a massive downzoning of much of the rural area that is not already subject to very large lot agricultural zoning (1 unit/50 acres).

The county's programs that result in protection of biodiversity and wildlife habitat are impressive and varied. The URDL, large-lot zoning, and tough development standards are the backbone of the initiative and have preserved huge tracts of open space, forests, and agricultural lands. While the southern half of the county is highly urbanized, the north remains mostly open, with over 800 working farms and significant agricultural production (corn, soybeans, horse breeding) and forestry as noted above. Because of the URDL, there is an abrupt and stark contrast between urban and rural areas, much like around cities in Oregon. Initially, wildlife habitat preservation was not the primary focus of these initiatives but was protected under the wing of water quality and agricultural land protection. More recently, the county has focused

The Hunt Valley business community is an example of planned development within the county's growth boundary. Photograph courtesy of Baltimore County, Maryland.

on issues such as forest habitat fragmentation and has put in place new regulations and acquisition programs that target rural character and habitat protection. The county has devoted significant resources to staff—the Department of Environmental Protection and Resource Management (DEPRM) employs over 100 people, and the Office of Planning another 50 (including community development).

The county has also looked inside the URDL to encourage both development and redevelopment, and has created designated growth areas into which it has poured millions of dollars of infrastructure investment to support higher-density development. The objective has been to direct development to areas that can be served in a cost-effective manner and to avoid inefficient development in more rural areas. In 2003, the county executive proposed a "Renaissance" strategy to further jump-start development on vacant infill and redevelopment parcels within the URDL. A goal of the strategy is to engage neighborhoods and prospective developers in planning development on these parcels with an eye toward speedy county approval of projects that comply with county regulations. The county also has a very ambitious stream restoration program in urban areas that is correcting serious erosion and other problems associated with past developments. A spin-off benefit is creation of a significant amount of wildlife habitat as well as improved water quality.

The county also has a number of partnerships with private land trusts and local conservation organizations, as well as the State of Maryland, to protect open space. Private land trusts in the county have protected over 12,000 acres, primarily through easement donations. Moreover, the county has worked closely with agencies from the State of Maryland, which until recently has strongly supported a host of land conservation and Smart Growth programs. (Budgetary problems and election of a new governor with different priorities have put many of those programs in question.) Additionally, the county has signed a number of important intergovernmental agreements with surrounding jurisdictions, notably in the area of water quality and watershed protection.

Importantly, the county is fiscally conservative and sees the clear link between sprawl in rural areas and providing services. The county has had to build only one high school in the last 25 years despite adding thousands of new residents. It sports a Triple A bond rating, which means the county is considered to have the highest capacity to meet its financial commitments.

The county also has an ambitious environmental educational program, particularly through its Green Schools Program, and some strong partnerships with local watershed associations and land trusts.

A final element of Baltimore County's success has been the prompting and support of the State of Maryland. A combination of state laws requiring local governments to focus on protection of critical areas, forest protection, and the Chesapeake Bay and several land acquisition/preservation initiatives backed by funding sources such as a real estate transfer tax have provided a strong foundation and impetus for many county programs.

Overall, the county has a balanced array of regulatory, acquisition, and other land protection initiatives that are supplemented by prudent capital investments, savvy professional staff, and effective public/private partnerships and educational programs. While watershed and agricultural land protection are often surrogates for biodiversity and habitat protection, increasingly these goals are specifically recognized in county policies and management efforts. And ultimately the proof is in the pudding of total acres of land protected through acquisition or easements—the county in 2004 passed the halfway mark toward its goal to protect 80,000 acres of land through acquisition, which is nearly one-fifth of the county's total area.

The county continues, however, to deal with a delicate balancing act between accommodating reasonable amounts of rural development and providing the best protection for sensitive environmental resources and its working lands economy. For example, it is sometimes difficult to take environmental issues into account for community plans in urban areas, because these plans are prepared by community groups who are more concerned with land use and traffic issues. But especially in rural areas, there are challenges in delineating responsibilities between the Office of Planning's traditional role of providing for development and the Department of Environmental Protection and Resource Management's mandate to protect resources and administer land preservation programs. For example, the county's master plan, adopted in 2000, called for investigating the concept of rural villages as an option for accommodating rural residential development in a manner less intrusive to rural character. After some preliminary analyses and review by an advisory group and the Department of Environmental Protection and Resource Management, the concept was rejected because it would have introduced negative environmental impacts in the reservoir watershed by concentrating development.

Moreover, while the county provides for some economic incentives through low-interest loans, it does not appear to have any effective rural economic development program to help farmers and other landowners look for realistic alternative, environmentally sensitive enterprises, although the master plan pointed out the need for such an effort.

Engaging minorities—a growing percentage of the county's population—in environmental programs has also been a continuing challenge. County officials report that the state tried to involve blacks in the region's Patapsco/Back River Tributary Strategy implementation team for the Chesapeake Bay Program's nutrient reduction efforts but could not get many people engaged on a sustained basis.

Finally, as agricultural protection/easement purchase programs come under fire at the state level as being a giveaway for the rich, some assert that the county needs to develop different environmental indicators other than acres of agricultural land preserved to make a stronger case for protection.

Key Program Elements

Program Structure and Administration

A strong testament to Baltimore County's commitment to natural resource and environmental protection is the funding it has devoted to building a deep, capable professional staff. The Department of Environmental Protection and Resource Management (DEPRM), which reviews developments for compliance with environmental laws, has over 100 employees, many with advanced degrees and years of hands-on experience in the field. Professionals include resource biologists, foresters, herpetologists, engineers, and planners. DEPRM, which was created in 1987, had an operating budget of $5.6 million in 2003. Additionally, the Office of Planning, which overseas comprehensive and long-range planning, has 50 people on its staff, many of whom are professional planners.

Because development review, environmental regulation, restoration programs, and land acquisition are all under the DEPRM umbrella, the county has a strong, unified conservation agency. This stands in contrast to many other jurisdictions in which such responsibilities are fragmented among many departments—planning, parks and recreation, and public works, for example.

If there is a disconnect in the organization and administration of resource protection, it is between DEPRM and the Office of Planning. The Office of Planning is responsible for long-range and area plans as well as periodic changes in land designations in zoning maps. While it formerly had the task of development review, that function was shifted to DEPRM in the 1980s. As a result, long-range planning may not be as well coordinated as one might hope. For example, the master plan produced by the Office of Planning promoted rural village developments that appear to be inconsistent with the county's historic rural development patterns and contrary to the county's natural area and agricultural land protection goals. DEPRM strongly objects to the introduction of new, dense human settlements in the middle of protection areas. On the other hand, what passes for rural planning in the county is, almost by default, agricultural land acquisition and strict development control. Seemingly only limited thinking has been given to the economics of agriculture and to assisting farmers and landowners in finding realistic environmentally sensitive enterprises. The county's master plan, completed in 2000, does devote a few pages to this issue, but reportedly there has been little implementation action by the county. However, DEPRM and other county agencies do have significant input to Planning's quadrennial comprehensive zoning map process, which provides an opportunity for environmental concerns to be included in decision making about zoning changes.

In addition to a strong staff, many (especially in the development community) view the organization of the county's development review system as a real plus. Instead of subjecting most applications to a lengthy process with numerous public hearings, most are heard before an appointed, independent hearing officer. DEPRM staff make recommendations to the hearing officer, and the public is given an opportunity to comment. Most observers feel that the system is much less political than in many other jurisdictions and is more efficient because it avoids multiple hearings by various review bodies. Additionally, the hearing officers have a great deal of experience in land use and environmental issues related to development, unlike many review bodies in other communities. One developer commented that while the process is lengthy and requires significant time and investment up front to produce plans and gather information, it is predictable and efficient, in no small part because of the hearing officer system. The planning commission and elected officials typically are involved mainly in policy issues and major land use decisions (such as comprehensive rezonings), not in day-to-day development review.

Another interesting aspect of land use administration in Baltimore County is the people's counsel, located in the Planning Office. The positions of the people's counsel and deputy were established by the county charter and are appointed by the county executive, subject to County Council confirmation. The function of the people's counsel may include appearing before local, state, and federal administrative agencies and courts to represent the interests of the public in general in any zoning matter. The people's counsel has the responsibility, under the charter, to defend any duly enacted master plan and/or comprehensive zoning map.

One of the most noteworthy elements of Baltimore County's resource protection initiatives is the numerous effective partnerships that have been created and nurtured with watershed associations (e.g., stream watch programs), local land trusts (five in county), and schools (Green Schools Program), among others. Cooperation with these private entities has leveraged the county's programs and taken them to a new level. On the other hand, it appears that intergovernmental cooperation with Baltimore County's neighbors, including Baltimore City and Anne Arundel, Carroll, Harford, and Howard counties, is still a challenge. However, in addition to a long-standing program for the protection of the city drinking water reservoirs, which serve 1.8 million citizens in the region, the local governments have worked together for the past decade in partnership and with the state to implement the Chesapeake Bay Agreement. In 2003, Baltimore City and County signed a formal Baltimore Watershed Agreement to address water quality issues in rivers and streams that flow through both jurisdictions.

Planning

While the planning and development review functions could be better coordinated, as noted previously, the county has produced a number of impressive watershed water quality management plans. They contain a detailed description of each watershed and its problems and threats, including pollutant loading, stream stability analysis, and restoration opportunities. These plans are geared to meet federal stormwater management requirements and state Chesapeake Bay Program commitments.

The plans have been supported by extensive mapping of watersheds, Chesapeake Bay critical areas/buffers, and detailed water quality data. While wildlife habitat mapping has been spotty at best, the county now pays much greater attention to mapping forest cover and buffers countywide in recognition of the impacts fragmentation is having on the forest base and wildlife habitat. The county's mapping of forest cover is accurate and comprehensive.

The MasterPlan 2010, completed in February 2000 by the Office of Planning and adopted by the county council, has a comprehensive discussion of urban planning issues, ranging from growth centers to historic resources. Almost 200 pages are devoted to the "urban county." (In contrast, the plan devotes only about 30 additional pages to the "rural county.") The plan discusses one of the key elements of the county's growth management strategy—directing new development to designated

Towson, Maryland, Baltimore County's seat of government, is the county's designated urban center. Towson, as all places in Baltimore County, is not an incorporated municipality. All of Baltimore County is governed by a single zoning authority. Photograph courtesy of Baltimore County, Maryland.

growth areas: Owings Mills in the west county, Perry Hall–White Marsh in the east, and the Towson urban area, which is the county's government center and "downtown." Owings Mills and Perry Hall–White Marsh were conceived in the 1979 master plan as planned communities that would provide housing, jobs, and a wide range of public and commercial services. They were a direct response to accommodating development following the downzoning in the mid-1970s of nearly two-thirds of the county in order to curtail low-density suburban sprawl, which was found to be inefficient and costly. Over the past 20 years, much of the county's growth has been directed successfully into these two growth areas and the Towson urban area, removing development pressure in rural resource areas.

To further encourage development within the URDL, the county executive in 2003 launched the Renaissance initiative to designate so-called opportunity districts. Seven sites will be selected, within which infill and redevelopment will be encouraged with incentives, speedier development approvals, and involvement of local communities to reduce development conflicts.

Acquisition/Funding

The county's extensive land use regulations and control on development in rural areas have been complemented by an effective and well-funded land acquisition program. The first easement in the county was in 1974, with the donation of an easement to the Maryland Environmental Trust. Since 1980, however, the county has been aggressively seeking conservation easements. Since that time, the county has preserved over 40,000 acres, largely through purchase of conservation easements and development rights.

The agricultural land acquisition program was adopted in the wake of a major, controversial downzoning of rural portions of the county in the 1970s that reduced allowable densities from 1 unit/acre to generally 1 unit/5 acres for parcels up to 100 acres. Later, permitted densities were further reduced to 1 unit/25 acres for tracts between 2 and 100 acres and 1 unit/50 acres for greater than 100 acres. Bond funding was made available to purchase land and easements as a way to take the sting out of the zoning restrictions. The acquisition program, linked to the State of Maryland's Agricultural Land Preservation Program, expanded in the 1980s. It focuses on wildlife habitat only indirectly—20 percent of the farmland protected through the program in the county is forest cover. It works like this: Landowners apply for designation as an agricultural district and make a five-year commitment that restricts the land to agri-

Farmland in Upperco, Baltimore County—Piney Rural Legacy Area, located in the midst of approximately 10,000 contiguous preserved acres. Photograph courtesy of Baltimore County, Maryland.

cultural use. The owner may then apply for the Maryland Agricultural Land Preservation Foundation or the county to purchase development rights on the property. Under the county program, a local agricultural board ranks farms for acquisition. A key aspect of this effort has been a dedicated funding source to ensure a steady and continuing source of funding. Baltimore County receives a local cut of the state real estate transfer tax and devotes those funds to agricultural land acquisition. Revenues have amounted to between $300,000 and $1 million annually over the last decade. Through the Maryland Agricultural Land Preservation Program and the sister Baltimore County program, over 18,000 acres of farmland have been preserved in the county.

Two other acquisition programs—GreenPrint and Rural Legacy—focus on preservation of forest lands, rural character, and wildlife habitat. Both have been initiated and primarily funded by the State of Maryland. The GreenPrint program, created in 2000 by the Maryland General Assembly, has three goals—to identify important unprotected natural lands, to link or connect these lands through a system of corridors, and to save them through targeted acquisitions and easements. The focus of GreenPrint has been on forests, with state funding coming from the state real estate transfer tax and bond funds.

The Maryland Rural Legacy Program is designed to preserve large blocks of rural lands for permanent protection through acquisition of conservation easements. Baltimore County has provided approximately one-third of matching funding to this state program. The county has five designated areas—the most in the state. Each area is sponsored by a private land trust (assisted by the county) and is governed by a state-approved protection plan. Landowners may donate or sell an easement to the county through this program. Each of the Rural Legacy areas has received county funds for conservation easement purchases. The program is designed to protect a combination of farm and forest lands, as well as natural resource lands such as wetlands, coastal areas, and wildlife habitat. Drawing on a combination of state and county funding, over 3,000 acres have been preserved through the Rural Legacy Program.

The Maryland Environmental Trust (MET) and local land trusts are another important element of the county's ambitious land acquisition program. Created by the state in 1967, the Maryland Environmental Trust seeks donated easements on farms and forestlands, wildlife habitat, natural areas, and scenic landscapes. County landowners have preserved over 12,000 acres through donations, taking advantage of an array of state and federal tax credits and deductions for the value of such donations. In addition to MET, eight local land trusts are operating in the county to protect important resource areas. The county DEPRM works closely with these land trusts, helping them with documentation, mapping, and grant implementation. Each of the land trusts has been awarded funds under Maryland's Rural Legacy Program and from other sources.

Regulations

The backbone of the county's natural resource and agricultural land protection programs has been a strong zoning and development control program. It has two main elements: large-lot zoning in rural areas to keep residential densities very low, and tough regulations that protect sensitive natural areas and trees.

The large-lot zoning requirements have an interesting history. When zoning was first put in place in the 1940s, lots of less than one acre were allowed throughout the county. After the landmark work of Ian McHarg's Plan for the Valleys and thanks to the help of citizen groups, the county began planning for future growth. Out of this effort came the plan to direct the majority of growth to the "Growth Centers" and to protect the rural resources of the county. In 1975, the county created Resource Conservation Zoning, which for the first time linked the appropriate zoning densities and regulations to the resources identified to be protected in the county. Among those new zones was an Agricultural Preservation Zone, known as R.C. 2. Although this R.C. 2 zoning was controversial and seemed like a good idea at the time, in practice not only was it ineffective in preserving open space and rural character, it actually contributed to sprawl—the countryside began to be peppered with five-acre farmettes

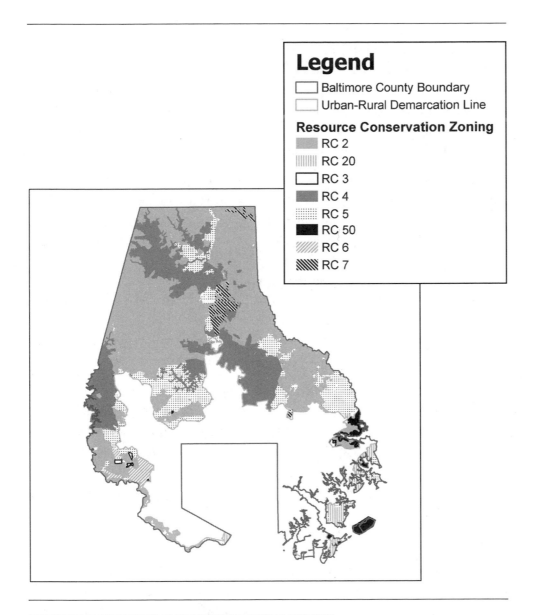

Legend

☐ Baltimore County Boundary
☐ Urban-Rural Demarcation Line

Resource Conservation Zoning

- RC 2
- RC 20
- RC 3
- RC 4
- RC 5
- RC 50
- RC 6
- RC 7

BALTIMORE COUNTY RESOURCE CONSERVATION ZONING DISTRICTS
Baltimore County's Resource Conservation zoning is designed to protect water quality in streams, reservoirs, and the Chesapeake Bay; focus urban growth inside the Urban-Rural Demarcation Line; and protect agricultural land. Map courtesy of Baltimore County, Maryland.

that carved up the landscape more quickly than ever. Consequently, the county in 1979 amended the zone to a more protective agricultural density—up to 1 unit/50 acres for tracts greater than 100 acres. This very large lot zoning has proven effective in protecting agricultural areas from encroachment while protecting big blocks of contiguous open space and habitat. More recently, the county has sought to address problems in the other original Resource Conservation Zones by creating new zones and rezoning large portions of the county.

In addition to the agricultural zoning, the county has also made good use of the conservation subdivision option that allows developers to cluster allowable density on smaller lots within a tract if they preserve a high percentage of the site in open space. The cluster subdivision option has helped protect over 2,000 acres. Interestingly, county staff do not favor using cluster subdivisions for protection of active farms, because introduction of houses in these areas has resulted in conflicts with existing farming operations. Moreover, resource protection regulations tend to force housing to be located away from sensitive natural areas and into arable lands. Conservation subdivisions work better, in staff's estimation, to create transition areas between suburban and rural areas and to promote the connection of environmental corridors.

The second key element of the county's regulatory program is a comprehensive set of natural resource protection standards that are applied to all new development in the project review process. Many of these regulations have been driven by the State of Maryland and are linked to protecting water quality/stream ecosystems and the Chesapeake Bay. However, Baltimore County was at the forefront of regulatory initiatives to protect water quality, streams, and wetlands, and began protecting these resources long before state requirements. For example, state law requires local jurisdictions to protect forests to prevent runoff into streams and the bay. Under county regulations, a specified percentage of existing tree cover on a site must be retained. If no trees exist, the applicant may be required to revegetate, either on- or off-site. Similarly, new development must avoid streams, wetlands, and associated steep slopes whenever feasible or mitigate impacts. The local regulations adopted in 1988 to implement state Chesapeake Bay Critical Area requirements designate land within 1,000 feet of tidal waters for protection of resources and enhancement. The rules limit impervious surfaces, require removal of pollutants from runoff, and protect wildlife habitat. Importantly, the county has sufficient staff so that all proposed developments are actually reviewed in the field on-site. This is unlike some jurisdictions where development review is a desk exercise, with no site visit to adequately evaluate the proposal and potential impacts on habitat.

Wildlife habitat protection has only recently been an important focus in the development review process. In the past, water quality protection and forest and stream corridor preservation have been surrogates for habitat protection. In 1993, the county began to focus on the continuing fragmentation of forest cover and the pernicious effects that such fragmentation is having on interior forest species habitat. As a result, development review staff are much more sensitive to proposals that require cutting of roads through intact forests and plans that spread development out over a site.

Because of the concentration of population within the URDL under the county's growth management strategy, the opportunities for significant habitat protection are greatest in rural areas. Nevertheless, riparian corridors and significant forests are protected countywide. including within the URDL. To account for lost and degraded habitat in older urban communities, the county has undertaken an aggressive stream restoration program.

The county's commitment to environmentally sensitive development is underscored by the fact that all county projects must comply all with development regulations—according to staff, there are no exemptions. The process by which county projects are reviewed is the same as for private sector projects, with the exception that the projects are not subject to review and approval by a hearing officer.

Restoration

Baltimore County has one of the most sophisticated, well-funded stream and shoreline restoration programs in the nation. Using natural channel design approaches, it has resulted in the restoration of miles of urban/suburban streams damaged by prior development and accelerated runoff. In 2003, the waterway improvement program had a staff of six people and a budget of almost $8 million. Some of these fees are paid by developers in lieu of on-site stormwater management. Most of the actual restoration projects are undertaken by contractors under supervision by county staff. The county has assessed 700 miles of streams and completed 26 restoration projects, with almost 10 miles of streams rehabilitated, at a cost of $12.4 million.

Additionally, the county has an ambitious forest and tree restoration program that is funded in significant part by state funds and by mitigation fees paid by developers who remove trees when constructing a project. Baltimore County also coordinates delivery of trees to citizens and community groups participating in the State of Maryland's Tree-Mendous Program. This state program was designed as an

Stream restoration and stormwater retrofit project along White Marsh Run, one of Baltimore County's planned growth centers. This project provides for stable streams, enhanced habitat, and treatment of runoff from a regional shopping mall. Photograph courtesy of Baltimore County, Maryland.

inexpensive way to allow citizen groups with trees and shrubs for planting on public land and within community open spaces.

Baltimore County is unique in that it is one of the few jurisdictions in the country to maintain its own native tree nursery to help accelerate reforestation efforts. Also, the county has a full array of heavy equipment to assist in planting programs.

Leading by Example

As noted previously, the county requires its agencies to comply with all county regulations when they engage in construction and infrastructure projects. The process, however, is different than that for private developers in that county projects are not subject to the hearing officer's process.

Perhaps the best indication of the county's environmental leadership is the attention it has received by agencies and organizations outside the county. Many of Balti-

Shoreline enhancement project in Bear Creek, a tributary to the Patapsco River and the Chesapeake Bay. Work included grading eroded banks and planting wetland grasses. Photograph courtesy of Baltimore County, Maryland.

more County's programs have been recognized widely and used as models of implementation. The county was ranked fourth among the nation's 40 largest urban counties for overall management (including fiscal management and information technology) in 2002 by *Governing* magazine and was recognized by the nonprofit 1000 Friends of Maryland as the most successful Smart Growth jurisdiction in the Baltimore region. It was also among the first urban jurisdictions to earn a Gold-level award under the Chesapeake Bay Partner Communities Program. The Local Government Advisory Committee of the Chesapeake Bay Program also conferred three Outstanding Achievement awards on the county, for its stream buffer regulations, for stream restoration projects, and for its green infrastructure analysis. Over the past decade, the county has also qualified as a Maryland PLANT Award community and as an Arbor Day Foundation Tree City USA.

Social Indicators

One of the most striking aspects of the Baltimore County story is that this is not a wealthy community or a jurisdiction with a college or tourism-based economy. On the contrary, while the county does have its horse country with large estates, the mean family income is only $65,000, second lowest in the six-jurisdiction region, reflecting the many working/middle-class families and large minority population. While its manufacturing industries have been declining, they still are an important part of the local economy. According to several observers, political support remains very strong for county environmental programs, in large part because of the rallying point that the Chesapeake Bay provides. The bay is a much beloved icon in the state and helps connect resource protection efforts together in a simple and understandable way for the average citizen. Support for land preservation and the protection of farmland also draws on a lingering cultural affinity and in some cases secondhand knowledge of farming in the area and respect for farm families.

The county's initiatives to foster infill and redevelopment also attest to its commitment to maintain and enhance existing older neighborhoods.

Education

Baltimore County has put into place a multifaceted environmental education program to supplement its regulatory, acquisition, and restoration programs. The initiative is staffed by a part-time professional in the DEPRM with a background in natural resources and education. DEPRM works closely with a variety of agencies and institutions such as the Alliance for Chesapeake Bay, schools, and watershed associations to further its education programs, which focus primarily on the Chesapeake Bay and water quality.

One of the most interesting programs is called the Maryland Green Schools Award Program, administered in cooperation with the Maryland Association for Environmental and Outdoor Education (MAEOE) and the Maryland Department of Natural Resources. The Green Schools Program recognizes schools that use the school site and curriculum to help understand key Maryland environmental issues, adopt model conservation management practices in their building and landscape design/maintenance, and build partnerships with the local community to design and implement projects to foster a healthier environment. Since 1999, 15 schools in the county have been recognized as Green Schools, the most of any county in Maryland.

The outreach for land preservation is through meetings, advertisements, and events that highlight preservation accomplishments. The land trusts and the county cosponsor these meetings and events.

Results

Each of the county's programs provides for assessments of progress. Land preservation, regulatory, and restoration programs all include extensive databases linked to the county's digital basemap (geographic information system), allowing continuing summary information and maps of accomplishments. Information is also summarized for several individual programs and forwarded to the state for use in assessing progress for statewide initiatives (e.g., Chesapeake Bay restoration, implementation of Critical Area and Forest Conservation regulations). Detailed information on restoration, regulatory, watershed planning, and water quality monitoring and facility maintenance programs is also summarized by major watershed and submitted to the Maryland Department of the Environment annually in response to requirements under the county's Phase 1 NPDES stormwater permit.

The success of Baltimore County can be clearly documented on the ground:

- More than 85 percent of the county's population lives within the urban growth boundary (URDL) on only one-third of the land.
- Strict Resource Conservation zoning covers more than 92 percent of the three regional drinking water reservoir watersheds, which comprise about half of the county's land area.
- Forty thousand acres of land have been protected through easement acquisition programs—halfway to the county's goal.
- Seven hundred miles of streams have been assessed by the county and 26 restoration projects completed, with almost 10 miles of streams rehabilitated at a cost of $12.4 million.
- Despite its significant urban complexion, the county has more trout streams than most other jurisdictions in the East, a clear indicator of high water quality.
- Submerged aquatic vegetation in the Chesapeake Bay within the county's jurisdiction is holding its own and recovering in many places owing to improved water quality.

- Sixty-five percent of forests on development sites subject to the Forest Conservation Act have been protected through implementation of those regulations.

- Watershed Management Plans have been completed for 10 of the county's 14 major watersheds, at a local investment of more than $2 million.

- Over the past 13 years, 420 community groups have planted more than 10,600 trees on public lands and community open spaces under the Tree-Mendous Maryland program.

- DEPRM's Community Reforestation Program, utilizing developer fees in lieu of mitigation under the Forest Conservation Act, has planted more than 22,400 seedlings and 1,040 large-caliper trees to reforest 53 acres in urban and rural areas.

This is not to say that the county has achieved all of its environmental management goals. Deer populations are booming out of control in some areas because of continued fragmentation of forest cover. At the same time, interior forest species are under stress and some are declining. Only recently has the county recognized this problem and begun to take steps in the development review process and in acquisition programs to address the issue. The county also recognizes the need to develop and use data indicators that provide program-related guidance about resource conditions, stressors, and progress.

Note

[1] Primary sources for this case study include Donald Outen, natural resource manager, Baltimore
County Department of Environmental Protection and Resource Management; extensive presenta-
tions prepared by DEPRM staff and other county citizens involved in land conservation; and the
Baltimore County Zoning Regulations.

CHAPTER 5

Dane County, Wisconsin: Stopping Sprawl and Promoting Infill

Dane County, Wisconsin, home both to the University of Wisconsin and to some of the richest farm country in the United States, is pulling off one of the most challenging natural resource protection juggling acts in the nation.[1] Led by a savvy county executive, Dane County has employed both an "outside" game and an "inside" game to advance its ambitious growth management strategy. Its outside game is built on a combination of regulatory, acquisition, and restoration tools to limit sprawling rural development and protect the county's numerous water-based resources—lakes, wetlands, and streams. The outside game is liberally spiked with incentives to secure cooperation from a myriad of independent local governments within its borders. On the inside, Dane County has worked closely with its constituent towns and cities like Madison to support infill and redevelopment as well as affordable housing strategies—all geared to focusing development within existing municipalities in a compact manner. Supported by some impressive private land conservation efforts and an active roster of nonprofit conservation organizations, Dane County has one of the most well-balanced and thoughtfully crafted natural resource protection programs in the nation.

Dane County, one of the fastest-growing jurisdictions in the Midwest (with an annual population increase of about 1.5 percent over the last decade), has a split polit-

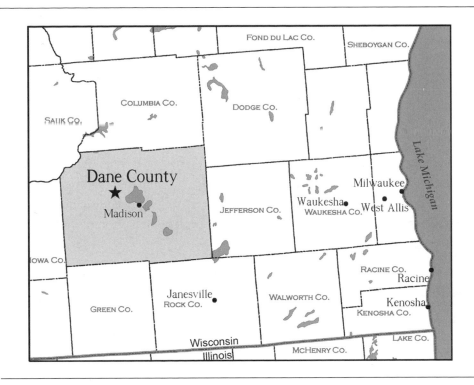

DANE COUNTY, WISCONSIN
Map courtesy of Clarion Associates.

ical personality reflecting its heritage as both a university center and center of a rich farm belt. Highly educated academics and city folk from Madison often debate politics with conservative farmers and small-town politicians representing the bulk of the county's land area. Permeating it all is the heritage of the great ecologist Aldo Leopold, who taught at the University of Wisconsin and whose presence is still felt in many policy discussions.

With a population of nearly 450,000, Dane County lies about 90 miles due west of Milwaukee. The county seat is Madison, home to the University of Wisconsin and its some 40,000 students. Madison, the state capital and home to about one-half the county's population, routinely wins national recognition as one of the most desirable, livable middle-sized cities in the country and kudos for its rich cultural and educational offerings. Part of its allure is the beautiful, often-rolling farm country that frames the city, laced with lakes, wetlands, and miles of trout streams. This is real farm country, not the hobby farms of the wealthy that edge many communities. Dane County is a farming powerhouse. Its 2,500 farms have direct combined sales of approximately $285 million. It is one of the top dairy counties in the state and leads Wisconsin in the production of corn. Soybeans, fresh vegetables, and flowers are also big money producers. Dane County is home to the World Dairy Exposition and the country's largest farmers' market.

Along with the farming comes a conservative political persuasion that creates some interesting dynamics when mixed with the more liberal politics of Madison. Throw in over 60 units of local governments ranging from cities to villages to townships, all with planning and land use powers that are zealously guarded, and you have the stage set for a political high-wire act when it comes to protecting natural resources.

The county is an interesting geologic and environmental mix. The northern part of Dane is relatively flat, reflecting the southerly march of the glaciers centuries ago. The southern part of the county is much more rolling, with occasional steep ravines. Limestone underlies much of the area, meaning that water percolates quickly into aquifers. The whole county is pockmarked by lakes, big and small, and marshes. Small, high-quality trout streams are threaded throughout glaciated portions of the county. These are not the rocky, fast-running waters that are pictured on trout fishing calendars, but quiet, clear-flowing creeks often overgrown by trees and full of mysterious-looking holes that beckon the angler. And they often hold big trout all out of proportion to their size. Not much remains of the county's original oak savannah—grasslands with scattered stands of oak. The plow took care of that a century ago.

Preventing sprawl and protecting water quality have been the rallying cries for resource protection in Dane County. The area's attractive quality of life has attracted almost 150,000 people since 1970, when the population was still under 300,000. Developed acres went from about 38,000 to over 130,000 in 30 short years. Dane County estimates it is losing about 5,000 acres of farmland per year, and experts predict the county's population will top 565,000 by 2030. Citizens watched uneasily as cornfields sprouted homes and apartments, leading to demands for action. At the same time, it seems as if just about everyone lives on a lake, or near a marsh, or has their favorite fishing stream. Indeed, Madison straddles two big lakes—Mendota and Monona. Declining water quality in these two highly visible and much-loved, much-used gems and other lakes set off alarm bells that have led to new programs and regulations, all with strong public support.

Beautiful rolling countryside in Dane County includes forests, farmland, and streams. Photograph courtesy of Dane County.

Despite these knotty challenges and its tough politics, Dane County has produced some remarkable and encouraging results to date, using an adroit mix of regulations, acquisition, and incentives. Two regulatory tools have been critical. The first has been exclusive agricultural zoning in 30 of 34 of the county's townships (each township has control of its own zoning). Spurred on by state tax incentives in the late 1970s, farmers voluntarily agreed to use their land solely for agricultural purposes in large areas of the county. The agricultural district zoning allows only one residential unit per 35 acres and greatly restricts any other uses except farming. The result has been preservation of large swathes of farmland in most of the county. The second has been an effective urban service boundary around all of the county's 14 municipalities. Cities and villages were not able to extend sewer service outside these boundaries without approval of the Regional Planning Commission. The result: an impressive 80 percent of all growth over the past two decades has been within incorporated jurisdictions. These regulatory programs have been supplemented by strong shoreland and environmental corridor protection laws (required by state law) and a new, ground-breaking stormwater management act that is one of the most innovative and far reaching in the nation.

The regulatory regime has been complemented and buttressed by an aggressive and well-funded land acquisition effort. Since 1990, the county has spent $1 million annually on open space and park acquisition, with an increasing emphasis on protection of natural areas and wildlife habitat. A 1999 bond issue upped the ante to $3 million annually for 10 years, with some of the funds targeted to purchasing development rights rather than full-fee acquisition. Private land trusts have also been active, preserving thousands of acres in close cooperation with the county, which provides grants to support their programs. A state stewardship grant program has been an essential partner for both the county and these nonprofits.

The county also has a very ambitious and successful stream restoration program that has produced notable results—miles of high-quality trout streams have been restored since the 1970s using increasingly state-of-the art techniques. These streams are often afforded further protection by numerous private, nonprofit watershed protection organizations that act as watchdogs for their favorite waters.

Perhaps most innovative of all the aspects of the county's multifaceted approach to land protection is what might be called its "inside" game. Led by a savvy county executive, Kathleen Falk, a former environmental attorney with a strong track record in social justice issues, the county has aggressively worked to encourage redevelopment and growth within municipal borders. The idea is that by creating incentives for infill and by removing unnecessary roadblocks to redevelopment, the county helps take pressure off for sprawling, greenfield development in rural areas. Falk also wants less well-off inner-city neighborhoods to benefit from growth and government investment in infrastructure. The county has a successful grants program to encourage planning and redevelopment within its municipalities. Behind the scenes, Falk also supported Madison's recently enacted, controversial affordable housing linkage regulations that require developers to provide a percentage of affordable units in every project. Falk sees sound land use planning and growth management as a crosscutting issue involving protection of natural resources as well as help for the economically disadvantaged.

Despite all of this progress, there are a few flies in the ointment. The State of Wisconsin, which played such a pivotal role in jump starting Dane's land protection program with its shoreland regulation requirements and agricultural land protection tax credits, appears to be retreating somewhat. The state is far more conservative on land use issues than it was in the 1970s, and since 2000 has been cutting back on funding for land acquisition and resource protection efforts. While the state legislature did enact some important Smart Growth legislation that encourages local governments to modernize their land use plans and development codes, shrinking resources for land protection and a general antienvironment/antiregulatory attitude are sending up warning flares.

Regional politics also are in a shambles. Opposition by powerful township politicians led to the abolishing of a regional planning commission that played an important role in assisting townships in preparing land use plans and in approving sewer extension outside existing service areas (often a major growth generator). The county is now scrambling to create a successor organization. Similarly, cooperative resource protection partnerships with surrounding counties are spotty at best. While some of this is understandable given the significant political and demographic differences between Dane County and its more rural neighbors, the results on the ground mean that resource protection often stop at county borders.

And local politics and land use planning remain challenging. Despite all of County Executive Falk's good work and attempts to work cooperatively with the villages and townships, growth management issues remain contentious. This tension is also reflected on the county commission, which mirrors the conservative/liberal split in Dane. Moreover, many townships and even some municipalities have no planning staff and cling to outdated zoning codes that make compact, "smart" developments difficult or impossible because of excessive road standards and large-lot requirements.

Overall, however, there is no denying that Dane County has made impressive strides in protecting natural resources and open space. The declining water quality in several lakes like Lake Mendota is being addressed aggressively, and many rivers are actually getting healthier—as witnessed by the healthy trout populations in numerous streams. Big chunks of open space are being protected through regulations and acquisition, and steps are being taken to preserve the remaining large tracts of prairie and old-growth oak patches that originally covered the county. At the same time, the county is paying attention to the social needs of town and city dwellers, an "inside" game that is one of the best in the country.

Key Program Elements

Program Structure and Administration

Dane County is governed by an elected county executive and, in typical Wisconsin fashion, a large and somewhat unwieldy 37-member legislative board of supervisors. The county executive is, in practice, the equivalent of a mayor with broad executive powers. Most departments report directly to her.

The system of local government in Dane County is fragmented and rather byzantine. There are over 60 governmental units within its borders, including cities like Madison; incorporated villages; towns (which would be called townships in other states); and a host of special entities such as the Lakes and Watershed Commission (an appointed body with regulatory powers). Many of the incorporated municipalities and some of the towns maintain their own planning staffs. Municipalities and towns have zoning powers independent from (and sometimes conflicting with) the county. However, all of the towns currently have opted to utilize the county's zoning ordinance. Because the towns generally do not have permanent planning staff, the county conducts development reviews for them. Until October 2004, a regional planning commission played a significant role in county planning matters, but it was abolished because of conflicts with some township leaders.

The key county staff involved in natural resource and wildlife habitat protection come from three departments: Planning and Development (which oversees the planning and development review functions), Land and Water Conservation (which focuses on soil conservation and water quality), and Parks (which oversees land acquisition and open space management).

The Planning and Development Department has a staff of 27, with its primary duties being drafting the county comprehensive plan, working with towns on their land use plans, and conducting development reviews in unincorporated areas on behalf of the towns. The department is also responsible for zoning enforcement, although the staff noted they do not have adequate personnel to conduct inspections of all development sites.

The Land and Water Conservation Department has a staff of 14 made up of engineers, soil conservation planners, geographic information system specialists, and an education director. It reports to a Land Conservation Committee that is charged statutorily with coordinating all matters relating to agriculture and soil and water use and conservation in the county. This includes the development of standards for best management practices to control erosion, sedimentation, and non-point-source water pollution. The committee is the successor to the local soil conservation district established under federal law to work with the national Natural Resources Conservation Service. The department, whose director is a lifelong county resident raised on a farm still worked by his brother, works closely with farmers on soil erosion and water quality issues. Staff also conduct inspections of development sites for compliance with stormwater management regulations. The department also coordinates with the Lakes and Watershed Commission, an appointed body with a small staff of two. The commission is important, however, in that it has authority to adopt countywide stormwater management regulations, which it did in 2003 (unlike zoning in which authority rests with the towns).

The third key department in the land use triumvirate is the Parks Department, with a staff of about 30 people ranging from parks planners and naturalists to operations managers and park laborers. The county parks system was founded in 1935 and today has 32 parks and resource sites covering over 6,000 acres. While the primary responsibility of the department is to manage and maintain the county parks, according to staff, they are fast making the transition away from a traditional local parks agency that focuses on "boat launches and picnic tables" to one concerned primarily about natural area protection. The Parks Department is responsible for preparing the county Parks and Open Space Plan, which, among its other purposes, is a blueprint for acquisition of natural resource sites. The plan also contains land evaluation criteria to guide potential land acquisition. County parks staff also take the lead in specific plans for new parks and negotiating land acquisitions. The department also works cooperatively with nonprofit land trusts, supporting their efforts with a small grants program that has been very popular.

Until October 2004, Dane County was served by a countywide Regional Planning Commission with a staff of 9. The commission was established in 1968 by the governor at the request of a majority of the local units of government in the county as provided under state law. Its 13 members were appointed by the county executive, the mayor of Madison, and others to represent the towns and other villages and small cities. One of its primary functions was to assist municipalities and the town in preparing and updating local plans and ordinances. It was also a useful source of regional data and served as the regional water quality and solid waste management planning agency. Political problems with the towns, some of whom apparently resented the commission's role in planning and designating urban service areas, recently led to the commission's being abolished by request of a majority of the local governments (most of which are the small towns). The county is now working to create an alternative agency that would assume some of the commission's essential functions.

Planning

When County Executive Falk took office in 1997, she undertook a series of intensive planning initiatives under the banner of "Design Dane." A variety of committees, meetings, and conferences contributed to her thinking. Beginning in 1998, she and her staff made a series of bold recommendations to grapple with the strong growth pressures that were eating up farmland and wildlife habitat. A July 2000 report entitled "Farms and Neighborhoods: Keeping Both Strong" captured the meat of her proposals. The proposals fell into three categories: (1) strategies to ensure that in Dave County enough farmland remains in workable configurations so that a wide variety of farming can prosper for the foreseeable future—recommendations included tougher regulations and a development rights purchase program; (2) initiatives to assist a wide variety of farmers to improve their profitability; and (3) proposals to assist the private sector and municipal governments in building and improving urban neighborhoods. Falk pursued these goals aggressively, including forging a coalition with area developers and realtors to push a major bond issue to fund acquisition of development rights. She also created an infill planning and investment grant program to aid smaller municipalities in their redevelopment efforts. Following up on "Design Dane," Falk is pushing another initiative she calls "Attain Dane." One of the key features of this latest plan is to identify areas both suitable and unsuitable for growth within the county to facilitate compatible, environmentally sensitive development in the right places.

The county executive's special initiatives are playing out against the background of a lengthier, more formal process to update the county's comprehensive plan. State law requires the county to have a new land use plan in place by 2010, and that land use decisions be consistent with the adopted plan. In 2002, Dane County along with 14 municipalities applied for and received a state grant to revamp the county plan. The county agreed to complete the new plan by 2006 and to address mandatory elements included in state legislation. Planning is now underway, with the appointment

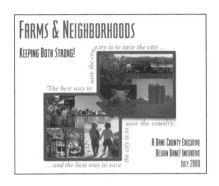

County policies include agricultural preservation efforts and encouraging infill development. Image courtesy of Dane County.

of a steering committee and involvement of many organizations and citizens. Three working groups are currently developing draft goals and objectives for each of the mandatory plan elements, such as housing, natural and cultural resources, and utilities and community facilities.

As previously discussed, in 2000 the county Parks Department completed a Parks and Open Space Plan that identifies high-priority natural resource sites for acquisition. These include marshes, lakes, and prairie lands.

Eventually, all of Dane County's constituent local governments, including the towns, must adopt a comprehensive plan. The town plans are particularly important. Any rezoning requests filed with the county (for example, from agricultural to residential) must comply with the town plans. While town plans have been rather rudimentary in the past, particularly from a natural resource protection perspective, some more recent efforts have paid greater attention to habitat and rural character. One example is the Town of Perry Plan, which calls for protection of "cliff" ecological communities. Most town plans are prepared with the assistance of private consultants. During its existence, the Regional Planning Commission also assisted with some town plans and worked with local governments to identify "environmental corridors" throughout the county. These corridors are environmentally sensitive lands—streams, floodplains, wetlands, wildlife habitat, and steep slopes—requiring protection. Once delineated and adopted, the corridors are used by local governments in reviewing development applications and were used by the commission to review proposals to extend utilities. With the demise of the Regional Planning Commission, it is not clear which agency will assume this function, although already Dane County staff members say they are putting a great deal more emphasis on assisting towns and municipalities with plans. All of this is in keeping with County Executive Falk's efforts to establish a more collegial relationship with these other local governmental units.

This and other planning processes have and will make good use of the county and state's extensive mapping information. The county appears to have useful mapping data related to, for example, land ownership, steep slopes, and endangered species. These maps focus more on ecosystem types than on specific habitats. The State of Wisconsin's Department of Natural Resources also receives plaudits from local planners for its extensive mapping resources.

As noted previously, one of the significant planning challenges facing Dane County will be replacing the Regional Planning Commission. Just as problematic is the seeming lack of interaction and regional land use planning with counties beyond Dane's border. While the county is cooperating with other jurisdictions to the south on protection strategies for the Rock River and has recently submitted a major multi-jurisdictional grant proposal with Iowa County to the west to preserve prairie habitat, overall the picture is not encouraging. County staff attribute the lack of cross-border cooperation to the significant political and demographic differences between Dane County and its more rural neighbors. Whatever the case, the result is that there is really very little effective resource and biodiversity protection going on at a truly regional level in this part of Wisconsin.

Acquisition/Funding

Dane County is somewhat unusual among counties in its region in that local officials believe it has a role in open space and park acquisition. Its extensive park system, covering some 6,000 acres, was started back in the 1930s. Since 1990, the county budget has provided around $1 million annually for park and open space acquisition.

These programs were ramped up significantly under County Executive Falk. When she first took office, Falk toyed with a number of ambitious and controversial ideas to preserve open space in rural areas. One proposal was to require developers to mitigate any open space lost as a result of one of their projects with an acre-for-acre replacement elsewhere in the county. In the face of strong opposition to that idea, Falk sat down with area homebuilders and developers to search for an alternative. What emerged was an ambitious proposal to float a bond issue to provide $30 million for land and development rights acquisition. Falk went so far as to sign a formal agreement to that effect with developers and realtors. With support from both environmental and development interests, the bond issue and resulting tax increases were approved by a substantial margin, providing the county with a steady and ample source of funding to acquire open space and sensitive resource areas. Jeff Rosenberg, president of Veridian Homes, was one of the champions in the development community, and according to observers played a critical role persuading fellow developers to join the cause.

The money is now being used by the Dane County Parks Department to purchase key parcels identified in the Parks and Open Space Plan—many of them natural resource lands and critical wildlife habitat. Acquisitions are almost always on a willing-seller basis. Ironically, Parks Department staff say they are having a difficult time spending all the money available because of staff shortages.

An interesting element of the new open space fund is that about 20 percent of the money is allocated each year for grants to local nonprofit land conservation groups and local governments that are attempting to acquire and protect resource lands identified in the county open space plan. The recipients must match the county dollars, among other grant criteria. The county holds a coeasement on any land or development rights acquired.

This type of partnership with the nonprofit sector has helped leverage the county's resource land protection programs. The Natural Heritage Land Trust, a countywide membership organization, is a frequent partner with the county and has protected about 3,000 acres in three watersheds through the use of conservation easements. Many of these lands have been preserved with the help of county funds and state stewardship grants that have supplemented federal tax credits available to

Dane County has spent around $1 million annually since 1990 for park and open space acquisitions such as this bike trail. Photograph courtesy of Dane County Parks.

landowners who donate conservation easements on key resource lands. Importantly, the county allows nonprofits to charge a small service fee in these transactions to cover their overhead; these fees are reimbursable through the county grant program. Thus, the county's acquisition efforts have been backed up by a strong bench of nonprofit organizations that have programs similar to the Natural Heritage Land Trust. Many of these focus on a specific stream or watershed. Dane County is also beginning to work more closely with developers to protect open space and provide trail links. A good example is the recent agreement with Veridian Homes to dedicate a substantial tract within a proposed development to complete a missing link of the Ice Age Trail, which stretches across the state.

The State of Wisconsin has also played an important role in Dane County's land acquisition programs. In 1990, Wisconsin voters created a state stewardship fund. It was reauthorized in 1999 to the tune of $60 million annually for 10 years. Of this, $10 million annually is earmarked for local government and private nonprofit land acquisition initiatives.

One final factor has contributed to the success of Dane County's acquisition program: major landowners have been very generous in donating land to the county for park purposes, and other citizens have contributed money to assist the county. This has resulted in the creation of several significant parks with important natural resources.

Regulations

Regulations have played a critical role in natural resource protection, even though the county has relatively limited land use authority. In Wisconsin, county zoning applies only in unincorporated areas; additionally, if the towns (townships) want to adopt their own zoning, they can do so. However, the towns can voluntarily choose to have the county zoning apply in their jurisdictions, which all have done in Dane County.

The Dane County development code is a fairly standard one, but it contains three key provisions that have resulted in significant rural land and natural resource protection. Two of these provisions were prompted by state laws adopted in the 1970s, when Wisconsin was at the forefront in agricultural protection nationally. The first is the county's exclusive agricultural zone districts. These districts typically allow only one residential unit per 35 acres and severely restrict nonagricultural uses (some towns allow only 1 unit/75 acres). Spurred by state income tax credits in the 1970s, many farmers in Dane County voluntarily agreed to have their property placed in these exclusive agricultural districts. Indeed, 30 out of the 34 townships in the county have adopted exclusive agricultural zoning districts in their township land use plans. Land cannot be removed from one of the exclusive agricultural districts without approval of the county board, and farmers must adopt conservation plans for their land that address issues such as soil erosion. The result is that in these towns, which cover the vast majority of the county, there is very little development in rural areas. While the agricultural zoning is aimed primarily at preserving farmland, a spin-off benefit has been keeping development out of sensitive wildlife areas and targeted within incorporated municipalities.

The second key element is shoreland protection regulations that have been required since the 1970s by state law. In brief, the regulations require that developments be set back from rivers, lakes, and wetlands a specified distance and that trees and other vegetation be preserved. The result has been significant habitat preservation along these water bodies.

Agricultural zone districts throughout the county keep development off rich farmland, as in this example of 1 unit/35 acres zoning. Photograph courtesy of Dane County.

The final piece of the land use regulatory triumvirate is what is called "environmental corridors." Working with the Regional Planning Commission, Dane County mapped in urban service areas sensitive environmental resources such as lakes, wetlands, floodplains, steep slopes, woodlands, and unique vegetation. The corridors are then used by the county in development reviews. For the most part, such resources are off-limits to development. Moreover, the corridors are also used in review of proposed sewer extensions and as a starting point for open space and recreation planning/acquisition. Major changes to an environmental corridor have required approval by the state Department of Natural Resources and the Regional Planning Commission.

Another regulatory regime that promises to have an important impact on preserving ecosystem integrity in Dane County is the recently adopted sophisticated stormwater management ordinance. As noted previously, one of the most serious environmental challenges in Dane County has been degradation of water quality in both streams and lakes. Runoff from agricultural areas has caused severe siltation and other problems in some trout streams, for example, and in the more urbanized areas, runoff from constructions sites is a major culprit in deteriorating lake water quality. In response, the county—through its Lakes and Watershed Commission (appointed by the county executive)—has drafted very strong stormwater management regulations aimed at preventing soil erosion and runoff of chemicals into streams and lakes. The new ordinance was adopted by the county board in August 2001. Under state law, this is one of the few areas in which counties have direct authority to adopt and enforce county regulations. The ordinance was adopted after a long arduous and collaborative process that included environmental, agricultural, and development interests. It relies on site runoff modeling and use of best management practices, and includes such novel features as a requirement for temperature controls on stormwater discharges into high-quality trout streams. Research has revealed that runoff from hot pavement can wreak havoc on cold-water creeks, with deadly effects on trout. The new regulations require more infiltration, underground detention, and other approaches to even out temperature spikes. As a follow-up to the stormwater management ordinance, the county has adopted an ordinance controlling phosphorus runoff. Phosphorus from lawns and farmland is one of the big culprits in deteriorating water quality in many lakes, causing algae blooms.

While the county has had success in the stormwater management arena, according to county staff its land use and zoning regulations are in need of updating. For example, the exclusive agricultural zoning provisions are less attractive today than 30 years ago because the value of the income tax incentives has eroded over time. The amount of the state income tax credit is based on a formula that uses household income and total taxes paid, with a cap on the total credit that can be claimed. The state has not made any adjustments in the cap for years to account for inflation or the growing value of farmland. As a result, few farmers will voluntarily subject their property to such controls today and there is not much financial incentive to keep lands in the exclusive agricultural districts. According to staff, agricultural use value property taxation is a more important incentive these days to keep land in farming—land that is being used for farming is taxed at very low rates, thus allowing farmers (and developers) to hold land with very low carrying costs.

The county staff are also working to refine and update the shoreland regulations. Today, the setback and other restrictions apply to shorelands uniformly—whether a lake or stream is in an urban or rural area, for example. County planners are working to tailor the setback, vegetative buffers, and other standards to the different types of water bodies. Thus a trout stream setback/vegetative buffer requirement may be more stringent than one applying to a lake.

Another challenge that the county faces is that a number of its municipalities have zoning provisions that appear to encourage sprawl. Counties in Wisconsin have no say over zoning within municipalities and little control over annexations. A number of villages and cities within Dane County have minimum density requirements of 1 unit/acre and subdivision standards that require very wide subdivision streets, for example. These regulations discourage more dense, compact development and result in more open space being chewed up to accommodate the larger lots. However, there have been some encouraging developments on this front. The State of Wisconsin recently adopted Smart Growth legislation that encourages more compact growth patterns and requires local governments to offer development options like traditional neighborhood development districts and clustered open space subdivisions. At the same time, progressive county developers like Veridian Homes are proposing and building mixed-use developments that are more dense and that preserve larger tracts of open space than the standard subdivision, but which are well designed and attractive.

On the township side, although an increasing number of local elected officials are recognizing the value of rural land and resource protection, there is a continuing clash between more conservative, economic development-oriented town and village boards. For example, Cross Plains Village officials recently promoted development of a large printing plant hard on the banks of Black Earth Creek, a nationally recognized trout stream. In the end, county regulations and other requirements discouraged the development, but some elected officials are still resentful. They are not persuaded of the economic benefits of the resource protection regulations and policies. For this reason, the county is hesitant to undertake any major comprehensive revisions to its zoning and subdivision regulations, many of which are seriously outdated, because under Wisconsin law, any major changes will give towns the chance to opt out of county zoning and adopt their own regulations—which would likely be somewhat weaker.

Restoration

Dane County has been heavily involved in mainly water-oriented restoration efforts since the 1970s, when it won national attention for its trout stream rehabilitation efforts. Initially, these efforts focused on fencing along streams to keep cattle from damaging the banks and causing erosion. Today, under the wing of the Land and Water Conservation Department, Dane County is undertaking much more sophisticated efforts that involve removal of streamside trees, which, surprisingly, actually do more harm than good. County research has revealed that large trees along the streams often topple over and open the banks to serious erosion. The county, in partnership with the state, Trout Unlimited, and other nonprofits, is now spending $250,000 annually to rehabilitate streams throughout the county. Between 1999 and 2004, 12 miles were completed, and 8 more miles are scheduled for restoration through 2005. Much of this work is being done in close cooperation with landowners, primarily farmers.

Stream restoration can include narrowing the channel and reshaping the banks. Photograph courtesy of Dane County.

This restored stream is narrow, deep, and cool—much better habitat for trout and other fishes. Photograph courtesy of Dane County.

The result, when combined with stormwater management controls on developments, has been steadily improving water quality in streams like the West Branch of Sugar Creek, a trout stream south of Madison. The stream was removed from the state Department of Natural Resource's impaired list, where it had been relegated due to sedimentation and bank erosion. Similarly, the Yahara River, which flows through Madison, has been taken off a U.S. Environmental Protection Agency watchlist as a result of reduced pollution from urban runoff.

One of the most significant challenges faced by the county is management of the lands it is acquiring. To date, most of the focus has been on the acquisition, and management has been more typically in favor of active parks use. However, with the increasing acquisition of sensitive natural resource lands, the county is grappling with the issues of use, public access, removal of exotic plants, and similar concerns. According to county staff, they would be overwhelmed if it were not for the help of over 3,000 volunteers—the Adult Conservation Team—who provided over 27,000 hours of free help to the county parks in 2002. Projects included prairie management (weeding, cutting brush, collecting seeds), work on trails, installation of a bluebird observation trail, and creek restoration, among others.

Leading by Example

The county has led by example in two areas. First, it complies with its own regulations in its own development projects—for example, the new stormwater regulations to reduce sedimentation. The county is also practicing what it preaches by managing its own open space and parks with a no-phosphorus policy—no phosphorus-containing fertilizers are applied in the parks.

Social Indicators

Dane County might be characterized as having multiple personalities when it comes to demographics and politics. At the core of Dane County is the City of Madison, a bastion of academia and liberal politics. At the same time, it has a significant minority population and what can only be called distressed inner-city neighborhoods. Like many cities, Madison is ringed by suburban growth, some in smaller villages and cities, some in sprawling residential subdivisions in the handful of unincorporated townships that have not adopted exclusive agricultural zoning. These suburbs tend to

Dane County's new stormwater regulations will help to control urban erosion such as construction site runoff. Photograph courtesy of Dane County.

be more conservative, but still concerned with the environment and quality of life. In the rural hinterlands, where farms and farming dominate, the politics are even more conservative. These multiple personalities are reflected on the county board, which is split almost evenly between conservative and moderate/liberal members. Thus resource protection policies and programs must be crafted to appeal to a wide range of interests.

County leaders have been extremely adroit in patching together strategies that appeal to all interests and that pay attention to human needs as well as resource protection. The cooperative processes that produced the stormwater management ordinance and the open space acquisition bond victory illustrate the success the community has had in reaching a general, if fragile, consensus on potentially controversial issues.

County Executive Falk's attention to inner-city residents and her push to help cities attract and accommodate growth are especially noteworthy. Few jurisdictions in the nation have strategies that are tuned so well to both rural resource protection and the needs of urban areas. Recall that the county has planning and rehabilitation grant programs to help its constituent cities and villages revitalize their main streets and neighborhoods. The county is also working with the cities to tune up their zoning ordinances to accommodate infill development and more compact residential growth. All of this is aimed at keeping the cities and villages economically strong, with vibrant, livable neighborhoods, while protecting against sprawling development that will adversely affect natural resource sites and wildlife habitat.

Education

In addition to the good work of the Adult Conservation Team with the Dane Parks Department and the acquisition efforts of groups like the Natural Heritage Land Trust, a bevy of other organizations provide strong support for county resource protection programs. Conservation groups like Friends of Lake Wingra, Friends of the Pheasant Branch Conservancy, and the Black Earth Creek Watershed Association lobby for protective regulations, conduct cleanup days, and have outdoor educational programs for students. Others, like the local chapter of Trout Unlimited, one of the most active in the nation, conduct actual stream-related research and were heavily involved with the stormwater management ordinance. One of the oldest groups is the venerable Dane County Conservation League, which has been around since 1933 and has about 300 members today. It owns 3,000 acres of prairie chicken habitat outside of Dane County and is involved in a variety of wildlife-related projects, such as building bluebird houses and undertaking stream bank improvements to Little Sugar Creek.

Sustain Dane is another nonprofit educational group, one with an interesting slant on conservation. The organization, which recently hired its first full-time executive director, concentrates mainly on educating city dwellers about growth and development issues, the philosophy being that it is difficult to focus on nature unless you get people to focus on how they live. For example, Sustain Dane conducts workshops on how communities can create a "sense of place." Another program seeks to create "eco-teams" in city neighborhoods that seek sustainable lifestyles.

The county complements these nonprofit educational efforts with a number of its own programs. The Parks Department has a full complement of outdoor educational programs, often run by volunteers. The Land and Water Conservation Department and the Lakes and Watershed Commission have instituted an aggressive educational program focusing on water quality and stormwater management, with funding provided for television and radio spots. However, an attempt to add an educational professional to the Lakes and Watershed Commission staff was recently turned down during the budget process.

Results

Even with its ambitious and often successful initiatives, challenges remain in Dane County. The county continues to lose farmland at the rate of several thousand acres a year as municipalities expand to accommodate suburban growth, often at low densities. Water quality in some lakes is barely holding its own or is declining. And of growing concern is the receding role of the State of Wisconsin, whose programs in the 1970s must be given much credit for jump-starting resource protection not only in Dane County but all over the state. Overall, however, the picture is encouraging and getting brighter from a nature protection perspective. Like Baltimore County, Maryland, and Sanibel, Florida, the results of Dane County's progressive policies can be seen on the ground:

- Ten thousand acres of high-value resource lands have been protected by the county and nonprofits.
- Twelve miles of stream have been protected from erosion or rehabilitated, with streams such as West Sugar Branch coming off federal pollution lists.

- There are now 86.6 miles of pure, high-quality trout streams.

- Over 80 percent of growth is taking place in incorporated municipalities.

- One hundred thousand dollars of grants are awarded annually to localities to support and encourage infill development.

- The county has several new initiatives to maintain and expand the original prairie/oak savannah habitat that once covered much of the county.

While some jurisdictions might have stronger regulations than Dane County and others more money to spend on acquisition, overall the county ranks among the best because of a judicious mix of strategies to protect natural resources. What makes it a exemplary community from a nature preservation and biodiversity perspective is its attention to the "inside" game and its efforts to make sure inner-city neighborhoods are strong and that roadblocks to infill and redevelopment are removed. These programs provide valuable lessons to other communities dedicated to effective nature protection.

Note

[1]Primary sources for this case study include Kevin Connors, Dane County Land Conservation Department; several other county staff members; representatives from nonprofits working on conservation issues; and the Dane County website, www.co.dane.wi.us.

CHAPTER 6

Eugene, Oregon: Shining Star of Wetlands Preservation

Eugene's nature-friendly programs and initiatives are a mixture of exemplary plans and programs and potential yet to be realized. The city helped to create a nationally recognized wetlands program for protecting the rare wet prairie lands discovered in the western part of the city, while allowing industrial development to proceed. The city also has one of the nation's oldest integrated pest management practices for city lands, an exemplary wastewater treatment program, a large number of natural resources staff, an impressive wetlands restoration program, and an admirable procedure for lobbying for federal funds cooperatively with other local jurisdictions. Progress could still be made on the stormwater management plan (a strong document, but implementation has been slow) and in protecting sensitive natural areas outside of the West Eugene Wetlands Plan boundary.

Eugene is the third-largest city in Oregon, with approximately 140,000 people and an area of 42 square miles (growing from only 36,000 people and 7 square miles in 1945). Set among rolling hills in the Willamette River valley in west-central Oregon, Eugene provides easy access to the Pacific Ocean to the west and the Cascade Mountains to the east—each reachable in a one-hour drive. Portland is approximately two hours north of Eugene.[1]

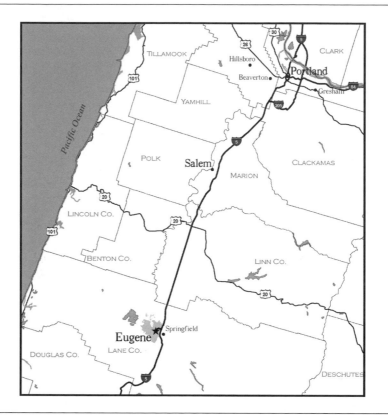

EUGENE, OREGON
Map courtesy of Clarion Associates.

The economy of the city struggled along with the state's in the 1980s and 1990s as extractive industries have become less dominant. Eugene was primarily a timber town until the 1980s, when it diversified with varying success to include a variety of retail, service, and manufacturing industries, including some high-tech companies. The University of Oregon is a major employer and influence in the community.

This primarily middle-class city has a council/manager form of government, with an eight-member city council, a mayor, and a city manager.

Eugene receives 43 inches of rainfall annually and has mild winters and a long growing season suitable for the agricultural activities prevalent throughout the Willamette River valley. Ecosystems found within city limits include riparian bottom-land forest (primarily ash, fir, cottonwood, alder, and willow tree species); hillside forest (fir, oak, and pine trees); oak savannah (grasslands interspersed with oak trees); upland prairie (several grass and wildflower species); and the now rare seasonally wet prairie (wetlands plant communities that thrive during the fall, winter, and spring owing to clay soils that become saturated with the annual rains). Of the original 360,000 acres of western Oregon wet prairie, only about 13,000 acres remain, and about 1,200 of those remaining acres are in Eugene. In addition, the Willamette River and its tributaries flow through the city limits, providing aquatic habitats.

Eugene citizens had an early interest in planning, livability, and natural resource issues. The city was the second in Oregon to form a planning commission (in 1925, after Portland did so in 1918), and was the third city in Oregon to have a planning staff of its own, forming its planning department in the early 1960s. The city held its first "Community Goals Conference" in 1966, in which 250 citizens participated. Air

Rare seasonally wet prairie is found in the west part of Eugene. Photograph courtesy of the City of Eugene Wetlands Program.

pollution and urban sprawl were the top two concerns, resulting from a growth spurt during the 1950s and 1960s. Based on guidelines from this initial conference, a new metropolitan plan (the "1990 Plan") was prepared in the late 1960s by the Central Lane Planning Council and adopted in 1972. This plan rejected the growth accommodation objectives of a regional plan previously adopted in 1959. A critical element of the 1990 Plan was the "urban service area" concept, which was created and adopted by the Eugene area before the state of Oregon required this element. The concept was actually used by the newly formed Oregon Land Conservation and Development Commission as a prototype for the "urban growth boundary" later required by the state for every city to incorporate into its comprehensive plan.

Oregon passed statewide laws in 1973 that were the first steps in creating detailed and strict land use regulations, including the urban growth boundary mentioned previously. Eventually 19 statewide planning goals were established that must be reflected in local comprehensive plans.

Many of Eugene's current nature-friendly efforts are guided by federal regulations as well as state provisions. The West Eugene Wetlands Plan is Eugene's primary nature-friendly program and was prompted by the discovery of rare wetlands in 1987. It has been studied and held up as a model since the plan was adopted in 1992, and will be discussed later in this case study under "Planning." As a result of the wetlands plan, Eugene has also developed large-scale restoration capabilities and an effective mitigation bank.

More recently, in 1999 the spring chinook salmon was listed as a threatened species under the federal Endangered Species Act and has prompted several actions. Because of the salmon listing, the city funded independent evaluations of city regulations and activities for environmental impacts and, in addition, surveyed aquatic and riparian habitat. Plans are underway to protect salmon habitat, but implementation will likely be slow owing to budget constraints. State Planning Goal 5 requires local governments to adopt programs that will "protect natural resources and conserve scenic, historic, and open space resources for present and future generations." To comply with Goal 5, the city has attempted to adopt a Natural Resources Inventory several times since 1988, but because of lack of approval from other local jurisdictions (the City of Springfield and Lane County), adoption has been delayed. This has resulted in sporadic protection for sensitive lands outside of the West Eugene Wetlands Plan boundary.

Other noteworthy city programs include one of the nation's first integrated pest management practices for city lands (begun in 1980); an exemplary wastewater treatment program; a large number of natural resources staff; an admirable procedure for lobbying for federal funds cooperatively with other local jurisdictions; and an impressive stormwater management plan (for which implementation has been slow). The city is also collaborating with several other local jurisdictions and the U.S. Army Corps of Engineers to identify waterway restoration projects.

Key Program Elements

Program Structure and Administration

Staffing

Eugene has dedicated significant resources to staffing natural resource protection programs. The two primary departments that work on habitat protection issues are the Planning and Development Department and the Public Works Department. The Planning and Development Department has had at least one planner dedicated to natural resource issues since 1987, when the wetlands plan process started. Development review is conducted by 7 planners. There are currently 18 planning staff overall. The Public Works Department has several divisions, including the Transportation, Wastewater, and Airport divisions, and the Parks and Open Space Division. The Parks and Open Space Division's mission includes natural area planning, acquisition, management, restoration, and volunteer and educational programming. This is where much of the city's portion of the wetlands program is administered. The division employs 80-plus full-time employees, 9 of whom are natural resource planners and managers. The division also employs approximately 30 seasonal employees each year, most of whom are dedicated to habitat restoration projects in the wetlands program. Also within Parks and Open Space, two employees oversee public education and work with volunteers on water quality and habitat enhancement for the city's Stream Team Program. In addition, the city employs a wetlands ecologist, sharing the salary costs with one of the other wetlands program partners. Public Works also has several employees working on stormwater management issues within its other divisions, including Engineering, Administration, and Wastewater.

Eugene's city departments coordinate on natural resource issues more than many jurisdictions. One example is the Environmental Policy Team. About five years ago, several concerned staff members (from several departments throughout the organization) formed an ad hoc group to draft recommendations related to environmental management for a new city manager who requested this input. They presented their ideas to the city manager, who supported their efforts.

One of the recommendations from this ad hoc group was to form an interdepartmental coordinating group for the city's environmental activities. This group was commissioned by the city manager in 1999, and is called the Environmental Policy Team (EPT). The team was intended to address the following recommendations from the ad hoc staff group: (1) coordinate environmental activities—externally and internally; (2) adopt an environmental policy; and (3) show the community that the city is complying with the same rules as the private sector. The group has evolved as the city has changed and become more responsive to a number of the group's initial concerns. As a result of this team's work, the city now has an environmental policy, an Endangered Species Act (ESA) team, an Environmental Review Team (which managed a study of city activities), a Green Buildings Team, and an extensive Environmental Management System project completed by the Public Works Wastewater Division.

An example of interdepartmental coordination is the Eugene ESA/Salmon Team (spawned so to speak from the previously mentioned Environmental Policy Team), which includes members from Planning, Public Works/Parks and Open Space, and Public Works/Engineering (stormwater).

An interesting aspect of Eugene's staff structure is that the parks staff, the wetlands restoration program, and the wetlands mitigation bank are all housed in the Public Works Department, Parks and Open Space Division. Wetlands program staff began to be housed here in the early 1990s because Public Works had reliable financing from stormwater fees and sales of credits from its mitigation bank. In other jurisdictions, the Public Works Department may be run quite separately from other natural resource topics, which can lead to competition among departments. In Eugene, because of the organizational structure, wetlands, planning, parks, stormwater, and other natural resources staff have to work together on a regular basis. Although there is still room to grow, the program structure has resulted in much positive collaboration, both internally and externally.

Partnerships

Eugene has also had a fair amount of success in partnering with other organizations. The West Eugene Wetlands Program is a model collaboration. The original wetlands management partnership formed in 1994 and included the city, the U.S. Bureau of Land Management, and The Nature Conservancy. As of 2003, five more partners had been added: the Oregon Youth Conservation Corps, the U.S. Army Corps of Engineers, the U.S. Fish and Wildlife Service, the McKenzie River Trust (a local land trust), and the Willamette Resource and Education Network (a local environmental education group). It is a loosely run group, with a one-page "Statement of Partnership" document, and since its formation has been the focus of several studies of how to successfully make such a diverse group work with limited bureaucracy. Major accomplishments include acquisition of approximately 3,000 acres of sensitive lands (inside and outside the official wetlands plan area), restoration of 700 acres, and establishment of an effective wetlands mitigation bank program.

In the 1980s, the city and other local communities came together to seek federal funds for wetland protection as well as funds for airport issues. They have expanded their federal lobbying efforts since then to include other capital projects but continue to focus primarily on land protection. The communities meet and agree on project priorities for the region. They prepare polished proposal packages and retain a Washington, D.C., lobbyist. Staff members also accompany and support their elected officials in annual trips to Washington. The project is known locally as the "United Front," and staff are not aware of any other group of jurisdictions in the nation that is as organized and as aggressive in this respect. Their approach enables them to take advantage of federal monies directly through Congress, in addition to, and sometimes instead of, going through established programs. The United Front has obtained about $37 million in capital since 1987.

Public Works staff are working with the City of Springfield, Lane County, and the U.S. Army Corps of Engineers in another interesting partnership to identify waterway restoration projects as part of a newer, groundbreaking Corps program. Projects in which environmental benefits outweigh the costs of restoration will be able to qualify for restoration funds from the Corps. Several Eugene metro waterways are being considered for restoration and potential implementation projects, and federal money has been identified. The next step is to estimate the environmental benefits, such as water quality improvement, habitat enhancement, and biodiversity. In addition, project cost estimates will be developed to help determine if these benefits warrant the cost of restoration.

The Eugene metro area was able to participate in this program because of its proven ability to collaborate in the past with various partners. For example, the City of Eugene, the Army Corps of Engineers, and the Bureau of Land Management are just completing a $6 million restoration project on 400 acres at Meadowlark Prairie, the heart of the wetlands area in West Eugene. Under construction since 1999, this project was undertaken through the federal Water Resources Development Act (WRDA), Section 1135. The city and the Corps are just beginning a $5 million project at Delta Ponds through another program of the WRDA (Section 206). Improvements will be made to the ponds, reconnecting them to the Willamette River, enhancing wildlife habitat, and providing passive recreation opportunities. The City of Eugene is funding 35 percent of the project.

Regional Cooperation

In addition to the wetlands program and the lobbying partnership, Eugene has several other formal and informal relationships with other jurisdictions in the region. The city often works cooperatively with the Lane Council of Governments, a regional planning agency, and in 2003 completed a regional open space vision and plan with the council (the Rivers to Ridges Project, mentioned later). Additionally, wastewater service is a metrowide system, governed by the Metropolitan Wastewater Management Commission.

Planning

Natural resource issues are addressed in a variety of local planning efforts and documents relating to stormwater management, wastewater treatment, parks and natural area management, and land use planning codes.

Regarding natural area management, Eugene has a strong plan and inventory for the West Eugene wetlands. The program is an excellent example of collaboration, transparent process, and long-lasting success as well as progressive restoration theory and practice. The West Eugene Wetlands Plan mentions biodiversity issues throughout, using such language as "protection of natural diversity" under plan highlights, and also specifically addressing rare species of plants and animals and other species to watch. This award-winning plan was adopted in 1992 to meet federal and state wetlands protection requirements, involving several years of work after rare wetlands were identified in West Eugene in 1987. The Lane Council of Governments provided project management, while city staff worked with other stakeholders on the plan with input from a Technical Advisory Committee consisting of federal and state agencies.

According to staff and community members, an important element of the wetlands program is that it makes a link between wetlands and public works (green infrastructure). Using the Public Works Department as the lead agency helped tie the wetlands program to other public works projects like stormwater and transportation, and helped tap a reliable funding source, the stormwater fee fund. The wetlands plan also has a capital improvements element.

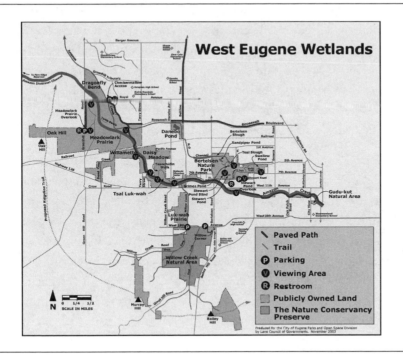

WEST EUGENE WETLANDS
Eugene has an exemplary plan and acquisition program for the West Eugene Wetlands. Map courtesy of the City of Eugene Wetlands Program.

Although many communities have faced federal and state species protection requirements, Eugene's process for addressing the wetlands issue was innovative. The plan has been extensively studied and documented because it was an early role model for collaboration among stakeholders and achieved an impressive balance between protecting habitat and encouraging development.

Planning and habitat inventory status has been weaker for land areas outside of the West Eugene Wetlands Plan area, despite statewide requirements that address both of these issues and despite the fact that Eugene began the process of complying with those requirements in the late 1980s. The primary reasons for this weakness have been inadequate funding, complex state law, and an initial state requirement for consensus of all local jurisdictions in the area regarding natural resources inventories (which was impossible to obtain early on). There have also been bureaucratic delays typical of any jurisdiction. The result is that there has been little protection for sensitive lands in the city outside the West Eugene wetlands, other than on lands owned by the city

The good news is that the region made headway in 2003 and 2004 in meeting all state requirements for habitat inventories and comprehensive plan review. The state has agreed to allow each of the three local jurisdictions to complete and approve separate inventories for lands within their own boundaries, which has made the adoption process easier than before. Once the inventories and updated local plan are adopted, the city can then start to formulate regulations to protect sensitive lands that have been identified. City staff have programmed this work to be completed in 2005.

The Metro Plan is the metro area's comprehensive land use plan and covers central Lane County, Eugene, and Springfield. The plan went through a state-required "periodic review" and update, with final adoption by all jurisdictions completed in 2004. It is unclear whether the update is as comprehensive and involves as much public participation as the original 1980s document. The Metro Plan has an environmental resources element, but because of the delays in adopting inventories, that portion of the plan has not been fully implemented. Eugene has had some separate neighborhood plans in place for several years that contain elements related to natural areas—in particular, the South Hills area plan.

Natural resource inventories of three types of habitat (wetlands, riparian areas, and upland wildlife habitat) are part of the state-required plan review. Although Eugene began this inventory process in the late 1980s (which is how the rare wetlands were discovered), it is finally in the home stretch of completing it. The riparian and upland habitat inventories were adopted in 2004, and adoption of the wetlands inventory (for wetlands outside of West Eugene) is expected in 2005. The wetlands in West Eugene are not included in these current inventories because the West Eugene Wetlands Plan has already met state requirements for protection.

On another front, a regional open space vision was completed in 2003, and a citywide parks plan will be completed in 2005. Eugene's Planning Commission and city council (as well as the elected officials of Lane County and Springfield) have endorsed the "Rivers to Ridges" vision, which is the first metrowide regional parks and open space study. This broad-brush regional vision was funded by several local entities, including the City of Eugene, and completed by Lane Council of Governments staff with heavy input from the same local entities. It will be used to help elected officials in the region find funding for regionally significant land acquisitions and recreation projects. The current city Parks and Recreation Plan dates from 1989 and does not break out natural areas specifically, although a large number of acres, even in recreational parks, are already managed for natural areas. An update to this plan is underway, and is moving in an encouraging direction of adding "natural area park" and "linear park/greenway" (greenways that are more than just a bike or pedestrian path) designations to the system. An inventory of established parks and open space has been completed that includes documentation of the natural areas within all parks. The completed inventory indicates that approximately 78 percent of the city's 2,900 acre parks and open space system is managed for natural resource values. The new Parks, Recreation, and Open Space Comprehensive Plan should be completed by early 2005.

The city's stormwater plan is a very strong document, but has been slow in being implemented because of funding problems, discussed below.

Acquisition/Funding

Natural areas preserved by the city thus far have been primarily either wetlands (with some accompanying upland habitat), Willamette River frontage, or open space associated with the Ridgeline Trail, a regional trail and open space system that incorporates some of the ridgeline and hilltop parks in the city. Although the following acre totals are not as high as totals preserved in several other jurisdictions featured in this book, the city's results are still respectable, and the wetlands plan has effectively acquired most of its targeted extremely rare habitat.

The wetlands program protects valuable wetlands while allowing development on lower-value wetlands. Of the total 1,491 acres of actual wetlands currently in the plan, the goal is to protect 48 percent (720 acres), restore 30 percent (444 acres), and fill 20 percent (304 acres) for development. There are only a few parcels remaining to be obtained to accomplish plan goals, and additional wetlands have been acquired outside the Wetlands Plan boundary, leading to a total of approximately 3,000 acres of lands owned in fee title or conservation easement.

On the parks side, about 2,300 acres of natural areas are present in the city's parks, which total 2,900 acres. The natural areas total includes parks that are comprised of chiefly natural areas (such as the ridgeline parks), as well as those portions of recreational parks that are managed for habitat.

The city's history of land acquisition for parks is sporadic. In 1938, citizens voted to purchase 280 acres on Spencer Butte, a prominent landmark at the south end of town. As development began in the nearby South Hills area in the 1970s, the city council requested a study that recommended housing developments provide for recreational space and preserve wildlife and vegetation. A $5 million levy in 1976 provided funding for several of the "ridgeline" parks identified in that study. In 1972 a bond measure paid for acquisitions along the Willamette River and protected part of the riverbank from development. The sluggish economy in the 1980s and 1990s prevented any other parkland bond measures from even being put to a vote until 1998, when another bond issue was passed that focused primarily on recreational needs. The $25 million 1998 bond measure (passed by a 3:1 margin) contained $3.7 million earmarked for expansion of the ridgeline parks (primarily natural areas) with a target of acquiring 232 more acres. As of early 2004, the city had exceeded the original goal and had acquired 354 acres, with some money still left. This success is attributable to good planning, some favorable deals, and donations, and in part reflects the character and values of the community, according to staff. In every case they worked with willing sellers/donors and have had mutually agreed on appraisals.

Although run separately from the city, the municipally owned Eugene Water and Electric Board should not be overlooked when considering acquisition of habitat in the Eugene area. The utility formed a formal, temporary partnership with the local land trust (the McKenzie River Trust) and gave them a $1 million grant to purchase

Spencer Butte was one of the first natural areas purchased by the city. Photograph by Cara Snyder.

land locally as part of federally required mitigation for relicensing small dams in the area. Usually mitigation funds go to public groups for public purposes; the unusual aspect here is that a private group has received the funds. While protecting ecosystems is becoming more acceptable as a green infrastructure mechanism to protect water quality, it is still not commonplace for a city utility, especially for a city this size, to be funding acquisitions of natural areas based on what they perceive to be their customers' water quality needs for the future. The city itself is also working with the same land trust to help purchase other threatened lands.

Funding land acquisitions is challenging in Eugene. Oregon does not have a sales tax, so this common tool in other states for raising land acquisition money is not available. In addition, the Oregon Constitution limits the amount of property value subject to taxation and also sets limits on the amount of property taxes that can be collected from each property tax account, creating another fund-raising obstacle for local jurisdictions.

Eugene's primary sources for funding acquisitions thus have been bond measures, stormwater funds, and federal monies. Although city bond issues are difficult to pass owing to a current requirement to get a "double majority"—half the registered voters must vote, and more than half of those voting must vote yes—this tool is still used occasionally to raise money for habitat acquisition. Since the two park bond issues in 1975 and 1998 passed readily, the challenge for bonds may be more that there has been a lack of political will to put parks bonds on the ballot in the first place.

One of Eugene's more innovative endeavors has been the participation in a regional strategy to obtain federal funding for a variety of projects, which often include some acquisition. This effort (the United Front) is discussed in the earlier section on "Program Structure and Administration," under "Partnerships." These partnerships have obtained about $37 million in capital since 1987, of which approximately $15 million has been for land acquisition and other nature-friendly programs, specifically for the city or the wetlands program.

Although little or no local general funds are used for land acquisitions, the city's general revenue fund provides monies for several natural resources staff members. Other staff funding sources include stormwater fees and mitigation bank funds.

The city's stormwater group has a modest budget of $150,000 per year for stream corridor acquisitions, and has used this money to acquire a small amount of land (about 35 acres). A 2001 study identified about $5 million in acquisition needs—stream corridors that are already in good condition and do not need restoration to be useful for stormwater management. A nominal increase in stormwater user fees was proposed several years ago to provide more substantial sums for acquisitions. The city council approved the fee increase and the proposed acquisitions, but action was not taken immediately, momentum was lost, and neither the fee increase nor the acquisition program was implemented.

Regulations

Eugene's natural resource protection regulatory efforts have been a mixed bag. Here again, the wetlands program shines, and areas outside of the wetlands are not as well covered. However, additional regulations are scheduled to be developed in 2005 to address sensitive resources inventoried outside the West Eugene Wetlands Plan boundary.

As part of the wetlands program, Eugene adopted three implementing ordinances that can be found in Chapter 9 ("Land Use") of the Eugene City Code. These ordinances established a Natural Resources Zone; a Waterside Protection Overlay; and a Wetland Buffer Overlay. The Natural Resources Zone is intended to protect outstanding natural resource areas identified in adopted plans and contains a long list of development standards that address such topics as buffers, vegetation removal, stormwater drainage, impervious surfaces, construction practices, design standards, and noise. The noise protection element is intriguing, and staff confirmed that they wrote that element particularly strongly since they felt they were protecting several rare species for posterity and that noise is a critical issue often overlooked. The Natural Resources Zone applies only to publicly owned property, to avoid takings issues on private property.

The purpose of the Waterside Protection Overlay Zone is to "protect water quality in designated waterways, riparian areas, and adjacent wetlands by maintaining an undeveloped setback area between these features and adjacent developed areas." Additionally, the setback area is intended to protect wildlife habitat, prevent property damage, and enhance open space next to water features. For example, minimum buffer setbacks from perennial water features in a floodway are 60 feet from the top of the bank and 40 feet if outside a floodway. The Wetland Buffer Overlay Zone is similar to the Waterside Protection Overlay but applies only to wetlands in the West Eugene Wetlands Plan. It also requires an undeveloped setback area between wetlands and developed areas. The amount of setback required is higher for high-value wetlands. For example, a setback of 100 feet from high-value wetlands is required with no site

Rare wetlands coexist with industrial development in West Eugene, with varying setbacks provided by the Wetland Buffer Overlay Zone. Photograph courtesy of the City of Eugene Wetlands Program.

enhancements, or 50 feet if site enhancement standards are met. Moderate-value wetlands require a setback of 50 feet with no site enhancements.

Currently, the city is only able to apply these natural resources zones to lands designated for protection in the West Eugene Wetlands Plan, since no other lands have yet been approved as sensitive areas (owing to delays on the natural resources inventory approval, noted previously). However, city staff will begin to apply these zones to areas outside of the West Eugene wetlands in 2005, since official inventories of the natural resources of those areas were finally approved by the city in 2004.

A developer representative commented that although any mention of wetlands puts up a red flag, the city is very helpful and provides wetlands maps and staff time to help navigate through the development process.

The city also has other regulations that could be considered nature-friendly, but these are not used often or are just coming into play: nodal development (mixed use, pedestrian/transit-oriented centers); a conservation subdivision option; and Planned Unit Development (PUD). A handful of nodal development projects were underway in 2003–2004, but some community members feel the city is not using this tool as effectively as it could to promote infill, since at least one of the projects is in an outlying greenfield site, possibly disconnected from some planned public transportation options (e.g., the planned Bus Rapid Transit System). The city's special standards for conservation land divisions are rarely used. However, the subdivision process in general has several environmental restrictions, and applications have been denied based on natural resource issues. Planned Unit Developments initially were useful for protecting some natural features, but during the 1990s a number of PUD projects demonstrated some deficiencies in the code related to natural resource protection. Some of these deficiencies were addressed through the adoption of an entirely new land use code in 2002. Other deficiencies will be addressed through the new regulations to be developed in 2005.

The development review process includes site review, with criteria for protection of natural features, tree preservation, and mitigation. However, because of the unapproved natural resources inventories, the code's language has been confusing, and criteria are currently more stringent for those lands that are not on the pending natural resources inventory—exactly the opposite of how it should be. As noted previously, staff are scheduled to address this inconsistency in 2005 and make the necessary code amendments to remedy this awkward situation.

An important component of the wetlands regulations is the program's wetland mitigation bank. It is widely praised as effective by the development community. This mitigation program (and the whole wetlands plan/program) has been featured in many wetlands case study books. It is discussed in greater detail under the heading "Restoration" in this case study.

The city's Salmon Protection and Recovery Program contains additional elements. It was started in response to the 1999 listing of the chinook salmon as threatened. The program was developed by the Eugene ESA/Salmon Team based on studies of Eugene's existing regulations, Eugene's existing internal practices, and riparian and aquatic habitat. The program proposed 10 strategies, including a salmon habitat protection overlay zone. In February 2003, the city council directed staff to pursue the 9 nonregulatory strategies proposed and for the tenth strategy (the salmon habitat overlay) asked staff to conduct additional public outreach and then bring the proposal back for additional council review. Unfortunately, funding was tied to stormwater fees, which have been frozen for now. Although the city already conducts many activities that protect salmon habitat, progress on the new strategies, including the proposed overlay district, will be slow because of funding constraints.

A new city policy in early 2003 prohibits the use of the most problematic and documented invasive plant species, discourages the planting of other species that are suspected to be problematic, and encourages the use of native plants on all city-owned lands and projects. Although not officially regulatory in nature, it is a promising effort.

Restoration

As has been mentioned, Eugene has developed the capability to conduct large-scale environmental restoration projects in-house. Most other jurisdictions, especially of this size, are more likely to contract out restoration work. The wetlands program again has been the driving force, and it has been the nature of the wetlands themselves that has inspired the community. Eugene has a unique type of wetland that is typically saturated or slightly flooded in the winter, but dry in summer and early fall. Eugene's wet prairie grasslands are the habitat for five species of plants and insects considered to be rare, threatened, or endangered. These are unique wetlands indeed, and the community, including city staff and other wetlands program staff, consistently appreciate that fact and show an admirable dedication to restoring what they can. Hundreds of volunteers work on restoration each year, as well as an impressive number of paid staff. A respectable system for monitoring successful restoration is in place (e.g., a certain percentage of native wetland plants must be present five years after restoration was begun). The first project in 1993 was 7 acres, and there has been a new project every year since 1993—up to 100 acres per project. Restoration typically involves an extensive site preparation process (to remove nonnative species), followed by replanting of native species and extensive maintenance and monitoring for five to seven years after planting. The total number of acres restored as of mid-2004 was 700.

The restoration projects are funded by a combination of federal funds (e.g., from the U.S. Army Corps of Engineers through Section 1135 of the Water Resources and Development Act, and from the U.S. Bureau of Land Management through the Cooperative Conservation initiative) and locally generated funds (e.g., the wetlands mitigation bank). Over the years, the mitigation bank has been the steadiest source of funding for restoration. A wetlands mitigation bank is a wetland area that has been restored or protected, and is then used to compensate for wetlands losses at other sites. Eugene's regulations require mitigation if a developer wants to fill in and build

Eugene has an impressive wetlands restoration program involving a number of paid staff as well as volunteers. Photograph courtesy of the City of Eugene Wetlands Program.

on high-value wetlands on a development site. Administered by the city's public works staff, the bank provides certified mitigation credits to developers, leads the implementation of plans to restore and enhance wetland communities, and collects fees from the sale of mitigation credits. Costs were initially $30,000 per credit and were increased to $50,000 per credit in 2002 to reflect the average costs associated with development, design, planning, construction, and monitoring of a credit. Future increases will be tied to inflation. About $2 million in credits have been sold in the past 10 years—and this money all goes back to restoration. The mitigation bank fund helps finance several employees—at least 1 full-time staff person and 16 seasonals. Sale of mitigation credits is starting to bring in about $400,000 to 500,000 per year (about eight credits per year at $50,000 per credit).

Native plant materials are one of the major expenses of wetlands restoration. Only native species from within 20 miles of the site are used. Seed is hand collected from remnant wetland areas, and staff are also working with local farmers to grow these rare plant seeds in bulk quantities. As a result, former grass seed farmers in the area have converted to native seed crops, which have become a good market for them, leading to markets outside the area as well. This is a win-win situation, since buying from a grower is cheaper for the city than purchasing handpicked seeds or attempting their own grow-out program.

Leading by Example

Eugene leads by example in several different ways. One illustration is the amount of self-examination the city has done in response to the 1999 chinook salmon listing. The city paid for independent studies of its regulations and its city activities to see what effect both are having on the environment. The results of the studies showed that Eugene is doing a good job overall. The city also has regulations in place to protect sensitive lands owned by the city.

The IPM (integrated pest management) program is another example of the city leading by example. Although not yet a formally adopted program (plans are in the works to institutionalize current practices in 2005), it is worthy of recognition. The city has had an informal policy of using IPM since 1980, and the program is one of the oldest in the nation, known nationally and internationally. Although pesticides are still used, it is only sparingly, and less hazardous compounds are chosen. Crews have had to spot-spray for weeds only once on 3 playfields out of Eugene's 25 fields in the last 16 years. Given that most of the threatened and endangered species in the Eugene area are water related (wetlands plants/animals and salmon), the city is a role model for the region in reducing one aspect of threats to these species.

The Wastewater Division has attained a very high water quality for wastewater. In addition, Eugene is one of the fortunate cities that have kept their wastewater and stormwater systems separate, so it never has to deal with stormwater causing overflow of wastewater into local rivers/streams. The city may also have been one of the first communities to stop using a toxic root removal chemical and switch to a nontoxic one.

Social Indicators

Eugene has modest programs for city infill, with fledgling transit node and mixed-use programs. The city park system is free to the public, and parks (including natural areas) are easily accessible throughout the city. Some local private groups are taking advantage of the wetlands presence to involve disadvantaged youth in restoration and education projects, but these are not directly city-sponsored programs.

Where Eugene shines regarding social indicators is in affordable housing. Both the City of Eugene and Lane County took a closer look at housing issues in the late 1980s because lack of affordable housing had become an obvious problem. The Eugene city council started adopting an annual goal related to low-income housing in 1989 and has had other policies in place even longer, including a policy to disperse low-income housing around the city and one to discourage low-income multifamily housing developments larger than 60 units. Since then, more policies have been adopted and refined, and more importantly, action and political will have accompanied these policies. Although Eugene does not own, operate, or build housing, since 1979 Eugene has purchased sites for future low-income housing, using primarily federal block grant funds, and then has given away the site for each low-income development that occurs. The city also approves 20-year property tax exemptions (as part of a state program), waives permit fees for developers, assists with down payments for homebuyers, and provides a density bonus for rent-controlled projects. Using these incentives and programs (and others), Eugene has built over 1,200 units of affordable housing since the early 1990s (over 100 units per year), which is admirable for a city of its size, and facing the challenges that it faces (e.g., tough state land use laws and scarce, expensive land). The cost of a typical acre of medium density residential land in Eugene went from about $20,000 per acre in 1990, to $40,000 in 1994, up to $100,000 per acre in 2001. The Eugene/Springfield area ranked twelfth in a 2001 National Association of Home Builders survey among 180 U.S. housing markets for least affordable housing for purchase, based on a ratio of median income and median sales prices. With these difficulties, good political support at both the city council and the county level has been critical. The city has been able and willing to try different incentives, and the resulting developments have been good looking and well maintained, thanks to a competitive proposal process and ongoing tenant surveys by city staff in respect to management, design, and other topics, to see if each project works on the ground.

Over 1,200 units of affordable housing (like these duplexes at Woodleaf Village) have been built in Eugene since the early 1990s—a notable accomplishment. Photograph courtesy of the City of Eugene Planning and Development Department.

Education

An overall educational bent is obvious to any visitor to the city's website: the Eugene city website makes it easy for Internet visitors to learn about its nature-friendly programs by providing an "Environmental Stewardship" button on its front web page.

Extensive wetlands education programs are present in Eugene and are primarily community-led. Hundreds of volunteers have already been involved in restoration projects in the wetlands areas since 1993, and a local high school has had science magnet classes focused on wetlands for several years. However, now that acquisition and restoration projects are well underway, the community is pursuing even broader educational goals. An informal citizens group that had started meeting to discuss educational ideas prior to 1999 has become the Willamette Resource and Education

Network (WREN). WREN is spearheading the planning of a new multi-million-dollar educational facility to house the variety of programs and groups that have already been involved in wetlands education projects.

The city sponsors an active environmental education program, Stream Team, which manages volunteers in wetlands, stream corridors, and other restoration projects, in addition to a wide variety of other stewardship activities throughout the city. This program also conducts frequent native plant salvage projects as well as managing a dedicated native plant nursery. The stormwater program also has developed an educational curriculum called "Splash!" that has been instituted in many local schools. The program covers water-related topics such as the water cycle, stormwater pollution, water use, and aquatic ecosystems, and includes teacher trainings, special programs, and a website geared to kids.

Steve Gordon admires a new interpretive wetlands sign. He led the collaborative process to protect the wetlands in the early 1990s. Photograph by Cara Snyder.

Several major environmental advocacy groups exist in Eugene, and many neighborhood organizations make environmental issues their number one priority. As a result, much public education occurs outside of city involvement, which when added to the city's public outreach and public involvement efforts, results in an active and informed public.

Results

The most important example of Eugene's attempts to measure habitat protection is the West Eugene Wetlands Plan, which has an impressive monitoring system in place. The system requires that after two years, 50 percent of the plant cover in the restoration area must be successful native vegetation, and after five years, 80 percent cover. "Successful" is defined as thriving living plants. Staff members visit each of the mitigation sites quarterly to conduct qualitative observations. Quantitative site visits occur in years 2 and 5 after restoration. The quantitative monitoring includes rare plant surveys, baseline sampling, tree and shrub censuses, seeding assessments, and herbaceous cover sampling. The city reports a 100 percent success rate on its restoration projects thus far, although some projects have needed fairly extensive maintenance to achieve the desired outcomes.

Overall, the City of Eugene has accomplished much in the realm of habitat protection:

- About 3,000 acres of land have been purchased in the West Eugene wetlands area, which includes upland habitat as well as almost all the targeted high-quality rare wetlands.
- About 2,300 acres of natural areas are preserved in the city's parks.
- 700 acres of rare wetlands have been restored as of mid-2004.
- Integrated pest management has been utilized on city lands since 1980.

Note

[1]Primary sources for this case study include Steve Gordon, program manager/natural resources, Lane
Council of Governments; Neil Bjorklund, senior planner, Eugene Planning and Development
Department; numerous other city, LCOG, and wetland team staff members; the city's website,
www.ci.eugene.or.us; and the book *Eugene 1945–2000: Decisions That Made a Community* (City
Club of Eugene, 2000).

CHAPTER 7

Fort Collins and Larimer County, Colorado: A Tale of Two Jurisdictions

This is a tale of two jurisdictions. Fort Collins is a city with strong regulations and a strong land acquisition program. Larimer County has more moderate regulations, a conservation development process that requires 50 to 80 percent open area, and a Rural Land Use Process that has a more voluntary slant. The county also has an acquisitions program. Both programs, while largely separate, offer an instructive contrast between different approaches that are both effective in their own way. These two jurisdictions also demonstrate that voluntary, cooperative regional approaches have some significant shortcomings.

These two related case studies of a neighboring city and county illustrate the challenges of regional biodiversity protection.[1] Fort Collins is a strong, financially viable, progressive city leading the region on several fronts—habitat protection via acquisition on a regional scale as well as tough regulations and education, ample staffing, and a commendable affordable housing program. The county also has impressive albeit quite different programs and is striving to improve its implementation record while working jointly with the city on growth management and planning. The county has

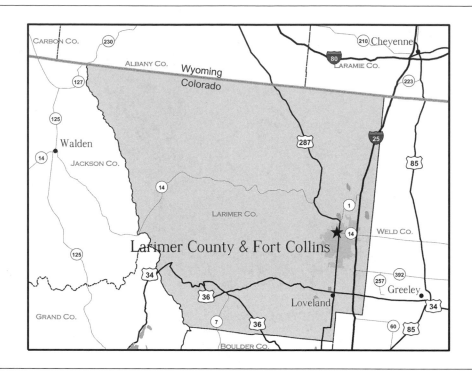

FORT COLLINS AND LARIMER COUNTY, COLORADO
Map courtesy of Clarion Associates.

also developed an award-winning transfer of density units program that the city has cooperated with.

Fort Collins is a rapidly growing university community about 75 miles north of Denver, nestled against the foothills of the Rocky Mountains and alongside the banks of the Cache La Poudre River. The city covers 47 square miles and in 2004 had a population of 126,800 residents, with an annual growth rate of over 3 percent for the past decade. It is the largest city in Larimer County and accounts for about half of that county's population, which was 251,226 in 2000 (a 35 percent increase over the 1990 population of 186,000). Larimer County's 2,640 square miles stretch from the mountainous Continental Divide on its western edge to shortgrass prairie and irrigated farmland in the east. Over 50 percent of Larimer County is publicly owned, including national forest lands and part of Rocky Mountain National Park. The climate is arid, with 14 inches of precipitation during an average year on the plains and foothills. Higher levels of rain and snowfall occur in the mountains. The area's diverse

Fort Collins and Larimer County have the Front Range of the Rocky Mountains in their backyard. Photograph courtesy of the City of Fort Collins.

economy includes strong agriculture such as wheat farming and ranching, tourism, education, and high-tech industry sectors. Approximately 23,000 students attend Colorado State University, based in Fort Collins.

Fort Collins is known for its innovative growth management initiatives like City Plan, big-box retail standards, and its New Urbanist–based code, as well as performance zoning. The county is more conservative but still active in growth management and open space preservation. It played a key role in passing the state's conservation cluster subdivision provision. The city and county have a long history of cooperative land use planning initiatives, including an intergovernmental agreement (IGA) for growth management (adopted in 1980) and joint planning areas.

Fort Collins is a home rule[2] city with a council/manager form of government. The city council is composed of six district council members who are elected on a nonpartisan basis for a term of four years, and a mayor who is elected at large for a two-year term. Larimer County has three full-time members on the board of county commissioners and a county manager. However, in response to requests from citizens, the board is considering alternative governance structures in 2004, including a five-commissioner board.

The ecosystems range from prairie in the east to mountains in the west. Since the high-altitude, mountainous portions of the county are already primarily publicly owned, the type of ecosystems that would most likely be considered for protection include the foothills (including mountain mahogany shrubland and ponderosa pine plant communities) and shortgrass prairie ecosystems, as well as agricultural lands.

Much growth in the county's unincorporated areas makes habitat protection challenging. Nearby fast-growing incorporated small towns like Johnstown and Windsor are spilling over from Weld County into Larimer County. Authority is fragmented, with no formal regional council of governments. Also, Colorado lacks strong statewide mandatory growth management legislation, which leaves cities and counties mostly to their own devices.

Significant growth since 1970 has been the driving force behind the countywide interest in protecting natural resources. The city grew from about 43,000 residents in 1970 to 118,000 in 2000. The county had a total population of 89,900 (including Fort Collins) in 1970, and has added 160,000 people since then to reach a population of about 250,000 in the 2000 census. To put this in perspective, both the city and the county population increased by about 35 percent from 1990 to 2000, an average of 3.5 percent per year.

Both the city and county had an early interest in open space and habitat. Fort Collins passed a seven-year, one-cent capital improvements sales tax in 1973, a portion of which was for the purchase of open spaces. The city created their first Open Space Plan in 1974. The county began purchasing sensitive lands in 1981. However, large amounts of land were not acquired by either entity until the early 1990s, when both the city and county residents voted to tax themselves specifically for acquisition of natural areas. As indicated in a 1993 county parks plan survey, citizens wanted "places with no houses."

There are quite a few natural resource professionals in the area because of Colorado State University (CSU), which has a nationally respected natural resource management program. The Colorado Division of Wildlife has formal affiliations with wildlife biologists at CSU. A substantial number of water and energy consultants also live in the area. Many of these people serve on boards for the city and county, and many additional citizens want to see the city be a leader in the area of resource protection.

Current programs that deserve mention include the acquisition programs for both entities. The Fort Collins Natural Areas Program conserved 9,700 acres from

1992 to 2003 and added over 13,000 acres to its program in 2004. The city is preparing to protect close to 40,000–50,000 acres of critical lands in the next 15 years. Larimer County's Open Lands Program will continue to steadily acquire open lands (not necessarily all habitat) at a slower rate, but has already protected over 16,000 acres. Both jurisdictions are using extensive mapping and geographic information system (GIS) data to guide acquisitions, and both have a dedicated sales tax to ensure funding for many more years. Both the city and the county have wildlife regulations in place that are actually used on the ground, with the city's being more prescriptive. The county's Rural Land Use Process is a model voluntary, incentive-based land conservation program that has protected over 6,500 acres as of 2003.

A key point made by both county and city staff is the importance of having a combination of tools and a range of options for protection of natural areas. Politics makes the county tread more lightly. For example, county staff say that even terminology can be tricky: the phrase "protecting the environment" is controversial—this approach has a negative aspect to some in their county. Instead, "protecting the character of the West, community character, and vistas" rang true with the public; it created something positive, and this specific desire of the citizens of the county led to the development of the county's cluster provisions in both its Conservation Development Process and its Rural Land Use Process. According to county staff, creation of opportunity should be the focus, not prohibitions. For example, instead of asking how to stop agricultural land conversion, ask how to increase economic opportunities so that landowners have affordable options other than selling their land.

There is a history of interjurisdictional cooperation in the area, although formal regional planning is weak. In 1980, Larimer County and the City of Fort Collins joined to adopt an intergovernmental agreement (IGA) to coordinate a Growth Management Area; this agreement has been maintained, updated, and adhered to. Other regional projects include the Northern Colorado Regional Planning Study, a multijurisdictional program completed in 1995 that provides a framework for cooperation among the participating jurisdictions in regard to growth management; the Northern Colorado Community Separator Study; the Northern Colorado Communities I-25 Corridor Plan; and other IGAs with some of the smaller towns in the areas. In addition, both open space acquisition departments (Larimer County Open Lands and Fort Collins Natural Areas) cooperate frequently. However, despite these laudable endeavors, a comprehensive and effective regional strategy to protect critical habitat has not evolved, largely because smaller jurisdictions are approving major developments with only limited environmental reviews.

This is a good illustration of two effective approaches under different political situations. Individually, both jurisdictions, especially Fort Collins, have commendable programs. But lack of a truly regional approach and competition among jurisdictions for growth and sales tax undermines the effectiveness of biodiversity and natural resource protection initiatives. Also, state involvement is mixed, while in other states it has proved to be a critical factor in resource protection. Great Outdoors Colorado (GOCO), which provides funds for open space from a statewide lottery, has been a godsend, especially since the state legislature seems intent on hog-tying local governments from using regulatory growth management tools. The GOCO Amendment to the state constitution was put in place by citizens, not the legislature, and assigns a portion of state lottery proceeds to habitat and open space protection.

Key Program Elements

Program Structure and Administration

Both the city and county have sizable planning departments, and each has one staff member who completes environmental review of development applications. Both have significant divisions dedicated to acquiring and managing open space.

Fort Collins has a Community Planning and Environmental Services Department that consists of Current Planning, Advance Planning, Natural Resources, and Building and Zoning divisions. The Current Planning Division staff (8 employees) review and evaluate annexations, rezonings, and development proposals. The Advance Planning Division staff (15 employees) prepare neighborhood and strategic area plans and administer affordable housing programs and historic preservation activities. Importantly, the Natural Resources Division is housed in the Community Planning and Environmental Services Department. It was created in 1985 and consists of four program areas: Air Quality, Natural Areas, Recycling and Solid Waste, and Environmental Planning and Information. The division has about 33 full-time staff members, 23 of whom work in the Natural Areas Program.

The Natural Areas Program was established in the late 1980s and adopted a policy plan in 1992 as a result of a citizen-initiated 1/4-cent sales tax initiative; it acquires natural lands and manages 39 natural areas for the city. The program has grown from a staff of 2 in 1992 to the current 23 staff members: 4 planners, 4 rangers, 6 seasonal technicians, 7 full-time technicians, 1 education coordinator, and 1 full-time restoration ecologist hired in 2002. Most staff positions have been supported by the sales tax since the program started, with only one staff position paid for by general revenues until 2004. Starting in 2004, all Natural Areas staff will be completely supported by the sales tax. In 2003, two staff members in the Real Estate Division were hired to work full-time on negotiating acquisitions and conservation easements. One staff person in the Natural Resources Division reviews all development applications for their environmental impact and acts as an in-house expert. The city has a separate Parks and Recreation Department that handles recreational facilities. Natural areas contain habitat and may have trails, but few other recreational facilities.

The Natural Resources Advisory Board was established in 1985 and reviews city policies and activities that affect the environment. The board is appointed by the city council and helped pass the tax initiatives: "They care passionately, they work their tails off, they raise the money to help pass the initiatives," according to Greg Byrne, director of Community Planning and Environmental Services. The language in the 2002 ballot initiative to extend the city's open space tax calls for a new open space board that will deal only with open space issues. This board had not yet been created as of late 2004 but is scheduled to be in place by 2006.

Housing planning and natural resources under one director ensures that internal coordination occurs, as does having one staff member doing environmental review of development applications. However, the Natural Resources Division, the Natural Resources Advisory Board, and the city's stormwater program all increased their activities after a major flood occurred in 1997, which has led to some power struggles. At the same time, the Natural Areas Program staff have worked cooperatively with the stormwater division of Fort Collins Utilities on at least three acquisition and restoration projects.

Larimer County has several departments that are involved with habitat protection. The Planning and Building Services Division assists the public with land use planning, zoning, land division, building permits, and building inspections. The Planning Department and the Rural Land Use Center are part of this division. The Parks and Open Lands Department falls under the Public Works Division and manages the outdoor recreational areas in Larimer County (including natural open space) and performs weed control on county lands.

The Planning Department has eight planners in Current Planning/ Development Review and three employees (including one GIS analyst) in Advance Planning, in addition to code administration and support staff. One of the current planning staff members works on development review focused on wetlands and wildlife. The Rural

Land Use Center (which runs a voluntary, incentive-based land conservation program) is leanly staffed with a director, one half-time technician, and one administrative assistant.

The Parks and Open Lands Department has 35 full-time staff members (including the recreational parks portion), a number that rises to over 100 with seasonal employees. Within this department, the Open Lands Program staff members include an open lands manager; a resource specialist who develops management plans and monitors conservation easements; a technician who reviews development proposals and oversees agricultural and trails programs; a fund development and outreach specialist; an education coordinator; a part-time accountant; two land agents who handle real estate deals; one full-time and one part time ranger; and a trail team with two supervisors. The Larimer County Weed Control District is now housed in this department and deals with exotic, invasive species on county lands and roadsides. Education is also part of their function. A special mill levy funds the district. Weed control funding for the Open Lands Program is discussed under "Acquisitions/Funding." The Open Lands Advisory Board approves all acquisitions for the Open Lands Program and consists of seven citizens appointed at large; one elected official or an appointee from the cities of Berthoud, Estes Park, Fort Collins, and Loveland; and one member from the Larimer County Planning Commission.

The city and county partner with each other and other groups in the region for various reasons. The city has partnered with Larimer County, the nearby city of Loveland, and nonprofit organizations (Great Outdoors Colorado, The Nature Conservancy, and Legacy Land Trust) for land acquisition. The federal government has also been involved in several partnerships with the city to restore gravel-mined sites along the Poudre River. Other regional examples are mentioned in the introduction to this case study.

The city and county have several intergovernmental agreements (IGAs) with each other, starting with one in 1980 regarding Growth Management Areas. This IGA designates urban growth areas and establishes land use policies for those areas. The agreement delineates common design standards, criteria for annexation, phasing criteria, supplemental zoning regulations for the urban growth areas, and a park fee collection system within urban growth areas. Other agreements include a cooperative plan for an area known as Fossil Creek and annexation agreements for several other areas. The county has also established IGAs with some, but not all, of the smaller towns in the county. Although there is general agreement that river corridors and community separators are important, annexations and growth management continue to be hot issues, and agricultural issues are not well understood. The county's inability to forge strong ties with all communities has resulted in development that does not always meet county goals. The county is mapping all annexations in 2004 to bring data to regional meetings in an attempt to create more understanding of the issues.

Regarding acquisitions, Larimer County Open Lands has partnered with Fort Collins, Loveland, Estes Valley, Rocky Mountain National Park, the U.S. Forest Service, and nonprofit organizations (GOCO, TNC, Legacy Land Trust, Estes Valley Land Trust). For example, Larimer County and Fort Collins have an IGA for the purchase of the Indian Creek Ranch for cost sharing. Fort Collins fronted 75 percent of the cost. and the county paid 25 percent and will then manage the land.

Notably, the region does not have a regional council of governments, which was abolished decades ago. As a result, regional growth management is voluntary and spotty.

Planning

Inventories/Mapping

Both the city and county have done extensive mapping using GIS and other data from a variety of sources.

The city uses two maps for its nature-friendly endeavors. The Natural Habitat and Features Inventory was developed from the April 1999 aerial photography used for land use planning and development. The items covered include aquatic, wetland, grassland, shrubland, and forest areas as well as potential habitats for rare and endangered species and other selected wildlife. These areas are delineated on the Natural Habitats and Features Inventory map, but the boundaries are subject to revision based on a site evaluation and ecological characterization. Staff acknowledge that this map should be updated, but it still provides a framework for applying the environmental standards (discussed under "Regulations") when new development is considered.

The Focus Area map for the Natural Areas Program is much more sophisticated and incorporates data from a wider range of sources, including the Natural Habitats and Features Inventory map, extensive data gathered by Larimer County for its Open Lands Master Plan in 2001 (discussed below), The Nature Conservancy's priority areas of high biodiversity, and the Colorado Natural Heritage Program's conservation sites, as well as several others. During the summer of 2002, city staff worked with a task force of local natural resource managers to identify high-priority resource protection areas. Resource areas were identified that have multiple conservation values (such as wildlife habitat,

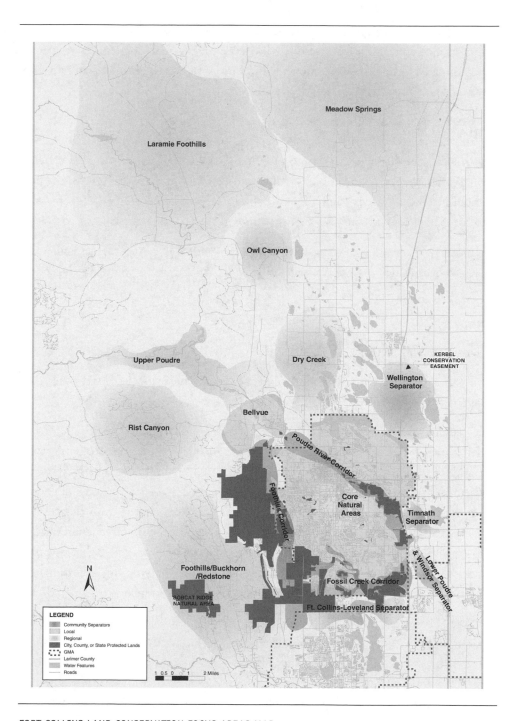

FORT COLLINS LAND CONSERVATION FOCUS AREAS MAP
The Fort Collins Land Conservation Focus Areas map shows the local, regional, and community separator focus areas, which are high-priority areas for future land conservation. Map courtesy of the City of Fort Collins.

recreation, education, scenic views, and watershed protection). The resource areas were mapped and grouped into focus areas. The Focus Area map was adopted by the city council in April 2003 and creates a framework for future land conservation.

The county's most extensive habitat mapping effort was completed for the 2001 update of the Larimer County Open Lands Master Plan. Using data from the county's geographic information system, previously completed planning documents, other sources, and on-site observation, a series of maps were prepared to illustrate existing conditions and resources. Data utilized include Colorado Division of Wildlife's wildlife areas (e.g., bighorn sheep lambing areas) and rare vegetation satellite data, public and protected lands, and an independent hydrology and wetlands study. The final result was the Open Lands Program Priority Areas map, which also incorporated public input from meetings and survey findings and is used to guide acquisitions for the Open Lands Department. Areas identified for protection include river corridors, important natural resource areas, important agricultural areas, and regional trail corridors.

Comprehensive Plan Elements

In October 1992, the city council adopted the City of Fort Collins Natural Areas Policy Plan as an element of the city's comprehensive plan. The city then implemented an award-winning comprehensive plan update in 1998 called "City Plan," which sets out a vision and a "Structure Plan" for the city. City Plan embraced mixed-use, New Urbanist principles for development and natural resource protection. The Natural Areas Policy Plan set a direction for "the future management of natural areas in Fort Collins that will meet the needs of the citizens of the City as well as the needs of the many other creatures with whom we share the land." The 10-year-old Natural Areas Policy Plan was rewritten and adopted in 2004 as the new Land Conservation and Stewardship Master Plan. The master plan lays out strategies for conserving land for the next 10 years.

The Larimer County Master Plan, updated and adopted in 1997, has several themes related to natural area protection: (1) land use shall be suitable for and compatible with the environmental characteristics of the site; (2) open lands shall continue to be a defining feature of the landscape of Larimer County; and (3) natural and cultural resources shall be identified, conserved, and protected. The Open Lands Master Plan uses some of the same base information. The current Open Lands Master Plan was prepared using a participatory public process and was adopted in December 2001.

Regional Coordination

The city and county partner together on acquisitions and planning for selected areas like Fossil Creek but do not have a coordinated plan for the region. However, the city has the potential to undertake large-scale protection in the region thanks to the amount of money produced by the current open space sales tax, and is moving in that direction, as noted under "Acquisition." But there is no truly regional approach to habitat protection except for acquisition; as noted earlier, there is no regional council of governments coordinating land use planning or other tools for habitat acquisition or protection.

Acquisition/Funding

Acquisition

Both the city and the county started their current acquisition programs in the early 1990s and have a strong partnership, frequently coordinating acquisition efforts. There are many similarities between the two programs. One difference is that the county staff must seek board approval for every purchase. County staff feel that this is a positive because the frequent media attention makes voters more aware of how their money is being utilized. Another difference, which will change soon, is that the county has a higher percentage of land in conservation easements (over 50 percent) than in full-fee acquisition. The city is just starting to focus more on easements, which in 2004 accounted for under 5 percent of total acreage preserved.

The primary acquisition program for the City of Fort Collins is the Natural Areas Program. In 1992, Fort Collins citizens by an overwhelming majority decided to tax themselves to establish the Natural Areas Program. Since 1993, the Natural Areas Program has helped conserve 9,700 acres—5,700 acres alone and 4,000 acres in partnership with other agencies such as Larimer County, the City of Loveland, Great Outdoors Colorado, the Legacy Land Trust, and other City of Fort Collins departments. Over 12,500 deeded acres were further acquired in 2004 (the Soapstone property near the Wyoming border), with an option to lease an additional 3,800 acres, adding approximately 25 square miles (16,300 acres) of relatively undisturbed shortgrass and mixed-grass prairie to the city's regional nature preserves. The city manages 7,700 acres (of the previously acquired 9,700 acres) in and around the city's Growth Management Area; partners manage the other lands. The Natural Areas Program has accomplished extensive protection along the Poudre River corridor (which runs through the city of Fort Collins) and has also preserved views of the foothills. In addition, a community separator between Fort Collins and Loveland has been partially protected and two incredible Natural Area complexes created: Fossil Creek and Coyote Ridge. The two tools used for protection are fee simple purchases (dependent on willing sellers) and conservation easements. Citizens voted to extend the sales tax that funds the Natural Areas Program, and the ballot language directed the program to consider acquiring land regionally instead of just locally. The Natural Areas Policy Plan, which was adopted in 1992 to guide initial acquisitions, is undergoing an update to address the changes in the program, including the more regional focus. The new plan is called the Land Conservation and Stewardship Master Plan and was adopted in 2004. As part of the update process, conservation focus areas were determined in 2002 (mapping of these was previously discussed under "Planning") and include local areas, regional areas, and community separator areas. Local conservation areas provide access to habitat closer to neighborhoods and schools. Regional areas are generally outside the city limits and protect large scenic views and large-scale functioning ecosystems, including migration routes from plains to peaks. Community separators are what they sound like—areas that, if protected, will help separate the city from the other growing communities in the region. The city has about $27 million for acquisition for 2004–2008 and will divide this amount equally (about $9 million each) among the three categories of conservation areas. The 2004 Soapstone property acquisition was the first major acquisition of this phase. Another $27 million will be spent in 2009–2013, with half going to regional conservation areas and the other half split between local and community separator areas.

With more focus on conservation easements, and the amount of money produced by the current open space sales tax, the city has the potential to undertake large-scale protection in the region. Protecting up to 25,000 additional acres is probable, but the city could possibly leverage over 40,000 acres for a Peaks to Prairie corridor from the Pawnee Grasslands to the Mummy Range. Public feedback has been positive, and the city council is supportive. A staff member commented, "It's like being in on the beginning of Yellowstone."

Larimer County also has an effective Open Lands Program. A Comprehensive Parks Master Plan was completed in 1993 that included protection of open space with particular emphasis on "areas of critical wildlife habitat or other areas that make an important contribution to the county's biological diversity." This plan led to the Help Preserve Open Space initiative (a sales tax for open space), approved in 1995 and discussed further under "Funding." The sales tax has helped the Parks and Open Lands Department to acquire and manage several thousands of acres of open space, a mix of

An example of collaborative acquisition efforts by city and county, Devil's Backbone Open Space Park contains one of the most impressive and visible geologic landmarks in Larimer County. Photograph by Rick Price.

recreational access and protected habitat. By the fall of 1999, over 8,000 acres of open space had been preserved, acquired from willing sellers only. By the end of 2003, the program had acquired a total of 16,400 acres of open lands (about half fee simple and half easements) using funds from the countywide sales tax ($19 million), partnerships ($25 million), and donations ($5 million).

The Parks and Open Lands Department manages a large chunk of these lands, while other entities manage the remainder. The staff also work with landowners to prepare management plans for the conservation easements. An updated open lands plan, called the Larimer County Open Lands Master Plan, was adopted in 2001 and is part of the county's Land Use Plan. Much energy went into this plan, including gathering of natural resource data to inventory existing conditions and resources. Public participation was extensive, from public meetings to a scientific citizen survey to determine public opinion about such topics as what types of land should be protected and what type of access should be allowed. Citizens surveyed preferred to acquire 55 percent of the land via fee simple purchase and 45 percent via conservation easements, knowing that public access was not allowed to the easement lands. The Open Lands Program receives no general revenues; administration costs are covered by about 15 to 30 percent of sales tax revenues.

Staff offer some advice for aspiring acquisition program managers:

- Keep an eye out on the future front despite pressure to focus on lands with the most development pressure.

- Realize that land purchased right before it is developed will have a higher price if the open space program is buying it.

- The last piece of the preservation puzzle should be a small acreage because you'll be held hostage for it.

- Make any funding tax renewable—this makes the program accountable and provides educational value for each new round of residents and officials.

- Remember to factor in management costs—it is expensive to manage land for public access so build management costs into initiatives.

Having an active open lands acquisition program for almost a decade in the county (and city) has had some interesting sociological results. Local property rights activists now see the open lands program simply as another viable option of what to do with land, instead of reacting vehemently when land shows up as a priority area for acquisitions on the map.

Funding

Both the city and county have sales taxes in place to fund acquisition of natural lands, as described below. The county has one funding source, which is shared with municipalities within the county, and Fort Collins has its own dedicated sales tax in addition to the portion it receives from the countywide tax.

Fort Collins voters approved an eight-year 1/4-cent sales tax in 1997, as part of a larger package known as Building Community Choices. The sales tax will be collected from 1998 through 2005, with total revenues for the Natural Areas Program projected at $27 million. Fort Collins voters then approved an extension of this tax with the Open Space, Yes! initiative in 2002. The 1/4 cent of the Building Community Choices sales tax dedicated to natural areas, trails, and parks was extended to the year 2030, all revenues going to the Natural Areas Program. The projected revenue from these taxes from 2006 to 2013 is $55 million.

In 1995, voters throughout the county approved the eight-year citizen-initiative sales tax known as Help Preserve Open Space. Voters then approved a 15-year extension of this sales tax on November 2, 1999. Total revenue from 1996 through 2002 was about $50 million—about 59 percent of this total went to six municipalities in the county, and the county received the remaining 41 percent. In retrospect, county staff have realized that since under Colorado law counties have more limited taxing authority than cities do, the county should have assigned a higher percentage of tax revenues to itself, instead of sharing such a high amount with the cities. However, this has been a boon for Fort Collins: the Fort Collins Natural Areas Program received approximately $22 million for the period between 1996 and 2003 from this county-wide tax and is projected to receive $33 million total over the next ten years.

Neither the city nor the county funds acquisitions programs with general revenues. However, the 10 staff members in the city's Natural Resources Department who are not involved in the Natural Areas Program have been entirely funded by gen-

Both Larimer County and Fort Collins contributed funds to purchase over 240 acres for the Cathy Fromme Prairie. The land is managed by Fort Collins and helps to provide a buffer between Fort Collins and Loveland. Photograph by Lesli Ellis.

eral revenues. For the Natural Areas Program, the city's general revenue fund provided for one employee prior to 2004. Starting in 2004, all employees and aspects of the program will be funded entirely by the existing open space sales taxes. The county's Open Lands Program receives no general revenues—all expenses, from acquisitions to heating and janitorial services for the offices, are paid by the sales tax. About 15 to 30 percent of the sales tax revenue is set aside for staff and management of the open space. Outside sources for funding are sought on top of any funds generated within the city and county. For example, both jurisdictions have received grants from Great Outdoors Colorado, which distributes state lottery proceeds to projects that preserve Colorado's wildlife and open spaces. In 2003, the county's Open Lands active grant-writing program was able to obtain $1.5 million in additional funds from outside sources (partnerships, grants, and donations from generous landowners).

The Great Outdoors Colorado Program has been a valuable resource for funding, and has provided $388 million in state lottery proceeds for more than 2,000 projects throughout the state since 1994, helping to protect over 350,000 acres of open space.

Land Dedication/Impact Fees

Both the city and the county have impact fees and code requirements that provide for land to be dedicated by developers. The city has a clustering provision in the Urban Estate District that provides for land dedication, but it is infrequently used. In Fort Collins, a new single-family home pays between $15,000 and $20,000 for city impact fees that are used to cover the costs of new streets, water and sewer lines, water and wastewater treatment plants, storm drainage improvements, parks, police, fire and library facilities, and so forth. The fees are calculated based on the square footage of the house (starting at $866 for up to 700 square feet). None of these fees goes to natural areas, but a significant portion of the fees is used for community parkland. Adequate funding from different pots for both natural areas and recreational parks keeps the two from competing for the same money.

The county has several ways that land can be dedicated by developers—as part of a conservation development or through the Rural Land Use Process. In conservation developments, the developer must reserve (usually by conservation easement) 50 to 80 percent of the land area as private open area in perpetuity. These areas are prohibited from future development and may be used to protect valuable wildlife habitat or natural areas. In the Rural Land Use Process, applicants must reserve at least 67 percent as private open area for at least 40 years. These areas are typically set aside for agricultural use or natural areas. In addition, there are Regional Park Land Dedication/In-Lieu Fee

Standards in the county code. A regional park is defined as providing "recreation opportunities associated with experiencing the natural environment" and is usually more than 250 acres in size. Owing to projected growth in the county, new development must set aside land for regional park expansion or the developer must pay an in-lieu fee that varies from $456 per unit for multifamily housing up to $701 per unit of single-family housing. The county shares open space impact fee revenues with the city.

Management of Lands

The Fort Collins Natural Areas Program manages 7,700 acres of the 9,700 acres in its program. The remainder is managed by partners. The city's primary mission is to manage the natural areas to protect their integrity, while providing educational, interpretive, and recreational opportunities to citizens as a secondary goal. To illustrate, the city adopted a zero-tolerance policy for off-leash dogs—dogs must be on leash at all times—in order to prevent disturbance to wildlife. A key future management issue is that the Natural Resources Advisory Board would like to keep more land off-limits to humans for protection of habitat, while some staff prefer multipurpose uses of open space. A citizen survey of Larimer County residents in 2001 by the Larimer County Open Lands Program showed that Fort Collins residents supported conservation of open lands as follows: with public use (79 percent), with limited public use (68 percent), and with no public use (66 percent). As more land is acquired by the city in the coming 10 years, this issue will become an important one to resolve.

In the county's Open Lands Program, when land is acquired, a management plan specific to the property is developed using a public process that includes both neighbors and future visitors. Easements are monitored annually, and a development plan is generated with the owner.

County lands that are protected during development through dedications and set-asides (what the county calls "residual lands") vary in how they are managed and by whom. Some are managed by Home Owner Associations, some by landowners or others. The planning department does not desire to manage residual land resulting from conservation developments and the Rural Land Use Process, so they modified the programs to minimize county involvement.

Transfer of Development Rights/Purchase of Development Rights Program

Larimer County and Fort Collins cooperated on a small-scale Transfer of Density Units (TDU) Program led by the county as an outgrowth of Larimer County's master planning process initiated in 1994, which identified buffers between communities as a major theme. The Fossil Creek Reservoir area is immediately southeast of Fort Collins. The award-winning TDU Program[3] was developed in 1998 as a tool to implement the joint Larimer County–City of Fort Collins Fossil Creek Reservoir Area Plan and the Plan for the Region between Fort Collins and Loveland.

The program is referred to as a "transfer of density units" program instead of a "transfer of development rights" program (the more commonly used name) because staff felt that the change in terminology helped with public perceptions. The "sending" area is the land area designated as a community separator, and it is located in unincorporated Larimer County where existing zoning allows more density than suggested in the 1995 Plan for the Region Between Fort Collins and Loveland. The "receiving" area is the Fossil Creek area, which is in the unincorporated county, located immediately southeast of the Fort Collins city limits. More density is desired there than existing county zoning allows. The program works like this: If the developer of a receiving area project 80 acres in size proposes 355 residential units (a density desired by the City of Fort Collins, which will ultimately annex the project), the number of TDUs needed in order to proceed would be 210 TDUs, as follows:

- County zoning in the receiving area allows 40 units on 80 acres
- Developer proposes 355 units, or 4.4 units per acre
- 355 minus 40 equals 315 additional units
- The transfer ratio is 1.5 for this program
- 315 divided by 1.5 equals 210 TDUs needed

The receiving area developer would need to acquire 210 TDUs from sending area landowners. The receiving area is annexed to the city following the transfer of density units and the recording of the final plat.

The program is close to completion and is an example of efficient and effective cooperation between the city and county. The program has protected at least 20 acres as part of the new Fossil Creek Reservoir Regional Open Space on the south side of the reservoir, containing important winter habitat for bald eagles, among other wildlife values. Also protected was a quarter-mile natural resource buffer on the north side of Fossil Creek Reservoir and 200 acres near the Fort Collins–Loveland airport.

County staff like this example of a TDU program because the property annexes immediately into a city or town jurisdiction (Fort Collins agreed to annex each lot after recording of the final plat), where the higher density "belongs."

Regulations

Zoning/Subdivision

Both the city and the county have environmental review staff members. There is one dedicated staff person in the city's Natural Resources Department who reviews all development applications for their environmental impact and acts as an in-house expert. The county still has one planning staff member dedicated to development review focused on wetlands and wildlife despite budget cuts in 2004. The county also has one Open Lands Department staff member who reviews all referred developments to assess impacts on adjacent parks and open lands, to determine if the development could provide open space or trail easements, and to determine if any land proposed for preservation is best located to protect or enhance agriculture, natural resources, and recreation.

Both entities have innovative zoning regulations that contribute to habitat protection, either directly or indirectly. Fort Collins has a Public Open Lands District and a River Conservation District. The Public Open Lands District is for large, publicly owned parks and open lands that have a communitywide emphasis, and very few uses are allowed, either by right or by special review. The River Conservation District is designed for the conservation and protection of predominately undeveloped land in the Cache La Poudre River corridor. The main purpose is to accommodate land use functions such as stormwater management, native wildlife habitat, and sand and gravel operations. New streets are prohibited in the natural area protection buffer (which extends 300 feet from the riverbank), and other site design standards ensure protection of natural area values. The city also allows clustering in the Urban Estate District, but it has not been utilized often. The city has several mixed-use districts, which have mandatory minimum densities to encourage more dense, compact development.

Larimer County has three options for rural development: conservation development, the Rural Land Use Process, and traditional subdivisions. All properties greater than 30 acres outside of the county's designated urban areas must comply with the conservation development provision unless (1) the landowner chooses to go through the Rural Land Use Process (discussed below); (2) the land will be divided into lots of 35 acres or more; or (3) the county commissioners grant an exception (e.g., if the site does not have environmentally sensitive areas or agricultural uses). The county's conservation development provision requires clustering and the preservation of 50 to 80 percent of the total developable land area of the site. The county's Conservation Development Process is the only one in the state of Colorado that requires clustering and the set-aside of up to 80 percent of land area in perpetuity.

The county also offers the Rural Land Use Process (RLUP) as a voluntary alternative to traditional 35-acre parcel development, a process over which Larimer County has very little review authority owing to statutory limitations on subdivision review. The RLUP invites landowners to submit to county review in exchange for additional development rights, or "density bonuses" subject to specific criteria. The process relies on a cooperative approach to review with the lure of incentives to encourage development that promotes rural land preservation. The process is voluntary, user-friendly, and flexible. The process may be used in the context of any residential zone district in the county.

The county has limited regulations for agricultural lands or open space and allows one dwelling unit per 2.29 acres in many places throughout the county, and one dwelling unit per 10 acres in some places. The county has two farming districts, two forestry districts, and an "open" district that allows all agricultural uses, single-family residential, and oil and gas development by right. Minimum lot sizes are 2.3 acres for the farming districts, 5–20 acres for the forestry districts, and 10 acres for the open district.

This development utilized Larimer County's innovative Rural Land Use Process, which is a voluntary alternative to traditional 35-acre parcel development. Photograph by Lesli Ellis.

Development Standards

Fort Collins and Larimer County have also both adopted development standards to protect wildlife and habitat.

The Fort Collins Land Use Code was revised in the late 1990s, with continuous updates since then. This revision established standards to ensure the protection of natural habitats and features on, and in the vicinity of, proposed development sites. (See Box 7.1.) Another key aspect of the revision is that almost all development reviews are administered by staff, making the process much more efficient. The standards include the establishment of buffer zones to protect sensitive wildlife species, as well as wetlands, streams, and other important natural habitats. A table summarizes the buffer zone standards, listing such items as "red-tailed and Swainson's hawk nest sites" and their associated buffer zones, in this case, 900 feet with the ability to drop down to 450 feet with mitigation.

With this ambitious revision, the city went from a performance standard system with much negotiation to one that is much more prescriptive to ensure protection. The issue now is that the wildlife regulations are so stringent that they can sometimes make infill development difficult. For example, raptors occasionally nest and feed in old-growth trees in urban areas, making it difficult to develop nearby parcels because of required wildlife setbacks. Although the regulations contain a flexibility provision to help avoid this type of complication, staff find it difficult to use in the current political climate and are considering future code revisions to make the buffers more flexible in infill situations and to help differentiate between values of land (infill versus rural areas).

Environmental review is triggered if city land is involved or if mapped natural features are on the site. Part of the city's process includes an ecological character study if deemed to be required by the environmental review planner during the conceptual review phase. This same staff person acts as an expert for the city, but occasionally obtains comments from the Colorado Division of Wildlife or other experts.

The county land use code also has development standards for wetlands and wildlife. However, these standards are much less prescriptive than the city's. For wildlife habitat, a preliminary staff review determines if the application should be referred to the Colorado Division of Wildlife for review of the criteria. Larger new development must meet a list of review criteria to determine if it will have an adverse impact on wildlife and wildlife habitats. Smaller sites (under 2 acres), smaller buildings (under 10,000 square feet), or sites that staff determine do not need to submit a

BOX 7.1

FORT COLLINS LAND USE CODE, DIVISION 3.4: ENVIRONMENTAL, NATURAL
AREA, RECREATIONAL AND CULTURAL RESOURCE PROTECTION STANDARDS

(B) *Purpose.* The purpose of this Section is to ensure that when property is
developed consistent with its zoning designation, the way in which the proposed physical elements of the development plan are designed and arranged on
the site will protect the natural habitats and features both on the site and in the
vicinity of the site.

(C) *General Standard.* To the maximum extent feasible, the development plan
shall be designed and arranged to be compatible with and to protect natural
habitats and features and the plants and animals that inhabit them and integrate them within the developed landscape of the community by: (1) directing
development away from sensitive resources, (2) minimizing impacts and disturbance through the use of buffer zones, (3) enhancing existing conditions, or
(4) restoring or replacing the resource value lost to the community (either on-
site or off-site) when a development proposal will result in the disturbance of
natural habitats or features.

wildlife conservation plan must comply with general standards, including a minimum
setback of 100 feet from any identified important wildlife habitat and use of native
plant species on-site. The wetlands provision requires buffers of 50 to 100 feet and
contains mitigation requirements (discussed later under "Restoration"). In addition,
the county's adequate public facilities standards have helped to keep development out
of areas that are more suitable for habitat.

Staff noted that the county's wildlife regulations were written to rely on input
from the state Division of Wildlife. Originally that worked well, but the state is not
always able to respond quickly. Additionally, although wildlife habitat and wetlands
were written as two separate sections to keep the topics separate, animals obviously
visit or live in wetlands areas, making the distinction fuzzy. However, the county is
still able to maintain a high level of protection in the conservation developments and
the zone districts inside the Growth Management Area. A strict buffer of 100 feet
from habitat/wetlands is consistently achieved in conservation developments, extending to 300 feet in many cases.

Similar to the city's raptor dilemmas, the biggest issue in conservation developments is eagle activity. There is a lack of good science for application of buffers and setbacks (for eagles as well as other species), and science can be used as a tool for obstruction as well as a tool for preservation.[4] Note that none of these standards applies in the Rural Land Use Process, which relies entirely on the negotiated process to achieve protection.

Stormwater Management and Landscaping

Other regulatory activities include stormwater management and landscaping ordinances. Fort Collins updated its drainage basins master plan for 2002–2004 (and working jointly with Larimer County on many aspects) after a major 1997 flood upped the 100-year flood standard. The city's stormwater staff rated quality of riparian habitat for all streams and require native vegetation be preserved in major stream corridors. Solutions considered for stormwater management include buying land and enhancing habitat. The Parks and Recreation Department is also working to expand riparian areas and increase curves in river channels. The county is not aggressively pursuing innovative stormwater management ideas, but will probably follow the city's lead.

Xeriscape (landscaping that conserves water) is an alternative available in the city's landscaping standards, but must be certified. It is encouraged in the application process, but no incentives to really undertake xeriscaping were included until 2003, when the city adopted tiered water rates because of an ongoing regional drought. The option had rarely been chosen in the past since it takes extra work and must be certified, and nonxeriscape landscaping is allowed. On a positive note, in 2003 an ordinance was passed that preempted homeowner association rules so that homeowners can use xeriscaping even if it is not allowed by their subdivision covenants.

Restoration

The city hired a full-time restoration ecologist in 2002, and the Natural Areas Program is planning to spend about $5.8 million on restoration projects from 2004 through 2008. Projects will include river corridor habitat acquired by the city over the past 10 years that is highly degraded because of gravel mining and agricultural practices. For example, at one time fields were covered with lime by-products of sugar beet processing. There are also many invasive species present.

The city also has tree protection standards with mitigation requirements, and the Environmental, Natural Area, Recreational and Cultural Resource Protection Standards contain mitigation and restoration provisions if development disturbs natural habitats and features in a designated buffer zone.

The county code sections regarding wetlands wildlife discuss restoration as part of a mitigation plan. The Larimer County Weed Control District is active in removing invasive species throughout the county, primarily in the eastern plains portion.

The Larimer County Parks and Open Lands Department restoration efforts are dependent on the resource management plan developed for each property managed by the department. Fossil Creek Reservoir Regional Open Space is the department's first major restoration project. The management goal is to restore 830 acres to short-grass prairie from dryland wheat. The project started in 2001, costs approximately $3,500 per year, and utilizes in-house weed control and seed drilling staff and equipment. The plan also calls for monitoring, but the process and staffing have not been determined yet. Otherwise, to date, several small 1- to 2-acre areas on various open space properties have been restored using hand seeding.

Leading by Example

Overall, the City of Fort Collins appears to follow the same regulations as required by private entities. Most relevant is that environmental review is triggered if city land is involved, so city land must comply with the same environmental standards as private lands. Capital improvement projects flow through the Natural Resources Advisory Board, and they ensure that requirements are met regarding impacts on the environment.

Larimer County requires all of the various county divisions to go through location and extent to ensure compliance with county environment policy and master plan policies. County projects must comply with the same wildlife and wetland standards required of private developers when and if a project goes through site plan review. Departments coordinate their projects as required with the Larimer County Environment Advisory Board (EAB) and with the Agricultural Advisory Board. The EAB, for instance, ensured that the new county office building and the new county justice building are energy-efficient buildings.

Social Indicators

Fort Collins has a laudable affordable housing program and may consider inclusionary zoning in the future. Current affordable housing incentives include priority processing, waived application fees, delayed impact fees, and sales and use tax rebates on materials used for construction. The city exceeded or met its goals for affordable housing in 1999–2002. It set out to assist in the production and preservation of 1,357 affordable housing units from 1999 to 2002 and assisted with 1,491 units. There was an overbuilt affordable housing environment in 2003, with vacancies available for residents with incomes below 40 percent AMI (area mean income), although this situation was only expected to last 12–18 months. Generally, the city does not have enough housing for low-income citizens but does not have the resources to provide all of the housing needed and instead utilizes programs that support builders in their efforts to obtain other funding for affordable housing projects. Most affordable housing in the city is provided by nonprofit housing developers. The city has about $2.5 million annually to invest in new affordable housing units (about 55 percent from federal programs and 45 percent from the city). Although housing costs are increasing faster than income, compared with other communities Fort Collins is making progress, partially since "fairness" has been identified as a community value in the planning process.

The picture in Larimer County is not as encouraging. Affordable rental housing is defined as that which costs no more than 30 percent of a household's gross monthly income for rent and utilities. According to the 2000 census, 42 percent of Larimer County renters were paying 30 percent or more of their household income for rent, a significant percentage. However, the county has chosen to be a rural-type area providing rural levels of service instead of urban levels of service. In keeping with this intent, the county does not approve upzonings to higher density in the unincorporated county, except where such higher density is planned in the Growth Management Areas (which are expected to be annexed) or in the LaPorte community. Outside of these areas, the policy per the master plan is to not upzone but to stay with the current zoning, which is generally no more dense than one dwelling unit per 2.29 acres. This low, rural-type density is not conducive to affordable housing because of the cost of the larger lots. Also, affordable housing should generally be located where it is close to urban levels of service, pointing to the municipalities as the logical places for affordable housing instead of in the unincorporated county.

In addition to its affordable housing efforts, Fort Collins does not charge fees for any of its natural areas nor for any interpretive or educational programs sponsored by the Natural Areas Program. The city has protected land along the river that flows through the city, making several city parks (improved recreational parks as well as unimproved natural areas) available for free access to the river for all citizens. In addition, its new plan for acquisition of natural areas calls for obtaining lands that are close to schools and neighborhoods to provide even more access for the general public.

Fort Collins also has some infill incentives in its development standards, Division 3.7 Compact Urban Growth Standards. These standards require that development occur within the urban growth area and adjacent to existing urban areas and provides an exemption from development application requirements for infill areas. However, there are still occasional roadblocks regarding regulations imposed by the utilities and public works departments.

The county code does not mention infill incentives, but the TDU Program promotes more compact development.

Education

The Fort Collins Natural Areas Program has an educational arm since one of the management goals for the natural areas is to provide educational and interpretive opportunities for citizens. Two educators are on staff (one full-time and one part-time), and they operate a Master Naturalist Program, consisting of about 85 volunteer naturalists who speak to local groups and take people on guided tours of the natural areas. These volunteers are trained and certified in ecology, including the plants and animals found in the natural areas, and donate about 1,300 hours each year. Approximately 33,800 people attended education programs from 1994 (program inception) to 2003; about 70 percent of these programs were field programs in the natural areas, and 30 percent were community events or classroom presentations. Many school programs (primarily walks and field trips to natural areas) are provided throughout the Poudre School District, which includes the city of Fort Collins in addition to several communities outside of the city limits. Educational material is provided that fits into required school curriculums and standards. Staff train teachers who are not familiar with field trips and provide a number of free bus field trips to natural areas. This outreach program is active year-round: during the summer volunteers work with day care and day camp programs. Staff also prepare interpretive signs for the natural areas, which are often interactive, providing a chance for the visitor to feel the fur of a local mammal, or smell the scent of sagebrush. A variety of printed materials is produced, including a list of native plants and where to get them locally. The entire budget for educational activities and staff comes from the sales tax.

The Larimer County Parks and Open Lands Department also has an active educational component and employs one full-time education coordinator. The department sponsors a variety of hikes, public tours, and education sessions each year with the help of about 40 volunteer naturalists. Approximately 700 people (children and

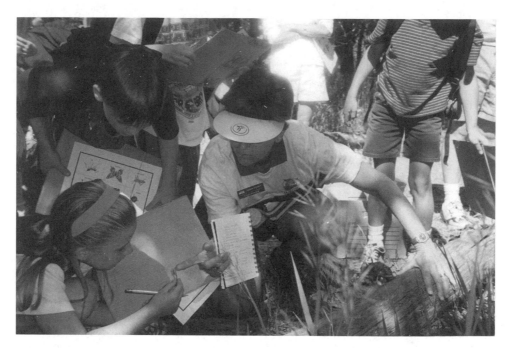

A goal of the Fort Collins Natural Areas Program is to provide educational and interpretive opportunities for residents young and old. Photograph by Sue Kenney.

adults) participated in Open Lands educational programs in 2003. Staff also work with a local school district to provide customized hikes for fourth-grade curriculums.

Results

Fort Collins has undertaken occasional monitoring projects. "Trends" is a report from the Advance Planning Department regarding economic and social data divided into four sections: business, labor and income, development trends, and demographics. Surprisingly, no environmental data (including habitat) have been included. However, the Natural Resources Division began producing an annual report in 2004 and intends to conduct six-month updates. As indicated in the initial annual report, the city has protected 11,472 acres of natural areas and open space as of the end of 2003. Of this total, 37 percent are local areas, 29 percent are regional, and 34 percent are community separator acres. Also promising is the City Plan Monitoring Project, begun by the city in 2001 to report on progress made toward achieving the goals of City Plan. The intent is to evaluate indicators every two years. Because of an update of the City Plan, the 2003 report was skipped—the indicators will be revised as part of this update and reporting should resume in 2005. The 2001 report contained indicators for population growth, land use (e.g., housing density, infill development), housing (including affordability), transportation, employment, and environment. The two environment indicators were air quality and open lands management. The latter tracks how much natural habitat or rural/open lands have been protected. As of 2001, the city had protected about 55 percent of the areas identified as natural habitat or features on the city's Natural Habitats and Features Inventory map (which is also used to identify items that require buffer zones). The 2001 report also indicated that about 46 percent of the areas designated as rural/open lands on the city's Structure Plan had been publicly protected from development.

The county has also begun to address the topic of evaluating and monitoring progress. Staff developed indicators and tracked them for 12 principles in the master plan in five major elements: growth management, land use, public facilities and services, transportation, and environmental resources and hazards. Examples include acres of intergovernmental agreement planning areas as an indicator of cooperative planning with municipalities and total acres of residual open lands as an indicator of rural development character. A public process determined which criteria would be used for each topic. The two "environmental resources and hazards" indicators are most relevant for biodiversity: (1) number of protected wetlands in new developments and (2) number of acres of protected important wildlife habitat in new developments as an indicator of wildlife habitat protection. The wetlands indicator data are not clearly presented and need refinement. Information is presented as "number of lots adjacent to wetlands" that have been protected by a buffer in new developments. Total acres protected are not listed, and one "buffer" was listed as "zero feet." Additionally, as acknowledged in the "Larimer County Master Plan Monitoring and Evaluation Report for the Year 2002," data are missing regarding the health of the wetlands—for those currently not affected by development, as well as those supposedly protected by the wetland buffer regulations. Field monitoring has been suggested but has not yet been implemented. The wildlife indicator was disappointing as well. None of the land divisions recorded in 2000–2002 protected important wildlife habitat as mapped by the Colorado Division of Wildlife. Another indicator tracks the amount of land protected through the Rural Land Use Process mentioned previously, which was about 5,560 acres of open space through the end of 2002. This is not broken down into habitat versus agricultural lands, although agricultural land is the primary type of land protected with this tool. Staff commented that it would have been easier to include benchmarks when the master plan was originally created. The plan goals were not written to be easily quantified, and it is difficult to determine what is

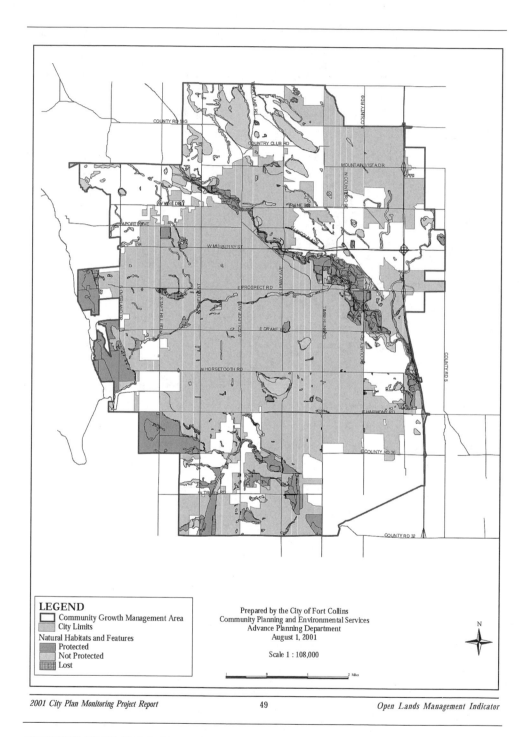

LEGEND
- ☐ Community Growth Management Area
- ▨ City Limits

Natural Habitats and Features
- ■ Protected
- ▨ Not Protected
- ▦ Lost

Prepared by the City of Fort Collins
Community Planning and Environmental Services
Advance Planning Department
August 1, 2001

Scale 1 : 108,000

N

PROTECTION STATUS OF NATURAL HABITATS AND FEATURES
The protection status of natural habitats and features was evaluated as part of Fort Collins's City Plan Monitoring Project. Map courtesy of the City of Fort Collins.

successful. However, even with these drawbacks, this effort is commendable, since most jurisdictions have no system in place to attempt this type of evaluation.

In summary, Fort Collins and Larimer County have accomplished much in the way of nature protection, using a variety of innovative tools, with solid funding, resulting in the following:

- The Fort Collins Natural Areas Program protected approximately 26,000 acres of habitat between 1992 and 2004, with tens of thousands of acres more slated to be to be preserved by 2020.

- By the end of 2003, the Larimer County Open Lands Program had acquired a total of 16,400 acres of open lands.

- The county's Rural Land Use Process had protected over 6,500 acres as of the end of 2003.

- Both the city and the county have wildlife regulations in place that are actually used on the ground.

Notes

[1]Primary sources for this case study include Russell Legg, chief planner, and K-Lynne Cameron, open lands manager, with Larimer County; Mark Sears, program manager, Natural Areas Program, and Ted Shepard, chief planner, Current Planning, with the City of Fort Collins; numerous other staff members with both the city and county; the Larimer County website, www.co.larimer.co.us; and the Fort Collins website, www.ci.fort-collins.co.us.

[2]Under "home rule" in Colorado, local governments have broad authority to adopt growth management regulations.

[3]There are two main components to the TDU program, a sending area where TDUs are transferred from, and a receiving area where TDUs are sent to. Development projects in the receiving area create the demand for TDU transfers from parcels in the sending area. Prior to receiving final approval, receiving area projects must show evidence of acquired development rights in the form of TDUs. The number of TDUs that must be acquired is determined by subtracting the number of residential units allowed by county zoning from the total number of residential units proposed. This number is then divided by the "transfer ratio" of 1.5.

[4]See report, *Conservation Thresholds for Land-Use Planners* (Washington, D.C.: Environmental Law Institute, 2003).

CHAPTER 8

Pima County, Arizona: Planning for and Investing in Habitat Protection

Pima County, Arizona, has pushed the envelope with its innovative Sonoran Desert Conservation Plan, which features protection of biodiversity at a landscape scale. The county has had the right combination of political will, public support, solid science, and state and federal pressure to move ahead relatively quickly on planning for biodiversity protection. The county has begun to implement some plan concepts (and has several other nature-friendly programs already in place). A successful bond election in May 2004 gave implementation a substantial boost, allotting $112 million specifically for acquisition of habitat identified by the plan, as well as significant funds for additional projects that will protect other habitat (e.g., community open space and floodprone land acquisition). As the county's Map of Priority Biological Resources states, "Protection of biological resources is considered an essential component of land use planning."

The classic image of the sun setting on desert mountains in the distance with a large saguaro cactus in the foreground is something citizens of Pima County see every day.[1] The days are sunny about 350 days of the year, and the desert ecosystem is evident everywhere; this is not a land where Kentucky bluegrass abounds. Quail and javelina visit suburban backyards.

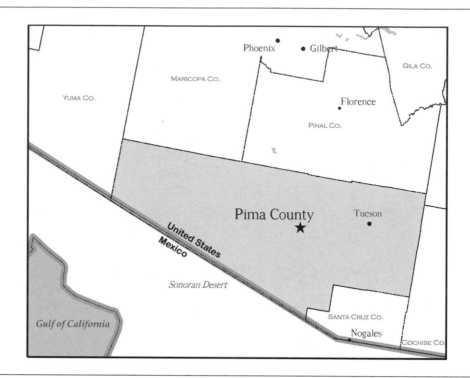

PIMA COUNTY, ARIZONA
Map courtesy of Clarion Associates.

The setting is beautiful—rugged mountain ranges (known as the Sky Islands) alternate with scenic valleys, and Sonoran Desert features such as the trademark saguaro cactus and the cholla cactus abound in the lower elevations near Tucson. Various desert ecosystems occur throughout the county, including desert shrublands and grasslands, while the higher altitudes encourage other ecosystems, such as coniferous forests. The Sonoran Desert is home to more than 2,500 known pollinator species and 500 migrating or resident bird species (almost two-thirds of the bird species in North America). Riparian areas are the lifeblood of the region, but few streams run year-round. The riverbed winding through downtown Tucson is mostly dry; one of the few perennial streams in the county was preserved in the 1980s owing to the scarcity of riparian habitat. Riparian ecosystems include cottonwood forests, mesquite woodlands (also known as bosques), and saltbush scrub. The first two plant communities are the first and second most threatened forest types in North America, respectively. Nearly all washes in the area are unimpaired by dams.

A typical Sonoran desert setting is found in Ironwood Forest National Monument, which was set aside as a result of Pima County's habitat protection planning efforts. Photograph by Chris Tincher, courtesy of the Bureau of Land Management.

Pima County covers 9,184 square miles (about 6 million acres) in south-central Arizona and contains the city of Tucson, as well as several smaller municipalities, such as the towns of Marana and Oro Valley to the north of Tucson and Green Valley to the south. The western half of the county is the Tohono O'Odham Nation. The population of the county is about 840,000, of which approximately 300,000 reside in the unincorporated areas. Tucson is the urban center, with a population of about 480,000 (more than half of the county's population) and is the second largest city in Arizona. The other towns in the county contain fewer than 30,000 residents each. The county has faced tremendous growth (as has the entire state of Arizona) since the 1950s. County population grew from 140,000 in 1950 to about 845,000 in 2000, according to the 2000 census. The population increase from 1990 to 2000 was 174,000 residents (an increase of 27 percent). About 20,000 people move to the county each year. Desert land is being consumed by development at about 7 to 10 square miles per year.

The county is a growing mix of transient job-seekers, retirees, residents with very long cultural ties to the area, and many citizens who are attuned to nature simply because the landscape is part of day-to-day reality—nature preserves have existed in the county, even immediately next to the Tucson city center, since the early 1900s. Because of the scarcity of surface water in this area, the urban areas did not replace native vegetation with turf as readily as Phoenix did, resulting in plentiful native vegetation reminding every citizen daily that they live in a desert. Water is extremely precious here, with only 12 inches of rainfall per year at the lower elevations. The communities obtain water from groundwater pumping and also from the Central Arizona Project (a large canal carrying water from the Colorado River basin to Arizona, built by the federal government because Arizona was overpumping its groundwater).

Although Pima County's urban areas do not have large expanses of bluegrass lawns, development has still increased water usage. Groundwater available to river ecosystems has decreased by about 95 percent in the Santa Cruz River basin owing to groundwater pumping (about 20 percent of this water has gone to golf courses), leaving many of the riparian areas dry more often than in the past. The three primary waterways in the Tucson area (the Santa Cruz River, Rillito Creek, and Pantano Wash) no longer run year-round.

Most of the land in the county is publicly owned. The federal government has been active in preserving land in Pima County since at least the early 1900s. Today, almost 30 percent of the county is federal land, including the Ironwood Forest National Monument (designated in 2000), Saguaro National Park, Organ Pipe Cactus National Monument, a national wildlife refuge, and Forest Service and BLM lands. Three tribes account for ownership of about 40 percent of county land, the majority held by the Tohono O'Odham Nation in the western half of the county. State lands comprise about 15 percent of the county, but much of this acreage is available for development. Discussions in 2004–2005 may result in some state lands being preserved instead of developed; it is unclear how much of the county's state lands would be affected.

The federal government and others started setting aside land in Pima County in 1902–1903, when national forest land and a university research area were established, thus beginning a long history of federal involvement in land preservation in the county. County involvement in preservation of land started in 1929, when the county helped to preserve part of the Sonoran Desert west of Tucson as Tucson Mountain Park. This popular 20,000-acre park provides the backdrop for Tucson's magnificent sunsets and is now surrounded by suburbia. The county then did not do much land preservation until the 1980s. Until the 1980s, interest in open space was more general—specific habitats or species were not really considered. Until the "bunny map." This map, affectionately and sometimes disparagingly known as the "bunny map" since it had a rabbit image in one corner, was put together in 1986 by the University of Arizona School of Renewable Natural Resources at the county's request and immediately spurred interest in the community. Although locations of specific animals, plants, and ecosystems were crudely located, the power of even a rudimentary map became apparent. This was the first map of biological resources in Pima County. The City of Tucson became one of the first jurisdictions in the country to zone for wildlife and natural vegetation, using the "bunny map" as a guide to protect dry creek beds (washes) throughout the city.

Pima County has gone through spurts of natural resource protection efforts. The county implemented several ordinances relating to natural resources in the 1980s and 1990s in response to various discrete concerns (hillsides, buffers for already-protected lands, and native plant preservation). In addition, two bond elections in 1986 and 1997 contributed about $18 million and $28 million, respectively, to open space acquisitions. The Natural Resources, Parks, and Recreation Department and the Flood Control District both acquire and restore habitat as part of their activities.

However, the primary nature-friendly program in Pima County is the Sonoran Desert Conservation Plan (SDCP). The plan was developed in the late 1990s and covers several million acres. It represents an innovative approach to urban planning, by looking beyond the species or park level to look at protection of ecosystems instead.

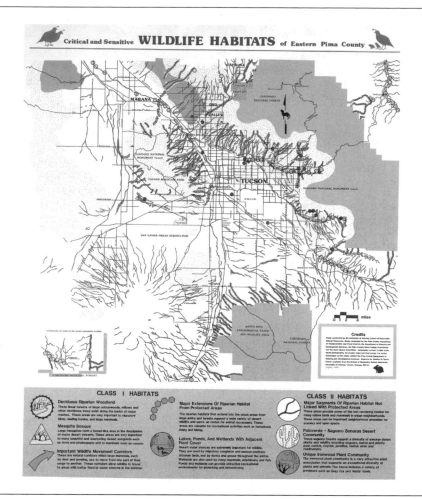

CRITICAL AND SENSITIVE WILDLIFE HABITATS OF EASTERN PIMA COUNTY
The so-called bunny map was the first map of biological resources in Pima County. Map courtesy of the Pima County Flood Control District.

It was a combination of several events in the late 1990s that led to the very progressive SDCP: (1) the listing of the cactus ferruginous pygmy-owl in 1997 as endangered by the federal government under the federal Endangered Species Act (ESA); (2) a state mandate to create or revise comprehensive plans by December 31, 2001; and (3) a board of supervisors with the political will to make it happen. As one environmental advocate stated, not every community has the hammer of the ESA, and not every community has the luck and timing to have elected officials who have the political will to make something like the SDCP happen. And not every community has the strong civic organizations in the natural history arena as well as the active neighborhood groups that Pima County has.

County residents support the SDCP and passed a $174 million open space and habitat protection bond package in May 2004 (with 65.7 percent in favor) that will partially fund the implementation of the SDCP. Another bond package for river parks and flood control improvements was also passed (by 59.2 percent) in May 2004, providing $5 million for a floodprone and riparian land acquisition program and another $28.7 million for several river park projects, several of which will involve ecosystem restoration or riparian habitat protection.

Key Program Elements

Program Structure and Administration

Three departments under Public Works are key players: the Development Services Center; the Flood Control District; and Natural Resources, Parks, and Recreation. There is one natural resources staff member in Development Services—an environmental review planner with a master's degree in natural resource public policy who worked previously as a habitat specialist. Staff numbers may be increased if the workload expands as implementation of the SDCP proceeds and if the federally required Habitat Conservation Plan is approved soon. The department also employs roughly 16 planners. The Pima County Flood Control District was formed as a result of Arizona State legislation passed in 1978 in response to a disastrous flood on the Salt River in the Phoenix area. The district has 43 full-time equivalent (FTE) employees. The Flood Control District established a new division in 2001, the Water Resources Division, with approximately 14 employees consisting of geologists, hydrologists, watershed management staff, 1 rangeland specialist, and 2 environmental resource planners. Its responsibilities include riparian habitat protection, floodprone land acquisition, water resources management, and environmental restoration functions. The Natural Resources, Parks, and Recreation Department has a large staff of about 150 FTEs and 200–300 seasonal employees, but none of these are biologists—yet. The department hopes to add a biologist and four FTE for specialized maintenance in sensitive areas. The total parks budget is about $10 million per year.

The county administrator also continues to play an important role. From plan inception to the current implementation phase, the county administrator, Chuck Huckleberry, and his staff have championed the Sonoran Desert Conservation Plan in the community as well as internally.

Cooperation is extensive throughout the county among the county, federal and state agencies, tribes, municipalities, and private groups. For example, several county departments are among many partners working to protect the Cienega Corridor (an area southeast of Tucson critical for linking several other protected sites to provide wildlife migration routes and protect archaeological sites). Several of the cities (including Tucson) and the county have agreed to share data for the Habitat Conservation Plan process for each.

There are some turf issues between the City of Tucson and the county. One source of friction is that two critical infrastructure services were split between the two—water service is provided by Tucson, and sewer is provided by Pima County. Although cooperation between city and county could be improved, staff members continue to work together on many projects such as parks issues, restoration projects, and the Houghton Area Master Plan. Tucson has been working on infill and design issues, which meshes well with the county's work on conservation to maintain overall quality of life for urban and suburban residents.

The county and other entities are part of the Pima Association of Governments, which is looking at a regional transportation plan—this organization has no regulatory teeth, but its efforts are promising.

Planning

The county attempted to pass a comprehensive plan several times over the years without success, owing to strong property rights sentiments. In 1992, a comprehensive plan was finally adopted. The 1997 federal listing of the cactus ferruginous pygmy-owl as endangered prompted the county to start looking more closely at habitat protection. Pima County's response to this listing became the Sonoran Desert Conservation Plan (SDCP). The State of Arizona then adopted Growing Smarter Plus in 2000, which required counties and municipalities to update comprehensive plans by the end of 2001 to include elements of land use, water resources, open space, environmental impacts, growth areas, and cost of growth. Pima County was able to incorporate many elements from the SDCP as part of their state-required comprehensive plan update in 2001.

Sonoran Desert Conservation Plan

The Sonoran Desert Conservation Plan (SDCP) is one of the nation's premier nature-friendly programs. It has won regional, national, and international awards. The plan covers 5.9 million acres; 850,000 human residents; about 25 threatened and endan-

The listing of the cactus ferruginous pygmy-owl as endangered by the federal government in 1997 was one factor leading to extensive habitat protection planning by Pima County. Photograph by Glenn Proudfoot, courtesy of the U.S. Fish and Wildlife Service.

gered plants and animals; and an even longer list (approximately 55 species) of what are called "priority vulnerable species"—a list of species used as a proxy for the biodiversity of Pima County. The plan includes five elements: Critical Habitat and Biological Corridors; Riparian Restoration; Mountain Parks; Historical and Cultural Preservation; and Ranch Conservation. The most impressive aspect of this plan is that it considers biodiversity protection at an ecosystem level, rather than simply at a species level, using a park or species approach. Although the concept is complicated, the basic notion is to protect ecosystems holistically—that is, protect land that has intact habitat and will serve as home to as wide a variety of native species (plants and animals) as possible, thereby avoiding listings of species in the future—by protecting the whole landscape and its process. If only a few species were to be considered, there is the potential for other species to become endangered if they do not share the same habitat as previously listed species. If the landscape and fundamental ecosystem processes such as fire and flooding are protected, the scientific data gathered for the SDCP assume that critical species are thus protected, and less comprehensive habitat can be developed without endangering other species later on.

The SDCP is the overarching program. It is an entity distinct from the county's comprehensive plan and the county's Habitat Conservation Plan (HCP) required by the Endangered Species Act. However, key concepts from the SDCP were incorporated into the county's revised comprehensive plan that was adopted in 2001. The SDCP data are also forming the underpinnings for the HCP process of obtaining a Section 10 permit that will allow some development to proceed under the ESA. A draft HCP—known as the Multi-Species Conservation Plan (MSCP)—was released in early 2004, and the U.S. Fish and Wildlife Service will review it and make a final decision on approval in 2005.

The SDCP is an excellent model for a number of other reasons:

- The process was open to the public.
- The scientific data created are excellent and defensible.
- The county kept scientists insulated from political processes, allowing the science to proceed on merit alone, and the science was peer reviewed.
- The county brought stakeholders to the table in the spirit of enlightened self-interest, keeping the focus on overall approach and how to use it to improve the community.
- The county prevented the process from becoming an "us versus them" relationship with the U.S. Fish and Wildlife Service.

Since the start of the SDCP process in 1998, over 205 reports have been prepared. Pima County has been fortunate to have a highly educated and highly involved citizenry to draw from who could act as intermediaries, speaking both the language of land use and the language of habitat conservation. There are also strong neighborhood and civic institutions here despite the somewhat transient population.

Citizen interest has been very high. When the county asked for volunteers for a steering committee, over 80 people showed up. Assuming that natural attrition would decrease that number to a more reasonable level, the county decided to let all interested parties participate. Only a handful dropped out over the four-year course of meetings.

Developers are concerned about the impact the SDCP and other nature-friendly programs may have on land availability and land prices. Already there is some concern about housing affordability diminishing. However, county staff point out that water is currently the most restrictive factor here. About 200,000 developable acres are in the Conservation Land System (CLS), a system that designates habitat to be protected in the county. About 285,000 acres are outside of the CLS, which means that 485,000 acres are available to develop. Current water supplies can serve only about 265,000 acres of development at current rates of density. The issue of how to balance the right to develop property with the right of citizens to direct growth thus becomes complicated by water scarcity. In this region, they do not just need environmental protection for its "feel-good" aspects, they need it for health and water. Yet even as Pima County gets its act together, the county to the north is allowing development right up to Pima's doorstep.

The draft federal MSCP says that from 7,000 to 28,000 acres should be protected in the next 10 years, and 34,000 to 139,000 acres in the next 20 years, to compensate for the environmentally sensitive land that would likely be developed in that time frame.

Mapping

One of the first comprehensive habitat maps of Pima County was produced in 1986 by the University of Arizona School of Renewable Natural Resources as part of a study conducted for the county. The Critical and Sensitive Wildlife Habitats Map became known as the "bunny map" and is still acknowledged as a landmark. It showed eight habitat types and associated wildlife. Another earlier map was created in 1992 by the county Department of Transportation and Flood Control District. The Flood Control District developed a definition and classification system of riparian habitat within the county that was later used for drafting of the district's riparian protection provisions, discussed under "Regulations." The classification system included vegetation types/species, densities, and water availability. The Arizona Game and Fish Department also completed a Wildlife Habitat Inventory Pilot Study, which was applied to eastern Pima County lands in 1996 using the geographical information system for mapping wildlife habitat values.

A multitude of maps have been produced as part of the SDCP. The primary one is the Priority Biological Resources Map, which includes the urban development guidelines adopted in the 2001 comprehensive plan update and explains the Conservation Lands System for the county. The map delineates the locations of several types of areas: important riparian; biological core; scientific research; multiple use; recovery; agriculture within recovery; and existing development. The two most critical areas are the important riparian areas and the biological core areas. Important riparian areas are described as "extremely important elements . . . and every effort should be made to protect, restore and enhance the structure and functions of these areas, including hydrological, geomorphic and biological functions." The biological core areas are "areas of very high biological importance distinguished by high potential habitat for five or more priority vulnerable species, special elements (e.g., caves, perennial streams, cottonwood-willow forests), and other unique biological features." The urban development guidelines, discussed under "Regulations," describe how much of the existing natural resources in each area should be protected if more intense land uses are proposed.

The draft Multi-Species Conservation Plan released in early 2004 contained a Map of Habitat Protection Priorities in Eastern Pima County, which consists of

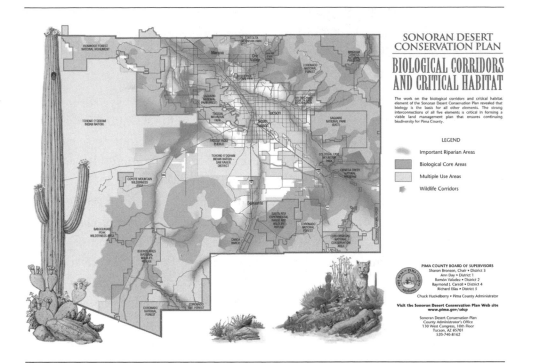

BIOLOGICAL CORRIDORS AND CRITICAL HABITAT, SONORAN DESERT CONSERVATION PLAN
This vision map of biological corridors and critical habitat was one of many maps produced early in the Sonoran Desert Conservation Plan process and provided a solid basis for the final Priority Biological Resources map currently used in the county. Map courtesy of Pima County Graphic Services.

criteria developed by The Nature Conservancy and the Arizona Open Land Trust applied to the county's previously identified Conservation Lands System. This map identifies about 525,000 acres for conservation in the county, which is about 26 percent of the Conservation Land System.

Acquisition and Funding

Pima County has acquired several large tracts of land over the years as part of its regional parks system. Funding for regional parks has come from several sources, but primarily bonds. A modest amount of general funds is dedicated each year for acquisitions (maybe $1–$2 million). Current parkland holdings are about 45,000 acres, including 4,600 acres newly acquired at the Canoa Ranch, which is undergoing restoration and is not available for public access as of 2004. The largest of these parklands are known as the "mountain parks" (there are currently three—Tucson, Tortolita, and Colossal Cave) and the natural preserves (currently one—Cienega Creek, purchased by the Flood Control District and jointly managed with the parks department). County involvement in preservation of land started in 1929, when part of the Sonoran Desert west of Tucson was preserved as Tucson Mountain Park. It was created along with the Pima County Parks Commission after a county agricultural agent and a U.S. senator convinced Congress to set aside thousands of acres of desert for protection, instead of allowing it to be homesteaded. Although the county did not have to spend money to acquire this area, this popular 20,000-acre park provides the backdrop for Tucson's magnificent sunsets and is still the largest of the mountain parks now managed by the county. Over 1,000 acres could be added to this park using funds for community open space approved in the May 2004 bond election.

The county board of supervisors has created a supportive environment for parks acquisition since the mid-1980s, when land acquisition by the county started in earnest. Tortolita Mountain Park is Pima County's second mountain park and was acquired in 1986. It is presently 3,500 acres in size, but could eventually exceed Tucson Mountain Park in total acreage as the Sonoran Desert Conservation Plan is implemented. The successful May 2004 bond package proposes over 9,000 acres could be conserved in the near future. The 4,000-acre Cienega Creek Natural Preserve was Pima County's first natural preserve, and its groundbreaking creation in 1986 set the stage for the ambitious efforts of the SDCP. It contains very rare Sonoran Desert riparian habitat. In 1987 the county worked with the Bureau of Land Management to purchase the Empire/Cienega Ranch in order to prevent development, and the board of supervisors increased the Flood Control District tax levy in anticipation of ranch acquisition. The ranch is now part of a federal conservation area, and the land area preserved is larger than that within the borders of Tucson. This ranch acquisition and preservation was one of the first major efforts of the county to halt urban sprawl. At 2,038 acres, Colossal Cave is Pima County's smallest existing mountain park, but it too has the potential to grow considerably to meet the region's conservation goals in the Rincon Valley area. It was acquired in 1992.

The Flood Control District is also active in acquisition of important habitat and owns 11,000 acres. Flood control districts were set up as special taxing districts under state enabling legislation, and this district receives over $13 million per year from its annual flood control tax. It also uses bond monies in conjunction with state and federal funding sources to build flood control facilities and to acquire floodprone land.

The district has purchased over 7,000 acres of floodprone land since 1984, primarily through its Floodprone Land Acquisition Program. Land acquisition was initially a means of removing buildings and residents from potential flood hazards. However, increasingly, the district is using this approach to preserve natural floodplain characteristics in upstream areas and to discourage development from taking place in vulnerable locations. One of the district's major purchases was nearly 4,000 acres of land located along Cienega Creek. The purchase of Cienega Creek Preserve provides significant flood control benefits, but also accomplishes important riparian habitat preservation and open space objectives. The preserve was acquired using flood district fees, but is now jointly managed by the district and the parks department.

A handful of communities in Arizona use sales taxes to fund acquisitions, but to do so requires a unanimous vote of the board of supervisors, which has yet to happen in Pima County. Bonds are therefore the primary source of funding. Two bond elections in 1986 and 1997 contributed about $18 million and $28 million, respectively, to open space acquisitions. Parts of Tortolita and Colossal Cave mountain parks were obtained with 1986 bond funds. Over 6,000 acres of open space and habitat have been acquired using the 1997 bond funds. The chief acquisition was the Canoa Ranch—a historic ranch on about 4,600 acres containing important riparian areas.

The county's most ambitious bond election yet for open space and habitat protection was held in May 2004, and it passed by a 65.7 percent majority. It includes funding for acquisitions of open space and habitat totaling close to $184 million. Included in this total are items that are not considered to be priority habitat but which contain habitat nonetheless. Specifically earmarked is $112 million to acquire a staggering 600,000 acres of the SDCP's habitat priorities. Another $37.3 million will be used to acquire "community open space"—these are not priority habitat areas but are adjacent to currently protected areas or have recreational, scenic, or cultural values. Another $10 million is designated for open space around Davis-Monthan Air Force Base (to prevent encroachment), and $15 million is marked for urban open space requested by various jurisdictions (small pockets of habitat or land adjacent to already protected areas). About $5 million of the $76 million approved in a separate bond for parks will acquire and restore habitat; the rest is for recreational facilities. Another $5 million is allocated for the Flood Control District to use for floodprone and riparian land acquisition. Not included in this total are several million dollars that will be used for habitat acquisition and restoration projects at river parks throughout the county; these costs are mixed in with flood control, parking lot, and

Cienega Creek Preserve protects important riparian habitat. Photograph by Cara Snyder.

trail construction costs. Several acquisitions occurred very quickly in 2004 after the bond issue passed in May. Approximately 700 acres of community open space were acquired at the Sweetwater Nature Preserve, the largest remaining parcel of privately held land in the Tucson Mountains. Additionally, 6,800 acres of the A-7 Ranch were purchased from the City of Tucson, containing about 1,300 acres of high-priority habitat, including globally rare cottonwood-willow forest that is habitat for the yellow-billed cuckoo, proposed for listing as threatened or endangered by the U.S. Fish and Wildlife Service.

Regulations

Pima County has had several ordinances relating to natural resources; staff are reevaluating and combining these with the intention of eventually strengthening them to help implement the SDCP. These ordinances include the Hillside Development Overlay Zone, the Buffer Overlay Zone, and the Native Plant Preservation Ordinance. Separately, the Flood Control District oversees a riparian area ordinance. In addition, some revisions were made to the development process to implement portions of the SDCP that were adopted in the 2001 comprehensive plan update.

The Hillside Development Overlay Zone was adopted in 1985 to conserve natural resources on hillsides and to regulate the density and reduce the physical impact of hillside development. Protected peaks and ridges are addressed. The Buffer Overlay Zone was adopted in 1988 with much public involvement and applies to development within one mile of a designated public preserve to provide aesthetic and resource buffering. The Native Plant Preservation Ordinance, adopted in 1998, contains provisions for the preservation in place, transplanting on-site, and mitigation of plants and plant communities native to Pima County. New development triggers this regulation if the grading area exceeds 14,000 square feet or if a development plan is submitted for a subdivision plat. Preservation requirements outlined in the ordinance apply to all riparian areas regulated by the Flood Control District's Riparian Protection Ordinance. If riparian areas are impacted, then mitigation must be consistent with the Riparian Protection Ordinance's mitigation standards.

In 1994, the board of supervisors adopted the Water Course and Riparian Habitat Protection and Mitigation Requirement Ordinance as part of the Flood Plain Management Ordinance under the authority of the Flood Control District. The ordinance was also linked to the zoning code by offering flexible development standards in exchange for protecting habitat. The ordinance does not prohibit development, but encourages habitat preservation by providing incentives to avoid damaging habitat. Initially the ordinance applied only to properties that went through the rezoning or subdivision process, but now it applies to all properties in unincorporated Pima County, including single-family residences. Any disturbance to higher-value habitat requires mitigation, while lower-value habitat requires mitigation only if over one-third acre of habitat is disturbed. The goal of the mitigation requirements has been to replace the vegetation volume of the habitat that has been disturbed within five years. Staff are considering lowering the mitigation triggers in 2004 in environmentally sensitive areas.

Until comprehensive land use plan revisions were adopted in 2001, the county had no standard requirements for habitat preservation on development sites. The Conservation Lands System (CLS) was adopted as part of the land use plan and came directly from work on the SDCP. The system kicks in when property is rezoned and sets conservation goals ("Urban Development Guidelines") for certain high-resource areas as follows:

- Areas that provide high potential habitat for *five* or more priority vulnerable species must set aside 95 percent of their existing natural resources. Currently, only the important riparian areas identified on the SDCP Map of Priority Biological Resources qualify for this requirement.

- Areas that provide high potential habitat for *three* or more priority vulnerable species must set aside 80 percent of their existing natural resources. Currently, only the biological core management areas identified on the Priority Biological Resources Map qualify for this requirement.

- The scientific research, multiple use, recovery, and agriculture within recovery management areas must set aside between 75 and 60 percent of their biological resources.

- Existing developments within the CLS should retain 60 percent of their existing biological resources.

- Urbanizing areas, which are generally not found within the CLS, should retain if possible 30 percent of existing biological resources.

The Development Services Department uses various tools, including site analysis, to meet these conservation goals. The concept of the Conservation Land System has been in place since 2001 but how it has been interpreted and implemented has been changing. Initially there were only rudimentary guidelines, but now the Biological Impact Report requirements are spelled out more—it is still a simple overview, and very easy for landowners to do using a county website. This provision may evolve as the Habitat Conservation Plan moves forward.

Development will continue to impact the lands included in the CLS and is projected to amount to 7,000 acres during the first 20 years; 34,000 acres during the second 10 years; and 110,000 acres at buildout. These losses will be mitigated by purchase of lands identified as Habitat Protection Priorities, and monies from the May 2004 bond election will help to fund this effort, as discussed previously.

The site analysis ordinance was adopted about 20 years ago and was considered avant-garde at the time. Site analysis is required whenever nonresidential or higher-density residential development (four dwelling units/acre or greater) is proposed on parcels greater than one acre, or whenever any parcels greater than five acres are rezoned. Wildcat subdivisions (subdivisions of up to five lots, allowed by state law) are not covered. The site analysis requires, among other topics, an inventory, map, and description of vegetative communities and associations and federally listed plant species, as well as a letter from the state habitat specialist regarding wildlife populations and habitat.

Other programs that are regulatory in nature include the county's conservation subdivision provision, but this is not used much since the incentives are not strong and the process is more complicated than the regular development process. The existing cluster provision is used more than the conservation subdivision provision, but does not clearly address natural resources. In addition, when rezoning, the parks department negotiates a buffer with the landowner along rivers for trail development with specific design standards (including requirements to use native vegetation).

Education

The Natural Resources, Parks, and Recreation Department began an environmental education program in 2002, when a staff person dedicated to education was hired. There are now two staff members who coordinate field trips for schools, provide programs about local habitats that are linked to academic standards, and provide adult and youth classes at recreation centers. They also run a docent program at the Agua Caliente Park hot springs area, where they are building an environmental education center. The park already gets 170,000 visitors per year. The department also sponsors an annual art and poetry contest that begins with education about watersheds.

Restoration

The Natural Resources, Parks, and Recreation Department undertakes mostly small-scale, riparian restoration that it contracts out or for which it receives volunteer help. The department often works with Desert Survivors (a local nonprofit native plant nursery that employs people with disabilities) and also Weedwackers (a community network of volunteers that removes exotic plants). In 2003, the department also adopted linear park landscaping requirements, which though not officially restoration, do require native vegetation to be utilized. Some park management plans also call for restoration.

The Flood Control District is involved with restoration in several ways. Some mitigation occurs as part of the district's regulations for watercourse and riparian habitat protection. Several small projects have been completed, such as 10 acres in the Cienega Creek Natural Preserve, several of which involve restoring cleared agricultural land to the native mesquite bosque. Another 27 acres of wetlands and riparian habitat were constructed in the Ajo Detention Basin in partnership with the U.S. Army Corps of Engineers for the Kino Ecosystem Restoration Project. Also, the district is actively pursuing restoration of sensitive environments in river corridors and

An environmental education facility is being built at Agua Caliente Regional Park, where warm springs flow into several ponds. Photograph courtesy of the Pima County Flood Control District.

floodplains throughout the community, often with the Corps. Although most of the Corps projects have not reached the construction phase yet, several of them will affect rather large land areas. An example is the Paseo de las Iglesias Environmental Restoration Feasibility Study that the Corps and the county (with input from Tucson, residents, and other stakeholders) completed in 2004. The proposed area for restoration includes over 1,000 acres of undeveloped land located along seven miles of the historic floodplain on the Santa Cruz River and the West Branch Santa Cruz River. If funded, restoration could begin in 2006. The Swan Wetlands Project will start construction sooner than that, and will reestablish riparian vegetation along tributary channels and banks. An important aspect of many of these projects is harvesting excess stormwater for use in other areas.

Leading by Example

In May 2000, County Administrator C. H. Huckelberry directed county staff to improve conservation activities at county-owned springs, including reestablishment of native fish and frogs where appropriate. In addition, county transportation projects and river trails require native vegetation in landscaping. The Flood Control District also removed livestock from riparian areas at Cienega Creek Preserve.

Social Indicators

In general, the social indicators for Pima County are modest at best. Although parks programs and entrance fees are free or negligible, the affordable housing situation leaves much to be desired.

In 2001, as part of the SDCP, Pima County conducted a survey of 35 counties nationwide and found that it spent much less per capita on affordable housing than the counties surveyed—Pima's growth pressures have been greater than most counties, but county program response has been less thus far. Lack of affordable housing has been widely accepted as an issue for some time (even before this study), and the 2001 comprehensive plan update includes policies related to affordable housing (e.g., inclusionary or mixed-income subdivision programs; strategy to ensure housing availability for population groups with special needs; and a program to develop strategy to provide affordable housing for families with incomes at median, low, and very low levels). However, these policies have not yet been implemented.

Wildcat subdivisions have somewhat filled the gap, but at a high cost to the community. These wildcat subdivisions, authorized by state law (landowners can subdivide their lot into up to five lots without review), can provide less expensive housing options because they are not required to invest in infrastructure—dirt roads and septic systems are the norm. Unfortunately, the costs of providing other basic services such as police and fire response to these areas are a drain on the rest of the community since they are not part of the tax base, ensuring that this initially low-cost housing option will never meet the affordable housing gap in a cost-effective manner for the county as a whole. Wildcat subdivisions have led to a 38 percent decline in the tax base.

What is needed is an affordable housing strategy, which has yet to be pursued. On the positive side, the county has been working on an affordable housing ordinance based on progressive model ordinances from other counties in the nation, and staff may create a policy in advance of the ordinance in 2004. In addition, a bond measure was passed in May 2004 that includes $10 million to "provide funding for the infrastructure to subdivisions that will make the homes or multi-family units more affordable to families at or below the 80 percent income level."

The City of Tucson also encourages infill development and has an impressive program in partnership with the Sonoran Institute called "Building from the Best of Tucson." Since 2001, the program has created and implemented urban policies that encourage high-quality infill development and downtown revitalization.

Results

The draft Multi-Species Conservation Plan has biological goals and an "effectiveness monitoring" component. The program is in the design phase in 2004 and will not be implemented for some time. Independent of federal requirements, the county is also preparing a "State of the Environment—Pima County" report as part of the Sonoran Desert Conservation Plan, to be released in 2005. This study will provide baseline statistical information on biological as well as cultural resources, with the intent to update this information regularly to monitor the county's progress.

Chiefly owing to passage of a major bond issue in 2004, Pima County will be able to start implementing one of the most ambitious biodiversity protection plans in the nation. However, the county has already made the following progress in protecting natural resources:

- Over 7,000 acres of floodprone land (primarily valuable riparian habitat) have been acquired since 1984.
- About 52,000 acres have been protected in county parklands and preserves through 2004.
- Extensive mapping of habitat has been completed, and other solid data regarding local species and ecosystems have been gathered during the course of the Sonoran Desert Conservation Plan process.
- A regulatory program has been adopted for riparian habitat that is more effective than the U.S. Army Corps of Engineers Section 404 rules at encouraging landowners to leave riparian vegetation and wash processes alone.

Note

[1]Primary sources for this case study include the Pima County Administrator's Office; Julia Fonseca, environmental program manager, Pima County Flood Control District; Sherry Ruther, environmental planning manager, Pima County Planning; several other Pima County and City of Tucson staff members; the Pima County website, www.co.pima.az.us; and representatives of several nonprofit organizations, such as the Sonoran Institute and the Coalition for Sonoran Desert Protection.

CHAPTER 9

Placer County, California: Leaving a Legacy

P lacer County, one of the fastest-growing communities in California, is also one of its most diverse ecological regions. Its approach to open space conservation and protection is a promising example of a program built on partnerships and collaboration. Operating in a very conservative political and fiscal environment, the county's elected officials and staff have demonstrated strong leadership in building a coalition between the region's development and environmental communities. While the California regulatory system represents its own set of opportunities and challenges that are unique to the state, Placer County's experience should be instructive to local governments elsewhere seeking to build a collaborative approach to protecting open space and natural resources.

Placer County is located 80 miles northeast of San Francisco and directly northeast of Sacramento.[1] It rises from the Sacramento Valley at elevations of near sea level to the high Sierra Nevada Mountains at the shores of Lake Tahoe. Founded in 1851, the county takes its name from the Spanish word for deposits that contain gold, which was discovered near Auburn in 1846, a town that still serves as the county seat. Part of Placer County's history is tied to the abundance of agricultural products harvested from its field and orchards. For many years, until a fungus attacked the region's

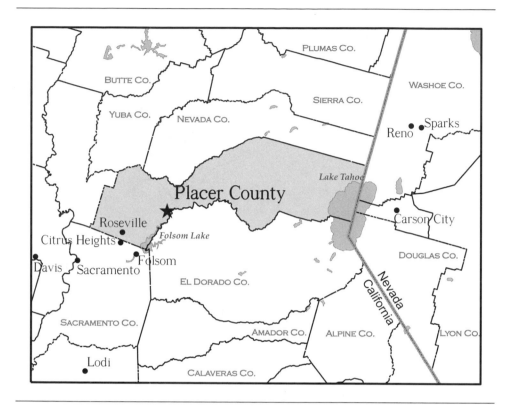

PLACER COUNTY, CALIFORNIA
Map courtesy of Clarion Associates.

orchards in 1960, Placer County was the fruit-producing capital of California. By the early 1920s, at the peak of the region's production, more than 100 million pounds of peaches, pears, plums, and grapes were produced and shipped annually. Completion of Interstate 80 in the 1960s began to open the region to Sacramento and beyond.

Placer County is one of the most diverse ecological regions in the West, containing an astonishing 62 percent of California's habitat types. Between the lowlands and deltas of the Central Valley and the Sierra summit, an elevation difference of more than 9,000 feet, lies a great diversity of natural communities, including foothills oak woodlands, and the forests, streams, and alpine meadows of the Sierra Nevada. The county covers an enormous area, containing more than 960,000 acres of land and water. The diversity of this land includes no fewer than 20 distinct vegetation associations over a distance of 80 miles, spanning six ecological zones and three major ecoregions, including the Great Valley, the Sierra Nevada foothills, and the Sierra Nevada upper slope. The western part of the county, which is experiencing the greatest amount of growth pressure, supports vernal pool–grassland complexes, numerous streams and rivers and their associated riparian areas, and freshwater emergent wetlands. Blue oak and valley oak woodlands, dominant vegetation types in the region, include some of the richest wildlife habitats in California, with over 300 vertebrate species relying on them for feeding, cover, or nesting sites during all or some parts of the year. Urban land uses comprise just over 60,000 acres in the county, of which 36,000 are intensively developed, mostly in the western portion of the county.

When the county adopted its first General Plan in 1967, the entire population of the county was approximately 77,000 people. By the year 2000, the population had reached 248,000 people, an increase of over 170,000. Placer County's strong growth

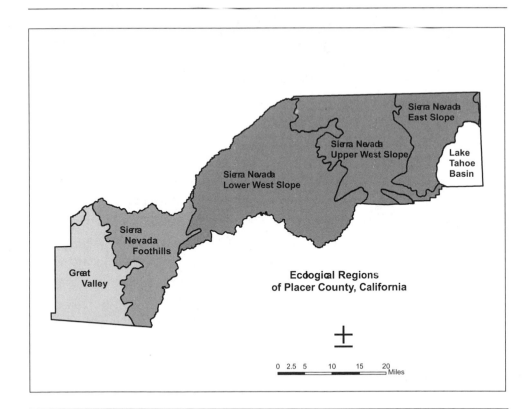

PLACER COUNTY ECOREGIONS
Spanning six ecological zones, Placer County is one of the most diverse places in the West. Map courtesy of Placer County.

Scenic woodlands, meadows, and mountains abound in Placer County. Photograph by Loren Clark.

can, in large part, be attributed to two main factors. First, Hewlett-Packard relocated from the San Francisco Bay Area to Roseville in the early 1980s. That brought thousands of new jobs and residents to the county. Today the county's job-to-population ratio is an enviable 2:1—which creates intense pressure to build more housing. Second, some feel that the area has become the Marin County of the Sacramento region, as many Sacramento Valley and even Bay Area residents convert their equity in pricey urban and suburban housing into foothills "estates" in Placer County. The county now has the sixth-highest disposal income of all of California, a significant change from the region's more modest demographics until recently.

For the past several years, Placer County has been among the fastest-growing regions in California, with annual growth rates of 4 percent. This high growth rate is expected to continue for many years to come, with Placer County's population expected to reach nearly 400,000 persons by the year 2020. As if to underscore the boom, four new high-end golf and skiing developments/resorts have been proposed in Martis Valley, near the Town of Truckee, just over the county's borders. This will attract not only more new residents to the region, but more jobs and job-hunters who will need housing.

The degree of change expected over the coming decades will convert a large portion of the existing open landscape in the county into urban and rural residential developments. Some of this future growth will occur within a relatively compact urban area, mostly in the southern portion of the county. However, up to 34,000 new rural residential dwellings could be constructed within 105,000 acres in the county's western area, which has been designated for rural residential land uses, more than quadrupling the current total.

The explosive growth in the more urbanized western portion of the county has led to a number of pressures and challenges, including increased suburbanization and loss of agricultural land and biodiversity habitat; encroaching urban development on the borders of the county and within the cities; and increased demand for urban services. Placer County's population growth was beginning to run head-on into the tough regulatory strictures of the California Environmental Quality Act as well as federal laws such as the Endangered Species Act.

In response to these pressures, in 1998 the county board of supervisors adopted the proposed goals and objectives of the Placer Legacy Open Space Conservation Program. Placer Legacy is a program that seeks to protect the county's diverse open space and agricultural resources. The stated goal of the program is to develop specific, economically viable implementation programs that will enable the residents of Placer County to preserve a sufficient quantity of these resources to maintain a high quality of life and an abundance of diverse natural habitats while supporting the economic viability of the county and enhancing property values.

Placer Legacy is a true example of a program designed in response to political realities. Placer County is fairly conservative politically; some have described it as California's "Orange County of the north." Thus, in order to be successful, county leaders needed to craft carefully a program that did not detract from the free market/private property rights conservative political environment of the region while still protecting citizens' desires to protect significant amounts of open space.

The county struck out on a new approach in 1997, with a county board of supervisors that was supportive of taking the county's General Plan to the next level. They held a retreat with county staff to discuss growth management, out of which came a commitment to support open space preservation—the foundation of what became the Placer Legacy Program. The program's goals are simple—to identify and protect high-priority resources in the county, including valley agriculture, riparian zones, vernal pools, historic resources, and passive recreation opportunities for residents of western Placer County. The overall goal for protected lands includes a total of 75,000 acres of lands to be managed through various implementation measures. In practice, the program is complex, since it involves a diverse range of protection activities that include acquisition, regulation through local development review, and mitigation as required under county, state, and federal standards.

Over the next few months, staff developed the goals and objectives of Placer Legacy, as well as a work plan to accomplish those objectives over a two-year period, by the summer of 2000. In order to accomplish this, three working groups were formed: a Citizens Advisory Committee, an Interagency Working Group, and a Scientific Working Group.

In addition to the formation of the three working groups to help develop the various aspects of the program, the county also established an important public/private partnership with an organization called the Sierra Business Council (SBC). (See Box 9.1.) Based in Truckee, California, the Sierra Business Council is a nonprofit business association whose mission is to "secure the long-term economic and environmental health of the 12-county Sierra Nevada region." Under a unique agreement, the SBC would oversee key aspects of the county open space acquisition program and provide two-thirds of the funding for it. The county would contribute staffing and some funding.

The Placer Legacy Program also has a regulatory element with two facets. The county is undertaking special habitat protection plans that will enable it to assume regulatory responsibility from the federal government and the State of California under the federal Endangered Species Act and other environmental laws. Currently, all development that affects protected habitat must seek approval directly from the federal government and state—a time-consuming and uncertain process. Additionally, the county has traditional zoning and land use controls that require large development lots in rural areas as well as compliance with natural resource protection standards (e.g., tree protection).

Will this hybrid strategy with significant private sector involvement ultimately be successful? The county has already protected thousands of acres through purchase or easements with the help of the SBC, and is putting into practice some strong local development mitigation requirements. It is also working hard on a Habitat Conservation Plan that will allow it to have greater say over federal endangered species regulation.

BOX 9.1

Sierra Business Council: A Unique Public/Private Partnership

The Sierra Business Council (SBC) is a nonprofit association of more than 600 businesses, agencies, and individuals working together to secure the social, environmental, and economic health of the Sierra Nevada region of California and Nevada. Founded in 1994, the SBC is an important resource for business leaders, government officials, and others seeking solutions to local and regional challenges. The fundamental premise of SBC's approach is that for a community and region to be successful, they need to grow all three forms of capital—social, natural, and financial—and ensure that increases in one form of capital don't come at the expense of another.

The SBC has become recognized nationally for its publications, which focus on how to measure, plan for, and invest in the region's prosperity, and which should be required reading for communities striving to become more nature-friendly. These publications include:

Sierra Nevada Wealth Index (2000) contains a set of indicators used to describe and track the social, natural, and financial capital of the region.

Planning for Prosperity: Building Successful Communities in the Sierra Nevada (1997) contains a set of principles for sound development to be used by elected and appointed officials and other community leaders who will be involved in making planning decisions affecting lands in the region, as well as a set of principles for involving and serving business and the public.

Investing for Prosperity: Building Successful Communities and Economies in the Sierra Nevada (2003) is a comprehensive guide to help rural communities create their own unique strategies for building long-term social, natural, and financial wealth.

More information about the Sierra Business Council can be obtained at www.sbcouncil.org.

On the downside, county residents soundly defeated a proposal in 1999 to earmark some sales tax revenue to fund open space acquisition. Moreover, critics point out that elsewhere in California habitat conservation plans have typically taken a long time (7–10 years) and will still likely face legal battles. In other areas, environmental groups have been unwilling to agree to the big-picture deal approach that a Habitat Conservation Plan represents, since they may view it as too much of a compromise between protection and development. The possibility also exists for conflicts between the goals of the Placer Legacy Program and a Habitat Conservation Plan—essentially the conflict between species habitat protection and passive recreation embraced by the Legacy Program.

Overall, the county has pieced together an impressive program with broad-based support and savvy partnerships—but is it is case of too little, too late? While the county has made important strides in planning for conservation, it is in the early stages of implementing various plans and regulatory initiatives. The county is at a pivotal point right now. Growth pressures are intensifying, and it will take some time before the county has all of its tools in place. If these efforts are successful, then the county will go a long way toward achieving its preservation objectives.

Key Program Elements

Program Structure and Administration

The lynchpin of the county's open space and natural resource protection efforts is the Placer Legacy Program. At the outset, the county entered into a unique agreement with the Sierra Business Council whereby they agreed to develop the Placer County Open Space Program as a joint project between the SBC and the county. Under the terms of the agreement, SBC agreed to oversee the funding for the development of the program from public and private funding sources (with private sources contributing $2 million, or two-thirds of the funding to the year 2000). SBC also was responsible for planning and implementing an extensive public outreach, education, and participation program. In turn, the county agreed to provide overall project management by assigning a planner to coordinate the development and implementation of the program, and by committing county funds to the program. Placer County provided general fund revenue to support staffing, land acquisition, maintenance, and monitoring. Additional funding has come from grants, gifts, and in-kind services from nonprofit partnerships.

Another key player in the early days of the program was an appointed Citizens' Advisory Committee (CAC). This was a diverse group of 11 citizens representing a broad spectrum of interests, including agriculture, land development, environmental organizations, businesses, and community organizations. In a unique approach designed to lend credibility to the CAC, two county board members who were on opposite ends of the political spectrum jointly selected their membership. An Interagency Working Group was also formed to ensure that members of state, federal, and local governments who had a stakeholder interest in the Legacy Program had a forum for participation. The Working Group included state and federal wildlife and land management agencies, local water agencies, and the cities of Placer County. The county also set up a Scientific Working Group (SWG), because program objectives are focused on the protection of biological resources as well as on the relationship between the program and state and federal agency permitting requirements. The role of the SWG was to ensure that the program is founded on sound conservation biology principles. The SWG included scientists from universities in Nevada and California.

The Placer Legacy Program is currently managed by Placer County itself. Decision-making responsibility rests with the Placer County board of supervisors, who serve as the program's board of directors. County planning staff dedicated to the program provide technical, administrative, and professional assistance to the board. As such, administration of the program has not proven to be much of a burden for the county.

In 2004, the county and SBC changed their relationship, and SBC is now a contract service provider to the county for the Placer Legacy Program outreach, focusing on producing a newsletter, private fund-raising, presentations, and establishing a "Friends of Placer Legacy" program.[2]

While it will continue to cooperate with the SBC, the county intends to form an Open Space Advisory Commission to serve as an advisory body to the board. Over time, the county will consider the formation of a Joint Powers Authority (JPA) to oversee administration of the program. In creating a JPA, Placer County would join with Placer County cities and potentially other public agencies to forge a partnership with the intent of working cooperatively to preserve open space.

Planning

The Placer Legacy Program has its roots in the county's 1994 General Plan, which is a document required by state law that serves as the community's "constitution" for land use and development. The county General Plan essentially accepts that growth will occur in the region but places a great deal of focus and emphasis on how and where that growth is to occur. Its policies state that urban growth be directed to urban areas of the county; discourage free-standing new towns; recognize the importance of agricultural and recreational activities to the county's quality of life; and place strong emphasis on protecting natural, agricultural, and forestry resources.

The General Plan also contains detailed policies for each of the seven types of open space that are addressed by the Placer Legacy Program. These include agriculture, outdoor recreation, scenic and historic areas, plant and animal communities, endangered and special status plant and animal species, separation of urban areas, and public safety (includes areas subject to flooding, areas susceptible to forest fires, and steep slopes).

The Placer Legacy Program does not constitute the open space and conservation elements of the Placer County General Plan; these elements are already contained in the *1994 General Plan Policy Document.* However, the Placer Legacy Program is seen by the county as the implementing element for those policies, as the primary tool through which the conservation policies of the General Plan can be implemented. As part of the process of updating the General Plan in 2004, the county will be incorporating the specific goals, objectives, and priorities of the Placer Legacy Program into the plan.

In addition to these more broad planning efforts, the county is in the process of developing and implementing a Natural Communities Conservation Plan (NCCP) and a Habitat Conservation Plan (HCP). Much of the available land for development in Placer County is privately held, and a significant portion of it has already received local approvals for development. However, if state or federally listed endangered species are involved, then permits are required to be obtained from federal and state agencies. If each development project must negotiate its own permits, mitigation tends to occur in a piecemeal, time-consuming fashion. However, if Placer County develops and successfully achieves approval of a Habitat Conservation Plan, then mitigation and conservation can be coordinated as part of a larger plan and a potentially more effective wildlife protection strategy. With this approach, the county can become the permit issuing authority for state and federal rules, thus retaining local jurisdiction over public and private development activities. This will add a level of certainly to the development process, while at the same time providing for the implementation of a conservation plan that is linked to the county's objectives for conservation and preservation.

A Habitat Conservation Plan (HCP) is a formal plan allowed under federal law that addresses the development of land that is designated as habitat for federally listed endangered species and outlines measures for conserving and enhancing habitat for these species in open space preserves. The HCP is intended to provide for the regional protection of natural wildlife diversity, while allowing for compatible and appropriate development.

Because the county is so large and conservation needs are more urgent in some parts of the county than others, the HCP will be undertaken in three phases. Phase 1, now under way, includes the more urbanized, rapidly developing western part of the county. This area is rich in ecological diversity and supports vernal pool–grassland

Vernal pool–grassland complexes are one of the high-priority resources targeted for protection under the Placer Legacy Program. Photograph by Loren Clark.

complexes, numerous streams and rivers and their associated riparian areas, and freshwater emergent wetlands. According to the report of the science advisers to the county for the HCP process, as much as two-thirds of the remaining riparian areas in the western portion of the county are threatened by urbanization.

To date, the county has released a draft Conservation Strategy Overview for the western area (September 2003), and its science advisors released their Phase 1 report identifying species and habitat protection objectives in early 2004. The NCCP/HCP is a complex undertaking, and will likely take several more years before the actual conservation plan is complete and ready for the structuring of agreements with state and federal agencies. The estimated completion date for the NCCP/HCP, including the implementing agreement with permits from federal agencies, is December 2005.

Acquisition/Funding

Land acquisition is a key feature of the Placer Legacy Program, and the partnership with the SBC has been essential to early progress. Under the terms of its original agreement with the county, SBC agreed to oversee the funding for the development of the program from public and private funding sources (with private sources contributing $2 million, or two-thirds of the funding). Placer County provided general fund revenue for staffing, land acquisition, maintenance, and monitoring. Additional funding support has come from grants, gifts, and in-kind services from nonprofit partnerships. To date, more than $5.7 million has been spent on acquisitions.

Unfortunately, county residents have been unwilling to create a revenue stream for county acquisition—a sales tax initiative in 1999 failed by a 73 percent to 27 percent margin, although the accompanying advisory measure passed with a 56 percent margin. Recent indications are that voters continue to oppose an open space tax measure. However, efforts are under way to see if there is support for a parcel tax, document transfer tax, or a bond as alternatives to a sales tax. Supporters believe that development pressures over the past five years may lead to support among the community, while detractors point to California's general antitax environment and the conservative politics of the region. It is noteworthy that while the county has set an aggressive goal of preserving as much as 75,000 acres of land in the county, the current revenue stream is estimated to only be sufficient to accomplish approximately 15 percent of that goal. The Phase 1 NCCP, independent of the 75,000 acres for open space conservation purposes, may need as much as 80,000 acres of protection area.

Another important aspect of the Placer Legacy Program has been other partnerships with land conservation organizations, such as the Placer Land Trust and the Trust for Public Lands, which have helped implement the acquisition of open lands in the county. One of the key partners is the Placer Land Trust, a modest program run on a shoestring that nonetheless has managed to accomplish the protection of open space lands along the American River and other areas in the county. Overseen by a diverse nine-member board of directors, the trust typically works in an informal

Spears Ranch in the Sierra Nevada foothills was acquired under the Placer Legacy Program. Photograph by Loren Clark.

partnership/coalition with Placer Legacy, the Trust for Public Lands, and the Sierra Business Council. They often serve as the first line of contact with property owners, who are often reluctant to work with government officials. The trust also holds and manages a number of conservation easements on open lands and agricultural properties in the county. The Trust for Public Lands, a national nonprofit conservation organization, has also participated in several land protection activities, primarily as a transactional partner.

Regulations

The regulatory side of the Placer Legacy Program has two prongs. In the near term, case-by-case review of compliance with both state and federal Endangered Species Acts and federal wetland regulatory laws will continue. As noted previously, these laws require permits for certain types of activities that can result in impacts on sensitive plant and animal species, or for impacts to regulated wetlands. Case-by-case negotiations will likely result in significant areas of sensitive lands being protected in the county as a part of project mitigation requirements.

In the longer term, the board of supervisors has directed the Planning Department to implement the Placer Legacy Open Space and Agricultural Conservation Program through the preparation of a Habitat Conservation Plan. This will enable the county to assume more direct regulatory authority.

Existing and updated county zoning and other land use regulations will also play an important role, both short and long term. In addition to the mitigation requirements for state and federal permit programs, the county is increasing its mitigation demands on developers through its normal development review process to address open space and agricultural land diminution, as well as more traditional impacts on environmentally sensitive lands. In response to these mitigation requirements being imposed on developers, entrepreneurs in the region are now setting up development mitigation banks—in essence, prepurchasing development rights on sensitive properties to sell to developers who must provide mitigation for the impacts of their proposed projects. Planners involved in administering the Legacy Program believe that the combination of county, state, and federal regulations and project mitigation, plus existing funding sources and grants, will be able to go a long way toward achieving the goals of the county.

The county has stated that it will not use regulations to achieve the objectives of the Placer Legacy Program other than the NCCP/HCP described previously, and views the strategy purely as an open space protection program, with all conservation

Placer County's Agricultural Exclusive District protects existing agricultural areas. Photograph by Loren Clark.

measures approached on a voluntary, willing seller–willing buyer basis. In reality, the county's planning department uses its regulations as a means of achieving many of the goals of Placer Legacy through its development review process. It is probably fair to say that the county would not be accomplishing as much as it has through the regulatory process if the Placer Legacy Program were not in existence.

For example, the county is in the process of updating a number of its regulations, such as its tree preservation ordinance, which previously required replacement of any trees removed. This ordinance is being revised to provide for a full woodland value replacement policy that is much more extensive and demanding. Similarly, the county's impact fee for active parks, previously set at 5 acres per 1,000 people in a new development, was increased to 10 acres per 1,000 people to provide a funding source for passive park development. The county is also proposing to add an open space conversion fee to offset impacts to open space that cannot otherwise be mitigated.

The county's traditional zoning regulations also protect much of the northern foothills areas through a series of agricultural, resource, and open space districts. The Agricultural Exclusive District, which has a minimum parcel size of 20 acres, is intended to protect existing agricultural areas. Other districts, including farm and forestry districts, have a minimum lot size of from 5 to 10 acres.

Finally, Chapter 18 of the county code requires an environmental review of both public and private development activities through the preparation of an "initial study," which can lead to the preparation of an environmental impact report. Such a report and accompanying mitigation measures are required by the California Environmental Quality Act.

Restoration

Placer Legacy has accomplished several watershed-level ecosystem restoration plans to evaluate a number of watersheds and restoration activities. The county has completed one restoration project and is preparing a second for implementation this next year. Over the coming year, it will have completed restoration plans for six major creek watersheds in the western part of the county.

Leading by Example

Other than for projects that are exempt (including such activities as minor alterations and actions for the protection of open lands or the natural environment), projects that are undertaken by the county are subject to the same environmental review process as private development projects.

Social Indicators

Placer County has implemented a number of programs to encourage redevelopment and provision of affordable housing. These programs are considered by the county to be part of a "total package," along with preservation of open space, to help limit sprawl. These programs include an aggressive set of policies designed to increase the supply of affordable housing. One example is the linkage between redevelopment projects designed to stimulate economic growth and the production of funding for low- and moderate-income housing. (California redevelopment law mandates that 20 percent of tax increment funds generated by redevelopment be set aside for affordable housing.) The county has adopted a mandatory inclusionary housing ordinance that requires 15 percent of housing units in market-rate developments to be affordable.

While the county's Placer Legacy Program does not have formal criteria with regard to open space accessibility, county staff and elected leaders have indicated that distance to population centers is an important consideration for open space protection. Particularly for projects with a public visibility, access, and/or recreational component, the program is placing a low priority on remote sites.

Education

Placer Legacy will be publishing a newsletter several times a year that provides updates on the program's activities. The program is also funded for a two-year public outreach effort with the Sierra Business Council to increase public awareness of the program and to initiate public education activities. In addition to Placer Legacy activities, the PlacerGROWN Program also includes an education component, including a significant amount of emphasis on working with the agricultural community on methods to keep agricultural land in production. One of the most challenging aspects of the program identified by its administrators is helping growers recognize the opportunities available to them in the marketplace. PlacerGROWN staff focus on educating the agricultural community about land conservation tools, such as state property tax benefits, conservation easements, and conservation and mitigation banking; and economic tools, such as agricultural tourism, farm stays, and farm-to-market activities.

BOX 9.2

PlacerGROWN

One of the more unique programs in the county is "PlacerGROWN," an initiative that focuses on the promotion of farm-fresh foods and agricultural products locally grown in Placer County. While PlacerGROWN does not have direct links to the Placer Legacy Program, it contributes to the county's agricultural preservation efforts. The program has its roots in 1989, when the county board of supervisors initiated a farmers' market. Under the direction of Joanne Neft, an energetic promoter and entrepreneur who now oversees the PlacerGROWN program, the farmers' market concept quickly took hold in Placer County, growing to eight locations and more than 10,000 people a week shopping the markets by 1994. PlacerGROWN now encompasses a dizzying array of programs and activities, including a Mountain Mandarin Festival that attracts 30,000 visitors over a two-day period each fall; a Placer Farm and Barn Festival, an educational and informational event that showcases Placer County agriculture and artists, including AGROart, a nationally known competition featuring sculptures created from locally grown and seasonal fruits and vegetables, farm tours, a barn photo contest, art show, farmers' market, and workshops; and a marketing program that produces an annual county Farm Trail Guide, directing consumers to local produce and agricultural markets and outlets. The program is beginning to show some benefits to farmers as well. When the program first began, there were 8 active mandarin orange producers in the county; today, they number more than 50. As a result of the PlacerGROWN county Farm Trail Guide and other marketing

—continued—

Results

Robert Weygandt, one of the county's elected supervisors, is an energetic leader whose personal experience in many ways reflects the story of the region. He describes the experience of moving to the county with his family from southern California when he was 10 years old as a turning point in his life. "Back then, Placer County was a very rural area," he says wistfully. "I thought that we'd moved to heaven. It was a great place to grow up, with natural resources everywhere, and hardly any growth." Weygandt describes the county's progress so far as a "glowing success" in terms of coalition building and developing a policy direction that is appropriate politically. He is spearheading an effort among members of the development and environmental communities and

---

Box 9.2 *(continued)*

Charlie Green, winemaker, checks grapes for ripeness before an early harvest in Placer County. Photography by Cindy Fake, Placer County Extension officer.

efforts, customer traffic for one iris grower in the county increased by 100 percent in the first year of their involvement in the program; the second year, their traffic increased another 50 percent. The region is now home to a specialty store that features a wealth of locally grown produce; regionally produced olive oils, vinegars, and other agricultural products; and locally produced meats and cheeses. Newcastle Produce, a storefront adjacent to the gold country town's former fruit-packing sheds, is owned by one of Placer County's farmers. A second produce market and café is scheduled to open in 2005 in Lincoln, a fast-growing town located in the western part of the county.

More information about the PlacerGROWN program can be obtained at www.placergrown.org.

area local governments to build a consortium for a three-pronged approach: support for the NCCP/HCP, a tax-based open space funding mechanism, and the county's General Plan policies regarding development standards and mitigation. According to Weygandt, three aspects have been the key to their success: good, committed staff; policies and regulations that mirror the will of the people; and "champions."

Results of the Placer Legacy Program can be measured in other ways: recognition on a statewide level, partnerships, and protected acres of lands. The program was recognized in 2002 as the recipient of the Governor's Environmental Economic Leadership Award. Clearly the partnerships forged between the county and the Sierra Business Council, the Trust for Public Lands, and the Placer Land Trust are a measure of successful results in collaborative program building. Another area of collaboration that is worth noting is the cooperative relationship between the county and state/federal resource agencies, academia, and a number of federal and state stakeholders in the NCCP. The county has been very fortunate to get extensive support from the resource agencies in participating in the NCCP program. Finally, the county has secured a number of conservation easements on agricultural properties as well as properties containing sensitive environmental features such as vernal pools, perennial streams, and grasslands. One of the county's most recent successes is the acquisition of the Spears Ranch, a 960-acre property that features pristine blue oak woodlands, a scenic creek, and a waterfall. Spears Ranch will become a county-owned passive park, where residents can hike, fish, and enjoy outdoor activities. The property was purchased by the county with major support from the Trust for Public Lands, the Sierra Business Council, and the State of California.

Notes

[1] Primary sources for this case study include Loren Clark, assistant planning director, Placer County; the Sierra Business Council; other county staff and elected officials; and the Placer County website, www.placer.ca.gov.

[2] The Sierra Nevada Conservancy was established in 2004 by the California legislature with bipartisan support. The Sierra Business Council has been asked to take a leading role in creating the conservancy in 2005–2006. This new nonregulatory regional agency will provide planning and grants to protect or enhance the Sierra's natural, cultural, and historic resources.

CHAPTER 10

Sanibel, Florida: Do Enjoy, Don't Destroy

S anibel Island, Florida, is home to a landmark wildlife habitat protection program that is as groundbreaking today as it was when conceived back in the 1970s. Shaped by renowned planner William Roberts from Wallace, McHarg, Roberts, and Todd and scientist John Clark of the Conservation Foundation, and defended by land use legal heavyweights Fred Bosselman and Charles Siemon, the Sanibel Plan was one of the first major land use plans based primarily on sound ecological principles. The plan has stood the test of time, supported by a judicious mix of regulations, acquisition, restoration, and education strategies. Habitat protection has become part of the culture of the island and a way of life. Sanibelians are proud they have demonstrated that humans can coexist with fully functioning natural systems without destroying them. They live with wildlife as part of the community instead of pushing it into a corner. And in the process, they have shown that resource protection can make good economic sense.

You know that you are in a place that cares about the environment when you drive off the causeway linking Sanibel to the mainland: the city's official logo sign greets you with this simple welcome: "Do Enjoy—Don't Destroy."[1] The point is reinforced when the silver-haired lady at the hotel check-in desk delivers a knowledgeable lecture about not picking up live shells or annoying nesting turtles on the beach with lights and points out the bicycles outside the lobby that are the best way to experience

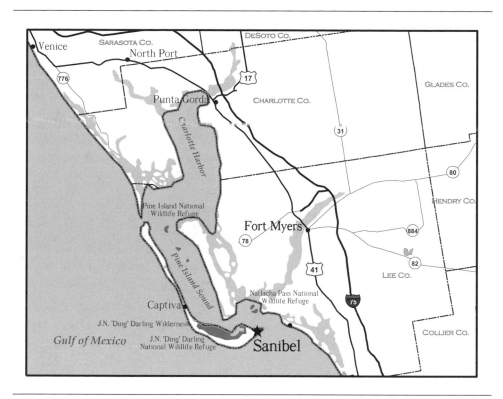

SANIBEL, FLORIDA
Map courtesy of Clarion Associates.

the island and its natural beauty. This is, as one wag put it, "a place where grown men stop for turtles on the road."

Sanibel is a 12-mile-long island located in the Gulf of Mexico off the southwest coast of Florida, approximately a two-hour drive south of Tampa. It covers about 20 square miles (12,000 acres) and has a permanent population of about 6,000 that balloons to over 18,000 in peak winter season. The economy is based mainly on tourism and second homes.

The island's ecosystems run the gamut from coastal beaches and dunes to upland ridges to freshwater wetlands to mangrove swamps. The coastal ridges are the most endangered habitat, a place condominiums like to grow as well as species like the gopher tortoise. The place teems with wildlife—birds, fish, manatees, turtles, alligators, and even a few wayward crocodiles.

In the 1970s, runaway growth was threatening Sanibel as Lee County politicians targeted the island for thousands of new condos and apartments. Development at densities permitted by Lee County would have let Sanibel mushroom to 90,000 people—too much for the island's ecosystems to sustain. Unincorporated at the time, the citizens of Sanibel organized and revolted, forming their own city and taking the growth management reins in their own hands. Under the leadership of their first mayor, Porter Goss (a former CIA intelligence agent and former U.S. congressman whom President George W. Bush has appointed to run the CIA), the new city council put a moratorium on development and fast-tracked a revolutionary new land use plan that was based on ecological principles.

The revolutionary land use plan for Sanibel was crafted with help from a leading planning firm out of Philadelphia, Wallace, McHarg, Roberts, and Todd (now WRT) and John Clark and his team of scientists from the Washington, D.C.-based Conservation Foundation (later merged into the World Wildlife Fund), led at the time by William Reilly (Reilly would later become head of the U.S. Environmental Protection Agency under President George H. W. Bush). It was based on three key goals:

Habitat protection has become part of the culture of Sanibel Island. Photograph by Chris Duerksen.

- Assure that the population would not exceed a level that would make safe evacuation of the island feasible. The two-lane causeway built in 1963 is the only way off the island other than by boat. Sanibel had been devastated in the past by hurricanes that washed over the island to a depth of nine feet!! Too much development on Sanibel would make evacuation impossible.

- Assure that the infrastructure of the island would not be overwhelmed. Much of the island's development was on private wastewater treatment systems or septics. Too much development might foul Sanibel's water supply and pollute wetlands. Too much development would also totally bollix up the island's narrow roads.

- Assure that the natural resources and wildlife habitat were protected.

The Sanibel Plan, a comprehensive land use plan for the island, designated six distinct ecological zones, and densities were assigned based on environmental attributes—the more sensitive the land, the less development was allowed. The plan recommended protection through a variety of tools, and the Sanibel city council enacted a development moratorium to give planners some breathing room.

Then the lawyers descended. The city council of this small, newly formed city was confronted with numerous legal suits brought on by developers and landowners, which the council fought vigorously and wisely. It negotiated settlements with a number of developers who already had approvals from the county and defused much of the opposition in that manner. By the early 1980s, a good deal of the legal wrangling had settled down, and the citizens of Sanibel began turning their attention to land acquisition and restoration of damaged ecosystems.

A key element of Sanibel's success has been a land acquisition program to supplement the regulations and zoning. Almost two-thirds of Sanibel is in public open space, the biggest chunk of which—over 5,000 acres—is the J. N. "Ding" Darling National Wildlife Refuge, designated in 1945. This national refuge is a heavily visited jewel. But perhaps the most critical and unique piece of the land conservation puzzle has been the good works of the nonprofit Sanibel-Captiva Conservation Foundation (SCCF). Founded in 1967 by citizens of Sanibel, it has acquired and preserved almost 1,800 acres of land through private donations, and it has been a leader in restoration projects to eradicate exotic vegetation and restore the acquired tracts to functioning ecosystems. The SCCF also maintains a native plant nursery to assist in these restoration efforts as well as a full complement of educational programs that supplement those of the national wildlife refuge. Its hundreds of volunteers are the secret weapon of the biodiversity protection of Sanibel. Moreover, the city and its citizens put their money where their mouths were. Millions of dollars have been raised by a special property tax levy enacted in the early 1980s for open space acquisition.

The partnership among the city, the federal national wildlife refuge, and the SCCF is exemplary. Because the tracts of land they own are intimately related ecologically and often physically interspersed, the three entities have struck a cooperative agreement that has them sharing management duties, staff, facilities and even equipment. This stands in stark contrast to the tense relationship with Lee County. While sour relationships with the county from the early days of Sanibel had mellowed in the 1980s, they have since 2000 become tense over the lack of upkeep to the island's causeway, which is owned and managed by the county.

The business community has also bought into the Sanibel Plan. According to the chamber of commerce, 75 percent of the economy is based on the environment. Business people recognize that wildlife and the environment are why people come to Sanibel. "If we commit change, we would destroy our businesses," says one chamber leader. Hotels, restaurants, condominiums, and tour businesses all rely directly on people coming to enjoy the fruits of the Sanibel Plan. The only real debate with the business community from time to time is how to implement the plan.

The success of the Sanibel Plan has, oddly, contributed to its biggest challenges. Because Sanibel is so desirable, real estate values have skyrocketed, and affordable housing is a serious problem. Few condos run less than a half-million dollars, and starter castles often go for $5 million and more. Few city employees can afford to live on the island unless they bought their homes 25 years ago. Just over 60 affordable housing units have been created by the island's nonprofit housing association and the city, but that is a drop in the bucket compared with the need. The Sanibel Plan stressed the importance of providing affordable housing, but it proved to be a challenge to implement that goal. Indeed, some citizens and developers opposed an inclusionary zoning program in the 1980s that would have required a percentage of all units in a new project to be affordable.

Since few city employees can afford to live on the island, they are forced to commute from less expensive areas of Florida. The deluge of workers and visitors has overtaxed the island's very modest two-lane road system. Traffic jams plague Sanibel twice in the morning and twice in the evening on many days—the first rush being workers followed by tourists and day-trippers. While some employers use van pools, public transit is virtually nonexistent.

There are also political fissures developing. A growing worry among many is the perceived lack of support for resource protection on the wildlife refuge by the Bush administration. Some fear the administration is tilting toward an emphasis on visitation and recreation and away from resource protection. Refuge managers are also facing a new threat from freshwater intrusions from water released out of Lake Okeechobee into the Caloosahatchee River, which feeds Pine Island Sound, bordering the refuge. Too much freshwater upsets the delicate balance of the area's ecosystem.

Locally, the solid consensus behind the Sanibel Plan and the unified, collegial atmosphere that has historically prevailed on the city council is showing some small, but disquieting cracks. Observers worry that the recent introduction of party politics on the city council and a truculent debate over reducing the size of the planning commission may foreshadow a weakening of development regulations and less commitment to land acquisition and management. The imminent retirement of several solidly conservationist councilors is creating a case of nerves among some citizens.

Despite these shortcomings and challenges, there is little debate that Sanibel has currently what is probably the most effective and progressive nature and biodiversity protection program in the nation. Only the traffic and affordable housing problems keep this sterling silver effort from earning a gold star.

Key Program Elements

Program Structure and Administration

Sanibel is governed by a five-member city council and a city manager form of government. It has a small, but highly professional and respected planning department that oversees development reviews as well as a two-person natural resources department staffed by resource biologists who assist in development reviews and oversee city natural lands acquisitions.

These two city departments—planning and natural resources—split the primary responsibility for development review and resource conservation on Sanibel. The planning department has five planners, a significant number for a relatively small local government. These planners are seasoned and highly respected professionally. The planning director, Bruce Rogers, has been in his position for over 25 years. His hands-on historical knowledge of the history of planning on Sanibel has, according to many observers, been a key element of the success of the program. He is known widely as the "keeper of the Sanibel Plan."

The planning department is responsible for all development reviews, a five-step process that involves significant hands-on evaluation by staff, including a site visit. Additionally, it handles any proposed revision to the island's comprehensive plan, known as the "Sanibel Plan." The department also takes care of proposed revisions to Sanibel's development code.

The natural resources department also plays a critical role in development review, providing advice and commentary regarding ecological impacts and vegetation issues to the planning department. Two full-time biologists staff the department, again extremely unusual for a small community. The natural resources department also has responsibility for land acquisition and resource management of city-owned natural lands. It has prepared detailed management plans for natural resource areas acquired by the city.

Both departments receive invaluable assistance from several citizen committees, such as the vegetation committee, which actually conducts on-site inspections of development to ensure compliance with Sanibel's strict vegetation protection regulations. These committees have, say staff, made themselves experts by study and hands-on experience.

According to developers, the development review process in Sanibel is not particularly speedy, but it is relatively predictable and reasonable. Even the planning staff concede that "our strength isn't efficiency." The staff and planning commission

BOX 10.1

SANIBEL DEVELOPMENT REVIEW PROCESS

1. Determine density allowed in applicable ecological zone.
2. Survey and map property with assistance of environmental consultation.
3. Walk site with staff to identify key features and natural resources.
4. Produce development layout that complies with environmental standards in development code.
5. Conduct formal staff review followed by planning commission review.

reportedly are sensitive to the context of each development and do not insist on a totally by-the-books compliance with standards and regulations. Overall, the staff and planning commission appear to command a good deal of respect in the community. A proposal by a council member in 2004 to reduce the size of the seven-member planning commission was roundly criticized as an effort to politicize a body that is seen as a thoughtful arbiter and protector of the island's natural resources.

Code enforcement is another critical element of the success of Sanibel's resource protection efforts. While the island's land development restrictions are tough, enforcement is done primarily through education and jawboning. Enforcement staff members reportedly bend over backward to work with owners to secure compliance with regulations such as vegetation protection and exotic removal requirements. They try to work out violations rather than take legal action. This has helped take the edge off a strong regulatory program.

As Sanibel nears buildout—there are only a few large vacant parcels remaining—the next challenge for the city will be management and restoration. Already the natural resources department is devoting an increasing amount of its time to managing the lands the city has acquired over the past two decades. It is also working with landowners and the SCCF to restore damaged ecosystems and rid the island of destructive exotics like the Brazilian pepper.

With regard to intergovernmental cooperation, it is fair to say, "It is the best of times, it is the worst of times." As discussed earlier, the relationship between the city, SCCF, and the national wildlife refuge is stronger than ever, and the results of this productive partnership are evident everywhere. Sharing of equipment and personnel, the new SCCF marine laboratory on refuge land, the cooperative restoration efforts—all add up to a model relationship.

In contrast, the relationship between the county (which still rules over neighboring Captiva Island) and the city appears to be cooling after a period of relative warmth. The county's handling of the causeway maintenance issue has been galling to city officials, and while county land use regulations and acquisition programs are far stronger than a decade ago, they remain relatively puny compared with the city's. While some of this city/county friction is not uncommon in other jurisdictions, it is worrisome given the growing regional ecological challenges facing Sanibel and the Pine Island Sound environment that it borders.

Planning

Based on detailed ecological studies, the Sanibel Plan was adopted in 1976 to much national attention and acclaim. Bound in an appropriately green cover, the plan broke new ground in several areas. Its main thrust is to conserve the "unique atmosphere and unusual natural environment" of this island community.

The linchpin of the plan is the six ecological zones (with subzones) into which the island is divided: Gulf Beach, Gulf Beach Ridge, Freshwater Wetlands, Mid-Island Ridge, Mangrove Forest, and Bay Beach. Each one of these zones has unique environmental characteristics, functions, and habitats. Development limitations are specified, feeding into the restrictions on density and environmental performance standards that overlie the six zones. Basically, the more sensitive the zone environmentally, the less density and the fewer uses are allowed.

The ecological zone approach was a significant departure from traditional planning thinking in the 1970s that typically focused development around a town center with businesses and houses feathering out into rural areas. In contrast, the Sanibel Plan begins by assessing the environmental capability of land and basing permitted development densities and uses on such analysis—a seemingly simple concept that was revolutionary at the time and still remains cutting-edge.

The Sanibel Plan also invokes hurricane safety and protection of groundwater as two major goals. Major hurricanes are far from unusual here. Sanibel was subject to a devastating hurricane in 1926 that wiped out the island's farm economy. With the only evacuation route being the two-lane causeway, the plan limits development density for safety purposes. Similarly, the plan identifies potential groundwater contamination from septic systems and stormwater drainage and recommends development restrictions to preserve the island's water supply and sensitive wetlands.

The Sanibel Plan remains the bible to citizens of the island, as witnessed by the continuing stream of letters to the editor invoking the plan during development debates. It has been updated several times since 1976, most recently in 1997, but remains faithful to the original vision and goals of Sanibel's citizens.

That is not to say the plan is without its shortcomings. Some planners feel the ecological zone system may be too complex and that fewer zones would be equally effective and easier to understand and administer. Also, the sophistication of the plan is not matched by the mapping and geographic information system (GIS) that the city uses to administer it. Wildlife habitat maps are not particularly accurate or compre-

Part of a mangrove forest at sunset—one of the ecological zones on Sanibel Island targeted for protection. Photograph courtesy of National Oceanic and Atmospheric Administration (NOAA).

hensive, according to staff, and they must rely on county aerial photos in their work. The city is reportedly putting in place a modern GIS, which should help matters.

Acquisition/Funding

The sensitive lands acquisition program on Sanibel has provided a strong underpinning for the ambitious planning and regulatory elements. It is an effective partnership between the federal government, the private sector, and the city, with impressive results—about 7,000 acres, or nearly two-thirds of the island, is in permanent open space.

The largest conservation landowner is the U.S. Fish and Wildlife Service, which manages the J. N. "Ding" Darling Wildlife Refuge. In 1945, through a combination of land purchase from local owners and a lease from the State of Florida, 2,400 acres was set aside to create the Sanibel National Wildlife Refuge. After years of lobbying and agitation by conservationists, in 1967 the refuge's name was changed to honor Jay Norwood Darling, a famous political cartoonist who had been a fiery advocate for conservation on Sanibel. Today the refuge covers more than 6,300 acres of wildlife habitat on and around Sanibel Island ranging from beachfront property on the Gulf of Mexico to mangrove wetlands, freshwater marsh, and upland ridges. It is a true birdwatchers' paradise.

The same year that the refuge was renamed, a group of visionary citizens founded the Sanibel-Captiva Conservation Foundation. Its mission is to preserve natural resources and wildlife habitat on the island and its environs. With the assistance of The Nature Conservancy, the SCCF immediately launched an ambitious drive to

Birdwatching at Ding Darling National Wildlife Refuge. Photograph by George Gentry, courtesy of the U. S. Fish and Wildlife Service.

raise funds to buy sensitive lands on Sanibel. It was a roaring success, with over $1 million pouring in to fund acquisition of a 207-acre parcel along the Sanibel River, which winds down the middle of the island. Today the SCCF owns an impressive 1,800 acres, all acquired with donated funds (1,300 on Sanibel and 500 in the Pine Island Sound Aquatic Preserve). According to the foundation's president, the organization has been fortunate that the island has generous well-to-do residents who open their pocketbooks when the call comes to purchase a critical parcel of land with outstanding natural values.

The third partner in the acquisition triumvirate is the city. In its early years, the city concentrated on planning and regulation. However, in 1982, members of the SCCF, recognizing that local zoning would not adequately protect sensitive wetlands, urged the city council to create a dedicated source of funding for land acquisition. The council agreed and passed a special property tax levy for land acquisition. As a result, with additional assistance from the State of Florida Community Land Trust, Sanibel now is able to spend between $750,000 and $1 million annually on land acquisition—a tidy sum for such a small jurisdiction.

An impressive aspect of the acquisition program on Sanibel has been the willingness of the players to form partnerships to buy key parcels. The Sanibel Gardens subdivision is a case in point. The subdivision was laid out back in the 1920s, a typical cookie-cutter development with small lots, sold over the next three decades. The lots carved up the parcel into a grid pattern laid out without any thought to protecting sensitive habitat. By the late 1960s, development was imminent, and the SCCF began purchasing lots. Over 350 had been purchased from willing sellers by 1987, but the going was getting tough because of the fragmented ownership pattern and the hundreds of lots still left to acquire. The SCCF and city agreed that Sanibel would take over the acquisition program, using its power of eminent domain as a last resort for the few remaining holdouts. The partners recently completed acquisition of the entire subdivision, with only a handful of lots having to be condemned by the city from recalcitrant owners. Today, the SCCF and the city have entered into a joint management program for the Sanibel Gardens Preserve, which encompasses the entire old subdivision, and are in the middle of an ambitious restoration program that will rid the area of exotic vegetation.

Regulations

The Sanibel Plan set the vision and laid the conceptual foundation for an aggressive implementation program by the city with regulations at the heart of the effort. Indeed, as soon as the city was incorporated, the city council adopted a controversial development moratorium that helped provide some breathing room for work on the Sanibel Plan. The moratorium was challenged by developers, who argued they had "vested rights" to proceed with their plan because they had received or relied on approvals from Lee County prior to Sanibel's incorporation. Many of these suits were settled, and a key victory soon after the plan was adopted made clear to landowners that the city was resolute. And it did not hurt that property values began to climb on the island—just the opposite of what many developers and realtors believed would happen. It became increasingly hard to argue in court that the plan would devastate property values and effect an unconstitutional "taking" of property.

However, as land use attorneys Richard Babcock and Charles Siemon wrote in their fine case study of the Sanibel litigation in *The Zoning Game Revisited,* the plan was not impregnable. It called for concentrating commercial development at strategic nodes rather than stripping it out along the island's main road—a well-accepted planning ideal that helps reduce congestion and potential adverse impacts on nearby residential properties. The result was that some landowners who had very valuable commercial zoning in Lee County were left with much less valuable residential zoning under the plan. These large diminutions in value led one court to strike down the commercial restrictions. The results are evident today along Periwinkle Way—commercial development sprinkled along the main thoroughfare, with multiple curb-cuts and dicey traffic and pedestrian circulation patterns.

As noted previously, the backbone of the Sanibel Plan was the establishment of six ecological zones, each with its own allowable uses and densities geared to the sensitivity of resources within a specific zone. The city's development regulations directly implemented these restrictions, so, for example, if a developer owns land within the Gulf Beach Zone, only passive recreation and conservation uses are allowed. In the adjacent Gulf Beach Ridge Zone, single-family residential cluster developments are allowed, with a minimum lot size of one-half acre, and, only 30 percent of a site can be cleared of vegetation. More intensive institutional and recreational uses require a conditional use permit and special hearing.

In addition to these use and density restrictions, the zoning ordinance imposes some overlay conservation district regulations that straddle several zones. For example, the Interior Wetlands Conservation District imposes restrictions on alteration of existing water bodies, controls the use of pesticides, and restricts vegetation removal.

Finally, the code sets forth on a zone-by-zone basis a number of tough environmental performance standards that address vegetation protection, landscaping, wildlife habitat protection, water pollution, and other similar topics. More traditional regulatory topics such as parking, lighting, and telecommunication towers are treated in other zoning articles.

These regulations are applied in the five-step development review process noted previously. According to staff, there is little controversy regarding the key regulatory elements. Developers work closely with staff and usually are willing to mitigate instead of litigate. Issues typically revolve around location of structures so as to avoid adverse impacts on wildlife habitat; removal of exotic vegetation; and trimming of vegetation to provide views without destroying mangroves and other key species.

Perhaps emblematic of the regulatory program's success is the fact that the hottest land use debate of recent years has been over what some call "monster houses." With

Sanibel's code has land use standards for landscaping and vegetation protection. Photograph courtesy of Clarion Associates.

skyrocketing real estate values, Sanibel is witnessing a phenomenon seen in other resort communities—the scraping off of modest one-story dwellings and replacing them with multi-million-dollar starter castles that can cover 10,000 square feet and more. Proposed regulations to control the look of such large homes and their impact on adjacent residences have been very controversial.

All in all, Sanibel's land use regulations remain as ambitious today as they were when adopted in the 1970s. According to most observers, they have worked because of a continuing preservation consensus among citizens; savvy application by staff and the planning commission, who know when to negotiate and when to be tough; and a strong education program for landowners. In the future, most observers expect the emphasis in Sanibel to be on restoration and management given the fact that there are only a few parcels—reportedly less than 100 acres—that are available for development. Thus infill and redevelopment promise to be on the rise—and along with them debates over compatibility with existing neighbors.

Melaleuca is an invasive evergreen tree from Australia that is now rarely found on Sanibel, thanks to a local eradication and maintenance program. Photograph by Ryan Hagerty, courtesy of the U.S. Fish and Wildlife Service.

Restoration

Just as Sanibel led the nation with its planning and regulatory efforts in the 1970s and 1980s, today it is at the forefront of local governments when it comes to habitat restoration and management. One of the first things that visitors notice is the large amount of grading and tree removal that appears to be going on scattered about on big parcels throughout the island. But closer examination reveals this isn't for development, but rather for rehabilitation. The city and the SCCF are removing exotic vegetation from acquired properties such as the Sanibel Gardens subdivision and restoring the historic flow of the Sanibel River, which had been disrupted with ditches, roads, and culverts. Both organizations are increasingly turning their focus to restoration and management.

One of the biggest threats to the island's ecosystem has been exotic vegetation. The warm, inviting climate is at the southernmost range of many temperate plant species and the northernmost for subtropical ones. The result is what a city brochure on exotics terms the "alien invasion." Literally hundreds of introduced species—some benign, like bananas and citrus, and others terribly destructive, like the Brazilian pepper. The invasive exotics pose a real threat to the island's ecosystems and wildlife as they crowd out native vegetation, on which native wildlife depend.

In response, the city has adopted some of the strictest laws regulating eight invasive pest species. These eight species (including Brazilian pepper, mother-in-law's tongue, and melaleuca) are not permitted to be grown, propagated, or sold on Sanibel and must be removed from a property that is given a development permit. Furthermore, homeowners on existing lots must remove all Brazilian pepper and melaleuca even if they do not apply for some sort of development permit. The city has a financial assistance program for those in the latter category, because removal of Brazilian pepper can be very difficult and expensive.

The cooperative effort by the SCCF and the city to restore the flows of the Sanibel River is also noteworthy. A slow-moving stream that would hardly qualify as a river in most places, the Sanibel River is nonetheless a critical piece of the ecological puzzle on Sanibel. It has been routinely diked, ditched, and diverted over the last century, thereby disrupting Sanibel's interwoven hydrologic system. Today, both SCCF and the city are undertaking restoration efforts on property they own, such as Sanibel Gardens, and the city is insisting on restoration when it receives a private development application for land through which the river meanders.

The national wildlife refuge has also undertaken some ambitious restoration projects. The original dike and wildlife drive that provides visitor access through the heart of the refuge was, according to the 1974 Sanibel Report, having serious adverse environmental consequences by blocking the free flow of water to parts of the refuge. That problem has been partially remedied by construction of culverts and ditches to restore flows. The refuge has also undertaken its own exotic removal program.

Some of the biggest habitat threats are, unfortunately, not completely under control of the refuge or city. Freshwater intrusion into adjacent Pine Island Sound from the Caloosahatchee River, the result of dumping of water out of Lake Okeechobee on the other side of the state, worries federal and city officials alike. Too much freshwater can easily upset the ecosystems of the area. Development-associated habitat destruction in Lee County is another worrisome issue to many, although everyone concedes that the county has made some strides since the dark days of the 1970s with its land use regulations to reduce development impacts. (Indeed, the county now also has its own ambitious multi-million-dollar land acquisition program.)

Growing visitor pressure at the wildlife refuge and on the island's beaches is another serious challenge that will test federal and local officials in the next decade. Currently, the national wildlife refuge hosts almost 1 million visitors annually—more than many major national parks. In the past, the primary focus of refuge managers has been on managing visitors and enforcement, not on managing the resource. All of that appears to be changing under the leadership of Rob Jess, the refuge's new energetic, likable manager who exhibits a bit of a contrarian, independent streak. Part Native American and from the dry West, Jess would on the surface seem to be an unlikely choice for managing an eastern coastal refuge with a lot of water. However, he has helped to establish some innovative partnerships with the city and SCCF—such as the new SCCF marine lab on refuge property on Tarpon Bay. Jess says he wants to know more about the biology of the refuge—things like the impact of fresh-water flows from the Caloosahatchee River—so the U.S. Fish and Wildlife Service can fulfill its primary mission to protect this rare and valuable ecosystem.

Leading by Example

Surprisingly, for all of its noteworthy work on development control, the City of Sanibel has partially exempted itself and other government entities from having to comply with the development code's density and environmental standards. As a result, projects like the new city library go through a limited, truncated review. The land use regulations provide that "the city is exempted from the specific requirements of this land development code . . . and limitations . . . shall be determined on a case-by-case basis, by the city council, but no such development shall be inconsistent with the Sanibel Plan."

When queried about this seeming contradiction and the vague standards, city officials said that the strict regulations that limit the amount of land coverage on a site (e.g., to 30 percent) would make major projects like the library almost impossible because of the cost of land. Following the regulations would mean acquiring more property so that more land would remain in open space.

While some might wonder about this "do as I say, not as I do" approach, in the city's defense, some of its major building projects, such as the city hall, have won environmental awards. The city hall fits softly within the landscape, with much of the native vegetation on the site protected and no paving on the parking lots, which allows water to filter naturally into the soil.

On the other hand, one critic maintains that the city has not taken aggressive enough steps to modify or relax its standards and density limitations to encourage affordable housing. City officials counter that Sanibel has on many occasions relaxed density limitations and increased density on parcels to allow for construction of below-market-rate housing.

Social Indicators

For all of Sanibel's progress in realizing the Sanibel Plan, there is one glaring short-coming: affordable housing. The Sanibel Plan includes a substantial element on affordable housing and housing needs. It contains a specific objective to "increase the total number of housing units that are available for persons of very low, low, and moderate income." Unfortunately, the results have been meager at best.

Few houses or even condominiums on Sanibel sell for less than $500,000. Most city workers commute from Ft. Myers on the mainland. Indeed, not one policeman working for the city actually lives on Sanibel. According to city officials, city and nonprofit housing programs have created only 64 affordable units on the entire island, mostly duplexes and multifamily units. In contrast, a similar high-end resort community with an effective wildlife protection program—Aspen/Pitkin County, Colorado—has created over 1,500 units of affordable housing through an aggressive program of exactions, development linkage, and direct subsidy.

The city did provide an early seed grant of $50,000 to a nonprofit Community Housing and Resources organization that was formed in 1979. However, according to housing officials, the city would not grant substantial density increases to make affordable housing economically feasible, and nothing like the substantial sums going into resource land acquisition has been raised for affordable housing. Moreover, developers and some citizens reportedly fought against the idea of inclusionary housing regulations—which require developers to set aside a certain percentage of units in any development for affordable housing.

Recently, the city has approached the nonprofit housing organization to address the issue of employee housing, but as one observer commented, it is probably too little, too late. With land values having skyrocketed, providing affordable housing on the island will be next to impossible without huge subsidies. It may be more cost-efficient to buy land or units on the mainland for employees, although redevelopment of existing lodges and apartment complexes could offer some opportunities to require a certain number of affordable units to be created.

While many worry that sky-high housing prices may make it impossible to maintain a real community on the island, it is interesting to note that local schools are maintaining strong enrollments. Some of this is due to the fact that a surprising number of wealthy newcomers are relatively young with families. A new middle school has recently opened, and the existing elementary school has been extensively renovated, which will help reinforce the central role that schools have always provided in "gluing" the community together.

On the other hand, the city manager worries that local merchants are being displaced by a growing number of offices that provide less tax revenue and tend to deaden the street for pedestrians. Loss of retail shops that serve local residents will further erode any sense of community as citizens are forced to drive to the mainland for their shopping needs. The city is considering regulatory and other steps to address this situation.

Education

Thanks to the Sanibel-Captiva Conservation Foundation and the Ding Darling National Wildlife Refuge, Sanibel has one of the most impressive environmental education programs in the nation available to its citizens. And not surprisingly, the island has a stalwart corps of volunteers who work on a wide variety of environmental education and restoration efforts.

The SCCF maintains an environmental education fund that reaches as many as 50,000 people annually. Programs include lectures, workshops, new-resident orientations, guided tours of SCCF properties, nature cruises, and beach walks. Participants include school kids, businesspeople, local realtors, church members, and civic

The Sanibel-Captiva Conservation Foundation sponsors Resident Environmental Orientations, introducing human residents to local critters such as alligators. Photograph by Chris Duerksen.

groups, among others. Similarly, the national wildlife refuge offers an impressive variety of programs on environmental subjects, anchored by a beautiful new visitor/interpretation center.

The foundation's army of volunteers wracked up over 20,000 hours in 2003, engaged in duties ranging from fund-raising to guiding nature walks to answering the phone. According to Erick Lindblad, SCCF executive director, this was the equivalent of over 10 full-time employees. Lindblad says that this corps not only stretches the reach of the foundation but also creates a strong group of advocates for the projects it has worked on, such as the Sea Turtle Conservation Program. Volunteers for this effort spent over 5,000 hours in 2003 walking and driving the beaches, marking nests, recording data, making signs, and educating residents.

Results

According to one local, the best test of Sanibel's progress toward the goals and vision of the Sanibel Plan came when John Clark, the biologist behind the influential Sanibel Report, on which the Sanibel Plan is based, visited the island in 1996 to celebrate the plan's twentieth anniversary. Clark said that things hadn't changed much since 1976, and that developments were where they should be.

Statistics on land acquisition and preservation buttress Clark's remarks. As noted previously, almost two-thirds of the island has been protected through acquisition. For the most part, developments built under the Sanibel Plan and development code are unobtrusive. In some ways, the island's ecosystems are in better shape today than 25 years ago.

Of course, challenges remain. Increasing visitor pressure, and external influences from development on the mainland and freshwater dumping out of Lake Okeechobee, are worrisome. Lee County is avidly promoting Sanibel's beaches as a centerpiece for a tourism campaign, while providing little assistance to cope with the impacts.

Note

[1]Primary sources for this case study include Bruce Rogers, former Sanibel planning director; Rob Jess, refuge manager, Ding Darling National Wildlife Refuge; Erick Lindblad, executive director, Sanibel-Captive Conservation Foundation; other city staff and local citizens; the City of Sanibel website, www.mysanibel.com; and the Sanibel Plan.

CHAPTER 11

Twin Cities Region, Minnesota: Toward Regional Habitat Protection

Notable nature-friendly programs in Minneapolis and St. Paul, Minnesota, the "Twin Cities," include collaboration among the many stakeholders throughout the region for funding purposes, as well as active identification, protection, and restoration of critical habitat. Although the Twin Cities region has a well-established regional planning entity, the Metropolitan Council, as well as established state-level programs, the area is just beginning to create a regional approach to habitat protection. There is no consistent regulatory approach, oversight, or guaranteed funding to ensure that habitat protection actually occurs in all local jurisdictions. The state Department of Natural Resources has also dedicated resources to the metropolitan region and has led initiatives to identify critical habitat, but also lacks the necessary regulatory teeth and funding required to be effective. Nevertheless, the Metropolitan Council's efforts in planning for transportation, wastewater treatment and collection, water supply and surface water management, and regional parks, along with its comprehensive plan conformance program, are excellent building blocks. In addition, a majority of the residents of the region were raised in-state, and many have local ties to the land, which presents a unique opportunity to maintain this region as one of the most nature-friendly in the country.

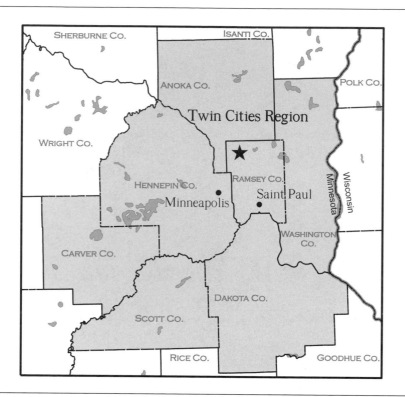

TWIN CITIES REGION, MINNESOTA
Map courtesy of Clarion Associates.

The Twin Cities region is where "the women are strong, the men are good-looking, and the children are above average." So proclaims Garrison Keillor in his nationally broadcast radio show out of St. Paul, *A Prairie Home Companion.* Indeed, this region is generally above average.[1]

Here is where a model public park system was created in the 1880s, and where one of the few regional planning entities with real power in the nation began in the 1960s. The lush greenery is still very much in evidence despite years of expansion around the hub of St. Paul and Minneapolis. Gently rolling farmland and forests scattered with wetlands, lakes, and small slivers of prairie characterize the suburban areas of the Twin Cities, set in the south-central part of the state. The downtown areas of both Minneapolis and St. Paul are set on either side of the dramatic Mississippi River valley, while other streams, including several trout streams, meander throughout the region.

The Mississippi is a focal point and appropriately so, as the granddaddy of the North American rivers. Its headwaters are in northern Minnesota, and as it makes it way to New Orleans, it drains 32 states. This made the metro area a logical place for a regional transportation hub for 150 years—river traffic first, then railroad traffic. The economy is diverse, but it wasn't always that way—this is the former flour mill and railroad capital of the United States. A major economic evolution has occurred beginning in the 1930s or so, with 3M, Target, and other companies representing banking, retailing, healthcare, insurance, and other industries becoming part of the current mix. Land ownership varies—some federal agencies and other public entities own land along the rivers. Away from the rivers, ownership is primarily private.

The metro area population is the fifteenth largest in the United States at about 2.6 million, up around 34 percent from 1980, when population hovered just below 2 million. Another million people are expected to move into the area over the next 30 years. Two-thirds of the metro population are originally from the State of Minnesota, and when people move there, they tend not to leave, providing a stable base. However, while growth has been moderate, as more and more newcomers move to the area, this relative stability may change and the number of people with ties to the land may decrease, making this the time to put policies and regulations in place to protect habitat.

The regional park system has 43 parks and park preserves, and Minneapolis in particular was fortunate to have visionaries set aside open space along the river and lakes in the late 1800s. But appearances can be deceiving: Less than 6 percent of the native landscape remains, and only about 4 percent of the native plant diversity still exists. An estimated 60 acres of open space are lost to development each day in the metro area. Ecosystems include riparian areas, upland prairie, and forests—bottomland and upland. Despite the decline in native ecosystems, the Mississippi River valley is used by about 40 percent of the nation's migratory waterfowl and is also home to a wide variety of fish, mussels, mammals, amphibians, and reptiles.

The Metropolitan Council, one of the first regional governments in the nation with real powers, provides a strong foundation for the region, with planning authority in several "systems" (transit, wastewater, parks, and aviation) that are more efficient to address at a regional level. However, its authority for natural resources beyond parks is either indirect or only advisory—primarily review and comment for consistency with regional policies or for compatibility with adjacent or affected units of government. It also establishes an area for development, the Metropolitan Urban Service Area (MUSA), in partnership with local governments. Communities at the developing

The Mississippi River provides valuable wildlife habitat as it runs through the Twin Cities. Photograph courtesy of the Saint Paul Riverfront Corporation.

edge are encouraged to maintain a 20-year land supply. The council's overall regional planning framework (the 2030 Regional Development Framework) and four regional system plans (the four planning areas mentioned previously), to which local jurisdiction plans must conform, provide an indirect way to advance natural resource protection. But they simply have no regulatory teeth, which is often required for on-the-ground change to occur. However, the most recent regional plan framework (adopted in January 2004) has incorporated a natural resource policy and goal to conserve vital natural resources, an important stride forward.

The council also created a regional park system, whose lands are managed by 10 regional park implementing agencies. The regional parkland acquisition phase has been generally completed in about half of the counties, with significant additional acquisitions needed in the other half, according to Department of Natural Resources (DNR) staff. It is unclear if additional acquisitions will become a priority again in the future. Other important council programs include the Livable Communities Act programs (which include support for development patterns that link housing, jobs, and services; brownfield redevelopment; and affordable housing), and water quality protection efforts (e.g., national award-winning waste treatment).

In addition to lack of regulatory authority, another potential issue is that the entire council is appointed by the governor and serves coterminous terms with the governor. Because of this, council priorities and policies can change every time the governorship changes. Until the mid-1990s, council members served staggered four-year terms, with half being appointed at one time, thus providing some consistency in policies.

The state Department of Natural Resources provides sound scientific information and data and has staff dedicated to the metro region. The department has a wide range of programs that protect habitat, such as trout stream protection and other water quality initiatives, and it has been the leader of the Metro Greenways Project and the Wildlife Corridors Program. However, the department also has very little ability to regulate, with jurisdiction only over state waters.

A large number of active, mature nonprofit conservation groups help focus resources on important habitat issues, including acquisition and restoration of sensitive lands. The list includes national groups such as the Trust for Public Land as well as local groups like the Minnesota Land Trust, Friends of the Mississippi River, Great River Greening, and 1000 Friends of Minnesota.

The region has several award-winning conservation design builders, and the development community in general has been supportive of efforts to identify habitat and standardize land cover information.

The biggest strength is that all of the previously mentioned groups, as well as other federal, state, and local entities, are collaborating and have successfully (though not without some disagreements) worked on several critical projects together.

Overall, there is much collaboration for acquisition, mapping, and planning what to protect among the many players throughout the region. The council, DNR, and citizen groups have reached some agreement about what habitat areas to protect, and cooperate on finding funds to protect them. Two of these more informal collaborations will be discussed later: the Regional Greenways Collaborative and the Natural Resources Task Force. They represent a promising future direction for the region regarding protection of natural areas at a regional scale by keeping all key players at the table.

While these developments are very promising, questions raised around the country are also being raised here by groups with a statewide perspective: Just how much should you try to save small pieces of land within an urbanizing area? How should *regional* be defined from a habitat perspective? Although there are some important ecological remnants that should be preserved within the seven-county metro region (e.g., the "Big Woods" area), staff at 1000 Friends of Minnesota feel that rampant sprawl *outside* of the official metro region is being overlooked, yet that is where the best farmland and most intact ecosystems are located that the group feels should be protected. While coordination is needed, more groups were focusing on this issue as of 2003–2004.

Despite the challenges facing this seven-county metro region, critical building blocks such as collaboration among many stakeholders for active identification of critical habitat and funding for protection, as well as regional planning and services efforts, make the Twin Cities a nature-friendly community with plenty of ideas to share.

Key Program Elements

Program Structure and Administration

The Metropolitan Council plays an important role in regional growth planning, indirectly contributing to habitat protection simply by coordinating basic services for transit, wastewater, parks, and aviation. It started in the form of a regional planning agency in the late 1960s in response to lack of coordinated water/sewer services in the rapidly growing suburban areas. Several commissions were created over the years and were subsequently added to the council's responsibilities, including transit and wastewater. The most recent reorganization was in 1994, giving the council its current form and authority, transforming it from a $40 million regional planning agency to a $600 million regional government operating regional sewer and transit systems. The council's jurisdiction covers seven counties (Anoka, Carver, Dakota, Hennepin, Ramsey, Scott, and Washington), which include 185 cities and townships. Many of these cities have their own planning departments, as do all the counties. Most apply their own development and zoning regulations.

The council obtains funding from a variety of sources: user fees such as wastewater treatment charges and transit fares (providing 42 percent of council revenue in 2003); state and federal funds (53 percent); property tax (3 percent); and other sources (2 percent). It is a large organization, with a governing body of 16 members who each represent a geographic district and 1 chair who serves at large. These members are all appointed by and serve at the pleasure of the governor. There are 3,718 employees in four major departments: Regional Administration (198 staff); Community Development, including the Housing and Redevelopment Authority (83 staff); Transportation (primarily Metro Transit) (2,718 staff); and Environmental Services (719 staff). The Community Development Department oversees the regional planning and conformance requirements, while Environmental Services addresses water quality, water supply, and surface water management issues, and operates the regional wastewater collection and treatment system.

The state Department of Natural Resources is the leader in habitat protection and has a region that includes the metro area—the DNR Central Region. The DNR Central Region used to cover the same seven counties covered by the council, but in 2002 the DNR regions were redrawn to make the Central Region larger, including about 10 more counties in the surrounding area and now embracing almost the entire growth corridor in the state. The DNR Central Region has a wide variety of programs and staff.

Compared with many other regions of the nation, there is significant collaboration at all levels and scales in the region—from the neighborhood level up to the regional level, and from township entities up to the Metropolitan Council, state departments, and federal agencies.

The Regional Greenways Collaborative is one example of this collaboration—it is a loose network of conservation professionals from public and some private entities from all levels as well as citizen advocates that has been meeting informally for several years, and formally since 2002. The collaborative holds half-day quarterly meetings about various conservation topics of concern to all and maintains a database of about 400 people in the network. It formed a steering committee in 2004 and has work groups, such as one defining vocabulary for habitat issues. The collaborative has developed benchmarks toward achieving its vision, goals, and objectives. This group has the potential to become an entity similar to the Chicago Wilderness coalition, discussed in Chapter 14—both started as a smaller group of concerned representatives from federal and state agencies and local conservation organizations.

Planning

Planning is where the strength of this region lies—in mapping and in regional plan coordination. The DNR has completed regional mapping of natural resources, while the council coordinates regional planning. Several programs will be discussed here, including the DNR's Metro Greenways, the Wildlife Corridors partnership, and the council's regional plan conformance. However, each program contains other key elements as well.

Mapping

There have been several attempts to map and identify critical habitat in the metro region, each one becoming more focused and incorporating more accurate data. The general process has been similar to that seen in other jurisdictions around the country: anecdotal and field information, land cover data, ecological value of that land cover, overview of the region, and then detailed analysis of smaller land areas.

For all mapping, the DNR provides many data layers regarding biological and other natural resources. The council has provided aerial photography every five years and has also developed world-class geographic information system (GIS) capabilities because of the need to coordinate many different types of programs and data requirements throughout the region. The DNR (with help from other local, state, and federal groups) created a new land cover system in the late 1990s called the Minnesota Land Cover Classification System (MLCCS) to help classify land in terms of land cover instead of land use. The MLCCS distinguishes among different types and amounts of land cover, vegetation, and impervious surfaces.

Original concept map   Mapping of critical habitat began in earnest in 1995 when the DNR sat down with a large group of planners, developers, and conservationists from around the region and created the original concept map to identify remaining known habitat. Staff had come to the conclusion that becoming active in identifying habitat would be more effective than waiting until the habitat was threatened by development. The initial map was crudely sketched using extensive field expertise regarding the last remaining green spaces in the region. DNR technical staff created a GIS-based map that showed the existing parks system in relation to important habitats with substantial natural resource attributes or wildlife habitat value. Potential greenways were drawn to stitch the natural areas into a regional network. The group wanted a graphic that could capture policymakers' attention, and it did—prompting the state legislature to fund a year-long collaborative process to explore how a regional concept for greenways and natural areas might become a reality. The 1997 report "Metro Greenprint: Planning for Nature in the Face of Urban Growth" was the culmination of many meetings by the Greenways and Natural Areas Collaborative. This led to the Metro Greenways Program, which was launched in 1998. This program will be discussed in more detail under "Acquisition/Funding."

Regionally significant ecological areas   In the fall of 2003, the DNR Central Region completed a landscape-scale assessment of the seven-county metro area to identify ecologically significant terrestrial and wetland areas. The Metropolitan Council provided satellite land cover data. The project developed eight separate GIS habitat models to evaluate these areas based on ecological principles and land cover characteristics (size, shape, connectivity, species diversity, and compatibility of adjacent land uses). The results from the individual habitat models were combined using another GIS model, and then proofed against the most current aerial photographs available. This assessment estimated that approximately 280,000 acres of regionally significant habitat remain, which is 14.7 percent of the total land area (including open water) in the seven-county metropolitan region, or 37 percent of the total remaining natural areas.

About 56 percent of the 280,000 acres, or 158,000 acres, include regionally significant wetlands and open water. Of this, 50,000 wetland acres fall outside of areas protected in regional, state, or federal parklands, but are protected by state wetlands law, the Wetlands Conservation Act of 1991. This suggests that 32 percent of regionally significant wetland areas may require additional protection if they are to retain their high ecological significance. Forested areas constitute 33 percent and grasslands about 19 percent of the regionally significant areas.

The council partnered with DNR fisheries staff to develop a preliminary aquatic assessment in 2003; DNR is planning to complete a more refined aquatic assessment in 2005.

Wildlife Corridors focus map   The Wildlife Corridors focus area map was created to determine where the partnership's funded projects should be targeted. This project concentrates on lands within corridors only and uses the Regionally Significant Ecological Areas map as a basis; it is discussed further under "Acquisitions/Funding."

Natural resources inventory   The natural resources inventory is a series of maps that describe natural resources in the region. The council prepared the inventory maps for its use in regional planning and for local governments to use in their local planning. The series of maps is a combination of the Regionally Significant Ecological Areas map mentioned previously with maps describing recreational and natural resources protection, river and stream corridors, and aggregate and agricultural resources. The council also incorporated some of the data from the natural resources inventory into the 2030 Regional Development Framework Map (the regional plan) as a conceptual

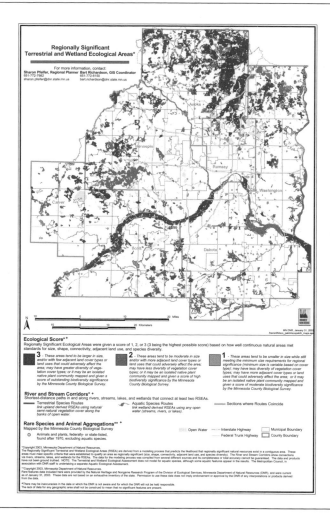

REGIONALLY SIGNIFICANT TERRESTRIAL AND WETLAND ECOLOGICAL AREAS, MINNESOTA DEPARTMENT OF NATURAL RESOURCES CENTRAL REGION
The Minnesota Department of Natural Resources Central Region is the area's leader in natural resource protection and has completed regional mapping of natural resources, as indicated in this map of regionally significant ecological areas. Map ©2003, State of Minnesota Department of Natural Resources. Reprinted with permission.

starting point only. The regional growth strategy map shows the regional natural resource areas. Every community can use the information as a foundation for locals to build more detailed maps of local resources for local natural resource planning and conservation activities.

The DNR, council, and other agencies are developing additional data and data of greater detail. A Natural Resource Task Force was formed in early 2004 by the council (with a DNR representative) to refine the process used by local communities to incorporate natural resource considerations into the comprehensive planning process. The refined process and added natural resource data will provide further support of the local comprehensive planning process, scheduled for completion by 2008.

Significantly, while the inventory was prepared under the previous administration, the current council retained as a new direction for its integrated, comprehensive strategy the use of the metrowide natural resources inventory to foster development that is more sensitive to the environment. The regional policy and planning framework is in place; however, the regulatory authority is still lagging, as discussed under "Regulations."

Local mapping efforts   As of summer 2004, about 75 percent of the seven-county area had obtained finer resolution data regarding habitat and land cover. This work has been driven by the DNR and funded by the Metro Greenways planning program, and about $1 million has been distributed to local jurisdictions for this purpose.

Regional Planning

Under state law, each city and township (185 total) in the seven-county metropolitan area is required at least every 10 years to prepare and submit to the Metropolitan Council a local comprehensive plan that is consistent with the council's metropolitan regional plan (which is updated at least every 10 years). The current regional plan, the "2030 Regional Development Framework," received an Outstanding Planning Award from the Minnesota chapter of the American Planning Association in 2004. It includes four system plans (transit, wastewater, parks, and aviation) that are being developed in 2004 and 2005. The next round of updated local plans will be due in 2008. The council walks a fine line of working with the local governments to achieve regional goals while acknowledging the importance of local decision making and the fact that most implementing authority rests at the local level. However, at the same time, the local plans must conform to the regional plan and related system plans. The process involves significant interaction between the council and each separate jurisdiction. There are sector representatives within the council staff who act as liaisons with the communities, while each of the 16 Metropolitan Council members visit their areas as well. When the council revises the regional plan and related system plans, input is obtained from the jurisdictions—it is not a completely top-down activity. When the regional plan and related system plans are finalized, staff members work with communities to help them update their local plans. The local plans must not only conform with the current regional plan and related system plans but must be consistent with current council policies in housing and water supply (water quality is considered part of a system plan) and must also be compatible with the plans of neighboring jurisdictions. Public participation is a council policy and is expected.

Something that makes this planning process more palatable to locals is that the Twin Cities region has had regional property tax sharing since the early 1970s. Council staff feel that this program has reduced competition for regional development projects. Communities are less interested in pursuing commercial development at all costs, which makes regional planning somewhat easier.

One criticism of the current regional plan (the 2030 Regional Development Framework) is that it allows development in rural areas at densities that promote sprawl and do not protect open space and agricultural lands. Rural residential areas can be developed at one dwelling unit per 2–2.5 acres, which critics claim is suburban, not rural. Council staff clarify that the regional plan is often simply a reflection of what is on the ground and not council policy.

On the other hand, an unexpected strength has been the inclusion of natural resources in the map used for the regional plan. Local communities will need to integrate natural resources into their plans. Also, the regional plan includes a clear goal of "preserving vital natural areas and resources for future generations." Local plans must reflect this goal. Another encouraging aspect of the new regional plan is the inclusion of benchmarks in 2004. Although none of them deals directly with habitat acres or species, several of the environmental benchmarks address water and air quality. Benchmarks will help the council evaluate the success of the plan and will inform any changes that may be needed or additional activities to be undertaken.

Advantages of having a regional plan conformance process are the following:

- Communities have some degree of assurance that there will be no drastic changes or development "surprises" around their borders—the regional plan assures some consistency and relative stability.
- Communities have ready access to information about innovative projects their neighbors are undertaking, which helps them visualize how they can do the same thing. Information and lessons learned from these projects helped to guide the policies and strategies of the regional plan and are being shared with communities across the region through the council's technical assistance.

- Communities all update plans at the same time using the same data set.

- The region has greater ability to plan infrastructure in a cost-effective and efficient manner.

- Many communities may not see a local need to update their community plans but participate in the plan updates because they are legally required to do so. Most jurisdictions comply readily and are accepting of the council because of the wide range of valuable services it provides.

The council has occasionally gone beyond regional planning to help coordinate local planning programs. One example is the "Mississippi Riverfront initiative" to produce a list of "priority projects" designed to preserve and revitalize the Mississippi River from St. Paul to its confluence with the St. Croix River below the City of Hastings. The initiative developed a process for identifying, evaluating, and prioritizing development, conservation, recreation, and other river projects.

For two years (2001–2003), 4 counties and 21 communities worked together to develop the list of priority projects and action plans along the 35-mile stretch of riverfront. The project built on extensive planning previously completed by local communities, nonprofits, business, industry, and public agencies. Major funding and guidance were provided by the McKnight Foundation (a regional, widely respected foundation). Individual local governments continue to implement the plan.

In addition to regional land use planning, the council also has broad responsibility for regional transit/transportation and wastewater treatment and collection, both of which have significant ramifications for habitat protection. They are coordinated and consistent with the regional plan.

Acquisition/Funding

Various entities acquire sensitive lands around the region, with no single player dominating. The region had an early emphasis on acquisition—the Minneapolis and St. Paul city park system, established late in the nineteenth century, kept significant portions of the Mississippi River bank free from development and is a national role model for early thinking about open space protection (and early acquisition).

In the 1970s, the council developed a regional park plan, which will be discussed further below. Around the same time, the Minnesota Valley National Wildlife Refuge was established about 10 miles from downtown Minneapolis. It consists of about 14,000 acres, and is the largest urban national wildlife refuge in the nation. Later, in the 1980s, the Mississippi River was designated as a national river and recreation area. However, this designation focuses primarily on history and tourism rather than on protection of the river, which prompted the formation of a citizen group, Friends of the Mississippi River, to focus on land acquisition and restoration along the riverbanks.

Since the early 1990s, grant money for acquisitions has been available from the state Legislative Commission on Minnesota Resources (which receives funding from state lottery proceeds). The DNR has been one of the primary funnels for these state funds. The DNR has also contributed significant building blocks of habitat to the metro area, as discussed later.

Metropolitan Council Regional Parks

The council is a player on the acquisition front primarily through its regional parks program. The regional park system was authorized by the Minnesota Legislature in 1974, and the enabling legislation required that acquisition should begin soon after adoption. About 31,000 acres already existed at that time and were folded into the system; another 21,000 acres have been acquired over the past 30 years. Over 70 percent of all the land is habitat. The regional parks system now includes 43 parks and park reserves, 22 trails, and 4 special recreation areas, totaling about 52,000 acres and 170 miles of trails, open for public use. The Recreation Open Space Policy Plan, amended in April 2004, calls for a park system of approximately 57,500 acres of land, so acquisition goals are nearly met. Parks are operated by about 10 partnering cities and counties. Funding for acquisitions has been provided primarily by council and state bonds. The council currently has about $5 million available for acquisitions, and properties will be acquired as willing sellers come forward. Funding has been consistently approved for acquisitions in every capital funding cycle, although since the goal of 57,500 acres is almost in hand, it is unclear if the council will set an even higher goal in the future or focus its money elsewhere.

The council has an AAA bond rating—it dealt well with the challenging economic times in 2002–2003. The council sells bonds to fund capital projects—40 percent of the parks capital budget comes from the council and 60 percent from the state.

DNR Metro Greenways

Over the years, the DNR has protected a large amount of habitat in the seven-county metropolitan area: 4 state parks (8,912 acres); 44 wildlife management areas (56,651 acres); 13 scientific and natural areas (2,401 acres); and 2 aquatic management areas.[2]

A walker enjoys Cottage Grove Ravine Regional Park in Washington County, Minnesota. Photograph courtesy of the Twin Cities Area Metropolitan Council.

The DNR has also sponsored programs to help local governments with acquisition and restoration initiatives.

The DNR led the Greenways and Natural Areas Collaborative funded by the state legislature in the mid-1990s. The group published the Metro Greenprint study in 1997, which recommended establishing an advisory committee that would guide creation of greenways and natural areas. The study also recommended an initial investment of $20 million to jump-start the program and protect priority areas. A grant program and an operating budget were also proposed. The legislature agreed to provide initial funding of just over $4 million to start a program to meet many of these goals, creating the Metro Greenways Program. The legislature has appropriated a total of $9.3 million to Metro Greenways for land protection and restoration, as well as planning grants from 1998 through 2004. This has leveraged $20 million in other state, local, federal, and private funds toward protection and restoration projects. To date, the Metro Greenways Program has protected through fee title and conservation easement acquisition more than 2,200 acres of sensitive natural areas, and has provided grants to restore 606 acres. Also, through Metro Greenways planning grants and the work of numerous local and county partners, land cover mapping has been completed for 1.9 million acres—about 75 percent of the seven-county region. Various groups can apply for grants, and this program is one of the best ways for local organizations and jurisdictions to get matching money for restoration and habitat inventory assistance, in addition to acquisitions. Since 2003, funding for Metro Greenways has been funneled through the new partnership called the Metro Wildlife Corridors.

Metro Wildlife Corridors

Metro Wildlife Corridors received state funding through the Legislative Commission on Minnesota Resources (LCMR) totaling $4.85 million for 2003–2005. One-fourth of this money is targeted for restoration and three-fourths for acquisition, which must be spent on wildlife corridors. Almost one-quarter of this money went to the Metro Greenways Program, discussed previously. Metro Wildlife Corridors was created to broaden organizational ownership of habitat protection efforts that had been dominated by the DNR. DNR staff still participate heavily, but partners play a more equal role. Current partners include several DNR units and nonprofit organizations. The group's strategies are to focus on strategic corridors, efficiently leverage the partners' resources, and enhance the cost-effectiveness of conservation programs by coordinating them within a regional framework. The project started in 2003 with the goals of restoring approximately 1,700 acres of habitat on public and private lands and permanently protecting approximately 600 acres of significant habitat. The first phase is to develop implementation strategies for each focus area chosen, with the intention of increasing local community interest, commitment, and capacity to protect natural resources.

Program partners have received an LCMR recommendation for $3.53 million in state funding (out of $17.7 million requested) to protect an additional 830 acres of habitat and restore another 570 acres. The group has added two more nonprofit organization partners and expanded into seven of the rapidly developing counties surrounding the seven-county metro region.

Nonprofit Activity

Other groups are actively acquiring land for protection in the region, including land trusts such as the Minnesota Land Trust and several other smaller, local land trusts, as well as nationally known organizations like the Trust for Public Land (a partner in

Metro Wildlife Corridors) and The Nature Conservancy. Several regional conservation groups like the Friends of the Mississippi River include acquisition strategies in their programs.

Local Efforts

Although a survey of acquisition projects in all 193 local jurisdictions (townships, cities, and counties) in the metro area is beyond the scope of this case study, recent progress in Dakota County is worth mentioning. Dakota County voters approved a $20 million bond referendum in November 2002 that will help protect key farmland and natural areas. Concerned about the rapid growth and development occurring in their communities, Dakota County citizens approved the measure by a vote of 57 percent to 43 percent. Dakota is the first county in Minnesota to adopt this type of measure.

Regulations

As indicated earlier, regulations are not the strong suit at the regional level. Perhaps that comes with the territory, or region, so to speak.

The current council, as well as its predecessors, has the philosophy that local jurisdictions should keep local control—that no local government likes to be told what to do by another governmental entity. However, other regional and nonprofit entities in the area feel that the council should use what authority it does have more aggressively in regard to habitat protection. The council has not been authorized by the legislature to directly regulate development issues, but it regulates indirectly through system plans, local plan conformity requirements, and the establishment of the Metropolitan Urban Service Area.

The council does have significant direct involvement with four "systems"—transportation, wastewater services, aviation, and regional parks. Having these regional issues discussed and addressed at a regional level is a big help. As discussed previously, the council has been directly involved in regional park planning and land acquisition. However, natural resources is not a separate "system" yet, and is unlikely to be in the near future. The state legislature and the governor, as well as other entities (such as the DNR) would have to come to an agreement about the council's scope and authority in this arena.

At the same time, some activities carried out by the council have a regulatory effect even if they are indirect and are not considered officially regulatory by nature.

Local comprehensive plan conformance with the regional plan is a type of regulatory tool. State law requires not only that each jurisdiction's plan should conform to the regional plan, but that the jurisdiction's zoning regulations must then conform to the updated local plan.

In addition, the Metropolitan Urban Service Area (MUSA) is not officially considered to be a regulatory tool, but it does help to slow sprawl and encourage more compact growth. MUSA is officially the seven-county metropolitan area for which the council is committed by policy to provide regional planning for sanitary sewer, highway, transit, park, and airport facilities. In the past, the MUSA was more tightly staged and acted somewhat like an urban growth boundary—services could not be extended outside the boundary except through a formal process to amend its reach. Today, the regional MUSA policy provides more flexibility for local communities; they can develop within a 20-year land supply. This moves away from a strict policy of contiguity of development.

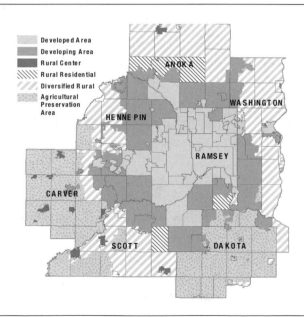

METROPOLITAN COUNCIL PLANNING AREAS
The Metropolitan Urban Service Area policy is now more flexible, providing for a 20-year land supply, rather than an urban growth boundary as in the past. Map courtesy of the Twin Cities Area Metropolitan Council.

In addition to indirect regulation through council MUSA policy and plan conformity requirements, state law requires environmental review for major projects. The state Environmental Quality Board writes the rules for conducting environmental reviews. The actual reviews are usually conducted by governing bodies, such as a county board, city council, or state agency. Not all development projects require environmental review. The nature, size, and location of a project determines whether environmental review is needed, and the specifics are spelled out in a detailed set of rules. If environmental review is required or desired, the governmental body with jurisdiction over the project works with the developer to complete one or all of the following documents:

- The *Environmental Assessment Worksheet* (EAW) is a screening tool to determine whether a full environmental impact statement is needed. The worksheet is a six-page questionnaire about the project's environmental setting, the potential for environmental harm, and plans to reduce the harm. About 150 worksheets are completed each year.

- The *Environmental Impact Statement* (EIS) is an extensive, in-depth analysis—often as thick as a book—used for a handful of major development projects that will greatly change the environment. The statement covers social and economic influences, as well as environmental impact, and looks at alternate ways to proceed with the project.

- The *Alternative Urban Areawide Review* (AUAR) is a study of the environmental impacts of development projects covering a large area, and is an alternative to conducting environmental assessments for individual projects. The Metropolitan Council is trying to encourage greater use of this approach.

Restoration

As with education, many organizations acknowledge restoration as a crucial element in their activities, and there are many small neighborhood groups actively restoring habitat throughout the region. But the shining example here is another nonprofit citizen group: Great River Greening. This organization came together in the 1990s, when a vision for St. Paul's downtown waterfront led to massive native plant restoration locally and now throughout the region.

Great River Greening restores valuable and endangered natural areas and open spaces in the greater Twin Cities by engaging individuals and communities in stewardship of the Mississippi, Minnesota, and St. Croix river valleys and their watersheds.

Since 1995, the nonprofit has engaged more than 14,000 volunteers and planted more than 40,000 native trees and shrubs and nearly 150 acres of prairie grasses and wildflowers. A key component of the volunteer work groups is education. Workshops are provided for supervisors and other volunteers on native ecology in addition to restoration techniques. More than 300 volunteer restoration project supervisors have been trained. The group also eradicates invasive species such as buckthorn on both public and private lands, and has completed a highly detailed map of the ecological characteristics of the entire Twin Cities Mississippi River corridor.

Leading by Example

The council's wastewater treatment plants all won national recognition in 2002 and 2003 for outstanding compliance with state and national water discharge permits. In addition, the council agreed to divert effluent away from its Empire Wastewater Treatment Plant to help protect high-quality trout habitat in the nearby Vermillion River.

Over 150 volunteers planted native trees, shrubs, and prairie plants in South Saint Paul's new Wild Flower Levee Park with the help of Great River Greening–trained supervisors. Photograph courtesy of Great River Greening, Saint Paul, Minnesota.

The council has promoted other nature-friendly activities. For example, two light-rail stations built by the council in Minneapolis will use native plant buffers planted by local school kids to manage stormwater runoff from the park-and-ride lots. Also, the council funded a natural resources management plan (completed in 2002 by the Friends of the Mississippi River and the DNR with other agency input) for its Empire wastewater treatment plant expansion southeast of the Twin Cities near Farmington and close to a sensitive trout stream. The management plan showed that the 459-acre site has about 180 acres that could be restored to native plant communities for wildlife value and ecological education.

Social Indicators

The Metropolitan Council Livable Communities Program is using incentives (not regulations) to encourage infill, brownfield redevelopment, and affordable housing. This voluntary program disburses monies from three grant funds—the Tax Base Revitalization Act, the Local Housing Incentive Account, and the Livable Communities Demonstration Account—and so far has awarded grants to approximately 106 communities in the region. To be eligible for any of these grants, a community must work with the council to set affordable housing goals.

The Tax Base Revitalization Act (TBRA) account provides grants to communities to help clean up polluted land and facilitate growth in tax base. Brownfields have been identified as a major obstacle to economic vitality in the Twin Cities area, especially in older parts of the region. Dollars available through this account total approximately $5 million per year. A bonding initiative in 2002 to promote turning brownfields into open space failed, but some metro counties are considering similar programs to turn brownfields into either greenspace or housing.

The Local Housing Incentive Account (LHIA) helps participating communities striving to create affordable housing opportunities. This account makes approximately $1.5 million a year available to assist the development or preservation of affordable housing.

The Livable Communities Demonstration Account (LCDA) provides grants to communities to encourage land efficient, connected development patterns, and reinvestment initiatives. Through July 2003, $42 million had been provided to revitalize older communities and to create new neighborhoods in developing communities by offering a mix of housing, jobs, and services connected by a variety of transportation choices.

The Livable Communities Demonstration Account provided funding to transform segments of Excelsior Boulevard into a vibrant, mixed-use corridor in Saint Louis Park, a first-ring suburb of Minneapolis. The Excelsior and Grand project adds almost 350 residential units and 160,000 square feet of retail to the area. Photograph courtesy of the Twin Cities Area Metropolitan Council.

The Livable Communities Program received a U.S. EPA Smart Growth Achievement Award in 2003. Some critics say that this award was given more because there are so few places attempting this kind of program than because the program itself was exemplary. The primary drawback is that the state legislation that created this program does not require any targeted quantitative goals. There is no measuring to see if affordable housing needs are actually being met, and as noted previously, the goals that are set by participating communities are not based on need.

Another social indicator is access by disadvantaged groups to natural areas. In the Twin Cities, the regional park system and the many rivers and lakes are accessible to all. One of the advantages of having a regional park system is that visitor data can more easily be gathered across the region. The council has begun to evaluate visitation. The 1998 regional parks summer visitor study showed that regional park visitors in 1998 were more racially and ethnically diverse than in 1982 (when a similar study was completed). However, this does not mean that lower-income folks are well represented, since the median income of visitors in 1998 was about $50,000, quite a bit higher than the $35,000 median income of the general population of the metro region. At the same time, several regional parks are located very near lower-income neighborhoods—for example, Phalen-Keller Park, which straddles north St. Paul and southern Ramsey County. Greater Ramsey County was the only park district that showed that visitors to the parks were similar to the general population in terms of income level; in all other areas, the income of park visitors was often substantially higher than that of the general population. Ramsey County was also one of a few metro park districts in which visitation by nonwhites was higher than their proportion of the general population in the area. Across the board, all regional parks showed that visitor education levels were higher than the general population.

The DNR also provides some programs that reach out to urban groups that might not otherwise get a chance to enjoy nature. Fishing in the Neighborhood (FiN) is a relatively new DNR program with admirable goals of increasing fishing opportunities, public awareness, and environmental stewardship within the seven-county metro region. DNR Fisheries staff have had an active urban fisheries program for many years. However, as the state's population has become increasingly urbanized, the need for angling options close to where people live became obvious. The 2000 Minnesota legislature provided funding for an expanded urban fishing program, which has evolved into FiN. FiN works with local partners to create safe, family settings situated in residential areas where people can enjoy a day in the park and good fishing. Along with these local partners, FiN stocks fish, installs fishing piers and platforms, restores shoreline habitat, and sponsors aquatic education to create quality fishing opportunities.

Education

The existence of so much parkland has been somewhat of a barrier to public understanding of biodiversity and the threats it faces in the region. The typical citizen sees the typical suburban wildlife critters like raccoons and various birds and plants and feels surrounded by nature. Fortunately, all of the major players in conservation in the region have educational aspects. Two private efforts will be highlighted here: Embrace Open Space and Friends of the Mississippi River. Education is critical.

The Embrace Open Space campaign is a joint program by 14 organizations concerned about protecting open spaces in the Twin Cities region. Coordinated by the

The Minnesota Department of Natural Resources Fisheries staff provide an urban fisheries program in the metro region. Photograph by Mark Nemeth, courtesy of the Minnesota Department of Natural Resources.

McKnight Foundation, the campaign began in September 2002 with print ads, publications, a comprehensive website, direct mail, and special events intended to mobilize Twin Citians to become more vocal in public decision making about land use and land protection in the region. It was intended to be a year-long project but has been extended and expanded to include an awards program ("Champions of Open Space") and other resources such as radio ads, highly creative and successful news strategies, action toolkits for citizens, a speakers' bureau, a half-hour television program, a monthly e-newsletter, and even a T-shirt. One of the project's slogans is "Not all of our assets are in the bank." And the small print for one of the newsprint ads available for any citizen to use reads:

> *The choice is yours. Right now, just minutes from your home, people are making decisions that will permanently change the landscape around you. Protect our open spaces like wetlands, woods and farmland, because when they're gone, they're gone forever. Your voice will make a difference.*
> www.EmbraceOpenSpace.org

The McKnight Foundation completed a detailed analysis of media coverage of open space issues after the campaign had been in place for one year. It found an increase in the number of stories about open space issues in the major daily newspapers in the region, and found that the media were beginning to frame the issues in new ways, similar to what the campaign is promoting. As of the end of 2004, nearly 500 people had signed up to receive monthly campaign e-newsletters. All of these materials are on the campaign website.

Friends of the Mississippi River draws attention to the river and provides a range of educational and recreational opportunities, stewardship projects, and information that get people to the river to learn about and enjoy its ecology and history. Their

This newsprint ad is one of several used by the Embrace Open Space campaign to encourage citizen involvement in land use decisions. Photograph courtesy of Embrace Open Space.

vision is of a large and diverse constituency of people committed to protecting the Mississippi River because they understand its place in the community's history, culture, and quality of life. The group sponsors an annual canoe trip among many other endeavors to get people outside enjoying the river itself. The group also undertakes restoration, acquisition, and policy advocacy along the river.

Results

At the regional government level, there is a transition to using benchmarks to affect policy. The new 2030 Regional Development Framework is the first regional plan to include benchmarks, and money has been set aside for the research department to gather the necessary data. This is a new step for the council. Current benchmarks include water and air quality, as well as transportation services. However, again, since habitat is not covered by any formal council system, the current benchmarks do not directly address habitat preservation.

Other indicators have been used by the council for the past several years, made available each year either through a report or through the State of the Region address given annually by the chair of the council. However, these indicators were not tied to policy, and again, none of the indicators directly addressed nature.

Other groups outside of the council have done some monitoring of various types, but not at a regional level, and data are not used to influence policy directly. The DNR Ecological Services Division includes the Minnesota County Biological Survey, which began in 1987 as a systematic survey of rare biological features in the state. The goal of the survey is to identify significant natural areas and to collect and interpret data on the distribution and ecology of rare plants, rare animals, and native plant communities. Survey work has been completed in 57 of Minnesota's 87 counties, including the metropolitan region. These data have been helpful and used in various ways over the years, but no one has yet to use the data to set actual goals for protection of various habitats or species at a regional level.

However, regardless of the status of monitoring, as of mid-2004, the Twin Cities region has protected a considerable amount of habitat.

- Approximately 36,000 acres are protected in the regional park system as park reserves—80 percent of these acres are to be restored to a state similar to what European settlers found when they arrived in the 1800s.

- Of the 1.9 million acres in the seven-county region, a minimum of 133,000 acres is currently protected for their recreational and habitat values—this is 7 percent of the current land base.[3]

- About 75 percent of the region's total land base has a smaller-scale habitat inventory and land cover data available as of 2004.[4]

- More than 40,000 native trees and shrubs and nearly 150 acres of prairie grasses and wildflowers have been planted in the Mississippi and Minnesota river valleys by Great River Greening alone; many other groups are active in restoration projects as well.

Notes

[1]Primary sources for this case study include John Kari, planning analyst, and several other staff members from the Twin Cities Area Metropolitan Council; Peggy Booth, Sharon Pfeifer, and several other staff members from the Minnesota Department of Natural Resources (DNR); the Metropolitan Council's website, www.metrocouncil.org; the DNR's website, www.dnr.state.mn.us; and representatives of a variety of local nonprofit groups, such as Great River Greening and Friends of the Mississippi River.

[2]Sharon Pfeifer, principal author, Minnesota Department of Natural Resources document in preparation for the Conservation Fund, 2004.

[3]Ibid.

[4]Ibid.

Focused Case Studies

These case studies focus on a single noteworthy element of a local or regional nature protection program. Several of these communities have comprehensive programs in place, of which only one aspect is highlighted here. For example, the benchmark program of King County, Washington, and the Greenprint Program in Pittsford, New York, are each only one facet of a larger effort to protect natural resources. Other jurisdictions have chosen to concentrate on specific topics of concern in their communities, such as the New Designs for Growth Program in the Traverse Bay area of Michigan and the Greenspace Program in DeKalb County, Georgia. As with the in-depth case studies, a range of communities is included, from small rural towns to urban counties.

CHAPTER 12

Bath Township, Ohio: Riparian Overlay District

Bath Township is an affluent bedroom community close to Akron in northeastern Ohio. It is also within commuting distance of Cleveland (about 20 miles).[1] The setting is a glacial valley with a rural atmosphere, containing rolling woodlands and agricultural land, but with increasing commercial growth and housing developments. The majority of Bath Township lies in the Yellow Creek watershed. Yellow Creek is 10 miles long and flows into the Cuyahoga River in Akron, which then flows north through the nearby Cuyahoga Valley National Park up to Cleveland and into Lake Erie.

The township was founded in 1818 and covers 23 square miles. The population in 2000 was about 9,500, compared with about 9,000 in 1990, a modest growth rate not unusual for this part of the state. The surrounding county (Summit County) experienced a similar increase in population, from about 515,000 in 1990 to about 543,000 in 2000 (after hitting a peak around 1970 of 553,000).

The issue in Bath Township then is not necessarily an excessive growth rate; it is that the citizens of Bath Township place a high value on natural features. In this primarily rural area, the community (which has had many longtime residents) has always been sensitive to the creek. Most of the township obtains drinking water from wells, which are recharged from surface water in the watershed.

The Yellow Creek watershed is also critical to the recovery of the Cuyahoga River and Lake Erie. The Cuyahoga River is the infamous "burning river"—fires erupted on the river several times from 1936 to 1969 owing to floating debris and oil. This circumstance has been given much credit for inspiring the Clean Water Act and the creation of the Environmental Protection Agency in the early 1970s. As such, the river was designated as an "American Heritage River" in 1998 for its "singular importance in the birth of the American environmental movement." It also has other historical significance, since it was the western boundary of the United States from 1795 to 1803.

While much of the conventional pollution has been cleaned up, the Cuyahoga remains an EPA "area of concern" because of the toxic substances still present. Yellow Creek is a headwater and one of the cleanest tributaries of the Cuyahoga and, thanks to its relative health, is helping to repopulate aquatic insect and fish populations in the Cuyahoga River and Lake Erie.

Bath Township citizens passed a bond issue in 1996 to preserve open space. Bond monies were used to acquire the 404-acre Bath Nature Preserve the following year. The township developed its comprehensive plan in 1996–1997. The plan, which included a Natural Features Analysis that mapped and analyzed many natural resources, such as waterways, wetlands, and watersheds, was accepted by the township in 1998. It also recommended incorporating best management practices from a regional watershed study.

The township undertook an extensive update of the zoning code in 1998–2000 to implement the new comprehensive plan. The watershed recommendations were not forgotten, and many elements were added to protect open space and the environment. The most notable of these is the Riparian Overlay District. The revised code earned awards regionally and nationally.

What is unusual about Bath is that it was the first township in Ohio to pursue riparian zoning. Several incorporated municipalities in Ohio had adopted similar programs before Bath did, but riparian protection was initially not considered to fall under a township's state-designated zoning authority. Because of this, Bath Township's program was controversial at the time. Since 2000, riparian protection in Ohio has become more accepted as a township zoning activity for public health and safety reasons—namely, flooding, erosion, and water quality.

Key Program Element: Riparian Overlay District

The Riparian Overlay District imposes additional development standards beyond those of the underlying zoning districts. The overlay now applies to streams throughout the township, using the Summit County Riparian Setback map and other data sources (e.g., U.S. Geological Survey) to determine applicability. Although the 1997 comprehensive plan update contained natural resource data, the boundaries of the Riparian Overlay District were initially based on more extensive ecological studies prepared in 1999 specifically to provide a defensible foundation for the zoning resolution update. Despite these data, the ordinance was still controversial but was finally

The Riparian Overlay District regulations help protect waterways throughout Bath Township. Photograph courtesy of Bath Township.

adopted. Public and private partners in the downriver cleanup efforts helped the township pass the Riparian Overlay District by testifying at public hearings.

Uses listed as permitted or conditionally permitted in the underlying zoning districts are allowed; however, the Riparian Overlay specifically prohibits land uses such as dry cleaners and gas stations (including some originally allowed in the underlying district) that could have a negative effect on the waterways. Additionally, the Riparian Corridor Overlay District establishes a streambank buffer. This streambank buffer defines a minimum distance between structures and streambanks that can be developed or disturbed.

When the Riparian Overlay District was created in 2000, it was the first such ordinance in Summit County, and possibly in northeastern Ohio. It included a minimum setback of 75 feet from named streams and 40 feet from unnamed streams. Summit County, within which Bath Township lies, then passed a more comprehensive riparian ordinance in 2002. When the township decided to add a steep-slope protection provision to their code in 2003, they also decided to amend the setback regulations to closely match those of Summit County. This revision allows variance requests from riparian setbacks to be heard by the township Board of Zoning Appeals instead of the Summit County Planning Commission. The board has had six requests for variances during the four years since the riparian ordinance was initially passed. One variance was denied; those variances that were approved minimized intrusion into the riparian corridor to the greatest extent possible.

The current Riparian Overlay District (in Bath Township and in Summit County) ordinance relates the amount of the setback to the amount of land area drained by the stream. The drainage area and consequent setback is assessed by the Summit County Soil and Water Conservation District during the development review process, but landowners may initially go to a county website to get a general idea of what type of setback might be required on their property.

The following setbacks were effective in Bath Township as of mid-2003:

- A minimum of 300 feet on each side of all streams draining an area greater than 300 square miles.
- A minimum of 100 feet on each side of all streams draining an area greater than 20 square miles and up to 300 square miles.

- A minimum of 75 feet on each side of all streams draining an area greater than 0.5 square mile (320 acres) and up to 20 square miles.

- A minimum of 50 feet on each side of all streams draining an area greater than 0.05 square mile (32 acres) and up to 0.5 square mile (320 acres).

- A minimum of 30 feet on each side of all streams draining an area less than 0.05 square mile (32 acres).

The regulation also requires setbacks for state or federally protected wetlands: 50 feet for Category 3 wetlands and 30 feet for Category 2 wetlands.

Another important part of the regulation is a steep-slope provision, included because of the presence of steep slopes throughout the township. Slopes with greater than a 15 percent gradient must add from 25 to 100 feet to the width of the setback.

Although the effects of the riparian ordinance have not been scientifically evaluated, county staff commented that the ordinance is redirecting development in Bath Township away from the riparian corridors (as intended), and that the potential for water quality degradation has been reduced.

Note

[1]Primary sources for this case study include Mark Fenn, Zoning Inspector/Administrator, Bath Township; Don Jenkins, Trustee, Bath Township; and the Bath Township Zoning Resolution.

CHAPTER 13

Charlotte Harbor, Florida: Ambitious Regional Critical Area Protection Program

C harlotte Harbor is a 270-square-mile estuary on the southern Gulf Coast of Florida located at the confluence of three rivers (the Myakka, the Peace, and the Caloosahatchee).[1] It is bounded by five barrier islands: Sanibel, Captiva, North Captiva, Cayo Costa, and Gasparilla. The harbor is the heart of a watershed 4,468 square miles in size, the nation's eighteenth largest estuarine system.[2]

The Charlotte Harbor estuary is unique in that it has a dynamic salinity balance as a result of the three rivers that empty into the harbor. As a result, it is home to a diversity of unique subtropical flora and fauna, including rare birds, manatees, cypress swamps, mangroves, and other biologically important species. The interface between land and water also makes the area very attractive for human settlement.

In part because of this abundance of natural resources and good weather, the three core counties in which Charlotte Harbor is located (Sarasota, Charlotte, and Lee) have had substantial population growth over the last half of the twentieth century. Between 1960 and 2000, population in these three counties increased by over 700,000 persons (a 518 percent increase) from 144,000 to 890,100. The population

The Charlotte Harbor estuary provides critical habitat for at least 42 federally and state-listed species, including the wood stork. Photograph by Ryan Hagerty, courtesy of the U.S. Fish and Wildlife Service.

of the area is expected to reach 1,382,500 by 2020.[3] The continuing desirability of the area for retirees, increased phosphate mining in upstream areas, more intensive agriculture/ranching in interior counties, and decreases in groundwater levels have all exerted great influence on the natural system in and around Charlotte Harbor. These forces have caused an overall decline in the quality of the estuarine resources.

In 1979, in response to this rapid growth and increased strain on the ecosystem in the three coastal counties bordering Charlotte Harbor (and the subsequent degradation of the adjacent natural resources), then-governor Bob Graham initiated a Resource Planning and Management Program for Charlotte Harbor by appointing a committee to study the area. The mission of the committee was to develop a comprehensive and coordinated program to resolve present and future problems that endangered the natural resources and burdened the public facilities within the area governed by multiple levels of government.

Key Program Element: Resource Planning and Management Program

The use and effectiveness of Florida's Resource Planning and Management Program can only be discussed in the context of the state's land management program, established to protect and manage environmental and natural resources of regional or statewide importance—the Area of Critical State Concern (ACSC) Program. Under Florida's "critical area" program, which was adopted in 1972, lands that are considered to have a significant impact on environmental or natural resources of regional or statewide importance can be designated as an area of critical state concern.[4] Following designation, an area of critical state concern is subject to a high level of review and regulatory control by the state to ensure that future growth and development does not adversely impact the environmental and natural resources of statewide importance (Section 380.05, Florida Statutes). In many instances, the critical area designation has been quite controversial and resisted by local governments because of the degree of state control that occurs over local planning, land use, and development decisions once the critical area designation occurs.

According to state law, prior to designation and establishment of an area of critical state concern, a resource planning and management committee must be established for the purpose of organizing "a voluntary, cooperative resource planning and management program to resolve existing, and prevent future, problems which may endanger those resources" (Section 380.045[1], Florida Statutes). The committee is required to consist of representatives from all local governments whose lands would be affected by the designation, as well as any state and regional agency representatives who are involved in the management and protection of the resources. The committee is required to either develop a resource management plan with detailed recommendations for local and state government action to resolve the resource protection problems identified to be of concern, or to recommend that no plan be adopted (Section 380.045, Florida Statutes). A major objective of the program is effective coordination among state, regional, and local planning agencies to protect and manage the resources of importance. If a Resource Planning and Management Plan is adopted, it is reviewed by the state, and a decision is made on whether or not to move forward with designation as a critical area. Typically, there is a strong incentive for local governments to work together to adopt and implement a resource planning and management plan as a way to avoid the additional regulatory hurdles that accompany designation as an area of critical state concern.

The Charlotte Harbor Management Plan process was initiated in January of 1979 when Governor Graham appointed a 39-member committee to study three elements: the area's rapid population growth, the need for facilities to accommodate that growth, and the effect of growth on the region's delicate natural environment. The committee was composed of one elected official and one planning official from each of the 11 local governments, representatives of regional and state government agencies, and representatives from private environmental and development interests. The initial focus of study was on the barrier islands, shoreline, and harbor waters, but the geographic focus quickly grew to encompass all land use activities affecting the estuary within the three-county area. After 30 months of deliberation, the Charlotte Harbor Management Plan was adopted by the committee, the local governments, and the state on June 5, 1981.

The plan includes two basic goals: "to maintain and improve the functional and structural integrity of the natural estuarine ecosystems and related coastal components through coordinated management of human impacts in surrounding uplands and freshwater systems" and "to identify and address the impact of growth so as to minimize or eliminate any adverse effects on the Charlotte Harbor area."[5] To accomplish these goals, the plan provided 15 different objectives and identified 43 specific implementation actions, which were then assigned to the various units of state and local government (including the Florida Legislature) as well as to various regional entities. The goals were designed to guide governmental decision making to accommodate projected population growth while also maintaining environmental quality. The objectives dealt with a variety of topics, including local government participation, intergovernmental coordination, land development in accordance with the plan, and monitoring of implementation. The plan strove to limit development within floodplains and wetlands, discourage substantial site alteration, improve stormwater runoff and drainage systems, and address wastewater and potable water supplies.

While the components of the plan are not necessarily that unique, what is interesting is how the plan seeks to create cooperation and coordination in planning and regulatory control across 11 different local governments, multiple regional entities, and the state government. Further, these actions are being taken not just to maintain the then-current conditions of the estuary, but to improve them for the future while at the same time accommodating more of the growth and development that led to the initial declines in estuarine quality.

The effectiveness of the Charlotte Harbor Management Plan was evaluated by the state five years after its adoption in 1986. Following adoption, the plan goals and objectives were integrated into the comprehensive plans of the three counties (Lee, Charlotte, and Sarasota) as well as seven of the eight municipalities in the Charlotte Harbor area. In addition, land acquisition programs were operating around the fringe of the harbor in Charlotte County, and the barrier islands in Lee County. Despite these early successes, the state found that "the effectiveness of the management plan has been hindered by the generalized, unmeasurable nature of its language."[6] Despite the fact that coordination among the local governments had not been as successful as hoped, no designation as a critical area was found to be warranted. One recommendation of the evaluation was to strengthen the role of the regional planning agency, the Southwest Regional Planning Council, through technical and financial assistance as a way to garner additional coordination across the various jurisdictions. In addition, there was a decision to use the then recently adopted statewide comprehensive planning system created under the 1985 Growth Management Act as a vehicle to promote continued implementation of the plan and its goals.

One of the lessons learned from the Charlotte Harbor experience is that the state can be a successful catalyst in encouraging coordination among local governments in protecting natural resources. While Florida's Area of Critical State Concern Program is often credited with being a primary tool for state attempts to address resource protection, the Charlotte Harbor experience demonstrates that the Resource Planning and Management Plan process, as a precursor to designation as a critical area, has an equally important place in the state's environmental protection and intergovernmental coordination initiatives as well. In Charlotte Harbor, the Resource Planning and Management Committee and the plan it recommended became the state's primary tool to engage the 11 local governments in the "voluntary" coordination of planning to protect resources. Environmental protection was established through the broad-based participation of local officials and citizens without the political difficulties and local resistance typically associated with critical area designation. In the case of Charlotte Harbor, the Resource Planning and Management Plan process was a sufficient agent for change in and of itself.

There are several examples across Florida in which the Resource Planning and Management Plan process has been used to stimulate voluntary participation in coordination and environmental protection without having to utilize the more "heavy-handed" mandatory compliance regimen associated with designation as an area of critical state concern. Such planning processes have been used to great success in other areas of Florida, such as Hutchinson Island; an area known as the "Northwest Coast" (including Okaloosa and Walton counties); Escambia and Santa Rosa counties in the

"Panhandle" area; the Kissimmee River valley; and a portion of the Everglades in western Dade County. The Resource Planning and Management process has also become a model for subsequent regional planning activities not initiated by the state in areas like the "Treasure Coast" area of central Florida.

Following the adoption and evaluation of the Charlotte Harbor Management Plan, Governor Lawton Chiles nominated Charlotte Harbor as an estuary of national significance in 1995, and as a result, Charlotte Harbor was accepted as one of the 27 estuaries within the National Estuary Program. As a result of the designation, "Committing to Our Future," a management plan for the Charlotte Harbor estuary was adopted in March of 2000. This plan was required under the National Estuary Program and had a broader scope with considerable more detail than the original management plan, but participation was voluntary and implementation was not mandatory. The plan also expanded the conservation objectives from the original 11 jurisdictions to include 8 counties, 15 municipalities, 3 regional planning councils, and 2 water management districts. The 2000 plan identified three main issues related to the protection of the estuarine ecosystem: hydrologic alterations (adverse changes to freshwater flows as a result of human activity), water quality degradation (due to increased pollution), and habitat loss (both on land and in the water). The plan put forth a series of priority actions and related projects to be undertaken within the estuary system to build upon the conservation activities already underway.

Notes

[1] Primary sources for this case study include the sources noted in the text; representatives at the Florida State Department of Community Affairs; and Craig Richardson, Clarion Associates.

[2] W. E. Daltry and David Y. Burr, *Base Program Analysis,* vol. 1, *Description of the Existing Laws, Policy and Resource Management Structures in the Greater Charlotte Harbor Watershed,* Technical Report No. 98-01 (North Fort Meyers, Fla.: Charlotte Harbor National Estuaries Program, 1998).

[3] Bureau of Economic and Business Research, University of Florida, *Florida Population Studies, Bulletin 138: Projection of Florida Population by County, 2003–2030 (median forecasts)* (Gainesville: University of Florida Press, 2004).

[4] Established in Chapter 380.05, Florida Statutes, the ACSC program protects resources and public facilities of major statewide significance. Designated areas of critical state concern are the Florida Keys, Big Cypress Swamp, Green Swamp, the City of Key West, and the City of Apalachicola. State Department of Community Affairs (DCA) staff review all local development projects within the designated areas and may appeal to the Administration Commission (the Governor's Office) any local development orders that they believe to be inconsistent with state guidelines. The DCA also is responsible for reviewing and approving amendments to comprehensive plans and land development regulations proposed by local governments within the designated areas.

[5] Division of Local Resource Management, Department of Community Affairs, *Charlotte Harbor Management Plan* (Tallahassee: State of Florida Press, 1981).

[6] Department of Community Affairs, *An Evaluation of Implementation of the Charlotte Harbor Management Plan* (Tallahassee: State of Florida Press, 1986).

CHAPTER 14

Chicago Wilderness: Biodiversity Recovery Plan

M ore than 250,000 acres of protected natural lands surround the nation's third largest urban area. These lands, as well as interspersed unprotected lands, contain regionally, nationally, and globally significant habitat—right outside of Chicago's back door.[1]

Early in the twentieth century, residents of Chicago and the State of Illinois created systems of publicly owned preserves in the region (e.g., Cook and DuPage county forest preserves). Since then, thousands of acres have been added to this network by county, state, and federal entities throughout the region (including parts of Indiana and Wisconsin). These publicly owned preserves now provide the core natural areas in the Chicago region. A 1978 Illinois Natural Areas Inventory found that one-fourth of the healthy, natural land that exists anywhere in the state can be found in the Chicago region, where only about 0.07 percent of Illinois land can be considered healthy and natural. Unfortunately, like other areas around the nation, consumption of land in the metropolitan region is increasing faster than the population is increasing, placing these healthy natural areas at risk. The Chicago metropolitan region increased in population by only 4 percent from 1980 to 2000, but the region's area of developed land increased by 35 percent.

The network of valuable, richly diverse habitat in the metropolitan area is known as the Chicago Wilderness. Its geographic area includes northeastern Illinois, northwestern Indiana, and southeastern Wisconsin. Ecosystems include tallgrass prairie remnants, as well as valuable forests, streams, and wetlands.

The Chicago Wilderness coalition was formed in 1996 when 34 institutions (including local, state, and federal agencies; centers of research and education; and conservation organizations) decided to work together to protect these ecosystems—those lands already officially protected as well as unprotected natural areas. Over 170 public and private organizations are now members of this coalition (as of 2004), and they are committed to the protection, restoration, and management of the Chicago region's natural resources.

Members of the coalition work together on projects in the areas of science, land management, sustainability, education, and communication. Partners have collaborated on more than 160 projects, such as ecological monitoring, prairie restoration, prescribed burn training, natural landscaping, and technical assistance to local governments.

Other projects of the group include an atlas of biodiversity for the region, a magazine for the public, a journal for conservation professionals, a family activity guide, a local government guidebook, and a conservation design manual. A new project to choose and track indicators for the health of the biodiversity of the region started in 2004.

Key Program Element: Biodiversity Recovery Plan

The Chicago Wilderness Biodiversity Recovery Plan was unveiled in 1999 by the coalition after a three-year initiative by over 200 people. It is the region's first comprehensive conservation and restoration plan. The award-winning plan identifies the ecological communities of the greater Chicago region, assesses their condition, identifies the major factors affecting them, and provides recommendations for actions needed to restore and protect and sustain them well into the future. The officially stated goal of the plan is "to protect the natural communities of the Chicago region and to restore them to long-term viability, in order to enrich the quality of life of its citizens and to contribute to the preservation of global biodiversity."

The plan identifies 49 different natural community types in the region, at least 25 of which are globally rare or uncommon. Approximately 1,500 native plant species occur in the region, one of the most varied plant populations in the United States.

Key recommendations of the plan include:

- Land that is already preserved for conservation must be managed in such a way that biodiversity is protected and restored.

- More land with existing or potential biodiversity benefits must be preserved.

- Management of streams, rivers, lakes, wetlands, and the surrounding lands must be greatly improved by state agencies, local agencies, water reclamation districts, and private landowners in order to protect water quality and biodiversity.

- More monitoring and other research need to be conducted in order to understand the effects that human disturbance and ecological restoration projects are having on biodiversity.

- Citizens' awareness of the importance of biodiversity conservation should be increased, as should the level of opportunity for participation in programs that enhance biodiversity.

- Local and regional development policies should reflect the need to restore and maintain natural areas and biodiversity.

The Northeastern Illinois Planning Commission adopted this plan in late 1999, becoming the first major metropolitan planning agency in the nation to adopt a biodiversity recovery plan for its region. The plan has also been adopted by the Northwestern Indiana Regional Planning Commission and 40 other government and private entities.

Note

[1]Primary sources for this case study include Catherine Bendowitz, Chicago Wilderness Program
Coordinator; the Chicago Wilderness coalition's website, www.chicagowilderness.org; and the
Chicago Wilderness Biodiversity Recovery Plan.

CHAPTER 15

DeKalb County, Georgia: Greenspace Program

The metropolitan region of Atlanta, Georgia, has been losing open space faster than most other areas of the nation—by one estimate it lost approximately 500 acres per week in the 1990s.[1] The Atlanta metropolitan region population grew from about 2.8 million in 1990 to about 4.1 million in 2000, a 45 percent increase. DeKalb County, which lies on the east side of Atlanta, grew by 22 percent from 1990 to 2000, with a population of about 666,000 in 2000.[2] The county is now growing at a slower rate—1.5% annually—than most of the other metro Atlanta counties, mostly because of lack of developable land.[3] In 2001, DeKalb County passed a bond to help acquire parkland before it was too late. It has also been participating in the state's greenspace program ever since.[4]

The county covers about 269 square miles (approximately 172,000 acres) and is the most densely populated county in the region and the second most populated county in the state. Over 70 percent of the county's land is developed.[5] The mostly suburban county varies from very urban (containing a portion of the city of Atlanta) to semirural, including some interesting ecosystems: granite outcrop communities, wetlands, and pine and oak forests. Stone Mountain Park, one of Georgia's most popular tourist attractions, is located at the east edge of DeKalb County. The county also

Davidson–Arabia Mountain Nature Preserve, the county's primary natural area, contains unique granite outcrop ecosystems, such as this one at Bradley Peak. Photograph by Don Saunders.

is the location of the Centers for Disease Control and Prevention, the only major federal agency headquartered outside of Washington, D.C.

The population of the county is becoming more diverse and more affluent while it is aging and household size falls. Over half of the residents are African American, with other minority populations increasing while whites have been decreasing. Income levels have been rising.

Key Program Element: Greenspace Program

Atlanta has the least parkland per capita for large cities in the United States, with 7.3 acres of parkland per 1,000 residents, as compared with Austin, which has 39 acres per 1,000 residents, and Oklahoma City, which has 43 acres per 1,000 residents.[6]

DeKalb County has taken bold steps to address this issue by taking advantage of state funding and stepping up to the plate with a local bond issue. The timeline for DeKalb County efforts to conserve park land has been impressively short:

- 1999: The State of Georgia elects a new governor (Roy Barnes), who promotes a goal of protecting 20 percent of the state's land.

- 2000: The state legislature earmarks $30 million annually for land acquisition for the newly created Georgia Community Greenspace Program.

- July 2000: The county adopts the DeKalb County Parks and Recreation Strategic Plan, which calls for $260 million for implementation, including $100 million for acquisition. It includes a survey of citizens that reveals their priorities for facilities: walking and biking trails (41 percent), neighborhood parks (37 percent), picnic facilities (25 percent), playgrounds (23 percent), nature preserves/environmental centers (21 percent), and large multiuse parks (21 percent).

- November 2000: DeKalb County and nine municipalities within the county finalize the Joint DeKalb County/Municipal Greenspace Program, which proposes to preserve 22 percent of county land area as greenspace (about 37,860 acres). Creation of this document helps to qualify the jurisdictions for state greenspace monies.

- November 2000: Vernon Jones is elected chief executive officer of DeKalb County and soon begins advocating for greenspace in the county.

- March 2001: A bond referendum is quickly proposed as part of a special election. DeKalb County citizens approve the issuance of $125 million in general obligation park bonds.

DeKalb County created an Office of Parks Bond and Greenspace to administer the funds that were obtained through the bond referendum ($130 million—$125 million plus $5 million from selling the bonds at a premium); from the state greenspace program ($5.5 million through 2002 for the unincorporated county); and from other sources such as local foundations and federal monies ($2.4 million through 2002).

The funds from the bond referendum will be split between land acquisition and improving existing parks. At least 70 percent (about $91 million) will be dedicated to acquisition of lands for parks and greenspace. This includes acquiring lands for active recreation, such as soccer fields and playgrounds, in addition to natural areas. No more than 30 percent of the bond funds will be used to develop newly acquired land and for improving existing parks. As of April 2004, a total of $54.38 million had been expended to acquire 1,924 acres. Of these, 300 acres will be used for active recreation, and the remaining 1,600 acres will likely stay as greenspace.

The public can nominate properties for acquisition, and the county has received over 600 nominations since the program began. The criteria used to evaluate properties are related primarily to active recreational parks (for example, ability to provide small neighborhood parks or larger community parks in underserved areas). However, two criteria are more relevant for biodiversity: (1) significant and measurable impact on water quality and (2) nature preserves and greenspace (must have public access and contain cultural, archaeological, and scenic features, or natural features such as wildlife or plant habitat, wetlands, rock outcroppings, stream buffers, and other features that are fragile and should be protected by the county).

Although the county has not defined how much of the bond money will be spent on natural areas, about 1,600 acres of the 1,924 acres that have been acquired as of April 2004 will likely remain as natural areas. This total includes 1,200 acres of sensitive lands that were bought as an addition to Arabia Mountain Nature Preserve, located in the southeast part of the county, and the county's primary natural area. The preserve contains granite outcrops (including rare vernal pool ecosystems in these outcrops), wetlands, pine and oak forests, streams, and lakes, all just a 20-minute drive from downtown Atlanta. Part of this acquisition provides a link between the nature preserve and nearby Panola Mountain State Conservation Park.

The funds obtained from the state greenspace program may only be used for what the state calls "greenspace." The Georgia Greenspace Program encourages urban and rapidly growing counties to set aside 20 percent of their land as protected greenspace as they continue to develop. The program defines greenspace as "permanently protected land and water, including agricultural and forestry land whose development rights have been severed from the property, that is in its undeveloped, natural state" or that has been developed or restored to be consistent with one or more of nine goals that include passive recreation, water quality protection, and scenic protection.

The Joint DeKalb County/Municipal Greenspace Program document provides the basic framework for these acquisitions. It was produced according to state requirements and included public participation and mapping of potential greenspace. The document identifies two tiers of land protection: sensitive lands and other greenspace categories. Sensitive lands include the 500-year flood-plain plus 100 feet, wetlands, riparian corridors plus 75 feet, rock outcrops, steep slopes and erodible soils, forests, historical sites, and agricultural lands. These potential sensitive area acquisitions total about 31,000 acres. Another 7,000 acres fit into the other greenspace categories. The county currently does not have the funding to obtain all lands identified, and the state funds received are small compared with the amount needed. Bond funds will certainly help the county move toward its ambitious goal of protecting 22 percent of its land area as greenspace; about 4 percent of the county is already publicly held and could be counted toward this goal.

The Office of Parks Bond and Greenspace has five staff members who administer the program and evaluate parcels that are nominated for purchase. All land acquisitions and capital expenditures require approval by the Board of Commissioners. Three citizen advisory committees help to guide various aspects of the program. The Parks and Greenspace Bond Advisory Committee provides advice regarding selection of bond projects and reviews bond expenditures. The Green DeKalb Advisory Council advises, advocates, and establishes a vision for DeKalb County's overall greenspace effort. The DeKalb Parks and Recreation Citizens Advisory Board provides advice related to the county's parks and recreational services.

As part of the greenspace efforts, the county established a Natural Resource Management section of the Parks and Recreation Department. This group is developing restoration and management plans for county lands. Programs will cover controlling invasive plant species and restoring native vegetation.

Notes

[1]"The Conservation Fund 2001 Year in Review" (Arlington, Va.: Conservation Fund, 2002), p. 13.

[2]*U.S. Census* (2000).

[3]DeKalb County Parks and Recreation Strategic Plan, July 2000, p. 9. Atlanta Regional Commission, *2003 Population and Housing* (Atlanta: Atlanta Regional Commission, 2003), p. 7.

[4]In addition to other sources as noted, the primary source for this case study is the DeKalb County's greenspace program website, www.dekalbgreenspace.com.

[5]*Local Greenprinting for Growth Workbook,* vol. 3, *How to Secure Conservation Funds* (San Francisco: Trust for Public Land and National Association of Counties, 2003), p. 32.

[6]Alycen Whiddon et al., *Open Space Acquisitions and Management Opportunities in the City of Atlanta and Adjacent Jurisdictions* (Atlanta: Research Atlanta, 2003), p. 4.

CHAPTER 16

Farmington Valley, Connecticut: A Valley's Biodiversity Project

S̲even towns (Avon, Canton, East Granby, Farmington, Granby, Simsbury, and Suffield) in north-central Connecticut are working with the Farmington River Watershed Association and the Wildlife Conservation Society's Metropolitan Conservation Alliance to protect biodiversity and wildlife habitats.[1]

These seven towns are in the Farmington River watershed in the rolling countryside west and north of Hartford, Connecticut. The Farmington River is the most fished river in Connecticut; the watershed also provides drinking water, either directly or through recharge areas to groundwater, for over 600,000 people in the Hartford region. About 14 miles of the West Branch of the Farmington River were designated as "Wild and Scenic" in 1994 by the National Park Service.

The forested valleys along the river have been primarily rural, growing more suburban closer in to Hartford, but since the beginning of the twenty-first century, residential development has expanded into agricultural and natural/forested areas. Fringe communities are growing more rapidly than urban areas—town populations throughout the Farmington Valley grew from 10 percent to 14 percent in the 1990s, while the City of Hartford lost almost 18,000 persons during the same decade. This fringe population growth has spurred local officials to participate in a regional study of biodiversity and land use programs that would help to protect natural areas and wildlife habitat. For example, Suffield is next to I-91 and Bradley International Airport, where suburban sprawl is increasingly a threat to the area's biodiversity.

Some of the habitats present include bogs, streams, ponds, mixed woods, rocky ridges, and grasslands. Although some portions of these habitats are already protected, such as the traprock ridge in Talcott Mountain State Park, much of the valley's biodiversity occurs outside protected areas. Reasons to protect biodiversity in this area are many. Bats, birds, and frogs keep mosquito populations down, which helps to control West Nile virus. Insects pollinate local apple orchards and vegetable farms. Marshy wetlands hold and absorb stormwater, helping to prevent flooding and to purify water as it percolates through to groundwater areas.

Key Program Element: Farmington Valley Biodiversity Project

The Farmington River Watershed Association (FRWA) is a citizen-based nonprofit organization that has been working on restoration and conservation issues in the Farmington Valley since 1953. The association invited Michael Klemens of the Wildlife Society's Metropolitan Conservation Alliance to speak a few years ago about his efforts to integrate biodiversity information into the land use planning process in other northeastern states. FRWA was intrigued, and asked the alliance to assist them with this issue in their watershed, starting the Farmington Valley Biodiversity Project. Seven towns are currently participating, with the hope that most of the watershed's approximately 25 towns will eventually participate. In addition, this process may someday be used as a model for how to incorporate biodiversity information into land use planning throughout the State of Connecticut and beyond.

The Farmington Valley Biodiversity Project is one of the most ambitious ecosystem studies in Connecticut and is intended to provide a scientific basis for keeping ecosystems intact through a combination of targeted preservation and improved local land use planning. The purpose of the project is to help towns plan development in a way that conserves existing ecosystems without stopping growth.

The Farmington Valley Biodiversity Project's objectives are field research, education, information sharing, and conservation, as follows:

- *Field research.* Establish a current and comprehensive biological data set by combining existing information with new data collected.

- *Community education.* Educate local officials (land use decision makers such as elected officials, town planners, and board members), land conservation organizations, and the public about biological resources and their value in the Farmington Valley.

- *Information sharing.* Distribute current biodiversity information, and the tools for using such information, to local land use decision makers and land conservation organizations.

- *Fostering conservation.* Foster the implementation of land use policies consistent with safeguarding local biological resources.

The biodiversity project started in 2001. As of May 2004, the following activities had been completed as part of Phase 1:

First, all available data were compiled. These included land use cover data from the University of Connecticut; road data layers from the state Department of Transportation; biological inventory data from the state's Natural Heritage Program; and stream survey information, including fish biodiversity. Holes in the existing data were identified. All of these existing data were then mapped.

The mapped data were then evaluated. The team looked at the maps for areas of land of varying sizes that could be valuable from a biodiversity perspective—criteria for size thresholds was 125 acres for forested areas, 25 acres for grassland, and 5 acres for shrub/scrub land. Potentially valuable areas were ranked as first, second, or third priority as follows: First-priority areas met the size criteria and had documented biodiversity, including endangered or threatened species. Second-priority lands met the size criteria and had a good diversity of microhabitats but lacked species information. Third-priority areas met the size criteria but had no existing evidence of biodiversity or specific habitats; however, owing to size, the areas could be useful for corridors.

A team of biologists (herpetologists, ornithologists, and a botanist) then conducted field visits to the first- and second-priority areas, as well as some third-priority areas, for six months in 2002 to collect additional biological data (e.g., information on sensitive species).

Ratings of the land areas were adjusted after these field data were incorporated and evaluated. The science team looked at how all of the land areas related to one another and started identifying and mapping "biotic corridors" in each town that would include core habitats. Biotic corridors are areas that provide connections between habitats, allowing species to move between them safely.

Another type of map, which appealed to the public and served as a helpful educational tool, was a map of ecoregions in the watershed. People could look at the map and see why one town had different habitats and species than another town, based on what type of ecoregion it was in (e.g., lots of rocky ridges, or floodplains).

Helpful to public officials was yet another kind of map—a "net buildable land map"—created by placing an overlay of habitat information on a map of buildable land in the community. This map made it more clear where to guide growth, and is also referred to as a "vulnerable habitat areas" map.

Throughout the process, outreach has been critical—with the public as well as with town officials. Biologists conducted several field trips in 2001 and 2002. For example, a canoe trip in Simsbury in August 2002 explored plant communities; other field trips allowed the public to join biologists while they inventoried species. Project leaders visited town commissions (inland wetlands, conservation, and planning and zoning commissions, or combinations of these) several times throughout the data gathering and mapping phase. This level of contact with public officials will increase as the implementation phase gets underway.

Peer review has been part of the process to ensure good science and "credible outcomes." In November 2001, FRWA hosted a workshop in which 32 federal, state, local, and academic scientists along with land use practitioners helped to develop field methods and figure out how local jurisdictions could use and implement the data.

As indicated, the process thus far has involved extensive data compilation, fieldwork, mapping of all data, and education. The steps required for these activities have a high degree of transferability within the State of Connecticut and so could potentially be used with great success in all 169 municipalities in the state. This is also true for the thousands of municipalities throughout the New York, New Jersey, and Connecticut region. Several other watershed associations are interested and could provide a solid infrastructure with good connections into the local communities, while working relationships have been established to obtain various data from state entities.

Phase 2, which started in early 2004, addresses implementation and is less transferable. The original intention for the implementation phase was to provide a tool book and best management practices to each town. However, this has been revised owing to the reality that each town has special circumstances and habitats, varying needs and community values, and different types of regulations already on the books.

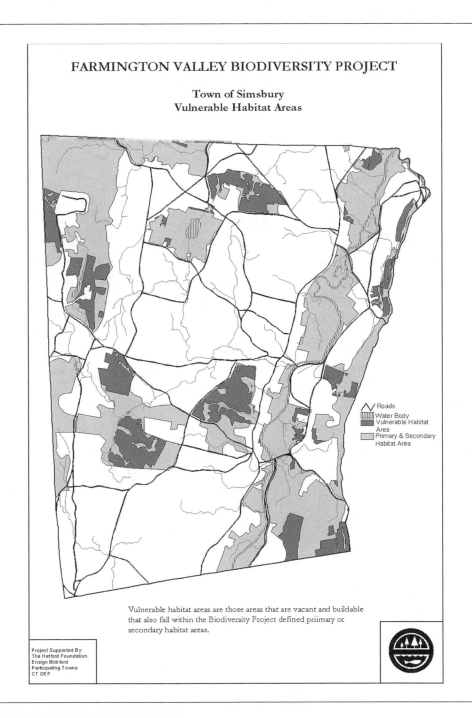

FARMINGTON VALLEY BIODIVERSITY PROJECT

Town of Simsbury
Vulnerable Habitat Areas

Roads
Water Body
Vulnerable Habitat Area
Primary & Secondary Habitat Area

Vulnerable habitat areas are those areas that are vacant and buildable that also fall within the Biodiversity Project defined priimary or secondary habitat areas.

Project Supported By:
The Hatford Foundation
Ensign Bickford
Participating Towns
CT DEP

SIMSBURY VULNERABLE HABITAT AREAS
This map of vulnerable habitat areas (also known as a net buildable land map) shows first- and second-priority habitat areas that are vacant and buildable in the Town of Simsbury. Map by Alex Persons, courtesy of the Farmington River Watershed Association.

The project leaders determined that providing maps and tool books would not be as effective as helping each town craft a unique approach. Initial steps for each town may be similar, although they may be revised as the project moves forward, and could include incorporating the net buildable land map into their comprehensive plan, adding a preapplication review procedure, and expanding the areas that require wetlands review.

Three towns have already incorporated the maps of net buildable land into their comprehensive plans (known as "plans for conservation and development" in Connecticut) and are beginning to review their existing regulations to determine ways to protect land as needed and to funnel growth into less ecologically sensitive areas. Some regulatory revisions have already been made. For example, the town of Suffield changed its curb law to require Cape Cod curbing—sloped curbs—on new or renovated roads. The old curbs made important habitats inaccessible to smaller species because they could not climb over them to cross roads. The new curbs do not cost more to install, and changing the regulation was an easy way to preserve biodiversity without hindering road construction.

The project's first phase was funded primarily by a $100,000 grant from the Hartford Foundation (a regional foundation), with additional funds provided by the Farmington River Watershed Association, the Wildlife Conservation Society, and several other private and public sources, including small amounts from each of the seven towns. The next phase, implementation, is being funded by a grant from the Connecticut Department of Environmental Protection.

Note

[1]Primary sources for this case study include Hank Gruner, Biodiversity Coordinator, Connecticut Programs, Wildlife Conservation Society and the Farmington River Watershed Association website, www.frwa.org.

CHAPTER 17

King County, Washington: Benchmark Program

H ome of salmon streams and aircraft manufacturing, King County is located in scenic western Washington.[1] On a clear day, Mount Rainier looms on the horizon to the southeast, while the Olympic Mountains appear across the large expanse of Puget Sound to the west. Water is everywhere—Puget Sound is a dominant feature, with freshwater lakes inland, and almost 1,000 wetlands, 4 major river systems, and 3,000 miles of streams. The county covers 2,130 square miles, which is about the size of Delaware. The City of Seattle is the county seat, the largest city in the Pacific Northwest, and is frequently cited as a "most livable city" in national rankings. The county's population is 1.7 million (including Seattle), up from 1.5 million in 1990 and 1.3 million in 1980. This was an increase of 15 percent from 1990 to 2000.

King County boasts more than 40 percent of Washington State's jobs and payroll, making it the primary economic engine of the Pacific Northwest. This engine slowed when the region's economy reached its lowest point in 30 years in 2001–2003. During that time, Boeing (the region's largest employer) laid off 18,000 people, the dot-com bust left its mark, and an earthquake in early 2001 left an even bigger scar on the region, resulting in expensive infrastructure repairs throughout the county. This has slowed the rate of growth slightly, but the local economy remains strong despite higher unemployment. Rural agriculture continues to play a role.

In the 1970s and 1980s, land was being developed in the region faster than the population was growing—developed land grew by 87 percent while the population increased only by 36 percent. King County reacted by becoming one of the first Puget Sound jurisdictions to delineate an urban growth boundary in 1985. It has managed to keep its urban areas relatively dense compared with other counties in the region, with approximately 3,600 people per square mile of urban land.

King County is a leader in an already progressive region. This is good news for the diverse species that call King County home—including the chinook salmon and bull trout that were listed as threatened species in 1999. The county has been taking a lead role for years in addressing regional environmental needs.

Key Program Element: Benchmark Report

King County prepared its first comprehensive plan in 1964 to manage growth in the unincorporated county. The county's plan update in 1985 defined an urban growth boundary and reaffirmed basic principles of protecting natural resources, among others. The State of Washington passed the Growth Management Act (GMA) in 1990 to protect the quality of life in the state by requiring all urban counties and their cities to prepare comprehensive plans and regulations to implement the plans. The GMA also required King County and its 39 cities to coordinate planning throughout the county. As a result of this directive, the King County Countywide Planning Policies (CPP) were put together by the Growth Management Planning Council, a group of 15 elected officials from jurisdictions around the county. These policies were adopted by the county and cities in 1994 and were used to refine the urban growth boundary to limit sprawl and protect open space and rural areas.

After the Countywide Planning Policies were put in place, the Growth Management Planning Council wanted a method for determining if the policies were achieving what they had set out to achieve, and they began to develop a monitoring and benchmark program. As a result, Benchmark Reports have been produced annually since 1996. A sister report, the Annual Growth Report, has been produced since 1982, so the groundwork was laid early for the Benchmark Report. The Annual Growth Report provides a broad range of growth-related data. Between the two reports, King County continues to be one of the few counties in the nation to track its progress on growth management goals.

The King County Benchmark Program is organized into 45 indicators for five general topics that are intended to measure progress in achieving the goals of the Countywide Planning Policies and the King County Comprehensive Plan. To set up the benchmarks, desired outcomes of the policies were determined, indicators were chosen for each outcome, and data were gathered. Some of the benchmarks have targeted, quantifiable goals. King County employs one full-time staff person to pull data together from a variety of sources: its constituent cities, outside agencies (e.g., regional air quality group), and the county itself, especially for environmental data, some of which the county's Department of Natural Resources and Parks provides.

In 2003, the format of the Benchmark Report was changed from a single annual publication to five bimonthly reports, one on each of the five topics. The publication cycle runs from August to May. All the reports are available on the web at www.metrokc.gov/budget/benchmrk.

The Benchmark Reports include the following topics and the specific indicators currently used for each topic:

- *Economic development:* real wages per worker; personal and median household income; percentage of population below the poverty level; new businesses created; new jobs created by employment sector; employment in industries that export from the region; educational background of adult population; high school "on-time" graduation rate.

- *Environmental issues:* land cover changes in urban and rural areas over time; air quality; energy consumption; vehicle miles traveled per year; surface water and groundwater quality; water consumption; change in groundwater levels; change in wetland acreage and functions; continuity of terrestrial and aquatic habitat networks; change in number of salmon; rate of increase in noise from vehicles, planes and yard equipment; pounds of waste disposed and recycled per capita.

- *Affordable housing:* supply and demand for affordable housing; percentage of income paid for housing; homelessness; home purchase affordability gap for buyers; home ownership rate; apartment vacancy rate; trend of housing costs versus income; public dollars spent for low-income housing; housing affordable to low-income households.

- *Land use policy:* new housing units in urban and rural areas; employment in urban and rural/resource areas, urban centers; new housing units built through redevelopment; ratio of land consumption to population growth; ratio of achieved density to allowed density of residential development; ratio of land capacity to 20-year job and household targets; land with six years of infrastructure capacity (there are currently no reliable sources for this indicator); acres of urban parks and open space; ratio of jobs to housing; acres in forest land; acres in farmland/number and average size of farms.

- *Transportation:* percentage of residents who commute one way within 30 minutes; transit trips per person; percentage of residents who use alternatives to the single-occupant vehicle; ability of goods and services to move efficiently and cost-effectively.

Several outcomes for each topic are listed, with one or more indicators used for each desired outcome. For example, under "land use," a desired outcome is "maintain the quality and quantity of natural resource lands." Two indicators are used for this outcome: "acres in forest land" and "acres in farmland/ number and average size of farms." Also, the reports provide commentary about each indicator, describing trends, data sources, specific examples of local situations, and what the county is doing to address the issues. Not all of the data is gathered annually, particularly data from specialized studies, such as from the U.S. census or for land cover changes (studies of Landsat images done in 1991 and 1999 were used for this indicator).

Many of these indicators have relevance for biodiversity in that they track growth and several address species and habitat issues directly such as "change in wetland acreage and functions," "continuity of terrestrial and aquatic habitat networks," and "change in number of salmon."

In the new format, each indicator is preceded by a citation from the Countywide Planning Policies that provides the policy rational for that indicator. Notes at the end of each report describe the data sources and the policy rationale. To illustrate: for the salmon indicator, the citation from the Countywide Planning Policies states that "all jurisdictions shall identify critical fish and wildlife habitats and species and develop regulations that promote their protection and proper management." It also cites sections calling for the protection of the overall health of the waterways. The salmon data sources are listed as the Washington Department of Fisheries, Washington Department of Wildlife, and Western Washington Treaty Indian Tribes.

The King County Benchmark Program can be considered to be past infancy, but not yet mature. Staff offer the following words of wisdom: Any jurisdiction starting a

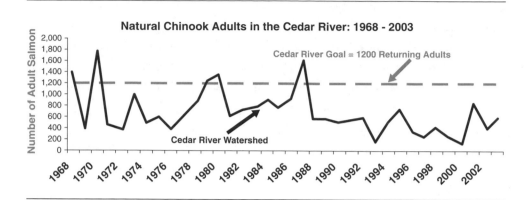

NATURAL CHINOOK ADULTS IN THE CEDAR RIVER, 1968–2003
The King County Benchmark Program contains an indicator for "change in number of salmon." Graph courtesy of Rose Curran, King County Benchmark Program.

benchmark program must understand it is a long-term commitment, and must be funded for at least 5 to 10 years to get good data and discern trends. Ownership by both elected leaders and managers is critical to provide clear lines of reporting and to offer a possibility of the data actually being used to affect policy.

As with any indicator project, there are pluses and minuses. Choosing appropriate indicators and ensuring adequate data to match can be challenging. Another concern is that the data may not be used to affect policy after all. However, the snapshots of various trends that can be seen in each of King County's Benchmark Reports are commendable and are an important start in monitoring the impact the county's policies may or may not be having on preserving the area's quality of life for all species.

Note

[1] Primary sources for this case study include Rose Curran, Benchmark Program Coordinator, King County Office of Management and Budget, and the King County Benchmark Reports website, www.metrokc.gov/budget/benchmrk.

CHAPTER 18

Pittsford, New York: Greenprint for a Town's Future

The Town of Pittsford is about eight miles from Rochester, near the Erie Canal in upstate New York.[1] The population of this historically rural community is approximately 25,000 persons; the town covers 24 square miles. The town has experienced pressure from the Rochester area to develop since the 1950s, with a peak in growth in the late 1980s and early 1990s. Growth has slowed from the 110 to 125 residential units per year during that previous spurt to about 80 units per year, with an expectation that population growth will continue at about 3.7 percent annually, a very high number for a northeastern jurisdiction.

Growth in and of itself was not the primary motive for this community to take steps to protect open space and ecological resources in the form of its award-winning "Greenprint"—the driving force was a desire to protect the community's rural character.

Much of the town's land area has been altered by agricultural and residential development. However, significant ecological resources are still present, including woodlots, meadows, streams, and wetlands, with the accompanying species of plants and animals that live in those habitats. The Greenprint states that even though there are few endangered species or unique natural communities in the town, the significance of these resources "lies in their diversity and availability to Town residents."

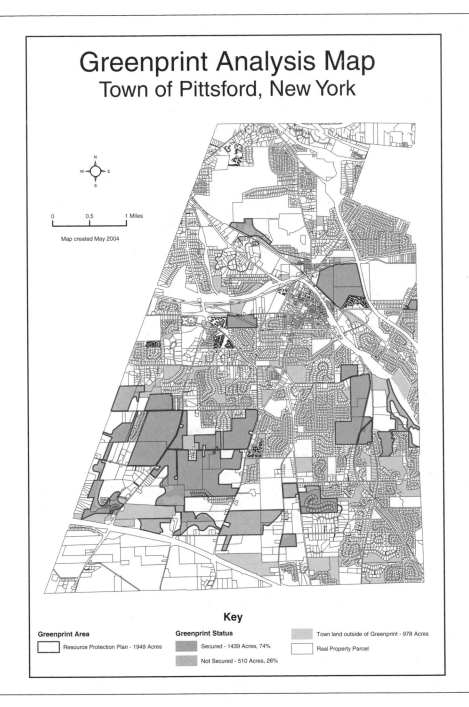

GREENPRINT ANALYSIS MAP, TOWN OF PITTSFORD, NEW YORK
This Greenprint analysis map shows that the town has protected 74 percent of the acres originally identified for protection. Courtesy of the Town of Pittsford, New York.

Key Program Element: Greenprint for Pittsford's Future

Pittsford has in place many key program elements that could be considered nature-friendly—community planning, inventory of resources, innovative implementation (purchase of development rights, transfer of development rights, and clustering), as well as providing funding for acquisition of lands identified for protection.

The program that has won the most recognition is the town's Greenprint, which is the implementation program for the town's comprehensive plan. However, many steps led up to this Greenprint and ensured its success.

The foundation was laid early—citizens drafted a Growth Management Plan in 1986 and in the same year rezoned all of the undeveloped land within the town's boundaries as suburban residential (SRAA) and rural residential (RRAA). The SRAA district requires that 30 percent open space be set aside for permanent protection, while the RRAA district requires that 50 percent be similarly set aside if the developer wants to increase the density from the standard 1 unit per 10 acres to 1.3 units per acre. A community visioning process was completed in 1992 ("Pittsford 2000") that established the high value citizens placed on the rural character of the town. In 1993, a fiscal impact analysis was commissioned and established a method that would be referred to again and again—a bottom-line sensitivity that showed that protecting open space while strategically planning for more development would be less expensive than business as usual. The town then undertook a comprehensive plan update in 1995 involving more than 100 public meetings and workshops. The revised plan recommended protecting about 2,000 acres of open space, while calling for economic development within ten existing nonresidential areas, and continued residential development on the remaining 1,600 acres of undeveloped lands.

In 1996, the "Greenprint for Pittsford's Future" was adopted to implement the revised plan. It was drafted when citizens realized they needed a process for deciding what land to protect on a parcel-by-parcel basis as well as what specific tools were needed to make the vision a reality. The Greenprint was the result of a citizens' committee to develop a rational way to prioritize resources. They hired a biologist to help. Ecological, open space, scenic, and agricultural resources were considered and ranked. Two-thirds of the remaining undeveloped land—about 2,000 acres—was slated for protection. Purchase of development rights (PDR) was planned for 1,000 acres (on seven farms in the area). Two existing regulations were intended to be utilized for the rest of the lands: incentive zoning (also known as a "transfer of development rights" program) for over 200 acres; and mandatory clustering (in the SRAA and RRAA zones) for over 600 acres.

The final step was to ensure funding for the PDR program, which the town accomplished later in 1996 when it authorized a $9.9 million bond for this purpose. As a fiscal analysis had indicated, it would cost an average of $67 per year per homeowner for this PDR program, versus the estimated $250 in taxes per year that homeowners would have had to shoulder if new homes had been built on the same land.

Throughout this effort, strong leadership from the town supervisor, Bill Campbell, was critical for community consensus and forward momentum. Additionally, a consultant, John Behan, provided much of the resource analysis and facilitated public meetings.

Innovative aspects of the Greenprint include the following:

- Citizens set a specific goal of permanent protection for 2,000 acres.
- A fiscal model was utilized for decision making, and prediction of future taxes based on future land uses was key.
- The citizen's advisory committee developed a rating system for evaluating all of the parcels.

The town produced a *Greenprint Policy Guidebook* in 1997 to assist the community in carrying out the Greenprint implementation programs.

Although Pittsford has taken many nature-friendly actions all along the way, the most relevant for biodiversity protection is the ecological resource evaluation that was completed as part of the Greenprint. In 1995, all 94 undeveloped parcels over 5 acres in size were evaluated by a consulting biologist for their ecological significance (as well as for their open space/scenic/agricultural value). This included a field inventory of each site, and rating of these sites based on presence, size, and quality of their aquatic, botanical, and wildlife resources. In addition, relationship to other property was considered, with a strategy of identifying corridors or blocks of undisturbed natural communities/habitat. The sites that scored highly were typically large sites with a diversity of natural communities; 14 sites were considered to have high ecological value. Of these 14 sites, 13 were included in the Greenprint, along with lower-value sites that provided connections to and buffers around other sites. As a result of this evaluation, the Greenprint includes three corridors of largely undeveloped wildlife habitat that radiate out into the town from its southwest corner and provide linkages to undeveloped habitats in nearby towns. These three corridors are described in detail in the Greenprint, which helps citizens understand why the areas are valuable ecologically. Most of this land is on private property. All three tools have been used to protect most of the originally designated 13 parcels with high ecological value. As of 2004, about 74 percent of all land designated for protection under the Greenprint had been protected.

The Town of Pittsford has shown that nature-friendly actions can make fiscal sense for a community, protecting habitat while encouraging strategic development.

Note

[1]Primary sources for this case study include Marty Brewster, Planning and Zoning Department, Town of Pittsford; the Town of Pittsford's Greenprint website, www.townofpittsford.com/community/greenprint; and the article "Planning and Financing Open Space and Resource Protection: Pittsford's Greenprint Initiative," by John J. Behan, available on the aforementioned website.

CHAPTER 19

Powell County, Montana: Rural County Wildlife Protection

A t a density of only 3.1 persons per square mile, Powell County is typified by vistas, big skies, and open range.[1] Culturally, the area is distinctly Western— its rich ranching heritage of cowboys and cattle drives reaches back to the 1850s. Powell County is also home to abundant wildlife, spectacular mountain and valley landscapes, and diverse plant species.

Today, the livestock trade and agriculture continue to underpin the local economy. Unlike other parts of the rural West that have experienced an influx of new residents in the 1990s, Powell County's population growth has remained relatively flat. Land prices, however, have increased significantly, particularly because of the construction of second homes in the county's northern end.

Despite this trend, Powell County is an unlikely candidate for rapid rural development. The county, which deeply values its rural character, has been active in laying the groundwork for preserving open space and mitigating the effects of development in the future.

Key Program Element: Important Wildlife Overlay District

In 1996, the county updated its comprehensive plan and adopted a series of development regulations. These regulations largely address existing development patterns throughout the county's large territory, which spans approximately 100 miles from end to end. Future growth in the county will be encouraged in rural centers—unincorporated towns with growth boundaries and preexisting infrastructure. A key objective of these regulations is to enact a series of minimum lot sizes and residential density restrictions intended to help preserve the county's largely pastoral character and protect existing residential areas from the impacts of future development. Wildlife habitat protection is another major plan element.

Implementing regulations include several overlay districts, among which is the Important Wildlife Overlay District. This district restricts residential densities to one unit per 80 acres in mapped elk winter ranges and excludes infill development in existing residential areas. It applies mainly to the county's northern end. Fortunately,

The Powell County Important Wildlife Overlay District protects elk winter range. Photograph by Lokey Lytjen.

to date there has been limited growth pressure in that area. Farther to the south, where lot size restrictions are less stringent, most of the important elk habitat is on public land. With the overlay district in place, however, the county is prepared for the future.

In addition to the Wildlife Overlay District, a committed county planning board has taken an active role with conservation easements throughout the county and is very supportive of habitat preservation efforts. The board has been negotiating appropriate language for each easement, trying to blend the easements with the goals of the comprehensive plan instead of using boilerplate language. The comprehensive plan states that conservation easements may be used to keep privately held land in agricultural production or open space uses, while keeping the land on the county tax rolls, provided that the conservation easements have clear statements of what values are intended to be protected. Over the past five years, the board has worked with the organizations responsible for many of the easements (two local private land trusts, The Nature Conservancy, and federal and state wildlife agencies) to craft language that identifies the conservation values they want to protect yet will allow more flexibility for adaptation to local circumstances without losing those same conservation values.

These types of regulatory and nonregulatory initiatives show that even small conservative jurisdictions can take simple steps to protect their rural character and wildlife habitat.

Note

[1]Primary sources for this case study include Ron Hanson, Powell County Contract Planner, and the Powell County Development Regulations.

CHAPTER 20

Teton County, Wyoming: Natural Resource Overlay District

T eton County, located in northwest Wyoming, is mountainous and heavily forested, with several broad river valleys, the most well known containing the Snake River.[1] At the center of the county is the town of Jackson, which is world renowned for its stunning scenery. Teton County also has a high concentration of critical wildlife habitat. At an average elevation of well over 6,000 feet above sea level, winters are long and cold in most of the county. Its lower valleys provide wintering ground for a wide range of wildlife.

The rise of Teton Range, as well as the erosion caused by eons of glaciation, has created the conditions that allow several plant communities to thrive—from ribbons of green riparian plants bordering rivers and streams, to sagebrush flats, lodgepole pine and spruce forests, subalpine meadows, and alpine stone fields. The wide range of plant communities in turn creates habitat for a variety of wildlife, including larger mammals such as black bear, grizzly bear, elk, moose, deer, and bison. Teton County's elk herd is one of the largest in North America, with approximately 15,000 animals. Teton County is also home to approximately 215 trumpeter swans, a threatened species.

The highest elevation is Grand Teton Mountain, at 13,770 feet above sea level, and the lower elevations are at 6,200 feet. Average annual rainfall is 17 inches, and

Teton County's Natural Resource Overlay District protects wildlife habitat through strong development standards. Photograph by Lokey Lytjen.

snowfall is 150 inches. The county encompasses a portion of Yellowstone National Park and all of Grand Teton National Park. All told, the federal government owns 97 percent of the county. As a result, the scarce remaining private land is under intense development pressure. Population has also risen dramatically. From 1990 to 2000, the county's population increased by approximately 63 percent to 18,250.

Wildlife resources are an essential component of the county's primarily tourist-based economy as well as a profound element of community character.

Key Program Element: Natural Resource Overlay District

The Teton County Land Development Regulations are a unified development code that implements both land subdivision and zoning functions. Development review is mandatory and subject to approval by the Planning Commission and the Board of County Commissioners.

The current process was adopted in 1994 as part of the Land Development Regulations and new comprehensive plan. These regulations implement two broad priorities: the protection of natural resources and scenic resources. Several overlay districts were instituted to accomplish these priorities.

Teton County's Natural Resource Overlay (NRO) District protects wildlife habitat in Teton County. For the purposes of the district, wildlife habitat is broadly defined by several "premier species" with "significant biological, ecological, economic, educational, and aesthetic values" for Teton County. The stated purpose of the district has seven objectives—namely, to protect and maintain:

- The migration routes and crucial winter ranges of elk
- The migration routes and crucial winter ranges of mule deer
- The crucial winter habitat of moose
- The nesting areas and winter habitat of trumpeter swans
- The nesting areas and crucial winter habitat of bald eagles
- The spawning areas of cutthroat trout
- The natural resources and biodiversity that support the wildlife population

All proposed developments that are located within the Natural Resources Overlay District are required to carry out an environmental analysis, including a habitat inventory and a development impact assessment. Development is prohibited in elk, moose, and mule deer migration routes and winter ranges as well as within 150 feet of cutthroat trout spawning areas unless the developer can demonstrate that the development will not negatively affect the species in question. Furthermore, development is completely prohibited within 300 feet of trumpeter swan nests, within 400 meters (1,312 feet) of bald eagle nests, and within the winter habitats of either species.

Additionally, fencing is recognized as an impediment to wildlife movement throughout the county. The NRO discourages the use of fencing; residential fencing is required to comply with fencing standards. The NRO also requires that domestic pets, particularly dogs, which pose a threat to protected wildlife, be either restrained or accompanied by a person.

The NRO prohibits development in 10-year floodplains and wetlands. Wetlands may be reconfigured in a limited manner in some cases, and on-site mitigation must be provided, wherever possible, at a ratio of 1½ acres of new wetland for every acre filled. Stream buffers are intended to protect the riparian plant community. Buffers for natural lakes and ponds are based on the same criteria. Buffer setbacks from specified resources are as follows:

· Rivers, 150 feet
· Streams and the riparian plant community, 50 feet minimum
· Natural lake or pond, 50 feet minimum
· Wetlands, 30 feet

The NRO also works in tandem with other county regulations. While the Land Development Regulations have designated the NRO as a priority overlay, in some cases the Scenic Overlay District (SRO) is also applicable and is another factor in site selection. The Rural District, which underlies much of the NRO, requires a large open space requirement and encourages "clustering," in which development is grouped together at higher densities in order to maximize open space.

The NRO serves as a powerful tool to protect Teton County's vast wildlife resources. It has worked well to ensure the appropriate placement of development and protection of sensitive areas. The NRO is widely used, with approximately 75 percent of all development applications involving the regulation. Like all comprehensive regulations, the NRO requires significant commitment of staff resources as well as local political will to be successful. On both counts, the NRO continues to be a high priority for the community.

In practice, rather than act as a typical zoning district boundary, the NRO is often used as a site locator to help guide development to the most wildlife-friendly location. By triggering an environmental assessment of proposed sites, the NRO ensures that wildlife concerns are considered as a part of development applications. For properties that do not fall squarely within the district, the site assessment works to determine precisely where the NRO boundary is located by considering a variety of factors, such as habitat type, the actual use of the property by animals, and migratory routes.

After 10 years in existence, the NRO continues to enjoy wide support. Given its many environmental variables and broad scope, it is difficult to evaluate the NRO's cumulative effect on wildlife, although a comprehensive study could help to address this issue. The NRO continues to serve as a model regulation that shapes residential development to coexist with and complement Teton County's rich wildlife resources.

Note

[1]Primary sources for this case study include Bill Collins, former County Planning Director, now with Collins Planning Collaborative, and the Teton County Land Development Regulations.

CHAPTER 21

Traverse Bay Area, Michigan: New Designs for Growth

In the northwest portion of the mitten-shaped lower peninsula of Michigan lies the Traverse Bay area.[1] The region consists of five counties (Grand Traverse, Antrim, Benzie, Kalkaska, and Leelanau), with Traverse City as the primary city. This five-county area contains about 130 miles of Lake Michigan shoreline and 100 inland lakes in addition to the scenic Grand Traverse Bay itself, and is known as the cherry capital of the world. Dense forests and beaches are some of the natural resources present.

The area has attracted new residents from around the Great Lakes region because of its scenic values and high quality of life. The economy has thrived, with an estimated 95 percent of the commercial activity in the region driven by small business. However, the burgeoning population is threatening to erode the very things people moved here to enjoy. For example, Grand Traverse County experienced a 17 percent population increase from 1980 to 1990. This growth rate increased during the next decade: The five-county region counted 154,000 residents in 2000, with an average 10-year growth rate of 26 percent for the area. The state as a whole is consuming land eight times faster than the population growth. Some impacts include a decrease in surface water quality, replacement of cherry farms with subdivisions, and a plethora of roads.

The Traverse Bay area enjoys a host of scenic and natural resources, including shoreline on Lake Michigan and Grand Traverse Bay. Photograph by John Robert Williams.

Key Program Element: New Designs for Growth

The Grand Traverse County planning commission started the ball rolling in 1991 when it conducted a citizen survey about development trends as part of a visioning process called Grand Traverse 20/20. Nearly 500 people attended 20 community visioning sessions throughout Grand Traverse County. Their input was used as a basis for a public opinion poll that was sent to over 800 randomly selected people. Over 85 percent of the poll respondents thought that scenic views, trees, and water quality should be protected. And 78 percent of those polled wanted uniform development guidelines for managed growth. At the same time as the citizen survey, the county planning commission approached the regional chamber of commerce (Traverse City Area Chamber of Commerce) and asked the chamber to survey their business members. When the chamber members showed even stronger concerns about growth and environmental quality, the chamber decided to become involved in the issue. To address the concerns raised about growth, Grand Traverse County, the chamber, and a local foundation (Rotary Charities) collaborated to produce the *Grand Traverse Bay Region Development Guidebook* in 1992 with the help of a Lansing-based planning consultant, Mark Wyckoff. The guidebook contains model development practices and strategies for managing growth. Despite initial interest in the guidebook, it became obvious that ideas were not being implemented. The chamber organized a steering committee that mailed out questionnaires to local planning commissions and boards to discover why the ideas in the guidebook were not being implemented. The 1995 survey showed that there were indeed barriers to using the guidebook, and a new organization, New Designs for Growth, was formed to overcome those barriers.

New Designs for Growth is a program of the Traverse City Area Chamber of Commerce and is a coalition of business associations, community organizations, and government officials determined to find a balance between development and resource protection in their neck of the north woods. What is unusual about New Designs is that it was one of just a handful of growth management initiatives led by business leaders around the nation in the mid-1990s when it began. Their mission has been "to formulate new patterns for land use that enhances northwest Michigan's natural features, regional economy, and cultural heritage by joining with communities to establish innovative tools to prepare for change." The group's position regarding growth is that growth is inevitable and desirable, but that it must be managed and planned.

New Designs set out to address some of the barriers identified: lack of training and technical assistance for local planning staff, commissions, and boards; outdated ordinances and comprehensive plans; and inadequate human and financial resources. As a result, New Designs created community workshops to train local stakeholders how to use the guidebook, strongly encouraging participation by the local planning commission and board of each municipality. Workshop participants utilize three-dimensional modeling processes to reach a consensus on what they want the future to look like, then draft ordinances to spell this vision out. Other technical assistance includes peer-to-peer consultations at a variety of stages along the way—including needs assessment, workshops on specific topics, using the guidebook, approaching the planning commission, preparing site plans, and implementing projects.

Another offshoot of their efforts is the Citizen Planner Program, which started in the region with the help of the Michigan State University Extension and has since become a statewide land use training and certificate program for volunteer land use decision makers. New Designs also created a Peer Site Review Committee, made up of planners, developers, real estate agents, and land use specialists, which reviews about 10 to 15 development proposals each year and secures modifications that meet the guidebook's smart growth principles.

As a side effort, Leadership Grand Traverse, a business leadership program that started in the region in 1980, was modified to include concepts regarding smart growth and natural resource protection.

Funding has come from local, state, and federal grants, with help from the chamber. The chamber is set up to have a nonprofit foundation portion that handles the grant monies. Over $1.5 million has been invested in managed growth activities since the start of the program, which has leveraged millions more dollars. New Designs provides partial funding for a program (e.g., a new public utility district ordinance in a community), while the community must match or exceed those funds.

About 82 of 93 local units of government in all five counties have been affected by New Designs in one way or another—71 of those governments have actually modified their master plans or ordinances to comply with guidebook principles. The final part of Phase 1 was in 2003, when the Kalkaska County Master Plan was completed, incorporating some of the guidebook principles.

Phase 2, starting in 2004, will focus more on general community education, expanding Citizen Planner activities in the region, and including more services and education for the development community. The latter portion is still being worked out, but experiences with the peer site review have indicated that developers will utilize the community's preferred design ideas if they do not cost more and there is a market for the product. Additional future plans include advocacy for state legislation and further revision of the guidebook. The guidebook has been revised twice before and has been reprinted three times. A previous revision added a segment about redevelopment options, and a chapter about roads is planned.

New Design's efforts have served as a role model for chambers of commerce around the State of Michigan, and several members of New Designs have served or are serving on a state task force regarding land use. The *New Designs for Growth*

Guidebook has prompted inquiries from out of state as well, and Keith Charters, the original consultant hired to run the New Designs program, has spoken around the country about the program.

A drawback is that the focus has been primarily on how development should look and its impacts, and not where it should be located, which is beyond the scope of what the chamber can address. This issue may be more likely to be addressed if a governmental entity were to be in the lead role. In addition, no attempts have been made to evaluate how the program has or has not affected growth in the region. Project leaders can point to examples of smart growth and "not so smart" growth but have no quantifiable measure of how much of each is happening.

Note

[1]Primary sources for this case study include Marsha Smith, Co-Chair of New Designs for Growth, and the Traverse City Area Chamber of Commerce website, www.tcchamber.org.

CHAPTER 22

Loudoun County, Virginia: Green Infrastructure Meets Green Money

Loudoun County, Virginia, points up the political challenges of wildlife habitat and natural resource protection efforts at the local level.[1] A sprawling county that reaches from the suburbs of Washington, D.C., west to the Blue Ridge Mountains, Loudoun County was one of the first jurisdictions in the United States to adopt a comprehensive land use plan that featured green infrastructure as a key element. Under the plan, natural resources such as rivers, streams, forests, and aquifer recharge areas are considered every bit as important to the economic well-being and quality of life of the county and its citizens as "hard" infrastructure like roads and sewer lines. The plan called for ambitious steps to protect these resources, and new regulations were quickly adopted by a pro-growth management board of county supervisors. Then political pandemonium broke loose. Loudoun's story is one that other jurisdictions contemplating upgrading their nature protection programs would do well to study.

Loudoun County, Virginia, is one of a growing cadre of local jurisdictions that has a split personality when it comes to development and land use. Located just outside and to the west of the notorious Washington, D.C., Beltway, Loudoun County is home to sprawling "edge city" commercial developments and mega-subdivisions that

Rolling horse country in the western part of Loudoun County contrasts with sprawling subdivisions in the eastern part. Photograph by Craig Richardson.

give way to rolling horse farms, vineyards, and thick forests in its western reaches on the flanks of the Blue Ridge Mountains. Many visitors to the Capitol probably don't realize they set foot in Loudoun County when they land at Dulles Airport.

The county is huge by eastern standards—it stretches almost 30 miles east to west and covers over 500 square miles. Its population stands at over 200,000, more than double what it was just a decade ago. Loudoun is a perennial member of the national fastest-growing county list, and in fact in 2004 climbed once again to the top of the charts. On average, 12,000 new residents have moved to Loudoun every year since 1990.

The county's eastern precincts are part and parcel of the burgeoning Virginia suburbs outside Washington, D.C. The line between sprawling Fairfax County, with its infamous Tyson's Corner shopping center and famous Reston new town, has long since been erased with suburban office parks, big outlet malls, and gigantic "planned" residential subdivisions with names like Stone Ridge and Brambleton. But there is an abrupt change at the county seat, historic Leesburg. This landmark-filled colonial town marks the transition between suburban and rural. And, at least for the time being, the transition is abrupt. West and north of Leesburg is a remarkably beautiful countryside featuring small villages with names like Round Hill, Purcellville, and Waterford; rolling horse farms; vineyards, dairies, and a rural way of life. Eastern Loudoun is four-lane highways, cul-de-sacs, manicured landscapes; western Loudoun is two-lane country roads, clean rivers, and lots of trees. Loudoun County's ecosystems are tremendously varied. The riparian habitats of the streams that feed into the Potomac River on the county's northern boundary are home to numerous birds and animals. The steep slopes and forests of the western reaches provide a dramatically different feel and environmental setting.

Loudoun Swings Like a Pendulum Do

Politically, the county has been Republican and fairly conservative over the past two decades, but its citizens and politicians have a track record of being favorably inclined toward land use planning and protection of natural resources. In a state that tightly controls and limits the growth management options of local governments, Loudoun County has been traditionally viewed as one of the more active jurisdictions when it comes to protecting natural resources. Indeed, it is home to many conservation and environmental organizations like the Piedmont Environmental Council, which counts scores of members in the county. By the same token, as growth has washed over the eastern portion of the county, big residential and commercial real estate developers and large landowners have not been shy in exercising their political muscles.

The tension between land preservation and development advocates has led to wild swings from pro-growth development policies to slow-growth policies. The latest chapter in this saga played out in the late 1990s when antigrowth sentiment boiled over in the face of 6 to 9 percent annual growth rates and projections that the county would reach 1 million residents in the not too distant future—sopping up almost 80 percent of the region's overall growth. One study cited the need for 184 new schools to cope with new students. Starter castles were popping up overnight on small three-acre lots allowed by county zoning in agricultural areas, carving up farms willy-nilly. The small villages were being surrounded by suburban subdivisions completely out of character with rural Loudoun, leading the Sierra Club to single out a development near the village of Round Hill as one of the worst examples of suburban planning in the nation. New residents worried that they weren't getting their fair share of services like libraries and schools, as even more new developments meant public funding had to be spread more thinly. Led by a political action committee called Voters to Stop Sprawl, in a landslide vote citizens swept in a new board of county supervisors committed to reining in the county's growth and protecting natural resources.

The new board, with a solid 7-2 majority in favor of growth control, was led by Scott York, a brusque, no-nonsense Republican with strong growth management credentials. The board wasted no time in redoing the 1991 comprehensive plan in an effort that involved hundreds of public meetings, numerous working groups that focused on key issues, and countywide town meetings. While the new plan could hardly be called a no-growth plan, it did cut the county's projected housing stock by about 24,000 to 136,000 homes. Most of this density reduction was to come in the western part of the county. Under the banner of green infrastructure, the plan also called for more stringent regulations to protect sensitive natural areas like rivers and streams, wildlife habitat, and steep slopes. At the same time, however, the plan recommended that rural landowners be afforded the opportunity to pursue compatible rural economic land uses, such as small conference centers and agricultural support services, as an alternative to subdivision.

The board also initiated a purchase of development rights program to work with willing landowners who needed cash but did not want to see their property developed. And at the state level, the county joined a coalition of other high-growth communities to lobby for greater enabling authority to grapple with development issues, including the use of impact fees to ensure new development paid its own way.

The plan was adopted by an 8-1 vote, and the board immediately set the wheels in motion to revamp the county's woefully out-of-date development code as a key to implementing the plan. They directed the staff to undertake a crash program to have the code revised and the county rezoned by early 2003.

County staff, with the assistance of a consulting team, plunged into the project, burning the midnight oil for months. Advisory groups made up of citizens, conservation organizations, landowners, and developers hashed out approaches to issues like riparian habitat protection, cluster development, and rural economy uses. While the process maintained a façade of civility, the effort was highly controversial from the beginning. Landowners from the rural western half of the county carried signs at various public briefings objecting to any reductions in density that might affect their land values. And large landowners and developers with holdings in the so-called transitional zone near Dulles Airport in midcounty served notice that they opposed the plan's vision for the area—low-intensity development and no extension of public sewer and water lines into the zone. Lack of these services would forestall the mega-residential developments that had developers salivating. These development interests also objected to application of the new natural resource protection standards to the east half of the county. Literally billions of dollars were riding on the outcome.

In record time, the new code was prepared and, in January 2003, adopted by a 7-2 vote of the Loudoun board. As a representative of the Piedmont Environmental Council observed, "Loudoun Supervisors have delivered on their promise to rein in uncontrolled growth in the county. They have made services for our existing suburban communities and protection of our rural heritage a priority." The new zoning ordinance contained four key features:

- It dramatically reduced the number of houses that could be built in the 300-square-mile rural countryside in western Loudoun—from one unit per 3 acres to one unit per 10, 20, or 50 acres, depending on the location and whether a cluster subdivision option was used.

- It permitted additional businesses, such as inns and retreats, in rural zone districts to provide a wider range of viable rural economic opportunities instead of housing development.

- It protected a wide range of natural resources and wildlife habitat—rivers, streams, wetlands, aquifer recharge areas, steep slopes, and forests—through tough new development regulations (though these standards were applied only in the west county in an attempt to assuage developers in the east).

- It zoned the transitional area to restrain suburban density housing development that would rely on water and sewer line extensions. Instead, the regulations promoted more compact "village" developments that would be surrounded by open space.

The board majority and its supporters had only a few days to bask in the satisfaction of following through on their promises to implement the Comprehensive Plan. Opponents filed a blizzard of lawsuits challenging the new code on a variety of grounds. The most serious claim was that the "downzoning" of land from one unit per 3 acres in much of the rural county to far lower densities amounted to an unconstitutional taking of property. Others alleged that the board's actions were illegal "piecemeal" zoning because they treated similarly situated landowners differently. Some developers claimed that they had locked-in "vested rights" to develop because they had invested time and money in securing, or had actually received, necessary county approvals before the law was changed. Several developer litigants admitted that the lawsuits were part of a larger, more concerted effort to push the growth control supervisors out of office in the election that was looming in November 2003.

The next few months were tumultuous. While the county attorney felt confident that the takings and vested rights claims could be defended for the most part, smaller landowners were portrayed sympathetically in the *Washington Post* and other newspapers. County planners and elected officials had ignored advice from several quarters to be more flexible in applying the new 1 unit/20 acres and 1 unit/30 acres limitations on property that heretofore had been zoned at 1 unit/3 acres. The new restrictions stung large landowners (e.g., those who owned 50 acres or more), but they were given the option to cluster their development densities and recoup some of the lots they had lost if they agreed to set aside large blocks of open space. This option was not available, however, in most cases for small landowners who held parcels of 5, 10, 20, and 30 acres, which were smaller than the applicable zone district minimum lot sizes. Thus an owner of a 30-acre tract located in one of the new 30-acre minimum lot size districts who could have developed 10 lots under the old ordinance suddenly found himself reduced to only one home on the parcel—the result being a large diminution in value. And because of the parcel's relatively small size, he was not allowed to cluster the development to regain density. However, if a neighboring landowner had 90 acres, he could recoup some of the lost density by agreeing to concentrate development in a cluster of smaller lots (e.g., 2 acres), preserving the majority of the parcel in open space.

The development community and homebuilders also began building a huge war chest to campaign against the "Smart Growth" supervisors—which amounted to almost $500,000 by election time. The chairman of the local building industry association was quoted as saying, "The way you get elected is by outspending your opponent!" In the end, the development community spent 10 times as much as they had in the losing 1999 effort. Between July 2002 and the election, contributions of more than $100 to candidates in Loudoun amounted to over $1 million—3 times the amount recorded in 1999. One candidate, Bruce Tulloch, who had refused to take developer money and had lost by a handful of votes to a slow-growth advocate, changed his mind without blushing, "In 1999, I pledged not to take any developer money. I was roasted on my petard and have regretted it every day since. I am proud to take your money this year . . . You have a voice, and it's Bruce Tulloch."

Tension ran high as the elections neared. The leader of one property rights group dressed up as revolutionary hero Patrick Henry and led a march on the county building in Leesburg. Growth control advocates countered by coming to a hearing with nine shopping bags full of red plastic Monopoly houses—100,000 of them—and dumped them on a large county map to illustrate how growth was out of control.

At the same time, in a stroke of bad luck for the "growth management seven," the economy began to weaken, and three of the counties biggest employers—WorldCom, United Airlines, and AOL—either stumbled or declared bankruptcy, cutting jobs and business operations in the process.

As the electioneering rolled on, the board began settling a number of vested rights cases in which landowners could make a credible case that they had secured approvals prior to the new regulations being put in place. Other lawsuits were dropped as developers realized that the new ordinance was not as draconian as some had feared. One major suit against the county challenging the new river and stream corridor protection regulations was successful because county staff had flubbed the required notice provisions, thus invalidating the regulations on a technicality.

But these settlements and compromises were not enough, especially in the face of the heavy campaign contributions that washed over the county. On November 4, in the populous eastern end of the county, voters threw out the growth management supervisors and elected six pro-growth Republicans in their place. Ironically, in the western rural part of the county, where the downzoning and new environmental regulations had the most telling impact, all of the growth management candidates were reelected, along with board chair Scott York, who had run as an independent after being jettisoned by the Republicans.

Thus, in an almost bizarre twist, it was the suburban eastern voters who threw the election to candidates who are pledged to supporting more development practically everywhere in the county. According to Michael Laris of the *Washington Post,* the sentiment among thousands of eastern county voters was that they were being treated unfairly. "A lot of the slow-growth is protecting western Loudoun, not here where we live," one eastern Loudoun voter told Laris. "They're protecting the landowners in western Loudoun and that's OK I guess. But I think we got the short end of the stick."

It didn't take long for the new board to act. At their very first meeting in January 2004, despite being fellow Republicans, they stripped Chairman York of all his powers to set agendas and preside over meetings. They rescinded a countywide historic preservation plan and took steps to kill the promising purchase of development rights program. They also voted to extend water and sewer services to a wide swath of central Loudoun that had been slated for low-density development under the 1999 plan and new code. Clearly, the new majority had met in secret prior to being installed in office and established a slash-and-burn agenda that they moved on immediately.

Things didn't improve in the coming months as several of the newly elected supervisors browbeat staff and threatened them with firing if they did not toe the party line to open central Loudoun for more development, despite evidence that this growth would have serious adverse fiscal consequences for the county. The board also indicated it would entertain new subdivision requests around some of Loudoun's western villages, which led to a loud outcry from village officials and citizens.

Time will tell if any of the 1999 Comprehensive Plan and code revisions survive in western Loudoun County. Rumors are flying that the new board is toying with the idea of relaxing the regulations in an attempt to settle some of the outstanding lawsuits. In any case, experience in other jurisdictions shows that it takes only a few years for a headstrong board to grant new development approvals that cannot legally be reeled back in by a subsequent board. On the other hand, there is increasing evidence that the new board may be overplaying its hand, setting the stage for another major political swing back toward growth management. Already, it has served notice that it will cut back county and school programs dramatically—not exactly what many voters in eastern Loudoun apparently had in mind when they cast their ballots.

Loudoun County's Comprehensive Plan and the nature-friendly regulations that followed would have established the county as one of the most progressive in the nation. Clearly, much of what was accomplished will be rolled back, leaving some important lessons in the wake:

- Ambitious land use plans and implementing regulations can be amended and repealed much more quickly than the time it usually takes to put them in place. Neither guarantees long-term protection.

- While land acquisition and development rights purchase programs are expensive, they establish "facts" in the ground that cannot be easily plowed under.

- Protective regulatory programs need to pay special attention to small landowners to ensure that their investments are not wiped out or largely diminished by stringent land use controls. This can be done through targeted exemptions, purchase of development rights programs, and other techniques.

- Planners like compact development and density, but citizens don't always agree, especially where smaller lots and more intense development are slated for areas already dotted with homes on larger lots.

- Successful implementation of ambitious nature protection programs takes several election cycles stretching over six to eight years.

Note

[1]Chris Duerksen and Craig Richardson worked with Loudoun County in 2002–2003 to draft revisions to the county's zoning ordinance. They are the primary sources for this case study unless otherwise indicated.

CONCLUSION

As the stories and communities in this book make abundantly clear, protecting the wild things is challenging, tough stuff. It is challenging because of economic pressures. The chimera of short-term economic gain is often alluring to local officials who—unlike the federal government—have to worry about balancing their budgets each year. Roads need to be patched, jails built, schools renovated, teachers paid. New developments' sales and property taxes often trump any serious thought about potential longer-term gains that protection offers. It is challenging politically, because imposing regulatory controls on property owners—often neighbors and friends—can raise hackles. As any former elected official can tell you, it is no fun to be yelled at and reviled. Passing an ordinance that might diminish the value of a property is the equivalent of fighting words in many places. And as much as anything, protecting nature is a challenge, because to be successful, local officials must take difficult stands. Long-term preservation efforts that succeed cannot be conceived and implemented in a single term in office. Persistence and tenacity salted with more than a little luck is the right prescription.

Despite those daunting prospects, now more than ever, local governments—elected officials, planning commission members, and planners—have an essential, indispensable role to play. It may not be politically fashionable to argue that government is part of the solution to practically anything these days, but there is no arguing the point when it comes to protecting wildlife and natural resources. Hoping or moping for renewed state and federal initiatives will not get the job done. That time may once again come as it did in the 1970s, but now it's time for local governments to step up. And they are. As the case studies so amply illustrate, there is much to be optimistic about. Places like Baltimore County, Sanibel, and Dane County are shining lights for their counterparts across the nation. But as our investigations show, there is still a long way to go and much to be done if we are to pass on our natural heritage to our sons and daughters to enjoy and benefit from.

There is also much to take comfort in the ways average Joe and Jane Citizen are pitching in as full partners in funding, educating, volunteering, and being watchdogs—all in the name of nature protection. That partnership is proving as powerful as it is impressive. It promises to be the strong right arm of the biodiversity protection movement.

In the end, it will boil down to political willpower, and sustaining and supporting local elected officials who create and maintain nature protection programs. That means getting involved in local political campaigns—licking envelopes, knocking on doors, sending out e-mails, and dipping into the wallet to support nature protection advocates. It will demand planning commissioners who spend long hours listening to their fellow citizens and landowners so they can craft wildlife protection programs that are palatable economically and politically. It will take fortitude by local planners to stick their necks out and act as voices for the critters when the time is right. All of this *must* be done. After all, as Edward O. Wilson, that eloquent and tireless advocate for biodiversity and nature has said, "Surely the rest of life matters." Be that our mantra.

INDEX